Ethics in Plain English

Ethics in Plain English

An Illustrative Casebook for Psychologists

SECOND EDITION

Thomas F. Nagy

AMERICAN PSYCHOLOGICAL ASSOCIATION
WASHINGTON, DC

Published by
American Psychological Association
750 First Street, NE
Washington, DC 20002
www.apa.org

To order
APA Order Department
P.O. Box 92984
Washington, DC 20090-2984
Tel: (800) 374-2721; Direct: (202) 336-5510
Fax: (202) 336-5502; TDD/TTY: (202) 336-6123
Online: www.apa.org/books/
E-mail: order@apa.org

In the U.K., Europe, Africa, and the Middle East, copies may be ordered from
American Psychological Association
3 Henrietta Street
Covent Garden, London
WC2E 8LU England

Typeset in Goudy by Stephen McDougal, Mechanicsville, MD

Printer: Victor Graphics, Inc., Baltimore, MD
Cover Designer: Michael Hentges Design, Alexandria, VA
Technical/Production Editors: Tiffany L. Klaff

The opinions and statements published are the responsibility of the authors, and such opinions and statements do not necessarily represent the policies of the American Psychological Association.

Library of Congress Cataloging-in-Publication Data

Nagy, Thomas F.
   Ethics in plain English : an illustrative casebook for psychologists / Thomas F. Nagy. —
2nd ed.
      p. cm.
   Includes bibliographical references and index.
   ISBN 1-59147-201-6
   1. Psychologists—Professional ethics. 2. Psychology—Moral and ethical aspects. I. Title.

   BF76.4.N34 2004
   174'.915—dc22   2004018052

British Library Cataloguing-in-Publication Data
A CIP record is available from the British Library.

Printed in the United States of America
Second Edition

To the memory of my father, who left this world
12 years ago, and my mother, whose final days
coincided with this book's completion.

This book does not represent the views of the American Psychological Association (APA); the APA Ethics Office; the APA Ethics Committee; the APA Ethics Code Task Force; or any other APA administrative, legal, or governance group. The plain English renditions of the APA Ethical Standards are wholly the creation of the author. They are not intended to serve as substitutes for the official standards, nor do they add to or reduce any requirements of the APA Ethics Code. All vignettes are fictional, and any similarity to actual people or situations is coincidental and unintended by the author. Where any conflict is perceived in interpreting the ethical standards or judging professional conduct, the official APA Ethical Standards, from which the plain English renditions are derived, must take precedence.

CONTENTS

ACKNOWLEDGMENTS

Many people were involved in generously offering their thoughts and wisdom in helping to create this second edition of *Ethics in Plain English*. I would like to thank them all— psychologists, psychiatrists, marriage and family therapists, social workers, attorneys, and even college students—for their constructive criticism about form, content, plausibility, and the many details that made the final product what it is. Some were close friends, some were colleagues, and some were utterly unknown to me prior to our discussions; however, virtually everyone I consulted about their particular area of expertise was willing to give generously of their time and energy.

There were a few individuals, however, who became involved with this project more extensively by reviewing several vignettes or more; evaluating concepts and story-line details; and enduring endless discussions, e-mails, and faxes concerning thorny clinical and ethical issues. I am very grateful to my friend José Maldonado, MD, cochair of Stanford Hospital's Ethics Committee and Chief of the Medical and Forensic Psychiatry Section in the Department of Psychiatry and Behavioral Sciences at Stanford University School of Medicine, for his creative and balanced contributions to the manuscript. I would also like to thank another friend, Bill Carroll, JD, Professor of Law at John Marshall Law School, for his contributions to specific vignettes and his friendly collaboration for over 20 years. In the Acknowledgments section of the first edition of this book I described Bill as indefatigable and saintly; I would say these still apply but would add that his zeal and attention to the finer points in his defense of mental health professionals who are under attack have likely saved the careers of many. I would also like to thank Lisa Butler, PhD, Senior Research Scholar in the Department of Psychiatry at Stanford University School of Medicine, for her goodwill in patiently reviewing vignettes and enlightening me about some of the more sophisticated (and gray) areas into which questions of ethics so often fall. And finally, I am indebted to Catherine Popell, PhD, for drawing on her vast experience to offer excellent contributions by teasing out some of the finer areas to highlight in certain vignettes.

Many other friends and colleagues were also willing to read one or more vignettes and provide detailed feedback about a particular specialty area of theirs. I am grateful for their willingness to participate in this project by putting energy into it and helping shape the final product. Some of the following individuals contributed to the first edition only, but having retained the vignette(s) in substance, for this volume, I owe them a debt of gratitude nevertheless. I would like to thank Margaret Lee, PhD; Hugh Baras, PhD; Stephanie Brown, PhD; David Brewer, PhD; Gerry Niewoehner, PhD; Michael Gottlieb, PhD; Brad Johnson, PhD; Alan Sklar, MD, and his wife, Alice Sklar, MSW; David Mills, PhD; Stephen Rao, PhD; Leonard Goodstein, PhD; David Spiegel, MD; James Schuerger, PhD; Mary Anne Norfleet, PhD; Karen Schlanger, MFT; Kerri Shandro, DVM; Mark Gardener; Paul Dunn, MSW; Leon Hoffman, PhD; Rodney Lowman, PhD; Bob Harris, MD; Marguerite McCorkle, PhD; Robert Boyd, PhD; Thomas Plante, PhD; Alex Caldwell, PhD; Barbara Brandt, PhD; Anne Berenberg, PhD; Ethan Pollack, PhD; Allan Berkowitz, MA; Jake Nagy, PhD; Matt Sorlien; Robert Garlan, PhD; and Paul Nagy. Without their diligence, hard work, constructive criticism, and, especially, a strong spirit of collegiality, this project would still have gone through many iterations, but it likely would not have evolved to its current state.

I am also indebted to my lawyer friends and multidisciplinary colleagues for their attention to details concerning legal matters and the psychology–law interface; this includes Harvey Ziff, JD; Julian Hubbard, JD; Lois Weithorn, PhD, JD; Alan Scheflin, JD; and George Alexander, JD.

As it was necessary to familiarize myself with animal research for some of the ethical standards, I am grateful to the staff at Stanford University's Animal Research Facility for allowing me to visit the laboratory. I am also grateful for the major assistance provided by Bruce Overmier, PhD, and Nancy Ator, PhD, for their kindness in sharing their expertise for the animal research vignettes, largely unchanged from the first edition, and to Steven Maier, PhD, for his contributions as well. I am also indebted to the Stanford University School of Medicine's Pain Management Clinic and particularly to its director, Raymond Gaeta, MD, for his helpful consultations.

I would also like to thank those who gave their time and effort in helping to generate some of the names for the characters in these vignettes. These included Stephanie Brown, Robert Harris, Mark Hendrickson, Don and Barbara Intersimone, "Fast" Eddy Vasquez, Arthur Bowen, Jean Halloran, Matt Sorlien, Marty Smith, and Michael Nagy. We had a great deal of fun in those brainstorming sessions, and I hope we contributed to lightening the tone of an otherwise weighty subject.

As with my first book, I am ever grateful to my loving wife, Kären, for her tangible contributions as well as her general support of this project, necessitating time away from family, and too many weekends spent with my Macintosh, instead of driving to the beach or the mountains. I am also indebted to Marty Smith for assiduously attending to the many formatting and countless details involved in preparing the manuscript for publication and for facilitating the transfer of late-breaking ideas to the printed page. I thank, too, the staff at American Psychological Association Books for their help. This includes Susan Reynolds, for keeping me on track and mindful of deadlines by means of gentle insistence; Judy Nemes, for the general overseeing of revisions to be made; and the reviewers whose close reading of the manuscript and excellent suggestions I found to be quite helpful. Also, I am particularly indebted to the careful review of the manuscript that was done by Stan Jones, PhD, whose characteristic fastidiousness and clarity of thought was greatly appreciated at the final stage of this project.

Finally, I thank all those who have served to stimulate my thinking about psychological ethics in recent years—psychotherapists, clergy, clients, patients, students, trainees, teachers, administrators, researchers, attorneys, plaintiffs, defendants, complainants, complainees, consumers of psychological services, and others who have consulted me and effectively contributed to enriching my knowledge in this fascinating, complex, and ever-evolving area of human interaction.

Ethics in Plain English

Frivolity, at the edge of a Moral Swamp, hears Hymn-Singing in the Distance and dons the Galoshes of Remorse.

INTRODUCTION

The second edition of *Ethics in Plain English*, like its predecessor, represents a rendition, in plain English, of the *Ethical Principles of Psychologists and Code of Conduct* (hereafter the *Ethics Code*), with illustrative fictional case vignettes.[1] The first edition of this book has been revised in form and structure to be used as a companion piece with the most recent (2002) revision of the American Psychological Association (APA) Ethics Code. The revised code of ethics has 10 sections, instead of 8, has deleted many of the original standards and added some new ones, and has changed the numbers of each standard. The six new ethical standards are 2.02 (Providing Services in Emergencies), 7.04 (Student Disclosure of Personal Information), 7.05 (Mandatory Individual or Group Therapy), 9.03 (Informed Consent in Assessments), 10.03 (Group Therapy), and 10.06 (Sexual Intimacies With Relatives or Significant Others of Current Therapy Clients/Patients). There are 12 new subsections; these do not have individual titles, as they are a part of the standard in which they appear as a lettered paragraph ("a," "b," etc.). I have attempted to loosely summarize the essence of each subsection in parentheses. The new subsections are: 2.01d (providing services when not fully competent if you are the only psychologist around), 3.10c (giving informed consent when services are court ordered or otherwise mandated), 4.02c (informing others about risks to privacy over the Internet), 8.02b (giving informed con-

---

[1] It is important to state clearly and for the record that the opinions about and applications of the ethical principles of APA contained in this book are simply those of the author and do not constitute official policy of any group, board, or body, including APA. The applications cited here are meant to stimulate awareness of ethical issues, not to make policy, define ethical behavior, or define enforceable standards of practice. Neither the vernacular versions of the APA standards nor the vignettes have been reviewed by any APA governance group or the APA Ethics Office or Ethics Committee. Any citations of this book in the forensic context should always make these caveats known. Psychologists and psychologists in training desiring to obtain official opinions of the APA Ethics Committee should consult statements issued by that body.

sent in intervention research), 8.08c (dealing with research participants who have been harmed by the research), 8.14b (obtaining consent for using others' research data that have been released to you for reanalysis), 9.01c (basing conclusions and recommendations on record reviews only and revealing your sources of information), 9.02b (using assessment instruments with established reliability and validity for your patient, or else providing disclaimers), 9.02c (assessing individuals in their preferred language), 9.04b (releasing test data only as required by law or a court order), 10.01b (giving informed consent for cutting-edge therapies), and 10.10b (terminating therapy with a dangerous client or patient).

This edition of *Ethics in Plain English* reflects each change, and more. Every vignette has been rewritten, resulting in a broader and more in-depth explication of the standard in question (and also contributing to the book's length). Also, questions have been added for every standard, provoking, I hope, thought about various ways of arriving at ethical decision making, raising related legal or clinical issues, and sometimes positing hypothetical situations that might have a bearing on the outcome. This book can be used as a companion piece to the APA Ethics Code and is meant to be read in conjunction with the original text from which it is derived.[2]

The ethical standards rendered into the vernacular, as any exegesis of a source document, are not meant to stand alone or to substitute for the APA Ethics Code. Neither are they intended to characterize the mandatory ethical behavior in a comprehensive or official fashion, although every effort has been made to retain the spirit and requirements presented in the original APA document. For this reason, the colloquial version of an ethical standard should not be relied on exclusively in considering matters of professional or ethical conduct of psychologists. Rather, readers are advised to study the original text for each ethical standard under consideration because its precise language defines that standard, with, I hope, little or no ambiguity. For this reason, the original wording of each ethical standard from the APA Ethics Code is presented in italics, directly before my rendition of it in informal language. This allows readers to benefit from the plain English rendition and to compare for themselves its derivation as well as any deviation from the original.

My intention in writing this book was to create a vehicle for conveying the essence of each ethical standard by means of a case vignette. Although fictional, the vignette relates a brief but plausible account of a psychologist's conduct, fleshing out the necessarily dry and precise language of the ethical standard. By studying fictional examples of both sound and questionable judgment on the part of psychologists encountering various dilemmas in their everyday work, I hope readers can gain an appreciation of the ethical stan-

---

[2]Readers may find it useful to refer to APA's Web site (http://www.apa.org/ethics/codecompare.html), which provides a side-by-side comparison of the old and the revised Ethics Codes.

dard under consideration as well as how it could be applied. It is my hope that the vicarious experiences gained from reading these case vignettes may help one to better grasp how ethical problems can naturally, and sometimes suddenly, emerge with competent and well-meaning professionals, even under the most ordinary of circumstances.

It should also be noted that the use of humor (e.g., unusual names of psychologists and other characters) in these vignettes is never intended to detract from the seriousness of the topic or to diminish the importance of a particular standard. Rather, it is my hope that the value of entertainment in this context may serve to lighten a weighty subject, thereby facilitating learning. The "thumbs-up" or "thumbs-down" graphic at the top of each vignette indicates conduct that is either exemplary or substandard. In some cases, it is not so clear cut, or the psychologist has started down an ethically tenuous path, only to be redeemed by a colleague who is more ethically competent. Here the graphic is a finger pointing straight ahead (presumably guiding the floundering or uninformed psychologist toward a more orthodox choice or strategy).

In reading the vignettes it is useful to bear in mind that the APA Ethics Code consists of two parts: (a) General Principles and (b) Ethical Standards. This book focuses exclusively on the 89 Ethical Standards, which are grouped under the following eight categories: (a) resolving ethical issues (8), (b) competence (6), (c) human relations (12), (d) privacy and confidentiality (7), (e) advertising and other public statements (6), (f) record keeping and fees (7), (g) education and training (7), (h) research and publication (15), (i) assessment (11), and (j) therapy (10). Many of these standards are divided into subsections, with additional rules to observe; taken together, there are a total of 151 ethical rules for psychologists. These standards essentially require psychologists to do something or to refrain from doing something when carrying out their work; they represent the musts and must-nots of psychological practice. They are enforceable, and the procedures for their enforcement and attendant penalties or sanctions are outlined in the "Rules and Procedures" of the APA Ethics Committee (APA, 2001b).

It should be noted that there may be times when a psychologist cannot necessarily guarantee a particular outcome in a complex situation. This is particularly true when the APA Ethics Code comes into conflict with a state or federal law, such as the Health Insurance Portability and Accountability Act or with an institutional policy or regulation. In these cases, it is important to at least make a good faith effort at complying with the ethical standard and to inform others of the existing conflict at the same time (e.g., a supervisor, manager, client, or patient). The key factor lies in making a serious attempt at complying with a standard rather than simply assuming that one will be overruled by a lax institutional policy or an individual in a position of authority who fosters a policy that is at odds with some ethical rule. Sometimes the state or federal law, or institutional policy, might have a higher standard than the APA Ethics Code; in these cases, naturally it is the psychologist's obligation to adhere to the higher standard, even though the code does not require it.

The General Principles, although not the subject of this book, also constitute an important part of the APA Ethics Code. These five guiding principles for all psychologists, as spelled out in this document, are as follows: A: Beneficence and Nonmaleficence, B: Fidelity and Responsibility, C: Integrity, D: Justice, and E: Respect for People's Rights and Dignity. The General Principles are generically broad philosophical constructs that do not set specific standards for professional conduct (i.e., behavior to be engaged in or avoided). Rather, they are aspirational in nature and serve to remind us of underlying themes that continuously surface in our work with others. As psychologists we are encouraged to strive always to exemplify these principles in the course of our professional activities.

DEVELOPING LANGUAGE FOR AN OFFICIAL CODE

An important decision in creating a document such as an ethics code involves the level of linguistic detail or generality that will ultimately convey the philosophical concepts and standards of behavior prescribed. As a participant in the drafting of text for the 1992 revision of the Ethics Code (APA, 1992), I, along with the other members of the APA Revision Comments Subcommittee, struggled with this very issue: How specific or generic should the language be in setting forth principles and standards of conduct? I suspect the task force completing the 2002 edition addressed the same concerns. If the language were too narrow in scope, it would not effectively address the specialty areas of many psychologists, unless the number of standards was to be greatly increased. This would result in a long and unwieldy document. However, if the language were overly broad and generic in scope, the document could be shorter, but many specific and important topics would likely not be included (e.g., specific research and clinical risks, evolving forensic issues, and computer- and Internet-related topics). The resulting document might also have less practical application for both psychologists and the public because many of the important topics in the science and practice of psychology would be excluded.

A way of resolving the dilemma of establishing a level of language that would be neither too general nor too specific is to use descriptors that offer precision to ethical rules while simultaneously facilitating their application in a broad array of circumstances. The use of these adjectives—reasonable, feasible, and appropriate—are examples of semantic descriptors that do, to some extent, accomplish this end. These words, unfortunately, seem vague at times, although they can serve the important purpose of accurately broadening applicability and interpretation.

The current version of the APA Ethics Code, in my view, appears to use language reflecting more common parlance and seems to offer fairly easy reading. The previously cited adjectives thankfully do not appear as often in the recent revision of the APA Ethics Code, yet there appears to have been little or no sacrifice to the meaning of the standards. For further information, readers may wish to consult the *Introduction and Applicability* section of the APA Ethics Code where the use and rationale of these modifiers are addressed (paragraph 6).

A VERNACULAR RENDERING OF THE APA ETHICS CODE

In creating plain English versions of the ethical standards I have provided a translation of the necessarily formalistic language used in the code. In doing so, I have used vernacular language, the very nature of which involves speaking plainly, in local or regional dialect, and avoiding the use of words that are literary, scientific, technical, or legalistic. It is clear that a double-edged sword hangs precariously over any attempt to render 89 standards of conduct (151 subsections) for researchers, teachers, practitioners, and other psychologists into a relatively easily understood series of maxims or rules, without significantly changing their meaning.

My attempt to meet this goal consisted mainly of making strategic cuts in language while being careful never to eviscerate, to remove excess verbiage while being careful to avoid transecting a conceptual nerve. Often, my rendition of a particular standard is longer than the original. Additional words were sometimes necessary to make the meaning clear. In creating a plain-English rendition of the ethical standards I eliminated qualifying adjectives from the text and attempted to substitute simpler language. As a result, it is possible that there have been some compromises to, or losses in, meaning.

However, I have endeavored to minimize the potential losses in meaning, such as overly narrowing, dichotomizing, or otherwise altering the applicability of the ethical standards while trying to maintain the heart of the concept under discussion. Although somewhat less precise than the original standards, it is my hope that the vernacular version might be more memorable to, and more easily taught and learned by, teachers and students, neophyte and experienced psychologists, and consumers of a broad array of psychological services.

CASE VIGNETTES

The case vignettes illustrating the standards are drawn, in part, from my years of serving on ethics committees (e.g., APA, various state psychological associations, other professional associations, Stanford University

Hospital) and consulting with those involved in legal and ethical disputes, both at the individual and institutional level. They are also rooted in my work as a participant in the previous revision of the Ethics Code (APA, 1992). This was a 6-year undertaking that involved evaluating thousands of proposals submitted by hundreds of psychologists and by APA divisions, task forces, committees, and other entities. It was my privilege to learn first hand of problematic areas that were of major concern to psychologists in many specialty areas.

Each vignette depicts an important aspect of the ethical standard under consideration and attempts to do so in a plausible setting. Ideally, a casebook might contain several or many vignettes for each standard, representing the various specialties and contexts in which psychologists work, such as teaching, research, forensic or clinical practice, and industrial and organizational consulting. However, this would have resulted in a considerably longer book than would be practical with the amount of detail I would hope to include. I attempted to approach this ideal by including, whenever possible, different areas of psychology based, in part, on the experience of other specialists with whom I consulted. However, some vignettes may be more reflective of my personal experience as a teacher, psychotherapist, supervisor, and consultant. I offer my apologies to those in specialties or work settings who may not find their work experience sufficiently represented in these pages.

Note that the vignettes in this book are fictitious, and any scenarios or names that may seem to reflect real life situations or people are purely coincidental and unintended. In addition, any case material that may have served as inspiration for the development of the fictional vignettes was significantly altered by changing such things as gender, age, topic, setting, and geographical location, to minimize any chance that a person would incorrectly believe that a real case was being discussed.

Some of the vignettes manifest exemplary behavior by psychologists, and some illustrate a woeful lack of knowledge about ethics or, even worse, a calculated indifference, resulting in a feckless application of the ethical standard in question. Although some vignettes may seem to be exaggerations or even caricatures of professional conduct, they are not as far-fetched as they might first appear, in my experience. Among individuals who may, at times, behave in an unethical fashion (any one of us), some are surprisingly capable of deviating far from the minimal expected standard with little or no effort. In fact, it is precisely this lack of effort that is unsettling in observing the unethical conduct of our peers. I have observed that what may first appear to be rather anomalous, or even hyperbolic or comical at times, is well within the range of unprofessional conduct encountered by the individuals bringing ethical complaints and engaged in by those who stand accused. If in perusing the activities of the protagonists in the case vignettes the reader can learn and grow as much as I did in creating them, then I am certain that the goals for this book will have been achieved.

SANCTIONS AND DIRECTIVES

It should be noted that someone who has a grievance against a psychologist or has had a disappointing or harmful experience has various options. He or she may complain to the ethics committee of the state psychological association of which the psychologist is a member, or to the APA Ethics Committee—if, again, the psychologist belongs to APA. In the vignettes there are examples of individuals complaining to both entities; it is a matter of personal preference. In many cases, however, the ethics committees of the state psychological associations no longer adjudicate complaints; they play an educative role only, leaving the complainant little choice but to submit the complaint to APA. Complainants may also choose to complain to the state licensing board, in addition to or instead of complaining to an ethics committee; this course of action may be taken if the psychologist's conduct is believed to be in violation of state law. In many states, the APA Ethics Code has been incorporated into the language of the law governing psychological practice; therefore, a violation of an ethical standard would technically be tantamount to a legal infraction as well. Finally, if the complainant chooses, he or she may initiate legal action against a psychologist by retaining an attorney and filing a lawsuit. This may be a costly option but may be appropriate in cases where substantial harm has been visited on the client or patient by a psychologist.

Upon concluding that a psychologist who is a member of APA has violated an ethical standard, the APA Ethics Committee may administer a *sanction* and may require one or more *directives*, or both. (Ethics committees of state psychological associations that still adjudicate ethics complaints may have similar options, but each has its own rules and procedures, and readers should consult them as needed). There can be a range of sanctions for each ethical violation, depending on the egregiousness of the act. A psychologist who exaggerates somewhat in a newspaper advertisement for his weight loss group will not receive the same sanction as a researcher altering data to achieve statistical significance, even though both have engaged in the publicizing of inaccurate statements. I next present a brief synopsis of the topic of sanctions and directives. For a complete list and explanation of the range of sanctions and directives, please consult the Ethics Committee's Rules and Procedures available on the APA Web site, http://www.apa.org/ethics/rules.html.

Sanctions and directives are the products of meticulous and comprehensive reasoning on the part of each member serving on an ethics committee that generally spends many hours over a period of months poring over documents, seeking answers to questions, studying the responses of the psychologist against whom a complaint was lodged, and weighing the evidence of wrongdoing. Available sanctions consist of (a) a *reprimand*, which is appropriate when there has been an ethics violation but not of a kind likely to cause harm to another person or substantial harm to the profession; (b) *censure*, which is appropriate when the ethical violation was of a kind likely to cause harm to another person but the violation was not of a kind likely to cause substantial harm to him or her or to the profession; (c) *expulsion*, which is appropriate when the violation was of a kind likely to cause substantial harm to another person or the profession or was otherwise of sufficient gravity as to warrant such action; and (d) *stipulated resignation*, which generally is appropriate when the violation merits expulsion from the association but extenuating circumstances might warrant specifying conditions for readmission to APA.

An ethics committee may also administer *directives*. These include a requirement that the psychologist participate in some action or some educational or rehabilitative experience. Available directives consist of (a) a *cease-and-desist order*, demanding that the psychologist stop engaging in the behavior deemed unethical, (b) *other corrective actions*, requiring the psychologist to take steps to remedy a particular violation or protect the interest of the association or the public (however, a psychologist cannot be required to make a monetary payment to the association or to aggrieved parties); (c) a *supervision requirement*, which places the psychologist under supervision for a specified period of time; (d) an *education, training, or tutorial requirement*, requiring an appropriate didactic experience; (e) *evaluation and treatment requirement*, necessitating a psychological evaluation and appropriate treatment, if warranted; and (f) *probation*, requiring monitoring of the offending psychologist by the Ethics Committee to ensure compliance with its directives while in force.

Sanctions and directives can be seen by psychologists as being both punitive and educational in nature. They carry significant weight, potentially, for the duration of the professional life of the psychologist receiving it. Receiving a sanction could have major implications on obtaining malpractice insurance, if it is severe, resulting in having to change carriers and pay a higher premium in some cases, or finding it impossible to obtain coverage at all in others. It could also have implications for one's ability to join various professional associations, as many inquire about one's history of ethical or legal problems as a part of membership screening.

The educational and rehabilitative aspects of a sanction or a directive can be profoundly helpful, such as (a) requiring a psychologist to have ethics training (e.g., continuing education workshops, individual consultations with an ethicist), (b) requiring that his or her practice be monitored by a senior clinician (clinical, business, legal, ethical, or professional aspects of the practice), or (c) requiring an impaired psychologist to engage in psychotherapy. Certainly, it can be a humbling experience, and generally a completely unanticipated one as well. Ultimately, in the long run, it will, it is hoped, be seen as having come at a time in the psychologist's life when it was sorely needed and can be experienced as timely rehabilitation that protects both the psychologist, against further risks in the future, as well as the public that he or she serves.

The sanctions that wayward psychologists occasionally receive at the hands of ethics committees in these vignettes are obviously not the product of an ethics committee's actual deliberations, and they should not be taken as such. Rather, they are the closest approximation I could develop, given the many years I have served on ethics committees in various venues, and I hope that they not only lend credibility to the vignettes but also are reasonable approximations of penalties that would likely be doled out.

A MODEL FOR ANALYZING THE VIGNETTES

In studying the vignettes and addressing the discussion questions at the end, it may be useful to analyze them according to the following three general categories: (a) ethical, (b) legal, and (c) professional. A fourth category would be composed of the psychologist's competence in his or her own subspecialty area, such as clinical, research, or supervision. As a reflection of real life scenarios, any vignette may be composed of a combination of ethical, legal, technical competence, and professional issues. The challenge for readers will be to identify the ethical rule or rules that are being addressed. Let us examine these three areas individually.

Ethical Issues

An *ethical issue*, for the present purposes, is one that is specifically addressed by any of the 89 ethical standards of the APA Ethics Code, or any ethics code of another professional association of which one is a member. These are essentially the musts and must-nots that govern our conduct as members of the American Psychological Association, or any state psychological association that relies on the same code of ethics to regulate the conduct of its members. These rules have evolved over the past 50 years in a teleological fashion; that is, the ethical rules of conduct are clearly connected to outcomes or results that are achieved by the actions of psychologists. The rules have developed to affect or limit the behavior of psychologists so as to maximize the safety and welfare of the recipients of their services and those who interact with them.[3]

Legal Issues

In many cases, state or federal laws exist that have a direct bearing on the conduct of psychologists. This would include such things as confidentiality and its exceptions, mandated reporting (e.g., child abuse, elder abuse,

---

[3]This is in contrast to rules of conduct that would be deontologically based, or founded on the concept that the moral content of an action is not wholly dependent on its consequences. That is, a higher value, other than one that exclusively relates to the outcome in a particular situation, is the origin of the rule (e.g., the injunctions to "always preserve life" or "always tell the truth" when, in fact, there may be specific situations that might invite a departure from this rule).

Tarasoff-type situations[4]), record keeping, regulations of the Department of Veterans Affairs, Medicare, and the Health Insurance Portability and Accountability Act. Also relevant would be the forensic activities of psychologists, whether in the role of fact witness, expert witness, assessor, respondent to a subpoena or court order, consultant to an attorney, in the role of *amicus curiae*, or any other role relevant to forensic work. Teasing out legal issues from ethical issues can be a challenge, and the importance of remaining current with ever-changing federal and state laws can never be overemphasized.

Technical Competence

Technical competence consists essentially of proficiency in one's specialty area, be it clinical work, research, teaching, or any other area. To show how it might apply with this model I will focus on the clinical area, as psychotherapists and those doing assessment seem to comprise such a large percentage of psychologists and so many ethical standards address their activities (and space prohibits an elaboration of every specialty area). The reader may substitute "research," "teaching," "supervision," "consultation," or other areas as appropriate while reading vignettes pertaining to their particular area of concentration. Many of the vignettes describe situations with patients and clients at various stages in their work with psychologists. In assessing, diagnosing, treating, and referring individuals psychologists must rely on their formal education, training, supervised experience, and continuing education experiences to provide the most current and effective services of which they are capable. At times their clinical service may be substandard, because of inadequate training, lack of competence, temporary personal impairment (i.e., poor health; mood disorder; life stressor, e.g., divorce, death of a loved one, etc.), personality characteristic, or some other factor. This may not constitute an ethical violation in and of itself; however, if left unchecked, and the psychologist continues to practice when clearly he or she should seek consultation or supervision, then this could possibly lead to harming the recipient of their services, which clearly *would* be an ethical issue. It is important to accurately distinguish clinical issues from ethical and legal ones and to develop clarity about the essentials of a particular clinical situation that may seem thorny or personally troublesome. This can help forestall the deterioration of one's work with a client or patient that could lead to harming them, and ultimately to harming the psychologist as well.

Professional Issues

It may be true that whatever issues fall outside the realm of ethical, legal, and technical competence in a subspecialty area land in the category of

---

[4]These are situations in which a client or patient has revealed to a psychologist his or her intention to harm an identifiable third party.

a professional issue. This includes the array of psychological activities found in academic settings, professional consulting activities, relationships with colleagues and those whom we mentor, some business aspects of independent practice, relationships with other health care professionals, noncontractual agreements in group practices, and many other areas. Often there are no specific guidelines or rules governing professional conduct, as distinct from ethical or legal requirements, and psychologists must make judgments reflecting their own values and idiosyncrasies appropriate to the situation. There are many decisions made by the professor, management consultant, researcher, or private practitioner about how he or she behaves with others that are not codified and probably never will be. These usually do not rise to the level of an ethical, legal, or clinical issue, although attempts may be made, at times, to drag them into one of these arenas (e.g., a client might complain that she found her therapist's use of four-letter words in a therapy session to be upsetting and file an ethics charge). Clearly discerning what falls into the realm of a professional issue will help simplify the task of grappling with any ethical issue that presents itself, in any subspecialty area.

ETHICAL DECISION MAKING

How can a psychologist have a reasonable amount of certainty that his or her conduct that may fall into a gray area (e.g., a new therapeutic strategy or consultative intervention) is ethically compliant? I have developed 14 topical questions that one can raise as guides in identifying higher risk situations, indicating the need for increased vigilance (see Table 1). Although many of these questions are oriented somewhat more toward clinical and research situations, they can be used as a means of troubleshooting for any subspecialty area. As can easily be seen, responding to these queries in a certain way would help cue one that an ethical or legal issue might be lurking and needs to be addressed. This is based in part on my earlier work (Canter, Bennett, Jones, & Nagy, 1994) and elaborated further in my chapter on competence (Nagy, in press).

Although the questions in Table 1 do not address every scenario, they at least can provide a basis for evaluating the ethicality of one's intended conduct when venturing into new territory (both theoretical and applied). Of course, consultation with a psychologist experienced in ethical matters is always an excellent recourse and should be seriously considered when in doubt. Decisions made in isolation may be regretted later on, when one could easily have contacted a peer, an ethics committee member of the county or state association, the APA Ethics Office, a lawyer familiar with psychological ethics, or some other resource. There is an abundance of help available; it is up to us as professionals to know when to avail ourselves of it.

TABLE 1
Topics and Self-Questions for Minimizing the Risk of Harm to Clients, Patients, Research Participants, and Other Recipients of Psychological Services When Innovative Techniques Are Contemplated in the Absence of Standards or Guidelines

Topic	Self-question
1. Boundaries of competence	Am I practicing within my boundaries of competence, according to my formal training, supervision, or experience?
2. State and federal laws and regulations, and institutional policies	Am I familiar with the current laws and regulations that pertain to my area of work that may provide guidance, though not actual answers to any questions (e.g., Health Insurance Accountability and Portability Act, confidentiality rules and exceptions, IRB guidelines for human participants, or the appeal process in managed health care settings for extending therapy)?
3. Ethics codes and practice guidelines	Am I familiar with the Ethics Code of the APA, that of any other professional association to which I belong, and any published guidelines or standards that may have a bearing on what I am about to undertake?
4. Innovative protocol, intervention, strategy, or approach	Am I about to engage in a new activity, research project, or intervention that has little or no referent in my training or professional experience (e.g., an inspired or intuitively novel therapeutic intervention)?
5. Uncertainty or apprehension about your work	Do I feel uncertain about how to proceed with respect to the impact of my work on others (e.g., research involving anxiety-evoking stimuli that I have never used before?)
6. Adequacy of data about the other person to avoid harming him or her	Can I be sufficiently assured of a client or patient's diagnosis, history, or psychological makeup so as to proceed ahead with reasonable certainty that no adverse reactions will be triggered?
7. Risk of harm to another	Is there a possibility of harm to an individual, group, or organization, as a result of my conduct, *even though remote*?
8. Impaired judgment or loss of objectivity	Is there a possibility that I may have impaired judgment or objectivity, or that I may be exploiting another as the

continues

	result of a conflict of interest or an emerging dual role relationship (i.e., Am I sexually attracted? Am I considering offering psychotherapy to my student or supervisee?)
9. Prejudice, blind spots, and bias	Do I judge or have strong feelings about certain individuals with particular personal qualities that could result in impaired competence? (e.g., gender, homosexuality, age, ethnicity, culture, religion, disability, socioeconomic status)?
10. Multiple role relationship	Am I altering my customary boundaries or limits by either engaging the individual in a secondary role (friend, co-author, or business associate) or attempting to increase or decrease my social distance (being artificially formal or inappropriately familiar)?
11. Exploiting the other for personal gain	Do I have something to gain by *using* the other for their knowledge or expertise, money, status, or some other attribute for my own personal or professional gain (e.g., "insider trading" on the stock market, free legal advice)?
12. Deceiving or manipulating the other	Are my statements accurate, or do they serve some secondary purpose for my own gain (i.e., am I attempting to prolong therapy for my own financial gain or influence others to behave in a certain way for my own benefit—such as referring their friends to me for counseling?)
13. Therapist avoidance or denial of reality	Am I systematically avoiding addressing certain topics or situations that I normally would confront (e.g., I never address the client's/patient's short temper or seductive behavior directed at me)?
14. Relinquishing your standard operating procedures	Do I find myself changing my usual and customary practices in dealing with a particular individual or situation (i.e., I begin to spontaneously extend the length of the therapy sessions, or agree to meet a patient or research participant for dinner)?

Note. IRB = institutional review board; APA = American Psychological Association.

1

RESOLVING ETHICAL ISSUES

1.01 MISUSE OF PSYCHOLOGISTS' WORK

If psychologists learn of misuse or misrepresentation of their work, they take reasonable steps to correct or minimize the misuse or misrepresentation.

If you find out that somebody has altered, distorted, misused, or otherwise misrepresented your work, be sure to make corrections, minimize the effects of the falsification, or at least make an effort to do so.

VIGNETTE

Seven investigators in the United States, England, and Australia had just published the results of a large 5-year study in an American Psychological Association (APA) journal examining the effectiveness of hypnosis for pain management and quality of life on patients diagnosed with fibromyalgia who also had an Axis II disorder.

Unbeknownst to his colleagues, one of the Australian coauthors, Dr. Last Gasp, who was nearing retirement, also had submitted a similar article to a journal of his local professional association, using the same data. He thought that the tone of the article published in America was far too modest in its claims, and he decided to unilaterally submit an article under his own authorship that would rectify this oversight. He made significant changes in the Results and Discussion sections of the article, citing the original authors but failing to inform any of them about this second publication. His motivation to take such a risky step was based, in part, on the fact that he held the directorship of a hypnosis training program at a major hospital and the fact that he had just submitted an application for a grant to fund additional research and training. A publication reporting strong clinical effects of hypnosis would certainly be helpful in his efforts to obtain additional funding, he reasoned.

Dr. Gasp reported specifically, as did his American and British colleagues, that hypnosis reduced the intensity of pain in all patients who had a moderate to high level of hypnotic ability. However, he went on to assert that hypnosis was also effective in ameliorating many symptoms associated with borderline, histrionic, narcissistic, and dependent personality disorders. This may possibly have been the case; however, the fact that the data failed to support these claims did not faze Dr. Gasp in the least. Instead, he backed his claims by altering the stated validity of an instrument developed for this study, the Chronic Pain and Life Adjustment Survey, to include the assessment of certain symptoms of personality disorders. He felt justified in doing so because he was one of the authors of the instrument and had always disagreed with his coauthors on its validity, thinking it could be used as a much broader indicator of mental health. To strengthen his arguments he also omitted from the publication any mention of pre- and posttesting using Millon Clinical Multiaxial Inventory scores, as they revealed disconfirming data concerning his assertions.

Several months after the publication of his article in an Australian journal, one of the American authors, Dr. Kara Ector, received an e-mail from a colleague "down under" that raised a serious question about the claims that were being made. Dr. Ector telephoned Dr. Gasp, only to have her worst fears confirmed: The research results had indeed been altered by Dr. Gasp, and unsupportable claims were indeed being made. She confronted Dr. Gasp, respectfully, with the unethical nature of his behavior and pointed out that the alterations and omissions of his publications not only violated the agreement among all coauthors concerning collaboration in publications but also constituted poor science and, in essence, corrupted the database as well.

Dr. Gasp was initially intransigent, wishing to end his career on a strong note, both by publishing a research article supporting hypnosis for broad application with pain patients and, he hoped, by bringing in additional funding for the hospital's hypnosis program. Also, as he no longer belonged to any professional associations, he knew that he was immune to any threats of an ethics complaint regarding his research.

However, as time went by, he was ultimately persuaded by the repeated and impassioned pleas of Dr. Ector and her associates and conceded that he was being shortsighted, selfish, and possibly even impaired in his objectivity and competence to carry out research any longer. He agreed to publish an erratum in the next edition of the journal and make corrective statements that were badly needed. Thanks to the persistence and compassion of Dr. Ector and her associates, a colleague with impaired judgment was helped to acknowledge his error and take remedial action. By acting swiftly, Dr. Ector and her coinvestigators helped nip this transgression in the bud and halt the further dissemination of distorted claims and misrepresentations concerning their research.

1. What other ethical standards might Dr. Gasp have violated in deciding to publish his article in the Australian journal?
2. If you had a colleague who misused and misrepresented your collective data, as did Dr. Gasp, you would have the choice of contacting the APA Ethics Office or discussing the matter directly with Dr. Gasp. What are the implications of each?
3. Does the APA Ethics Code ask psychologists to discriminate between impaired judgment on the part of a colleague and willful unethical conduct for personal gain of some sort? Would you be able to make such a distinction and, if so, what difference would it make in your choice of action to rectify the situation?

1.02 CONFLICTS BETWEEN ETHICS AND LAW, REGULATIONS, OR OTHER GOVERNING LEGAL AUTHORITY

If psychologists' ethical responsibilities conflict with law, regulations, or other governing legal authority, psychologists make known their commitment to the Ethics Code and take steps to resolve the conflict. If the conflict is unresolvable via such means, psychologists may adhere to the requirements of the law, regulations, or other governing legal authority.

If an ethical rule clashes with a legal regulation, be sure to let others know that you have an obligation to follow your profession's Code of Ethics, and then take some positive action to resolve the dilemma. Sometimes it may require coming up with a creative solution; if not, however, you are allowed to simply adhere to the requirements of the law, regulation, or other governing legal authority, even though it might mean technically violating the Code of Ethics.

VIGNETTE

Captain Nathan Black, an Army psychologist stationed in the Middle East, had been providing psychotherapy to an enlisted man for alcohol abuse over a 3-week period. One day, the soldier's commanding officer, Colonel Snoopy, telephoned Captain Black to inquire about the progress of therapy. Captain Black knew that he must address this request, because confidentiality rules in a federal installation preempt state laws and permit such disclosures. He also knew that under the federal rules of patient confidentiality he was required to reveal some information to his patient's commanding officer, relevant to his deployability on a particular mission, if requested. In fact, his input could be critical in assessing the man's fitness for active duty. He also was aware that his client had authorized such communication in the informed consent that he had signed at the outset of the psychological referral by his physician. Captain Black suspected, however, that at some point the colonel might well attempt to seek information above and beyond what was minimally necessary to address issues of direct strategic concern (e.g., deployability).

Captain Black attempted to adhere to his ethical duty to protect his patient's confidentiality by informing Colonel Snoopy of this ethical obligation and the risks of breaching confidentiality in a therapy relationship, even though the law might permit it (and even though a general consent form had been signed). Captain Black artfully explained to the colonel that psychotherapy was generally most effective when there was a trusting relationship with the therapist, allowing the client to disclose anything of importance that he or she might wish to discuss. Captain Black further informed the inquisitive officer that this trust would be undermined if he were to reveal the topics and specific details that were discussed in therapy. Unless the client had some confidence that his discussions with the therapist would remain private, it was likely that he would begin to selectively withhold important information that he would not want his commanding officer to know but might be a contributing factor to his ongoing psychological problems. If this were to happen, then it was possible that either the client would eventually drop out of treatment with no substantial benefit or the treatment might drag on unproductively because important issues were not being addressed.

Colonel Snoopy seemed to understand the psychologist's resistance to disclosing the details of treatment; however, he persisted in at least discovering whether any progress was being made. There was a critical mission scheduled to take place in 1 week, and the colonel had to know whether his soldier would be fit for active duty at that time. Captain Black knew that he could divulge treatment progress in a general way without compromising the trust he had established, but he followed his normal protocol of discussing the matter with his client first. Part of a therapy session was devoted to addressing the colonel's request for information, how it should be handled, and what could comfortably be revealed that would satisfy the colonel's need to know but would not disclose private information that should remain in the consulting room. Captain Black and the client devised a strategy for how to provide both a general overview of the therapy progress and an educated guess about the enlisted man's probable readiness to be deployed.

The client appreciated being included in the discussion of such a complicated ethical and clinical issue and was able to be an active participant in its apparent resolution. Colonel Snoopy was not quite as easily appeased, however; it was difficult for him to grasp the nature of the therapy process and the importance of confidentiality. Furthermore, he tended to interpret Captain Black's reticence as an attempt to "pull rank" on him and pamper a soldier who was shirking his duties in the desert by duping his psychologist into thinking that he had "some mental problem." Colonel Snoopy became somewhat testy with Captain Black, informing him that this soldier was badly needed in combat missions, if at all possible, and that he thought the soldier might be malingering.

Time was running out, and Captain Black knew that he had to resourcefully deal with the colonel's point of view or else the therapy might be compromised. To satisfy the colonel and, he hoped, maintain his patient in treatment, he disclosed information that the colonel considered a core issue. The colonel already knew about the alcohol-related incident that had precipitated therapy, and he was relieved to learn from Captain Black that the enlisted man was not an alcoholic. Apparently his drinking was related to a diagnosis of "adjustment disorder with anxiety," relevant to the pending deployment. Captain Black respectfully and patiently described the type of therapy he was providing, the prognosis, and the probable etiology of the disorder, with enough specifics to convince the colonel that the soldier was not malingering. He emphasized that the soldier would likely constitute more of a risk than an asset, were he to join his unit in the field, possibly jeopardizing the safety of others because of poor concentration, anticipatory anxiety, and significant memory deficits. The colonel inquired about the man's homosexuality, as he suspected that he probably was gay, because of some pornography that had turned up in his sleeping quarters. Captain Black gently but firmly reminded the colonel that homosexuality was not a medical issue; he indicated that it could contribute to social alienation at times but would not in and of itself have any bearing on this soldier's fitness for duty.

Captain Black was able to convince Colonel Snoopy of the validity of his patient's impairment. Once again he had struggled with the Catch-22 of trying to comply with the requirements of ethical standards pertaining to confidentiality and the federal laws pertaining to patient privacy in a military setting. He was satisfied that instead of simply yielding to the colonel's requests for information he had followed his usual regimen of attempting to openly thrash out with his patient and the colonel the relevant issues as he saw them: (a) the importance of confidentiality of psychological records, (b) limits to that confidentiality in the military setting, (c) the clinical issues that contribute to therapist–patient trust and efficiency in treatment, (d) the psychologist's need to obey his or her professional ethical standards concerning confidentiality, and (e) the commanding officer's real need for information about whether a soldier is fit to be deployed. As a result, the colonel's awareness of the importance of therapy confidentiality was heightened, and the patient emerged with a realistic understanding of his rights and heightened respect for his therapist, who had attempted to preserve them.

1. What is the extent of confidentiality for enlisted men and women consulting with mental health care providers in a military setting?
2. How might Captain Black have handled Colonel Snoopy's inquisitiveness about the client's homosexuality if it seemed to be creating a problem of morale or harassment in the unit?
3. As a psychologist in the military, or in a Veterans' Affairs hospital, what are some of the other issues you might confront, besides confidentiality, in attempting to be a resource to your patients while simultaneously adhering to policies and legal regulations?
4. How might different confidentiality rules, such as those in a military setting, affect how you would maintain your clinical record of consultations?

1.03 CONFLICTS BETWEEN ETHICS AND ORGANIZATIONAL DEMANDS

If the demands of an organization with which psychologists are affiliated or for whom they are working conflict with this Ethics Code, psychologists clarify the nature of the conflict, make known their commitment to the Ethics Code, and to the extent feasible, resolve the conflict in a way that permits adherence to the Ethics Code.

If you find a conflict between the policies of your workplace and the Ethics Code, explain the nature of the conflict and let others know about your obligation to comply with this code. Then do your best to resolve this problem in a way that permits maximal adherence to the Ethics Code. It may not be a perfect solution, but at least you will have made a good-faith effort to address the problem.

VIGNETTE

Dr. Ida Listig accepted her first postdoctoral position as a staff psychologist in a suburban private hospital that specialized in the treatment of chronic pain and chemical dependency. After working there for 1 month, she realized that some long-standing hospital policies concerning diagnosis and treatment were not necessarily in the patients' best interests; neither were they in conformance with APA's Ethics Code. Staff frequently used diagnostic procedures that were unnecessary and costly for the patient and third-party payors. For example, every chronic-pain patient was given a battery of neuropsychological tests as part of the initial evaluation, even though this was a significant departure from the usual and customary assessment procedures for chronic pain. Also, testing and psychotherapy were routinely carried out by unqualified staff, such as registered nurses and unsupervised psychological assistants. Furthermore, most patients were routinely admitted to the hospital for "state of the art diagnostic procedures and observation," according to the statements in the hospital brochure, regardless of the source of their pain, history of treatment, and equal outpatient treatment.

Chemical dependency patients were treated by an interdisciplinary team of therapists who often did not agree on treatment plans and were outright divided on such fundamental matters as abstinence, controlled drinking, and the benefits of 12-step programs. Also, it was a routine practice in the hospital to use photocopied versions of various copyrighted instruments of assessment (e.g., the Beck Depression Inventory, Symptom Check List–90, etc.). The staff simply used a copier to duplicate these tests when supplies were exhausted instead of ordering new materials from the publisher and paying for them.

Many of these practices contributed to improving and maintaining the financial health of the institution and were well entrenched by the time Dr. Listig began working there. With some misgivings, she approached Dr. Sly Hardrock, chief of the psychology service, to discuss the reservations she had about carrying out duties that appeared to violate the Ethics Code. Specifically, she raised two major issues: (a) financial exploitation of patients (Standards 3.04, Avoiding Harm; 1.01, Misuse of Psychologists' Work; and 3.08, Exploitative Relationships) and (b) staff incompetence (Standards 2.01, Boundaries of Competence; 2.04, Bases for Scientific and Professional Judgments; 9.02, Use of Assessments; 9.07, Assessment by Unqualified Persons; and 10.01, Informed Consent to Therapy). She addressed several other areas of concern that seemed to be either unethical, illegal, or unprofessional as well.

Dr. Hardrock was distinctly unimpressed with the ethical questions raised by his new employee. He had not been a member of the APA or his state psychological association for many years, and he believed, therefore, that the APA Ethics Code had no jurisdiction over him. As for his staff members who were active members of APA, they would have to make ethical compromises if they wanted to keep their very well-paying positions at the hospital. It was clear that Dr. Hardrock had no intention of altering hospital policies that reflected his own personal stratum of an unethical quagmire.

Reluctantly, Dr. Listig began her search for another position, although she was not successful for nearly 1 year because of the poor economy and few job openings. During that period, she did what she could to maximize her own compliance with the Ethics Code and to enlighten other psychologists on the service about these matters that had significant clinical and ethical implications. In the last few months of her job at the hospital, she initiated a formal complaint against Dr. Hardrock with the state board of psychology. Although it was true that he was not a member of APA or the state psychological association, he held a psychology license and was therefore bound to comply with the state licensing laws that mandate compliance with the Ethics Code.[1]

1. Would you characterize Dr. Listig's response to the hospital practices as naïve or overly idealistic in light of the economics of the situation?
2. Would Dr. Listig be vulnerable to a possible ethics complaint, board of psychology complaint, or civil suit, by continuing to participate in a system that blatantly ignores the ethical standards of psychologists?
3. If Dr. Listig were the sole psychologist practicing alongside psychological assistants, anesthesiologists (pain specialists), psychiatrists, technicians, clinical social workers, psychiatric nurses, and registered nurses—all with their own codes of ethics—how might her risk to a malpractice claim, from a disappointed and litigious former patient, change?

1.04 INFORMAL RESOLUTION OF ETHICAL VIOLATIONS

When psychologists believe that there may have been an ethical violation by another psychologist, they attempt to resolve the issue by bringing it to the attention of that individual, if an informal resolution appears appropriate and the intervention does not violate any confidentiality rights that may be involved. (See also Standards 1.02, Conflict Between Ethics and Law, Regulations, or Other Governing Legal Authority, and 1.03, Conflicts Between Ethics and Organizational Demands.)

If you believe that a psychologist has violated some ethical rule and an informal approach seems best, bring it directly to his or her attention, rather than automatically contacting an ethics committee or state psychology board. In any case, do not simply turn a blind eye; make an attempt to get in touch with the individual. However, do *not* do so if it would jeopardize the privacy of others in these situations; bear in mind that a client or patient may not want or feel ready to bring an ethics complaint even though you think that they should. (They may need some "recovery time" after experiencing unethical conduct at the hands of a psychologist that could take months or even years, depending on the severity of the transgression.)

---

[1]Laws concerning compliance with the APA Ethics Code vary by state.

VIGNETTE

Dr. Gary Greavers was on the faculty of a small professional school of psychology and was well-known for his enthusiastic teaching style and affable nature. During the winter months, however, his spirits had begun to sink, and it was becoming increasingly clear to his colleagues that he was inexorably headed toward depression. A colleague, Dr. Sylvia Reacher, noticed that he was keeping rather unusual office hours and several times each week was having dinner with a few select female graduate students. Although there was nothing specifically unethical about this practice, it raised a question in Dr. Reacher's mind, and she began to wonder whose needs were being met—the supervisor's or his supervisees'. It seemed likely to her that Dr. Greavers might be starting to seek the emotional support of his female students to lift his spirits during this time of apparent low mood.

She also took note of the fact that one of his trainees, Inga, had begun seeing Dr. Greavers for supervision at 7:30 p.m. each evening, when the building was usually empty. After the supervisory session, the two would go out for dinner to a nearby restaurant. Dr. Reacher waited, watchfully, to see if Inga would raise a question within the department or bring a complaint about her supervisor's apparent changing relationship with her. This never happened, however, possibly because Inga ascribed a significant amount of social power to Dr. Greavers, and they were still in the early stages of a possible romantic relationship. Dr. Reacher also noted that on the mornings that she and Dr. Greavers cotaught a seminar she sometimes smelled alcohol on his breath, noted that his words were almost slurred, and observed that his usual eloquent style of presenting seemed quite different.

One day, Dr. Greavers openly confided in Dr. Reacher that he was having difficulty sleeping and that he had been very dejected about his brother's recent positive HIV diagnosis. She listened empathically to her friend and took the opportunity to mention that perhaps the stress of his brother's ill health was affecting his objectivity and ability to carry out his work in his usual competent manner. Pointedly, she also raised the question of his late-night tête-à-têtes with his supervisee, Inga, and his possible overuse of alcohol.

Dr. Greavers was resistant at first and denied that he had behaved in any way that was questionable or that he was drinking too much. The next day, however, he contacted Dr. Reacher and told her that he was relieved that someone had finally raised these questions with him. He told her that he actually had increased his daily alcohol consumption lately and, to manage his strong anxiety in the morning, was even drinking before he left his house for work. He also acknowledged that he did have amorous feelings for Inga that were leading him closer to a full romantic relationship with her, although there had been no sexual contact yet.

Slowly, Dr. Greavers had become more impaired in his ability to provide competent and objective supervision to Inga and probably would not have taken any steps to remedy this situation until he had traveled farther down the road of an intimate relationship with her. Attempting to provide supervision while pursuing a romantic relationship was clearly at cross-purposes, but he had continued to engage in both these roles until his friend and colleague had called his attention to what was happening.

Because of Dr. Reacher's efforts, Dr. Greavers began the process of his own rehabilitation by consulting with a therapist and started to consider attending 12-step meetings to explore his heavy reliance on alcohol. He understood that it would be best if Inga were to change supervisors and explained to her that he needed to withdraw from that role, given his current state of emotional stress. Dr. Reacher was pleased that her friend was responsive to her suggestions and obviously saw no immediate need to formalize a complaint to an ethics body or licensing board. Dr. Greavers seemed well aware of his temporary incompetence and was taking appropriate steps to remedy it.

1. Was Sylvia Reacher too slow in bringing her observations about supervision to her colleague, deciding instead to see whether Inga would initiate a question or complaint?
2. How likely is it that Inga would have complained against her supervisor's romantic interest in her if it were reciprocal in nature?
3. What would you recommend as the next series of steps that a friendly colleague such as Dr. Reacher should take, both within the professional school and outside, if Dr. Greavers persisted in resisting her attempts to point out his alcohol dependency, depression, and risk of unethical conduct with the supervisee?
4. Does Dr. Reacher bear any ethical, legal, professional, or moral responsibility to follow up with her friend, who now has begun treatment for alcohol dependency and depression?

1.05 REPORTING ETHICAL VIOLATIONS

If an apparent ethical violation has substantially harmed or is likely to substantially harm a person or organization and is not appropriate for informal resolution under Standard 1.04, Informal Resolution of Ethical Violations, or is not resolved properly in that fashion, psychologists take further action appropriate to the situation. Such action might include referral to state or national committees on professional ethics, to state licensing boards, or to the appropriate institutional authorities. This standard does not apply when an intervention would violate confidentiality rights or when psychologists have been retained to review the work of another psychologist whose professional conduct is in question. (See also Standard 1.02, Conflicts Between Ethics and Law, Regulations, or Other Governing Legal Authority.)

Situations can arise in which a psychologist's unethical conduct has significantly harmed or is very likely to harm someone or some organization, and bringing your concern to their attention would not be wise (e.g., the conduct is egregious, or you have already approached the individual directly and have been stonewalled or threatened to be sued by that person if you persist in "bothering" him or her). This would apply to major transgressions, such as sex with a patient, fraudulent research, or defiant refusal to change after he or she has already been confronted about the unethical conduct. In these cases, don't hesitate to contact an ethics committee of your state psychological association (if it still accepts complaints for adjudication) or the APA, the state licensing board, or other authorities (hospital or university ethics committees, other professional association ethics committees, or institutional review board, etc.).

VIGNETTE

Dr. Heddy Bong was skilled in hypnosis and had been using it extensively in her practice with many patients. She was also a recovering cocaine abuser and had been drug free for almost 5 years. She attributed her success in stopping cocaine use to her unique application of hypnosis and thought that she had discovered a foolproof cure for chemical dependency in general. She was so pleased with her innovative techniques and convinced of their superiority to all other programs that she founded her own self-help movement called Alcoholic Hypnotics Anonymous (with the spirited acronym AHA!).

She borrowed heavily from the 12-step program model and added her own hypnotic training as a central feature, teaching hypnosis to all participants and encouraging them to teach others as well. Her groups were open to all comers; she did not "diagnose or discriminate," welcoming those who were depressed or had panic disorders right alongside those who were actively suicidal, paranoid, or had a bipolar or dissociative disorder. Hypnosis was "for one and all" who wanted to stop drinking, and "each one should teach one," as she believed that AHA! was the true cure for everybody and that conventional individual therapy was rapidly becoming an anachronism.

In reality, Dr. Bong was engaging in a range of potentially dangerous professional activities. She was systematically assembling the very ingredients that could result in serious harm to individuals: a nonspecific treatment for those who are chemically dependent—some with dual diagnoses, some with serious developmental disabilities, and some with grossly impaired judgment—and attempting to teach a specialized technique (hypnosis) to them regardless of their history or capability to engage in it, with little apparent concern for risk.

Several colleagues approached Dr. Bong over a period of 6 months and questioned her professional activities, but she was unwilling to consider their objections to her professional practices. She told them that she was not acting as a psychologist in the groups because, as a recovering cocaine addict, she considered herself a "patient" too, and therefore the Ethics Code did not apply to her conduct. The fact that she used her doctoral title, promoted the groups with newspaper advertisements and on local radio and TV talk shows, and charged a fee for group attendance did not, in her mind, constitute rendering a psychological service.

Dr. Bong's concerned colleagues soon discovered that little would be gained by further attempts to point out the grave risk of her amateurish conduct, and the high probability, ultimately, of harming others who were in need of treatment. They brought a formal complaint to the APA Ethics Committee, citing Standards 2.01, Boundaries of Competence; 3.04, Avoiding Harm; and 2.04, Bases for Scientific and Professional Judgments. Furthermore, a participant in one of her groups who had become actively suicidal while under her care also brought a complaint against her for malpractice. The ensuing investigation by the Ethics Committee revealed that several other standards also were pertinent. The psychologists were confident that they had followed the most effective course in reporting such egregious conduct to the Ethics Committee, especially in light of the fact that Dr. Bong had made vague references to suing them for slander if they continued to "harass" her.

The Ethics Committee took approximately 1 year to process the complaints against Dr. Bong. Ultimately, APA censured Dr. Bong and required several directives. The directives included (a) a cease-and-desist order for her irresponsible and potentially harmful practices involving the application of hypnosis in such a highly heterogeneous group setting; (b) required psychotherapy (including quarterly brief reports to the Ethics Committee); (c) required monitoring of her practice by a psychologist; and (d) 12 hours of continuing education in ethics, with a focus on competence, dual-role relationships, therapist impairment, and business practices. This meant that Dr. Bong would be required to stop the use of hypnosis in her groups; consult with a psychologist who was experienced in chemical dependency and hypnosis, who would monitor and review her practice; begin individual psychotherapy on a weekly basis; and enroll in continuing education courses and meet with senior psychologists specializing in ethics training. This was a major blow to Dr. Bong, resulting in significant and costly restructuring of her professional and personal life. However, it was a badly needed intervention for a psychologist who was judged to be impaired, in danger of harming others, and unwilling to accept the wise counsel of her peers.

1. How would Dr. Bong's concerned colleagues have gone about the process of confronting her with their reservations about her conduct? As the "ethics police"? As "their brother's (or sister's) keeper?" Some other approach?
2. Did Dr. Bong's colleagues violate the Ethics Code by making an informal contact instead of filing a complaint as soon as they became aware of her behavior?
3. What dilemma is presented when one of Dr. Bong's former group members seeks outside individual treatment, because of a bad experience with her, but is unwilling to formalize a complaint against her or participate in the complaint process? Keeping in mind the requirements of confidentiality, what, if anything, could or should the treating psychologist do?
4. What would you consider in making the decision whether to confront a colleague with his or her possible unethical conduct or report him or her directly to an ethics committee?

1.06 COOPERATING WITH ETHICS COMMITTEES

Psychologists cooperate in ethics investigations, proceedings, and resulting requirements of the APA or any affiliated state psychological association to which they belong. In doing so, they address any confidentiality issues. Failure to cooperate is itself an ethics violation. However, making a request for deferment of adjudication of an ethics complaint pending the outcome of litigation does not alone constitute noncooperation.

If the APA or your home state Ethics Committee comes knocking on your door, open it! You must cooperate with the investigation (e.g., respond to letters and requests for information within the time limits specified). Never simply ignore a formal complaint because you think you have done nothing wrong; you could lose your membership, because failing to respond is an ethics violation in and of itself. You may certainly defend yourself and explain your side of the story, with or without consulting an ethicist or a lawyer, but always comply with the Rules and Procedures of the APA (2001) or state Ethics Committee. If you have been sued, and litigation is still going on, you may ask the Ethics Committee to defer your case until it has been completed.

VIGNETTE

Dr. Ari Gant was the human resources director of a large hospital system with many franchises in different cities. One day, Dr. Gant received a certified letter from the APA Ethics Office notifying him that a formal complaint had been brought against him for his conduct as a psychologist. An African American man, Jackson Williams, who had applied for work at the hospital, was claiming racial discrimination in the hiring practices of the human resources department, a direct violation of Standard 3.01, Unfair Discrimination. Mr. Williams faulted the department's policy of screening potential employees by using a structured interview and a 30-item, multiple-choice test that attempted to assess candidates' professional judgment and interpersonal skills in a variety of typical hospital emergency and nonemergency situations.

Dr. Gant was a busy man; he was responsible directly or indirectly for the hiring, firing, and promotions of thousands of employees in eight different cities. He felt that he "could not be bothered" with an ethics complaint from APA, particularly when he felt that he had done nothing wrong and that the job applicant was just harassing him with a frivolous complaint.

Dr. Gant was given 30 days to respond to the charges in writing, according to the APA Ethics Committee's Rules and Procedures (APA, 2001b); specifically, he was asked to write his account of the complainant's assessment process at the hospital and show that it was not unfairly discriminatory. The complainant had signed a consent form allowing such disclosures and had submitted his own written version of the purported discrimination to the APA Ethics Office. Unfortunately, however, Dr. Gant considered an ethics complaint from APA to be relatively unimportant—it did not carry the force of a civil lawsuit or the potential serious consequences of a psychology licensing board investigation. Therefore, he decided to disregard it and did not even inform the hospital attorneys or his own professional liability insurance carrier that a complaint had been filed against him. Furthermore, being caught up in daily personnel crises at the hospital and the need to travel more than usual because of staff problems in other cities, he felt he had no time or energy to seriously address this problem or to provide a reasonable response to the Ethics Office. He failed to respond to additional attempts by the Ethics Committee to contact him, including letters advising that (a) he was in violation and was being recommended for expulsion from APA; (b) he had waived his right to a hearing by failing to respond to that recommendation; and (c) he could submit a statement to the Board of Directors, the body that would make the final decision whether to expel him.

Ultimately he received a letter expelling him from APA. He was further informed that he could reapply for membership after 5 years. Dr. Gant valued his membership in APA and was deeply distressed that such a severe sanction had been imposed for his failure to cooperate. He would have been better off had he responded to the complaint regardless of his feelings of guilt or innocence; if he was hopelessly overwhelmed with work obligations, he could have petitioned for a delay in responding. Even if he had cooperated fully and the complaint was adjudicated, it might well have failed to meet the threshold of an ethics violation, and he could have been fully exonerated. Failure to offer any response whatever was clearly a poor choice.

1. Although involved with work "emergencies," how might Dr. Gant have proceeded if he had accorded the complaint the seriousness that it deserved?
2. By failing to respond to the letter, how did Dr. Gant increase the risk of another sort of complaint from Mr. Williams, thereby "upping the ante"?
3. How would Dr. Gant know that he is cooperating adequately with an Ethics Committee investigation?

1.07 IMPROPER COMPLAINTS

Psychologists do not file or encourage the filing of ethics complaints that are made with reckless disregard for or willful ignorance of facts that would disprove the allegation.

Filing an ethics complaint is serious business. Before filing a complaint, or encouraging someone else to do so, consider what facts you actually know, or could easily learn, that would invalidate the charges.

VIGNETTE

Dr. Mohammad Essabar was a practicing Muslim and psychologist working in the psychiatry department of a large county hospital. For the past 18 months, he had been carrying out exploratory clinical research with chemically dependent adults who used street drugs, principally, Oxycontin, heroin, and Ecstasy. His research involved examining the psychologically healing properties of forgiveness by having his clinical patients participate in a forgiveness workshop as an adjunct to their standard treatment. Although patients were not randomized to receive this intervention, and there was no real control group other than patients who chose not to participate, Dr. Essabar observed that those who went through the forgiveness workshop were more likely to report reductions in their use of street drugs and improvements in mood.

A colleague in the department, Dr. Goldberg, had been scrutinizing Dr. Essabar's clinical work with a somewhat jaded eye ever since he had arrived on staff, and he had been generally critical of his research. Dr. Goldberg himself had been struggling with chronic depression and unresolved personal losses for many years. His parents had endured the concentration camps of the Holocaust and, more recently, he had lost his only sibling, a beloved sister, who was working in the World Trade Center when it was destroyed in the terrorist attacks of September 11, 2001. He felt he was justified in reacting strongly to what he saw as religious extremism and bigotry; indeed, he had always viewed Dr. Essabar's commitment to Islam as a significant problem—it was a conflict of interest, the way he understood Islam. More recently, however, his judgment was becoming more distorted, and he had started to believe that Dr. Essabar was truly a malevolent force, in spite of the fact that others saw him as a successful clinician carrying out consistently innovative research.

Dr. Essabar had presented some preliminary results of his exploratory research at a professional conference indicating that, although based on case studies, his protocol appeared to have value in the rehabilitation of some patients who were addicted, and he thought it warranted further research in a randomized clinical trial format. Even the media had taken an interest in his work by publishing a brief summary of his presentation in the local newspaper. Unfortunately, however, it was presented in a superficial and sensationalistic manner, with important disclaimers missing, and Dr. Essabar's clinical interventions were described as a panacea for virtually any drug addict. He immediately contacted the newspaper about the tenor of the article and substantial distortions, but unfortunately the editor refused to print a retraction or correct the misstatements.

This was all the ammunition that the smoldering Dr. Goldberg needed to give vent to his ever-increasing ill will. Obviously there was no way that he could formally complain about his colleague's religious convictions, but at least he could criticize what he considered to be shoddy research and false claims. He expressed his antagonism indirectly by avoiding questioning Dr. Essabar about the newspaper article, even though this would have been an obvious step to take, as advised by Standard 1.04, Informal Resolution of Ethical Violations. Instead, he immediately contacted his state association's Ethics Office to initiate a formal complaint.

Dr. Essabar was very surprised to receive a letter from the Ethics Committee charging him with several violations of ethical standards involving public statements and research methodology, as reported in the newspaper article. His attempts to contact Dr. Goldberg were futile, as the latter would not return any phone calls or e-mails and refused to even speak with him on the rare occasions when they encountered each other in the hospital. Dr. Essabar knew that he was obliged to comply with the Ethics Committee's rules and procedures by responding to the charges within a specified time frame. This took a considerable amount of his time and energy and was personally stressful as well. Dr. Essabar took his membership in the state association seriously and did not wish to jeopardize it, even though he thought that this was an unjustified complaint triggered by personal feelings of animosity, not ethical considerations. Therefore he gave his full attention to the complaint process, responding to each of the charges and providing answers to all questions, complete with requested documentation. The task was time consuming, taking nearly 6 months, and it was somewhat anxiety evoking to submit to the scrutiny of one's peers, even though he felt that he had committed no ethical infraction. He felt the complaint warranted this amount of effort, however, and provided the fullest response possible. Ultimately, he was exonerated, and all ethical charges were dropped.

Dr. Essabar gave much consideration to the actions of his colleague and suspected that Dr. Goldberg must have been aware of his strong ethical commitment in research and clinical work, as they had been on the same staff for many years. He concluded that the complaint brought by Dr. Goldberg must have been an attempt to hurt him, based on his own feelings of prejudice against Muslims and, possibly, his own untreated (and unacknowledged) depression.

After much reflection, Dr. Essabar decided to attempt to approach Dr. Goldberg one last time and raise the question that he had filed an improper complaint. Certainly Dr. Goldberg would have known that it was unfounded when he filed it, and he should have approached Dr. Essabar directly, rather than contact an ethics committee. As it turned out, Dr. Goldberg's mood had deteriorated to the point that he was required to take a medical leave and begin long-overdue treatment for depression. Dr. Essabar had no need to file a countercomplaint, citing Standards 1.07 (Improper Complaints) and also 2.06 (Personal Problems and Conflicts), as Dr. Goldberg finally acknowledged that he had behaved improperly and with vindictiveness, and eventually he formally apologized to Dr. Essabar for his actions.

1. What steps might Dr. Goldberg have taken before filing his complaint that might have averted his taking that step, assuming he still had some objectivity left?
2. If the Ethics Committee took a long time to conclude that there was no basis for a complaint, after examining all the possibilities of technical violations based on research methodology, would this provide the basis for Dr. Goldberg to argue that his complaint, in fact, was not improper? (See footnote 1.)
3. List all the ways that Dr. Goldberg harmed Dr. Essabar by filing an improper complaint.
4. Whom might you consult, before filing a complaint, to make sure that it was not falsely grounded?

1.08 UNFAIR DISCRIMINATION AGAINST COMPLAINANTS AND RESPONDENTS

Psychologists do not deny persons employment, advancement, admissions to academic or other programs, tenure, or promotion, based solely upon their having made or their being the subject of an ethics complaint. This does not preclude taking action based upon the outcome of such proceedings or considering other appropriate information.

The fact that someone has either brought an ethics complaint, or has been named in a complaint by someone else, must not be used against him or her in the following situations:

- potential students or trainees seeking admission to an academic program or some other professional setting and
- faculty or staff seeking employment, professional advancement, promotion, or tenure.

If you are the one to make decisions in these matters, however, you may take into consideration the outcome of such a complaint, or other collateral information that you have obtained that would have a bearing on that person's eligibility.

VIGNETTE

Dr. Handler was an assistant professor in psychology, up for tenure and promotion to be an associate professor, and he also had a small private practice two evenings a week. Being ambitious, he was attempting to increase his practice by one extra night per week and add Saturday mornings, and he did so by seeking out many managed health care panels on which to serve. He also had two young children at home and had recently purchased a new house. He was finding that, given all the demands on his time and energy, he occasionally would lose track of things and fail to fulfill some of his professional responsibilities.

He had never felt that this was a serious problem, however, until the day he received a certified letter, with return receipt requested, from the APA Ethics Office, informing him that a complaint had been filed against him by one of his former patients. Unfortunately, he had not been as attentive as he should have been about completing the patient's health insurance claim forms promptly and following up when the case manager refused a claim. A particularly angry female patient whom Dr. Handler had diagnosed with borderline personality disorder, Ms. Brenda Pryor, had broken off treatment 6 months earlier and had relapsed into alcoholism. She had telephoned Dr. Handler on several occasions, months later, leaving messages for him to complete the forms for her sessions to date, so that she could obtain reimbursement. Her health insurance claim forms and related correspondence from the managed-care company had gotten lost in a pile of papers and likely had been discarded.

Recently Dr. Handler had been involved with the task of converting his practice to be compliant with the HIPAA (Health Insurance Portability and Accountability Act) regulations, as several of the managed-care companies required electronic submission of documents, and he knew that this was likely to be the case with most other companies in the future. He had been spending a great deal of time rewriting his authorization forms and informed-consent documents to be consistent with the HIPAA rules. Unfortunately, he had lost track of several patients' third-party payor forms, and many months elapsed. Ms. Pryor was the only patient who initiated a complaint with APA; the two other patients, who were continuing to see Dr. Handler, simply brought additional forms to their therapy sessions when he was unable to locate theirs.

Dr. Handler was understandably upset about this complaint, particularly that three standards had been cited: Standard 6.06, Accuracy in Reports to Payors and Funding Sources; Standard 2.06 (b), Personal Problems and Conflicts; and Standard 3.04, Avoiding Harm. Ms. Pryor felt that she had been harmed by his failure to fill out the forms in a timely fashion, as she counted on the financial reimbursements to meet her ongoing living expenses. In a vindictive mood, she also sent a copy of her complaint letter to the chairman of the psychology department at the university, as she knew that her former therapist was on the faculty there, and she wanted to spread the word about Dr. Handler's incompetence in any way she could.

Dr. Handler worried that this complaint might affect his good reputation within the department and, more specifically, that it would negatively affect his pending promotion. The chair of the tenure review committee, Dr. Stickler, was well aware of the many responsibilities of university professors, such as participating in committee work, following through with difficult students, meeting deadlines of various sorts, and dealing with departmental fiscal matters as well. He was disappointed to learn that Dr. Handler was so lax in his business practices that a patient had actually filed charges against him with APA, and he privately wondered how this might portend of future lapses within the department if Dr. Handler were to be promoted.

Dr. Stickler and the committee deliberated on these matters and carefully reviewed the facts concerning Dr. Handler's performance within the department of psychology. One younger member of the committee pointed out that, according to the most recent revision of the APA Ethics Code, psychologists were not supposed to deny a person advancement simply on the grounds that a faculty member had an ethics complaint pending with APA; however, they did have the option of delaying their decision until an outcome was reached by the Ethics Committee.

They ultimately decided to proceed with their decision, and promoted Dr. Handler to associate professor, in spite of the fact that the complaint had not yet been adjudicated. They reasoned that his performance within the university had always been strong, his publications were excellent, and he generally received high teaching evaluations by students. It was unfortunate that he had mishandled an important aspect of his business practices, outside of his academic work, but that seemed to have little bearing on his responsibilities as a faculty member.

Dr. Handler was pleased with the outcome, obviously, but nevertheless sought out a senior faculty member to discuss his recent tendency to overextend himself. Over time, this mentoring friendship resulted in some important lessons for Dr. Handler that affected decisions about his professional life for many years to come.

1. What sort of complaint might get the attention of the tenure review committee and warrant the delay of Dr. Handler's promotion until after it was adjudicated by the APA Ethics Committee?

2. What if Brenda Pryor were applying for admission to the doctoral program in psychology during the time frame of her troubles with Dr. Handler? How might an admissions committee be influenced by her current complaint against a member of their faculty, such as the one against Dr. Handler, in light of the requirements of this standard?

3. What steps might an advanced doctoral student take against a professor who committed a serious ethical violation, such as plagiarizing the student's work in a journal article?

2

COMPETENCE

2.01 BOUNDARIES OF COMPETENCE

(a) Psychologists provide services, teach, and conduct research with populations and in areas only within the boundaries of their competence, based on their education, training, supervised experience, consultation, study, or professional experience.

Do only what you are competent to do. Always stay within your depth when doing psychotherapy, assessment, consultation, teaching, supervision, research, or any other psychological work, even though at times you may be tempted to push yourself. Make sure that your professional work is based on at least one of the following:

- your formal graduate or professional education,
- other postgraduate training or ongoing education,
- supervised work by a competent and credentialed supervisor,
- consultation with someone who is qualified in the area in question,
- independent study on your part, or
- some other fitting professional experience.

VIGNETTE

Dr. Overschoot had recently relocated to a new city to join a group practice and was eager to build his reputation by accepting as many new patients as he could schedule. He agreed to accept into treatment a young woman who requested hypnosis for alleviating her long-standing anxiety symptoms. His only exposure to hypnosis had been a half-day workshop, which he took several months previously with no follow-up consultation or supervision.

The woman had magical beliefs about hypnosis and was quick to place her trust in Dr. Overschoot; she was particularly encouraged by his strong endorsement of hypnotic techniques for anxiety management. Unfortunately, however, shortly after beginning the hypnotic induction she experienced a panicky flashback, and she began to gasp and weep and manifest other signs of obvious distress. Dr. Overschoot was ill prepared for what appeared to be an intense dissociative reaction, and his efforts at working with her with the meager hypnotic strategies that he remembered only made things worse. The patient eventually opened her eyes, ended her trance, and attempted to orient herself and make sense of what had just occurred.

Dr. Overschoot had such little training in hypnosis, dissociation, or posthypnotic processing that he was unable to provide much help to his patient, who was attempting to analyze and understand what appeared to be a traumatic memory, as he did not understand it himself. As a result of this experience, Dr. Overschoot wisely resolved to avoid using hypnosis until he acquired substantially more training and supervision.

The experience of working outside his area of competence by using hypnosis, unfortunately, did not deter Dr. Overschoot from overextending himself once again in a different subspecialty area. He agreed to accept for divorce mediation a married couple, Mr. and Mrs. Wolf, who had a long history of alcohol abuse and violence, in spite of the fact that his only relevant training consisted of a 2-hour presentation on divorce mediation and a slight amount of reading about couples who were violent. He felt he had some innate experience, however, as his own parents had had a turbulent marriage and divorced when he was a teenager, and there had been many occasions when he had intervened to help calm things down.

The couple showed up 10 minutes late, with the husband appearing mildly intoxicated and the wife apologetic. As the counseling session began, Mr. Wolf was sullen while his wife began to criticize and blame. Dr. Overschoot's attempts to structure the session were ineffective. Slowly, Mr. Wolf became increasingly belligerent; in response to his wife's thinly veiled taunting and Dr. Overschoot's clumsy confrontations, his temper began to flare, and his face turned red. Rising out of his chair suddenly, he slapped his wife in the face and bumped Dr. Overschoot out of the way as he stormed out of the office, breaking a lamp and an antique table in the process. Mrs. Wolf remained behind, tearfully speaking about how difficult their marriage had been and pleading with Dr. Overschoot to help them to separate once and for all, without the expense of having to retain separate lawyers. Dr. Overschoot sadly informed Mrs. Wolf that he did not think he would be able to assist the couple, given the intensity of their dynamics. In reality, it was clear that Dr. Overschoot's amateurish interventions only served to provoke the husband's aggression, and it was obvious that he possessed few skills to facilitate such a loaded situation that exploded out of control almost before the session got under way.

As a result of these two incidents, Dr. Overschoot began to appreciate the potential dangers of practicing outside his areas of competence. By being willing to accept into treatment almost anyone seeking his services, regardless of their presenting complaint and his level of competence, he not only risked harming consumers but also increased his vulnerability to ethics complaints or civil lawsuits by dissatisfied clients. For the first time in his professional life, he began to own up to the fact that he simply did not possess the competence to provide therapy to anyone who might request it, even though the person's motivation to seek treatment from him might be quite high. He learned a painful lesson from his unskilled attempts at hypnosis and divorce mediation. He now could see the importance of selecting patients with concerns clearly within his areas of competence and the necessity of obtaining more training and consultation before moving into new areas.

1. How would Dr. Overschoot be able to determine that his training had been sufficient to undertake a new area of practice, such as hypnosis, high-conflict couples, biofeedback, attention-deficit disorder, or any other area?
2. What course of action would you recommend for Dr. Overschoot to remedy the situation with his hypnosis patient, to minimize harm?
3. Describe several scenarios in which inadequate preparation and training on the part of a psychologist in your specialty area could result in significant harm to someone.
4. What risks does a psychologist face from a disappointed and angry consumer who wishes to take some action against him or her?

2.01 (b)

Where scientific or professional knowledge in the discipline of psychology establishes that an understanding of factors associated with age, gender, gender identity, race, ethnicity, culture, national origin, religion, sexual orientation, disability, language, or socioeconomic status is essential for effective implementation of their services or research, psychologists have or obtain the training, experi-

ence, consultation, or supervision necessary to ensure the competence of their services, or they make appropriate referrals, except as provided in Standard 2.02, Providing Services in Emergencies.

When you know that a client or patient's personal attributes will probably affect your work with him or her, make sure that you have the right training, experience, consultation, or supervision to do a good job in carrying out clinical work, consultation, research, or any other psychological service. In doing so, please consider the following:

- age (chronological age or developmental stage; e.g., child, adolescent, adult, or elderly);
- sex (male or female);
- gender identity (how the person views him- or herself—male or female—regardless of genotype);
- race (differentiated by skin and hair color, physical traits, etc.);
- ethnicity (shared cultural traits; e.g., Asian, Latino, etc.);
- culture (shared beliefs, customs, practices, and social behavior; e.g., Native American or Cajun);
- national origin (Mexico, China, India, etc.);
- religion (Catholic, Jewish, Buddhist, Muslim, etc.);
- sexual orientation (gay, straight, bisexual, etc.);
- disability (medically diagnosed condition; e.g., blindness, deafness, chronic pain, degenerative illness, etc.);
- language (English, Spanish, and dialects); and
- socioeconomic status (income level, social class, etc.).

If you are unable to accept or well tolerate one of these attributes of a person or group to whom you are rendering services, refer the client to someone who is! Otherwise, obtain adequate training, consultation, or supervision to compensate for your deficiencies (see American Psychological Association [APA], 1993a).

VIGNETTE

Mrs. Lopez, a 60-year-old Puerto Rican woman who had been visiting relatives in Manhattan, was brought to the emergency room of a downtown hospital following a relatively minor automobile accident. The taxicab she was riding in made a turn onto a one-way street near Times Square and collided with another car. The cabbie blamed her for the accident and belligerently cursed at her for distracting him. When Mrs. Lopez was examined by the physician, she appeared to be inconsolably irrational and overexcited. The physician detected no evidence of a head injury or any other significant injury and no evidence of drug or alcohol use. She found Mrs. Lopez's apparent cognitive impairment, anxiety, and intense emotionality to be excessive and triaged her to the psychologist on call, Dr. Terry O'Reilly.

Although she was highly anxious, appearing to be delusional at times, and was struggling to speak English intelligibly, Mrs. Lopez was able to provide a sketchy history in response to questions from Dr. O'Reilly. He was able to glean from her excited presentation that she had come to New York 3 days ago and was visiting her two sons and their families. Unfortunately, her oldest son had been diagnosed only the day before with a rare neurological disorder, and his prognosis was uncertain. Also, tragically, she had lost her husband, to whom she had been married for 40 years, to an unexpected heart attack 2 months before.

Dr. O'Reilly noted that many of Mrs. Lopez's symptoms—such as trembling, shortness of breath, lightheadedness, dizziness, and a feeling of warmth in her chest along with a cold sweat—were consistent with a panic attack. However, he also found her speech to be incoherent at times and observed that she persisted in talking about her deceased family members. Their "presence" in her life appeared to be consistent with delusional thinking. He diagnosed her as having a brief psychotic disorder and recommended that she be admitted to the hospital and assessed by the attending psychiatrist, who would likely advise treating her with a neuroleptic agent.

As he was about to implement his recommendation, he was joined by his colleague, Dr. Carlos Mendoza, a Hispanic psychologist, who fortuitously was just beginning his shift at the hospital. After hearing Dr. O'Reilly briefly review Mrs. Lopez's case, Dr. Mendoza was intrigued by her symptoms and asked if he might interview her. After doing so, he concluded quickly that Ms. Lopez suffered from no psychotic disorder at all but that she had the familiar signs he had witnessed many times before among Hispanic women who had recently experienced a major loss in life. This is called *ataque de nervios* and is characterized by many symptoms similar to anxiety and psychotic disorders. The death of her husband and the illness of her son had all caused mounting levels of stress in her life, and the automobile accident was the final stressor that triggered this reaction. The treatment of choice, as many Hispanic families knew from experience, was decidedly not hospitalization, which would isolate her from her social support network and would likely worsen her symptoms. The administration of neuroleptic medication, which would only cause side effects and not substantially affect her mental health, was not the answer either. Instead, Mrs. Lopez needed the solace, love, and support of family members who would virtually surround her with a functional therapeutic milieu. This could readily be accomplished, because Mrs. Lopez had many extended family members living in New York. After making the diagnosis and recommending the family's supportive involvement as the only treatment needed, Dr. Mendoza contacted Mrs. Lopez's sons to help facilitate its implementation.

Dr. O'Reilly learned a valuable lesson about taking cultural variables into account when diagnosing and treating mental disorders. Had it not been for his colleague's intervention, he would have made a formal recommendation for treatment that would have been quite inappropriate and likely would have exacerbated the patient's symptoms. He resolved to learn more about treating Hispanic patients by taking a continuing education workshop at the next available opportunity.

1. How might Dr. O'Reilly's decision to hospitalize Mrs. Lopez have negatively affected her, in a worst-case scenario?
2. What steps might you take if you suspected that cultural, sexual, ethnic, or religious variables were significant factors in treating or mentoring a particular individual, but you were unclear as to their exact nature or what to do about it?
3. How might a psychologist conducting a child custody assessment make significant errors because of his or her naivete about the couple's culture, religion, or race?
4. Think of several examples in your own specialty area where you might possibly increase the risk of an ethics complaint or other kind of grievance action due to a failure to consider variables such as culture, race, sexual orientation, disability, or ethnicity.

2.01 (c)

Psychologists planning to provide services, teach, or conduct research involving populations, areas, techniques, or technologies new to them undertake relevant education, training, supervised experience, consultation, or study.

When considering an area of work that is new to you, such as a different population (adolescents, Mormons, lesbians, etc.), psychological topics, techniques, or technologies (computers, the Internet, etc.), offer your services, teach, or research only after first completing education, formal training, supervision, consultation, mentoring, or some suitable independent study. Approach these new areas and innovative techniques with prudence, caution, and customary scientific rigor. (If you want to be on the "cutting edge" of a therapy or intervention, be vigilant, because it may "cut" both ways—you could harm someone or ultimately be harmed in the process, by an ethics complaint, complaint to a licensing board, or a lawsuit.)

VIGNETTE

Dr. Thinnice was a psychologist in independent practice who specialized in health psychology and stress-related disorders. Because the combination of a slowed economy and the limitations of managed health care had taken quite a toll on his practice, he decided to seek new ways of diversifying.

Because he was friends with Mr. Borge, the chief operating officer of a successful pharmaceutical company, he thought this might provide an opportunity to offer his services as an organizational consultant to the company.

The pressure of diminishing income prompted him to move ahead on his idea with only a minimum of training in corporate consulting. He had taken a 1-day workshop in management consulting, and thought that he was now ready to begin offering his services in this area.

Mr. Borge was enthusiastic about Dr. Thinnice's offer to work with his firm. Although the company had been successful to date, it had recently suffered in its financial health, and the CEO was considering beginning a round of layoffs. It would be very helpful, Mr. Borge thought, to have the input of a psychologist he could trust about how to assess employees and streamline the layoff process; he envisioned that Dr. Thinnice could work closely with the company's human resources department in facilitating this reduction in force.

Dr. Thinnice was eager to get started. He hastily developed an assessment process consisting of a questionnaire for the employee, a brief structured interview to be carried out by managers, and a checklist appraising recent job performance. His protocol was largely intuitive, based on the stress management training and counseling he had done with clients in his private practice in recent years. He had given a slightly different version of his questionnaire to psychotherapy clients during the previous 2 years, and he felt that this provided good enough validation to proceed ahead. He presented this to the human resources staff for their consideration, stating that he had used this procedure before with good results. The truth was that he had neither empirically validated his technique nor carried out either a pilot study in an organizational setting or done any formal research in this area.

The reduction in force had to move ahead, and Dr. Thinnice's employee assessment program was implemented. Although some managers disagreed with the program, they knew that Mr. Borge strongly supported it and that resistance would be futile. However, many subordinates admitted to their managers that they had lied on the questionnaire to help save their jobs. Dr. Thinnice thought it would be wise to attempt to gather systematic data that would validate his three-part protocol. In this way he might eventually publish it—if, in fact, it turned out to be a useful tool. Specifically, the protocol was designed to assist managers faced with the problem of identifying employees who could be retained, those who should be referred for stress management counseling or other intervention (suffering incipient burnout or other problems), and those who should be laid off in times of economic necessity.

Dr. Thinnice appreciated the increase in his revenue resulting directly from working for the company, and he enjoyed the exhilaration of "really making a difference" and seeing the tangible results of his work in a short time frame. However, after a short time, some problems began to surface.

First, employees began to complain about the selection process for the stress management seminars or counseling with an Employee Assistance Program therapist that they felt they did not want or need. Second, some complained that the meetings were too much like group therapy, and they did not want to talk about their stress with fellow workers whom they did not necessarily trust, given the psychological climate of the layoffs. Third, and most important, one employee who had been laid off had begun a wrongful-termination suit against the company, naming Dr. Thinnice, specifically, as one of the defendants.

In light of all the complaints, and the pending lawsuit, the CEO and his executive team had good reason to reevaluate Dr. Thinnice's protocols; it did not take them long to reach a consensus about discontinuing it and terminating his contract. The CEO and the human resources department now had to focus energy on their own legal defense, something that was costly and time consuming. Unfortunately, Dr. Thinnice's malpractice insurance did not cover this particular professional activity, as he had never informed the insurer that he had added industrial–organizational consulting to his professional responsibilities. The charges against Dr. Thinnice focused on competence—chiefly, his failure to use methods for which he had adequate education or training, and his use of instruments of assessment and techniques that did not meet scientific standards for validity and reliability. By the time his legal defense was complete his expenses had rapidly escalated to over $40,000, a cost he was ill equipped to meet.

Indeed, the ice had finally become too thin for the ambitious doctor, and his painful fall into icy waters of litigation taught him some valuable lessons. He learned that there are no shortcuts and, regardless of the level of confidence he had in his abilities, he should never stray from his area of professional competence and always obtain formal training and consultation when venturing into new areas. Also, he gained a new respect for adherence to generally accepted standards of test development, including such basic factors as reliability and validity. Finally, he learned a costly lesson about the risks of harming the very people he intended to help and inadvertently increasing his own liability to lawsuits and ethics complaints in the process.

1. What sort of training or educational experiences should Dr. Thinnice have obtained before entering the area of corporate consulting?
2. What could Dr. Thinnice ethically have offered the employees that might have been of more value?
3. Would it have been ethically acceptable, and professionally wise, if Dr. Thinnice had used his experimental protocol with the pharmaceutical company but had included a disclaimer about its experimental nature?

When psychologists are asked to provide services to individuals for whom appropriate mental health services are not available and for which psychologists have not obtained the competence necessary, psychologists with closely related prior training or experience may provide such services in order to ensure that services are not denied if they make a reasonable effort to obtain the competence required by using relevant research, training, consultation, or study.

If you are asked to provide services to persons in need, and you are their only hope (i.e., no other services are available), you may do so, even if you do not have the ideal training, as long as you have some preparation or experience that is closely related. Make sure, however, that you get yourself up to speed by using pertinent research, training, consultation, or study.

VIGNETTE

Dr. Green had recently moved from Denver, Colorado, to a small town in Montana, to escape the intensity of city life and to establish a private practice in a part of the country he loved. There had been two other psychologists in practice in this town, but one had recently retired, and the other had declining health and was often unavailable. One day he received an urgent call from Mrs. Fields, a panicky mother who had just learned of her 17-year-old daughter's "terrible psychological problem." Mrs. Fields had come home from work early one afternoon to find the kitchen littered with open food containers—potato chips, two burrito wrappings, a pint of ice cream, an empty package of hot dogs, an empty box of cookies, and a pizza box. She then heard some noise in the back of the house and discovered her daughter vomiting loudly in the bathroom. It did not take long for her to learn that her daughter had been privately bingeing and purging for more than 10 months. Apparently, she had also been using laxatives regularly during this time as well. Mrs. Fields pleaded with Dr. Green to help her daughter, as soon she would be going away to college, and there just was not much time. She further relayed that her daughter had been losing weight recently, that her health was not very robust, that she was anxious and depressed, and that even her teeth were beginning to show the effects of all the vomiting. Her daughter admitted to using her computer for regular e-mail exchanges with a "friend" in Los Angeles whom she had met on a Web page for girls who relied on bingeing and purging to cope with stress. At first, her daughter adamantly refused to consider meeting with a psychologist, but after a few days, as her anxiety and depression worsened, she relented.

Dr. Green had seen adolescents in his practice, but he had never treated one with an eating disorder before, although he had had some didactic training in graduate school many years earlier. It was not a diagnostic category in which he was particularly interested or competent, and he had always been able to refer such patients to nearby colleagues or clinics. However, in this rather remote area he had no colleagues nearby; he was truly a solo practitioner—the nearest psychologist was over 75 miles away. He agreed to meet with the troubled teenager and her mother to explore the possibility of treatment.

Before the appointment, however, he telephoned his colleague and friend in Denver to discuss this case. His friend referred him to another psychologist in Denver, Dr. Sage, whose specialty was eating disorders. Dr. Green was pleased to have this resource available to him. After a brief consultation with Dr. Sage it was clear that he would probably be able to offer therapy to the teenager that would be helpful. Dr. Sage agreed to be an ongoing consultant on the case, for a fee, and to provide Dr. Green with some excellent resources. He immediately e-mailed Dr. Green a reading list, as well as several journal articles and chapters. It was apparent that technology would prove to be quite helpful in assisting with carrying on a practice in such a rural area. With access to a fax machine and e-mail, and using the Internet for searching electronic journal articles and databases about eating disorders, Dr. Green was able to augment his knowledge about theories and treatment options for bulimia. He wisely consulted regularly with Dr. Sage after he began treating the teenager, to provide the highest quality of care that he could under these less-than-optimal circumstances. In the meantime, he scoured the continuing education workshops that were being offered in his part of the country and felt fortunate to find a professional workshop on eating disorders being offered in Salt Lake City, Utah, which he attended so he could further develop his knowledge and skills.

1. What risk would exist if Dr. Green had simply accepted the teenager into treatment without consulting an experienced clinician as a resource?
2. What liability, if any, might Dr. Green incur if he had simply refused to treat the teenager and she deteriorated to the point of committing suicide?
3. How else might Dr. Green have found a resource to consult if none of his friends or colleagues could refer him?

2.01 (e)

In those emerging areas in which generally recognized standards for preparatory training do not yet exist, psychologists nevertheless take reasonable steps to ensure the competence of their work and to protect clients/patients, students, supervisees, research participants, organizational clients, and others from harm.

If there are not any standards or guidelines that relate to your ground-breaking work (or the work of others that you are following), take steps to assure your competence and to avoid harming clients, patients, students, supervisees, research participants, organizational clients, and others in the process. Remember, harm can come in a variety of ways: psychologically (unintended results of "successful" treatment or failed treatment, worsening of symptoms), therapeutically (loss of trust in treatment and therapists), socially (impact on other family members, friends), professionally (interfering with a client's ability to work), financially (unwarranted fees and expenses), legally (depriving others of rights), and in many other ways.

VIGNETTE

Dr. Wow was a psychologist practicing in a large midwestern city who felt that he had pioneered highly effective treatment interventions involving meditative and trance states. He had studied and received much training in different forms of meditation over the years and had most recently developed a radically different form of therapy, which, he thought, incorporated the best of Eastern and Western philosophy. He called this therapy *existential somatic shifting*, and he described it as a "miraculous intervention for resistant clients." In this therapy, he typically touches patients on both shoulders while staring at the center of their forehead for 5 minutes. He then places the patient's "soma" within his own. By noting the patient's skin color, hand temperature, and breathing pattern, and synchronizing his own breathing to match, he begins "a psycho-metabolic shift in the patient's soma." With much clever and persuasive advertising in the print and electronic media, Dr. Wow soon convinced many individuals to consult him for treatment.

Unfortunately, Dr. Wow never attempted to validate his intervention with clinical trials; neither did he inform patients that it was essentially an experimental technique. He also made no effort to publish his theories or present them at scientific meetings. He saw no reason to do so because he was convinced that his approach was effective, posed little or no risk to consumers, and was far superior to conventional therapies.

Certainly his approach worked well in a financial sense; Dr. Wow's bank account experienced a "metabolic shift" of major proportions because many patients sought him out for treatment. Some patients reported a "miraculous" improvement in their symptoms and were very pleased with the treatment. These patients became strong advocates of Dr. Wow's work. Other patients, however, experienced poor clinical results in the long run, with either no beneficial changes or a worsening of their symptoms over time.

One patient who was alcohol dependent continued drinking to excess while under Dr. Wow's care; Dr. Wow saw no reason to monitor the patient's drinking, refer him to a chemical dependency unit or 12-step program, or recommend any other conventional treatment for alcohol dependence. After all, he thought, his revolutionary interventions helped everyone, regardless of their behavioral problems or history. Unfortunately, this patient continued drinking to excess and one evening, while speeding home from work, had a near-fatal automobile accident, striking two cars in an intersection. All eight passengers and drivers in the other cars sustained major injuries necessitating hospitalization, although fortunately nobody was killed.

It was clear that Dr. Wow's therapy did not meet any standard of care for treating alcohol dependency. Because of his overconfidence, he had also failed to inform his patients, orally or with handouts or consent forms, that the therapy he offered was experimental and not necessarily a valid, safe, or effective intervention, or a substitute for other empirically validated treatments. By recklessly assuming that his groundbreaking treatment was a panacea for everyone, he contributed to harming not only one of his patients but also others involved in the patient's life—in this case, the occupants of the other vehicles in the automobile accident. This patient and several others ultimately decided to initiate formal ethics complaints against Dr. Wow, claiming that they had been harmed by his fraudulent advertising, false claims and reassurances, incompetence, and unconventional treatment, without any disclaimers or warnings as to possible risk or harm. Several patients also brought civil suits against him for subjecting them to a treatment far below the standard of care and causing substantial harm to them.

The APA Ethics Committee reviewed the complaint over a period of 16 months, seeking all available clinical information about Dr. Wow's infamous existential somatic shifting and any supporting information that he could supply. Finally, the committee reached a consensus that the charges not only had merit but also were sufficiently egregious to warrant expulsion from APA. A letter was sent out to Dr. Wow informing him of his expulsion and of his options for appealing the decision; the board of psychology in his home state also was notified. On the strength of this notification the state board began its own investigation of Dr. Wow, and he eventually lost his license to practice.

1. What should Dr. Wow have included in an informed-consent statement to better protect his patients and, ultimately, himself?
2. How far must a therapist go in informing patients in advance of innovative strategies or untried interventions?
3. Do you think Dr. Wow's malpractice insurance would pay for an attorney to defend him in both (a) the civil suits and (b) the state board of psychology investigation? If not, how could he change his malpractice insurance to cover attorney's fees for board of psychology investigations?

2.01 (f)

When assuming forensic roles, psychologists are or become reasonably familiar with the judicial or administrative rules governing their roles.

Know the judicial or administrative rules that pertain to your work when in a forensic role. (This would include such things as knowing the basic rules governing direct and cross-examination of witnesses, responding to a subpoena and a court order, being an expert or fact witness, acting as a consultant "behind the scenes" to an attorney, releasing clinical records and test data, and conducting court-appointed psychological assessments with its attendant confidential obligations to various parties.) You may not consider yourself to be a forensic psychologist, but you can easily be drawn into litigation, regardless of how ethically or professionally you behave. It only takes one of your clients or patients to be sued by someone, or one who decides to sue a former employer, physician, or ex-spouse, to engage you in the process.

VIGNETTE

Dr. Sparsely received a subpoena *duces tecum* requiring her to produce all records of her patient and appear for a deposition. Her patient had been fired from his job as a supervisor in a construction company and had sued his former employer for wrongful termination.

Because Dr. Sparsely had never been deposed before, she was unfamiliar with the rules concerning the payment of fees for appearing at a deposition. She was of the opinion, however, that she would be playing the role of an expert witness and therefore should be paid her customary professional fee plus compensation for the time required to drive to and from the attorney's office. Shortly after receiving the subpoena, she brashly informed the attorney by letter of her expectations about being paid her professional fees and indicated her desire to receive a check in advance of the deposition date, or at least a letter of agreement that her fee would be paid. She stated that she would not appear for the deposition in person, although she would release the patient's records, if the fee were not paid.

Several days later, while discussing the matter with a colleague experienced in forensics, she began to have grave misgivings about her actions. Her friend told her that her threat to refuse to appear for the deposition unless paid in advance was not only unwise but also risky. Simply refusing to respond to the subpoena would likely involve her personally in lengthy, costly, and testy controversy with the subpoena-issuing law firm. Furthermore, it ultimately might require her to explain her position in court and bear the cost of legal representation. The colleague said that he could understand Dr. Sparsely's reluctance to reveal clinical records or make herself available to be deposed about them, but she should always follow well-established procedures when interfacing with the legal system, not make up her own procedures, in order to best protect her patient's interest. His general advice was that psychologists follow these five simple steps whenever they receive a subpoena:

1. Contact the patient directly to discuss the matter.
2. Learn from the patient how he or she wishes to proceed—either comply with the subpoena or take other steps.
3. Obtain the patient's authorization to discuss the matter with his or her attorney in order to understand exactly what is being requested and review the protections against the demands of the subpoena that may be available in this case under state and/or federal law (e.g., moving to quash the subpoena, discussing a limited release of information, etc.).
4. If compliance with the subpoena is the strategy on which the patient and attorney decide, then invite the patient to come into your office first to review the records, so that the patient will be well versed about your diagnostic impressions, treatment plans, and so on.
5. Obtain the patient's signed consent authorizing release of the records.

Dr. Sparsely's colleague further advised her to consult with the state or county psychological association for advice if it is ever needed, as an attorney or knowledgeable psychologist might well be available.

He also suggested that she review the forensic literature, including documents such as APA's (1991) "Specialty Guidelines for Forensic Psychologists." In addition, he gave Dr. Sparsely a relevant journal article: "Strategies for Private Practitioners Coping With Subpoenas or Compelled Testimony for Client Records and/or Test Data" (APA, 1996b), as well as a reading list for ethics and forensic matters that he happened to have from a recent workshop.

Dr. Sparsely was grateful to her colleague for timely advice that had averted potential serious consequences she might have encountered if she had followed her own initial plan. She promptly contacted an attorney specializing in mental health matters. He reaffirmed what her friend had told her, that according to the court rules of her state, she was obliged to appear for a deposition even if a fee agreement had not been reached in advance. The lawyer further informed her that at this point it was uncertain whether her formal role would be as an expert witness or a fact (percipient) witness. As a fact witness, she might only be expected to testify to the fact that she personally had met with the plaintiff (her patient) on the dates indicated by her clinical and billing records. Or she might be asked to verify that her patient had in fact revealed certain information to her in the course of their consultations. In any case, in this jurisdiction, Dr. Sparsely could not demand that her appearance for the deposition be contingent on payment of a professional fee in advance, and failure to show up could indeed expose her to a possible contempt of court ruling, as her friend had stated. As for her expected financial remuneration for her appearance, she may well have to wait until she had provided her testimony or seek a court's ruling if it were disputed.

Because of Dr. Sparsely's lack of experience in judicial and administrative matters, she arranged to explore several other topics at a later time on the subject of preparation for providing testimony. The lawyer was particularly useful in helping her to discriminate between information she learned from others (i.e., hearsay information) and her knowledge of facts that she herself witnessed. The rules of evidence governing her testimony would not allow her to introduce information learned from her client unless it was for the sole purpose of perhaps explaining her client's beliefs and his state of mind, rather than as evidence of actual fact. This was an important distinction because, as a therapist, Dr. Sparsely was inclined to accept what her clients told her as accurate reports of others' behavior, believing what they said and accepting as valid their characterizations of third parties. As a result of this tendency, she had already formed opinions about her client's supervisor and other individuals in the company on the basis of her client's disclosures during therapy. Her naive inclination would have been to volunteer that she knew the supervisor to be a crafty, belligerent, and sadistic man and that her client had been unfairly treated by him for more than 5 years.

The lawyer firmly reminded Dr. Sparsely that she actually knew nothing about the supervisor aside from the subjective perceptions of her client. It would be essential for her to consistently indicate, if asked, that her *client* alleged that the supervisor was belligerent or abusive, not that the supervisor actually *was* this way. Because Dr. Sparsely had never met or observed the supervisor, she should never make evaluative statements about him based on her patient's perception, accurate or not. It was always important while testifying, the attorney emphasized, that she distinguish between what she was aware of by means of her own experience and what she had been told by another person or had read in a report. If she did not accurately make this distinction, the attorney warned, then she was at risk for investing the opinions of others with her own professional validation, when in fact she had no legitimate grounds for doing so.

This consultation with the attorney provided some badly needed remedial knowledge about fundamentals pertaining to judicial proceedings and participation of psychologists therein. Dr. Sparsely had the benefit of her attorney's wisdom concerning many aspects of interacting with the court system and continued her association with him when involved in future forensic matters. She also planned to take a forensic workshop at her earliest convenience to further supplement her knowledge.[1]

1. How might Dr. Sparsely balance maintaining her objectivity as a psychologist while simultaneously feeling as though she were an advocate for her patient?
2. What are the various role conflicts that Dr. Sparsely might experience, at different times of the trial, if she were asked to serve as an expert witness on a psychological topic and as a fact witness, on the subject of her treatment of the patient?
3. What steps can you take to learn about the judicial and administrative rules governing your behavior when assuming a forensic role?
4. How might you respond at a deposition or trial when compliance with a request from an attorney or judge for information or an opinion seems to place you in conflict with a particular ethical standard?

2.02 PROVIDING SERVICES IN EMERGENCIES

In emergencies, when psychologists provide services to individuals for whom other mental health services are not available and for which psychologists have not obtained the necessary training, psychologists may provide such services in order to ensure that services are not denied. The services are discontinued as soon as the emergency has ended or appropriate services are available.

In an emergency, such as domestic violence, natural disasters, accidents, terrorist attacks, or some other urgent situation, you may offer your services, assistance, or consultation even if untrained, if no other help is available. However, do so only as long as you are needed or until the person in need can obtain help from another, more qualified person.

VIGNETTE

Mrs. Haddit was the divorced mother of three adolescents, living separately from her former husband for 3 years, with joint physical and legal custody of the children. The parents lived close to each other, and both had made good efforts to be actively involved with their children's lives—including school activities, sports, and friends.

---

[1]Judicial and administrative rules governing the roles of psychologists may vary by state. Consult your state board of psychology or an attorney knowledgeable about such matters if you become involved in forensic work.

However, recently Mrs. Haddit was finding that the combined stress of working as a newspaper journalist and providing single parenting was wearing her down. She began to have such severe migraine headaches and poor sleep, with anxiety and agitated depression, that she sought treatment from her primary-care physician. After evaluating her, the physician prescribed medication for her migraines but wisely refrained from offering psychotropic remedies, referring her instead to Dr. Bridge, a psychologist specializing in adult depression and anxiety. Mrs. Haddit promptly began consultations with Dr. Bridge on a weekly basis.

At her seventh session, Mrs. Haddit appeared in Dr. Bridge's waiting office with her 16-year-old son, Dominic, sobbing anxiously that he had just gone on a rampage in her house, smashing their TV set, several treasured works of art, and one window in her bedroom. The son was subdued, sullen, disheveled in appearance, had several long scratches on his arm, and smelled of alcohol. Mrs. Haddit pleaded with Dr. Bridge to please meet with her son "and talk some sense into him" or else she was going to call the police.

Dr. Bridge did not treat children, adolescents, or families, and he did not have much professional experience with alcohol dependence. However, the situation seemed to be an emergency, and he was concerned about the safety of the boy and his family. After considering other options, such as referral to a colleague in the community (on the spot) or hospitalizing the youth at a large county hospital, he decided to meet alone with him and spent the next hour and a half learning about his life. The boy's father was a recovering alcoholic, sober for 2 years, and had recently relapsed to his old drinking habits. He was also spending more time with the two daughters, and played them off his son, resulting in great sibling rivalry and tension within the family.

The session went better than Dr. Bridge had hoped; he gained Dominic's trust and determined that he was not a danger to himself, that his violent behavior this morning was out of character for him, and that he had much remorse for what he had done. He had felt betrayed by his father, and rageful, yet he feared expressing these feelings to him. He also was angry that his mother could not observe the dynamics and intervene somehow, as she had in the past.

Although Dr. Bridge considered the therapy session to be productive, he knew that ongoing treatment, as well as some therapeutic intervention that would address the changes in Dominic's relationship with his father, was probably desirable. He also knew that because of his lack of experience and training in this area, he was not the one to carry out this therapy. After carefully evaluating the boy for any further impulse control problems or dangerousness, Dr. Bridge decided to refer him to a colleague in his practice who specialized in family therapy and worked with adolescents, particularly where alcohol dependency was a factor.

Dr. Bridge explained to Dominic that he could not meet with him on a regular basis because he already had established his role as his mother's therapist, and it would be confusing for everyone concerned if he were to try to offer counseling to both. He reassured him, however, that he would confer with the new therapist, with his and his mother's consent, and continue to play a collaborative role that would likely help the family situation. Finally, he asked Dominic to agree to a sign a contract, before he left the office, that he would telephone Dr. Bridge if he ever felt like drinking alcohol again or acting out with violence. This contract would be in effect until Dominic began treatment with his own therapist.

That evening, Dr. Bridge telephoned his colleague (who had been out of the office that day) and discussed what had happened—specifically, how he had handled the intense emotionality of the situation. He had some doubts about Dominic's ability to comply with a behavioral contract and his willingness to actually appear for the counseling session with his new therapist. The colleague processed the session with him and advised that he follow it up with a telephone call the next day just to see how the boy was doing and possibly even meet one more time with him before the new therapy began. At this second meeting Dr. Bridge could personally introduce the boy to the new therapist, and the transition might be easier. The colleague also acquainted Dr. Bridge with literature about adolescent alcohol abuse, the 12-step program Alateen, and other community resources that might address his needs in the future.

Dr. Bridge was aware that he was prudent to limit his work with the teenager, even though Dominic had quickly developed confidence in him and wished to meet with him again. This was not his area of expertise, and he knew it. He also realized, however, that it was better to have met with Dominic on the spot rather than to refer him to another therapist or hospitalize him, because of the risk of suicide or danger to others. He also greatly valued the feedback from his colleague and learned much that would help him in the future. Following this episode, Dr. Bridge's interest was sparked by the liveliness of family work, and he decided to attend a workshop on the topic.

1. How might Dr. Bridge have dealt with Dominic if he had refused to agree to a "no violence and no drinking" behavioral contract?
2. What if Dominic reveals that his mother also drinks to excess, practically nightly, and occasionally invites him to drink with her as well?
3. What are the options if Dominic wishes to continue treatment with Dr. Bridge and will not agree to see anyone else?

2.03 MAINTAINING COMPETENCE

Psychologists undertake ongoing efforts to develop and maintain their competence.

Continuously stay on top of new developments in your area of research, teaching, clinical practice, or consultation, and keep your skills sharp at all times. Do this by reading journals and books, attending workshops and conventions, writing articles and giving presentations, joining a peer consultation group, using the Internet, and seeking any other resources that will refresh you professionally. Do not rest on your laurels for very long; there is an ever-changing and expanding knowledge base that may directly affect what you do.

VIGNETTE

Dr. Able routinely treated adults who had a history of childhood sexual abuse and used hypnosis occasionally as a part of treatment. She made an ongoing effort to keep abreast of the current research on memory and its unwitting contamination with the use of hypnosis. She knew well the caveats and risks concerning the use of implicit suggestion by less skilled therapists who could be overenthusiastic about using hypnosis as an adjunct to psychotherapy with patients who have an increased ability to dissociate.

Dr. Able was also aware of the ongoing controversy on this subject within various professional associations. She closely monitored the research and publications of APA, the American Psychiatric Association, the American Society for Clinical Hypnosis, the Society for Clinical and Experimental Hypnosis, and other professional associations reporting research on this topic. She was familiar with the publications by researchers and therapists in APA's Division 30 (Psychological Hypnosis) as well as other relevant psychological and psychiatric journals. She also regularly taught and attended continuing education workshops on the subject of hypnosis.

Her philosophy of hypnosis emerged from her long experience as a psychotherapist working with trauma patients. She understood well that hypnosis was not a "truth serum" and should not be used to aggressively seek and corroborate impressions about early childhood abuse. As a part of informed consent with new patients, she was fastidious about discussing the various applications of hypnosis and describing her views about the potential benefits and dangers. She generally advised new patients to respect the potential that hypnotically refreshed memories held for contributing to the overall therapy experience, but she also advised them to invest somewhat cautiously in them. Although she did not discount the memories and general impressions of an exploratory hypnotic session, she believed that their accuracy could not necessarily be assumed in every detail, and she knew that hypnotic recollection could enhance conviction that a memory was true without improving its accuracy. She also was careful to alert patients to the risks of using hypnosis if they were currently engaged in any legal proceeding (e.g., litigation). Consistent with professional guidelines and state laws concerning hypnosis, the testimony of any witness in a judicial proceeding who had undergone hypnosis could possibly be discounted as having been "contaminated" by the hypnosis itself, if it related to the subject of litigation. Dr. Able knew of many therapists who never provided such informed consent to their patients, but she also knew the risks of failing to do so, including ultimately harming the patient's credibility in a legal venue by making it impossible for the person to testify in court.

Dr. Able viewed hypnosis as a very useful vehicle to help move the therapy along and to gain new information about the patient's original trauma as well as the thoughts and feelings associated with it. She also saw it as helpful to patients in containing the emotional impact of traumatic memories by helping them to better manage their physiological responses to them and the time spent thinking about them. She was skillful in applying hypnosis for symptom management, many years after the trauma, and in teaching many patients how to use self-hypnosis on an as-needed basis.

Because of Dr. Able's ongoing interest in and awareness of the clinical, ethical, and legal aspects of the use of hypnosis with this patient population, the efficacy of her work was increased while the welfare of those who consulted her was protected. She had a good appreciation of the concept of competence as an ongoing phenomenon and of the need to continually sharpen her expertise commensurate with the current research in her field. As a result, her interventions with patients were safe and effective, and she maintained only a minimal risk for a patient complaint about operating outside of her level of competence.

1. Is Dr. Able at a greater risk for a complaint or lawsuit from third parties (e.g., parents) because she accepts hypnotically induced information as factual with patients claiming childhood sexual abuse?
2. Hypnosis is a specialized technique; how would a psychologist using conventional methods know if he or she is doing enough to maintain an adequate level of competence regardless of continuing education requirements?
3. To what extent are APA members expected to be familiar with the content reflecting their specialty area that is printed in the *American Psychologist* or the *APA Monitor*, as official organs of the association?
4. Does your state have requirements about continuing education for psychologists?

2.04 BASES FOR SCIENTIFIC AND PROFESSIONAL JUDGMENTS

Psychologists' work is based upon established scientific and professional knowledge of the discipline. (See also Standards 2.01e, Boundaries of Competence, and 10.01b, Informed Consent to Therapy.)

Your work must be firmly grounded in established scientific and professional knowledge. Do not make "factual statements" in your classroom, your consulting office, the courtroom, on radio or TV, in print, on the Internet, or anywhere, about psychological matters that go beyond supporting facts, unless you include a disclaimer. Resist the temptation to overgeneralize or oversimplify, regardless of the setting or pressure from others. It's better if your statements are a little more tentative, but accurate, rather than flashy and flawed.

VIGNETTE

For the past 10 years, Dr. Dippy had been a strong supporter of the integrative-medicine movement and had been encouraging other psychologists to update their skills in this area. She personally had gained much relief from chronic back and leg pain through the use of interventions such as biofeedback, hypnosis, and acupuncture. She had also experienced improvement in her chronic depression and overall health by experimenting with a combination of herbal remedies.

Unfortunately, Dr. Dippy's scientific approach to her clinical work was becoming less rigorous over time, as she seemed to increasingly rely on her own intuitive thoughts about psychological interventions based, primarily, on her own personal successes coping with various physiological and psychological problems. She followed with great interest recent developments in homeopathic medicine, at the expense of keeping current with the psychological literature—indeed, she had stopped reading psychological journals altogether and saw little value in attending most psychological conventions or workshops.

When dealing with patients with chronic pain, mood disorders, eating disorders, and other chronic problems, Dr. Dippy relied increasingly on advocating the use of certain vitamin and mineral supplements and other herbal remedies. She became less willing to engage patients in psychotherapy, believing instead in the potency of natural substances to treat mental disorders. Although she knew of little valid empirical support for these theories, she frequently passed them off as factual and "clinically proven" in many trials in the United States and abroad. In short, she cited research that would never appear in refereed journals, because of poor design, yet she was highly persuasive with gullible patients.

Dr. Dippy had many books and articles on herbology and other alternative medicine interventions in her office, and she freely distributed them to patients without any caveats or disclaimers. She also endorsed specific products and brand names and encouraged patients to purchase them at a nearby health food store. If they had difficulty locating a particular product, patients could purchase directly from her, as she maintained a large supply at her office, at a slight markup.

Unfortunately, her unscientific approach in treating a variety of ills helped few of her patients in the long run, although some reported improvement in their health from time to time. For those whose psychological symptoms or physical pain became exacerbated over time, Dr. Dippy usually recommended additional herbal remedies and her own special concoction of teas and infusions.

Dr. Dippy seemed unconcerned about dispensing therapeutic advice that had little or no scientific basis, and she occasionally underestimated the danger to clinically depressed individuals who were at risk of suicide. Because she rarely referred patients to other mental health care professionals for psychotherapy or antidepressant medication, she increased the likelihood that such patients' depressive symptoms would become more extreme and possibly result in self-destructive behavior. She ultimately was harmful to many patients who believed in her competence and followed her professional advice. When a young male patient nearly carried out a suicide attempt, the man's wife became quite concerned about Dr. Dippy's idiosyncratic treatment methods and decided to formally raise the question of her competence by initiating a complaint to the state licensing board.

1.   Which standards, in addition to 2.04, has Dr. Dippy possibly violated?
2.   What would the impact on therapy be if Dr. Dippy had informed her patients that the remedies she proposed were not validated, yet they had frequently been effective with her own symptoms? Consider your own theoretical orientation when you answer.
3.   How do Dr. Dippy's actions differ from those of a competent, creative, and open-minded therapist who wishes to share new knowledge or unvalidated clinical interventions with patients?
4.   What is the least stringent sanction—reprimand or censure—that might be imposed on Dr. Dippy by the APA Ethics Committee if a depressed patient complained that her mood had been deteriorating as a result of using some of the recommended herbal remedies? (See APA Rules and Procedures of the Ethics Committee, available on the APA Web site: www.apa.org/ethics/rules.html.)

2.05 DELEGATION OF WORK TO OTHERS

Psychologists who delegate work to employees, supervisees, or research or teaching assistants or who use the services of others, such as interpreters, take reasonable steps to (1) avoid delegating such work to persons who have a multiple relationship with those being served that would likely lead to exploitation or loss of objectivity; (2) authorize only those responsibilities that such persons can be expected to perform competently on the basis of their education, training, or experience, either independently or with the level of supervision being provided; and (3) see that such persons perform these services competently. (See also Standards 2.02, Providing Services in Emergencies; 3.05, Multiple Relationships; 4.01, Maintaining Confidentiality; 9.01, Bases for Assessments; 9.02, Use of Assessments; 9.03, Informed Consent in Assessments; and 9.07, Assessment by Unqualified Persons.)

Whenever you assign tasks to others (e.g., employees, supervisees, research or teaching assistants), or whenever you use the services of others (e.g., interpreters), make sure that

- you never delegate responsibilities to someone who already has a relationship with the individual being served that would reduce his or her objectivity or increase the risk of exploitation (e.g., a friend or relative, employee);
- the individual is competent in regard to his or her level of education, training, or experience, either unaided, or with the level of supervision that you are prepared to provide; and
- you follow up with the individual to ensure that he or she did a competent job.

It is important to note that there could be serious legal, scientific, and professional consequences for you in any psychological role you play, as the one who delegated responsibility, such as clinician (e.g., lawsuits by a disgruntled consumer against both your supervisee and you, ethics complaints, loss of malpractice insurance), researcher (e.g., threats to the validity of your data, future funding), or academician (e.g., formal grievance, diminished academic standing), to name a few.

VIGNETTE

As the owner of a large, interdisciplinary group practice, Dr. Cagey, an aggressive entrepreneur, paid his employees for their professional services. However, he was only minimally aware of their skills and training and did little to monitor their work. As referrals decreased over the years, the income of the business also declined, leaving some staff members with a very small caseload. More concerned about the financial success of his personal friends on staff than the company as a whole, Dr. Cagey frequently carried out the task of in-house patient referrals on the basis of the welfare of his associates and his corporation rather than that of the patients. For example, he referred patients in need of psychological testing to his closest friend on the staff, a clinical social worker, who actually had little formal training in assessment. He also routinely referred patients for biofeedback training to one of his psychological assistants, an unlicensed practitioner accruing supervisory hours toward licensure, whose entire biofeedback training consisted of a 4-hour workshop at a convention and no follow-up supervision or training in carrying out biofeedback with patients.

By consistently referring individuals to his personal friends, whose competence was questionable, Dr. Cagey was placing patients at risk of receiving a poor quality of service or, even worse, of being harmed. He thought that his obligations to carry out the administrative work of the group practice and to vigorously promote their psychological services within the community took precedence over consultative or supervisory duties or any obligation to make careful in-house referrals. Unfortunately, several patients were significantly damaged by Dr. Cagey's lax referral policies and eventually brought formal complaints against the unlicensed practitioner and Dr. Cagey himself.

One case involved a child custody dispute. Both parents had been formally assessed by one of Dr. Cagey's employees, resulting in a report submitted to the court. However, the psychologist doing the assessment had used improper and biased methods while evaluating the family and wrote a report that was neither objective nor comprehensive. The litigation was prolonged, in part because of the problematical psychological report, which nearly resulted in a decision by the court to award sole custody to the less competent parent.

Another case involved a clinically depressed cancer patient with pain and nausea from chemotherapy. The patient was referred by a social worker on the oncology team for biofeedback training to help manage her physical discomfort and anticipatory anxiety about further treatment. Dr. Cagey referred the patient to his psychological assistant and subsequently took little interest in her treatment. Unfortunately, the psychological assistant's theoretical approach in the application of biofeedback was unsophisticated and rather mechanistic. He overlooked her significant depressive and anxious symptomology and proceeded directly with electromyographic and thermal training on the biofeedback equipment. The patient did poorly with biofeedback, failed to practice at home on her own, became increasingly despondent, and eventually dropped out of treatment after 3 weeks.

Dr. Cagey's irresponsible practices not only resulted in harm to many individuals consulting his employees but also contributed to the further decline in the financial health of his group practice. He learned, too late, that an extensive working knowledge of his employees' competence and ongoing monitoring of unlicensed employees is essential whenever professional duties are delegated to subordinates.

1. What might Dr. Cagey have done to promote the growth of his group practice while remaining ethically compliant?
2. What is the responsibility of psychologists in his practice who are aware of Dr. Cagey's transgressions?
3. How might you deal with the conduct of an employee in Dr. Cagey's practice who has a different code of ethics (social

worker, marriage and family therapist, or psychiatrist) but clearly is not qualified to carry out his or her assigned duties?

2.06 PERSONAL PROBLEMS AND CONFLICTS

(a) Psychologists refrain from initiating an activity when they know or should know that there is a substantial likelihood that their personal problems will prevent them from performing their work-related activities in a competent manner.

Never undertake professional work when there is a good chance that your personal problems and troubles will interfere with your ability to do a good job. Psychologists, like everyone else, experience stress, illness, losses, and life changes and have personal foibles and weaknesses. Be aware of these, and avoid situations that would compromise your work.

VIGNETTE

Dr. Hotspur was an excellent researcher and highly respected professor at a large, prestigious university. For the past 6 months, however, he had been experiencing increasing stress from his difficult marital situation: His wife had recently sued for divorce and was demanding that he move out of the house. The situation was becoming more painful as the months went by, because his wife's attorney was aggressively pursuing his client's goals of obtaining custody of the couple's two young daughters and a large financial settlement.

It was clear that the ongoing stress of Dr. Hotspur's personal life was beginning to intrude on his research and teaching responsibilities, impairing his concentration and competence. He was in the final stages of completing data collection and analysis for the last year of a 3-year research project of an examination of the communication style of couples engaged in marital therapy. Unfortunately, he found that he could no longer be impartial in evaluating the subjective oral and written comments by the wives participating in the study. His personal feelings of anger and loss from the ending of his own marriage were ever present, causing him to transfer his negative feelings toward his wife to women in general. His negative mood also was beginning to contaminate his cognitive process, resulting in a consistent antifemale bias in analyzing the data. He wondered if he should seek a colleague's assistance in completing the final phase of his research.

Of more immediate concern, he also noticed that he expressed stronger feelings of irritation toward female colleagues in response to relatively minor provocation or disappointments. Several friends and colleagues called attention to his reactions and offered to assist him in some way if he wished. Dr.

Hotspur was beginning to appreciate the deep impact of the stressful divorce on his mood, his professional competence, and his professional relationships, and he considered discussing his situation with a therapist.

In addition, one of Dr. Hotspur's younger female research assistants, Dawn, was showing obvious signs of compassion for him in his distress. Although she was his student, she felt a special affinity for him, as a needy male, in this time of major life transition and loss. Dr. Hotspur, in his loneliest hours, indeed felt himself beginning to respond to Dawn's gentleness and kindness, and he soon experienced feelings of affection and sexual attraction for her that grew with each passing day. With little concern for his professional role or the possibility of harming one of his students, he began to yield inexorably to the growing romantic pull of this wonderful new woman who had so easily entered his life.

1. How would you advise Dr. Hotspur if he asked your opinion about his ability to continue with his project?
2. What would be your obligation, as Dr. Hotspur's psychotherapist, if he confided in you that he is deliberately distorting the research outcome to show a negative bias toward women?
3. What are the ethical issues of beginning a romantic relationship with your research assistant? Is this specifically unethical? How could the assistant, or the research, be harmed?

2.06 (b)

When psychologists become aware of personal problems that may interfere with their performing work-related duties adequately, they take appropriate measures, such as obtaining professional consultation or assistance, and determine whether they should limit, suspend, or terminate their work-related duties. (See also Standard 10.10, Terminating Therapy.)

When you become aware of personal problems that interfere with your performance, do whatever is necessary to help restore your own good mental health and your ability to work. This might include temporarily suspending or narrowing the scope of your work, consulting with a respected colleague, or obtaining psychotherapy or any other assistance or rehabilitative experience that would help. You have an ethical duty to be mentally healthy!

VIGNETTE (CONTINUATION OF PRECEDING VIGNETTE)

Dr. Hotspur's conversation with his friend and colleague, John, helped him to see the extent to which his deteriorating marital situation was affecting his professional life in a variety of ways. He now could accept the extent to which his mood affected his work in the final phase of his research project. He noted that sometimes, during the final face-to-face interview, he had been argumentative with the participants in his research project, particularly the wives. He also realized that he sometimes made systematic distortions in his interpretations of the data from the transcripts and ratings of the therapy sessions, ascribing ulterior motives to the women that were clearly unwarranted by the data.

With John's help, Dr. Hotspur concluded that it was essential to distance himself from the interviewing and data analysis at this particular time, because he clearly was not competent to continue doing the work. Fortunately, he was able to engage several senior research assistants to help carry out his responsibilities. Although the project was slowed down considerably, taking 6 more months to complete than originally planned, at least the research team no longer ran the risk of significant threats to the study's validity due to the work of an impaired and biased researcher.

As for the budding relationship with Dawn, his research assistant, Dr. Hotspur acknowledged to her that he was very appreciative of her friendship but that the professional boundary would remain intact. As he processed the painful feelings about his own divorce in therapy, his intense feelings for Dawn began to subside, and he no longer felt the need to act on his initial sexual attraction to her.

Although he had entered the most emotionally demanding transition of his adult life, Dr. Hotspur appreciated the fact that friends and colleagues came to his support, guiding his judgment and encouraging him to obtain the psychological treatment that so benefited him. Because of their help, he was able to acknowledge the immediate need to limit his work responsibilities and make sound decisions about his personal life.

1. How would you approach Dr. Hotspur if you were his research assistant and had noticed some flaws in his professional work?
2. How does a researcher balance time deadlines for a project with his or her own mental health and the need to take steps that might slow things down?
3. How do you recognize your own signs of stress or impairment, and in whom would you confide to obtain feedback or use as a resource when needed?

3

HUMAN RELATIONS

3.01 UNFAIR DISCRIMINATION

In their work-related activities, psychologists do not engage in unfair discrimination based on age, gender, gender identity, race, ethnicity, culture, national origin, religion, sexual orientation, disability, socioeconomic status, or any basis proscribed by law.

At work, do not treat people unfairly; provide them with a lower quality of care; or be influenced by bias, bigotry, or prejudicial feelings just because they are outside your personal experience in some basic way. Whether your client or patient differs from you by being straight or gay, male or female, of a lower socioeconomic background, physically disabled, elderly, Hispanic, Native American, or atheistic, remember that state and federal discrimination laws may apply to your work. Treat others impartially and evenhandedly (as you would want to be treated).

VIGNETTE

Dr. Festige, a young faculty member in a small professional school of psychology located in a rural, conservative part of the country, had never felt comfortable with the idea of homosexuality. He believed that gay men and lesbians were essentially abnormal and in need of treatment to change their sexual orientation, regardless of their inclination to do so. In point of fact, during his short teaching career Dr. Festige had never had any personal contact with students whom he knew to be gay, nor had he and his wife ever had any friends who openly acknowledged their homosexuality.

One year, however, two openly gay men, Richard and Sal, were admitted to the doctoral program. Both were highly competent students and well experienced in clinical settings. It was not very long before Dr. Festige found himself in the position of supervising Richard in an individual psychotherapy practicum course. Dr. Festige began to notice his feelings of personal conflict increasing as the supervisory relationship got under way. As the weeks went by, he identified emerging feelings of fear and hostility, which raised some questions in his own mind about his ability to remain objective and provide good training for Richard. At first, he thought that his reactions would pass—indeed, he was hoping that he could overcome years of thinking a certain way that reflected conditioning from his family and religious background. He honestly hoped that he would be able to accept a student whose sexual orientation conflicted so fundamentally with his own, and he wondered whether he could bring himself to raise the topic of "what it was like" to live openly regarding one's homosexuality as a part of the supervisory sessions; however, he felt utterly unable to discuss these topics with Richard. To the contrary, he continued to feel vague apprehension before each supervisory session and sometimes found himself looking for excuses to cancel a meeting or end it early. Although Richard perceived no blatant discriminatory behavior on the part of his supervisor, he became aware of Dr. Festige's general avoidance of him and began to wonder whether and how he should raise the question of his sexual orientation as a contributing factor.

Dr. Festige decided that he should consult a trusted senior psychologist about the advisability of continuing in his role as Richard's clinical supervisor. Also, for the first time he began to seriously and formally explore his philosophy and feelings about homosexuality as a mental disorder. He was willing to consider, in light of the emerging research, that his conceptions might be overly rigid and outmoded. As a result, he vowed to make an effort to deliberately expose himself to gay men and lesbians to help overcome these uncomfortable feelings. He thought this was the logical step to take, as he valued his career as a psychology professor and knew that it was increasingly likely that he would have more encounters with openly gay students and faculty as time went on. As a part of this effort, the senior consultant referred Dr. Festige to an openly gay colleague at another school, also a psychologist, who was willing to further explore these issues with him.

With this help and support, Dr. Festige was able to continue working as Richard's supervisor, and eventually he overcame his anxious and avoidant reactions. Ultimately he consulted a psychotherapist for a time to make further progress with these deep-seated feelings. He eventually was able to feel compassion for his gay and lesbian students, as he felt for the straight students he was mentoring, and he gained a greater appreciation for some of the unique stresses inherent to the homosexual lifestyle.

1. What impact could Dr. Festige's bias have had on the quality of supervision and, ultimately, on Richard's development as a budding psychologist?
2. How could Dr. Festige have raised the topic of his bias in a responsible, mentoring fashion as a part of supervision?
3. What steps could Dr. Festige have taken in dealing with Richard's need for practicum supervision if he could not let go of his strongly negative feelings?
4. Should you attempt to deal with a strongly held belief of yours (e.g., bias, prejudice) before it results in the kind of dilemma experienced by Dr. Festige? If so, how would you go about this?

3.02 SEXUAL HARASSMENT

Psychologists do not engage in sexual harassment. Sexual harassment is sexual solicitation, physical advances, or verbal or nonverbal conduct that is sexual in nature, that occurs in connection with the psychologist's activities or roles as a psychologist, and that either (1) is unwelcome, is offensive, or creates a hostile workplace environment, and the psychologist knows or is told this or (2) is sufficiently severe or intense to be abusive to a reasonable person in the context. Sexual harassment can consist of a single intense or severe act or of multiple persistent or pervasive acts. (See also Standard 1.08, Unfair Discrimination Against Complainants and Respondents.)

When at work, avoid harassing, pestering, annoying, or stalking another person because of his or her sexuality, gender, gender identification, sexual orientation, sexual characteristics and appearance, or related factors. Sexual harassment consists of saying, writing, or doing something that is sexual in nature *in connection with your professional activities or role as a psychologist* (a) when you have been told that this is offensive or unwelcome or that it creates an intimidating atmosphere at work by focusing on sex, or (b) that it is so excessive that most men and women in the situation would consider it rude, insulting, or abusive. Never engage in the latter, excessive behaviors, and immediately stop engaging in the following if you have been told that they are offensive or unwelcome:

- flirting, asking someone for sex, and other sexual solicitation;
- standing too close to someone, physically touching, patting, stroking, hugging, or kissing him or her;

- engaging others in titillating conversations, such as telling sexual jokes, inviting or alluding to sexual activity, disclosing your sexual fantasies or activities, commenting on others' sexual and physical attributes, sending sexualized mail or e-mail, and so on; and
- using nonverbal communication that is overtly sexual, such as leering, staring, making inappropriate gestures, displaying sexual photos or materials, leaving pornography or sexual screen savers on your computer, and so on.[1]

Also do not assume that others will necessarily welcome your brand of sexual humor or conduct in the workplace, particularly when there is a difference in ascribed or real power or authority. Distinguish between showing your romantic interest in another person and harassing him or her by, for example, such tactics as embarrassment, violating his or her personal space, or initiating unwanted touching.

VIGNETTE

Dr. Dents was a new psychology instructor on a predominantly male faculty and had little awareness of how the concept of sexual harassment applied to him. He occasionally told his female supervisees sexual jokes that were tasteless and offensive, both during supervisory hours and in social settings. They tolerated these indiscretions, as deference to an authority figure required, but they generally avoided being in his presence alone. Once in awhile Dr. Dents and his male colleagues brought pornographic DVDs to work to swap by placing them in each others' office mailboxes; they were oblivious to the effect their conduct might have on both female and male students, even though one of the DVDs "accidentally" found its way into a graduate student's mailbox. Furthermore, he and a few colleagues would regularly spend time connected to the Internet, in their offices, exploring pornographic Web pages and trading their latest discoveries with each other, sometimes carelessly within the earshot of students and other colleagues.

One of Dr. Dent's older colleagues, Dr. Libidish, often sat too close to his female trainees, touched them, or even put his arm around them while observing group therapy sessions through a one-way mirror in the darkened observation room. Students reacted differently to these touches: Some felt quite flattered that a senior faculty member would behave so affectionately, but others felt quite agitated and were distracted from what was supposed to be a didactic experience. Dr. Libidish also attempted to pat his supervisees on their lower back or even give them a "fatherly" hug at the end of supervisory sessions. He sometimes referred to them as "darling," or "gorgeous," or in

---

[1]Some of these are examples of behavior that is excessively abusive as well and should obviously be stopped if you have been told that they are offensive.

some other unacceptably familiar or affectionate manner, and he implied in many subtle and not-so-subtle ways that their mentoring relationship might readily take on an amorous dimension if the student were so interested. The ambiguity he presented was interpreted by some as friendly and welcoming and by others as seductive and inappropriate.

Such pervasive sexualizing of the workplace also included the female clerical workers, receptionists, cleaning staff, and any other woman connected to the institution who could be a likely target. Indeed, sexual harassment was rampant in the psychology department and created a consistently hostile workplace environment for any woman who was unfortunate enough to work there. Judging by the frequent turnover of staff and high use of temporary workers supplied by an agency, the dissatisfaction level was quite high, yet apparently unlikely to change.

On occasion, a particularly assertive student would complain to Dr. Dents, Dr. Libidish, and other offending faculty members but usually was met with denials of and rationalizations for the sexualized behavior. Complaints to the administration generally resulted in little or no action; although the department chair and provost had heard these complaints many times, they apparently were unable to act or to issue sanctions that were more than a proverbial slap on the wrist. Most students simply dared not say anything about the offensive behavior and just endured it, as they were all too aware of the power differential and their professional vulnerability. The pattern of sexual harassment was extensive in the male-dominated department and had deep roots, a long history, and a tradition that was consistent with the "good old boy" network. There was seemingly no way to bring a successful in-house grievance, because sexual harassment was endemic to the institution and was considered to be an acceptable part of campus life, even within the graduate departments and, in a more sophisticated way, the upper administrative levels.

This pattern of abuse ultimately led to significant disappointment among many female students and some male students as well and caused some of them to drop out of the program. The students remaining behind, who were predominately male, unfortunately received much social validation in their graduate school experience for any culturally sanctioned sexist views that they previously held. It would be many years before any of them would begin to view their behavior as problematical; for some, it would take a formal ethics complaint or civil suit for them to recognize how destructive they were being to female colleagues and clients in overt and covert ways.

1. Some men and women hold the opinion that there is no such thing as sexual harassment—that women should simply be more assertive with men who harass. How would you debate this point of view?
2. What steps could one take in dealing with sexual harassment in the following roles: (a) as a student in graduate school,

(b) as a faculty member whose tenure is on the line, (c) as a staff psychologist in a group practice, (d) as a research participant being exploited by a research assistant, or (e) in other settings?

3. How can you recognize your own thoughts, feelings, or patterns of behavior that could indicate your own tendency to sexually harass, under certain circumstances, even though you might think of your actions as humorous, flirtatious in an acceptable fashion, or just plain "fun" with someone of the opposite sex who seems to be a likely sparring partner?

3.03 OTHER HARASSMENT

Psychologists do not knowingly engage in behavior that is harassing or demeaning to persons with whom they interact in their work based on factors such as those persons' age, gender, gender identity, race, ethnicity, culture, national origin, religion, sexual orientation, disability, language, or socioeconomic status.

Never make fun of, belittle, badger, humiliate, mock, harass, or otherwise disparage your colleagues, staff, clients and patients, students, supervisees, research participants, or others with whom you work on the basis of factors such as their age, sex, race, ethnicity, country of origin, sexual orientation, disability, native language, or social class.

VIGNETTE

Dr. Merth was an administrator and part-time psychology faculty member in a small university. He suffered from subclinical hypomania, which made for an entertaining teaching style, but he had a reputation for having a sardonic sense of humor. He thought that teaching was maximally effective when it could be made amusing for both the student and the professor. He also believed that a good administrator should be able to engage others on various levels and that humor was the social lubricant that could facilitate most administrative interactions.

At his best, Dr. Merth's style was somewhat reminiscent of the comedian Don Rickles; he was able to comment spontaneously, creatively, and humorously on the behavior of others and sometimes got them to laugh at themselves. At his worst, however, he could be offensive and even crudely insulting, arousing feelings of hurt, anger, and even shame in those who were the butt of his humor. At these times, it seemed that his intention was to humiliate others or simply to vent his own hostility, and he often would tell his jokes or imitate the style of his intended targets to their faces or well within their earshot.

Part of Dr. Merth's repertoire included sarcastic comments and jokes about women, African Americans, Jews, gay men and lesbians, older people, immigrants from Asia and Eastern Europe, and various other members of groups to which he did not belong. When teaching his statistics classes, he made a point of telling jokes or weaving a humorous story into his lecture that was based on the minority-group distribution present in the class. If there were Mormons or African Americans in a particular class, for instance, then his humor would focus on the values and behavior of Mormons and African Americans. As an administrator, he frequently participated in meetings with the same mix of individuals he had derided; hence, his humor and harassment tended to be repetitive, becoming more tedious than funny.

At times, Dr. Merth was endearing to others and succeeded in charming them or lightening their mood. Indeed, his behavior sometimes seemed rooted in attempts to gain their approval or validation. However, Dr. Merth was generally less successful in entertaining, and more often he simply seemed hostile, inflicting humiliation and insults on students and colleagues. His deeply held prejudicial views and harassing behavior were not successfully balanced by respectful comments or disclaimers, resulting in a general negative effect on the individuals who were the unfortunate targets of his hostility. By his consistent pattern of harassment in the workplace, he made himself vulnerable to valid ethics complaints from those whom he estranged.

1. Would Dr. Merth's behavior be considered unethical if there were no power differential between him and his targets (e.g., if he never disparaged secretaries or graduate students, but only his fellow colleagues)?
2. Does this standard really require that one be "humorless" or insipid in one's interpersonal style? Where does humor end and hostility begin?
3. How would you approach a colleague who is either having a manic episode; or has another mental disorder that contributes to inappropriate interpersonal behavior; or who simply chronically harasses others in little ways, alienating them and creating a generally negative mood in the workplace? What steps would you take if you were on the lower end of the power differential in attempting to deal with this person?

3.04 AVOIDING HARM

Psychologists take reasonable steps to avoid harming their clients/patients, students, supervisees, research participants, organizational clients, and others with whom they work, and to minimize harm where it is foreseeable and unavoidable.

> Never harm clients or patients, students or trainees, supervisees, research participants, or anyone else with whom you work. In cases in which it is inevitable that someone will be harmed by your actions (e.g., child custody change or a clinical judgment of competency to stand trial), make an attempt to minimize harm, if possible.

VIGNETTE

Dr. Lastlap's reluctant new patient, Anthony Flake, was an automobile mechanic who had been experiencing panic attacks and binge drinking for several months. He had recently lost his job, and his wife was due to deliver her first baby in about 2 months. Although his health insurance was still in effect, it did not cover psychotherapy sessions with a psychologist who was not on the panel of providers. Mr. Flake had never consulted a mental health provider in the past, and never would have this time, if it were not for his wife's appeals and, more recently, her threats to leave him and go live with her mother.

Dr. Lastlap wanted to do what he could to help Mr. Flake ease the financial burden of treatment. After the initial meeting, there seemed to be a good match, and Mr. Flake's apprehension about treatment largely subsided. By coincidence, Dr. Lastlap's passion was racing cars, and one of his older cars, an Alpha Romeo, had been in need of a new transmission for several years. Because his patient was financially needy and in their first session had actually offered his automobile repair skills as a means of in-kind payment for psychotherapy, Dr. Lastlap agreed to consider seriously a bartering arrangement. The risk seemed minimal, the patient was motivated and presumably competent, and Dr. Lastlap thought that he could keep the professional boundaries clear.

The two men discussed the details of this plan and calculated that parts and labor for a new transmission for the Alpha would easily pay for 25 therapy sessions. Mr. Flake appeared to be enthusiastic with this plan and was much relieved that he could now afford an adequate number of sessions of psychotherapy in this fashion. He worked on the car after hours in his friend's shop, successfully installed the new transmission, and returned the car to Dr. Lastlap 3 weeks later.

The following weekend, while driving on a busy highway on the way to the racetrack, Dr. Lastlap noticed an odd smell coming from the Alpha Romeo's engine. It was the transmission overheating, and suddenly it failed, causing Dr. Lastlap to lose power while in the passing lane. He was able to swerve off the road into a ditch in the center divide and escape a potentially dangerous accident. Ultimately, on inspection, it became clear that the problem was due to an oversight on the part of Mr. Flake in working on the car. As a result of driving into the ditch, Dr. Lastlap unfortunately suffered a neck injury, which required medical treatment and physical therapy over a period of 6 months. He suffered constant pain and began harboring some negative feelings toward Mr. Flake that interfered with his continuing effective treatment of him. Dr. Lastlap finally found it necessary to end therapy with Mr. Flake; unfortunately, this was at the same time that Mr. Flake was able to begin processing his feelings of guilt about the role he played in the accident and worry that he had alienated Dr. Lastlap and would lose him as his therapist.

After therapy ended, Mr. Flake felt abandoned by Dr. Lastlap and was somewhat fearful of entering therapy again with someone else, even though he had names of several potential new therapists. Originally, he thought that his idea of bartering automotive skills in exchange for therapy was a good one, and he was very pleased that his therapist had agreed with him. He had never engaged in such an exchange of services before with a health care professional, and the possibility of any negative consequences never occurred to him. It clearly was Dr. Lastlap's responsibility, however, to have considered all the potential risks of bartering for services with his patient and the possibility of long-term harm that participating in such an agreement could cause. He had failed to do this, thinking instead that he was helping his financially needy patient. Ultimately, however, Dr. Lastlap had placed the professional relationship at risk by agreeing to such an arrangement and harmed the patient he was hoping to help.

1. How did Dr. Lastlap's enthusiasm and goodwill cloud his judgment in considering a bartering-for-services arrangement?
2. Were there other ways Dr. Lastlap could have responded to his patient's financial neediness?
3. Could Anthony Flake have had insurance (as an unemployed mechanic) that might cover the costs of the care for Dr. Lastlap's injuries, or damage to his vehicle, if the accident had been more serious?[2]

3.05 MULTIPLE RELATIONSHIPS

(a) A multiple relationship occurs when a psychologist is in a professional role with a person and (1) at the same time is in another role with the same person, (2) at the same time is in a relationship with a person closely associated with or related to the person with whom the psychologist has the professional relation-

---

[2]Standard 3.04 is a very broad principle, which states, generically, the most important rule of all. There are at least 151 ways that psychologists could visit harm on someone, that is, by violating any one of the 151 standards or subsections in the Ethics Code. It is wise to consider the various professional roles that you play in carrying out your work and the ways that each of those roles could result in harming somebody personally, emotionally, cognitively, physically, sexually, professionally, financially, or legally, or in some other way.

ship, or (3) *promises to enter into another relationship in the future with the person or a person closely associated with or related to the person.*

A psychologist refrains from entering into a multiple relationship if the multiple relationship could reasonably be expected to impair the psychologist's objectivity, competence, or effectiveness in performing his or her functions as a psychologist, or otherwise risks exploitation or harm to the person with whom the professional relationship exists.

Multiple relationships that would not reasonably be expected to cause impairment or risk exploitation or harm are not unethical.

Keep your professional and scientific relationships (e.g., with patients, clients, students, supervisees, research participants) clear, simple, and straightforward. As a psychologist, generally play only one role at a time with a consumer, unless certain that adding a secondary role would not (a) interfere with your objectivity, (b) impair your competence or effectiveness, or (c) in some way harm or exploit him or her. The original relationship could suffer, your psychological work could be compromised, or both, and things could permanently change between the two of you. Specifically, observe the following when you have a professional relationship with another individual:

- Never add a second role to a preexisting professional role, or vice versa, such as a family member, relative, friend, neighbor, or close associate (e.g., offering therapy to your house cleaner or your dentist, or asking your patient for advice in the real estate market).
- Never have a professional relationship with someone who is close to someone to whom *you* are close, by virtue of family, friendship, work setting, and so on (e.g., offering therapy to your husband's friend, or to your boss's wife, or dating your adolescent client's mother).
- Never promise a second role to someone with whom you have a professional relationship or to someone to whom that person is close (e.g., agreeing to coauthor a journal article or a book with your current patient, discussing the hiring of your supervisee's best friend as a receptionist in your office).

However, it is acceptable to have a compound relationship with another individual if it plausibly would not lead to taking advantage of that person, or risk harming or mistreating him or her in any way.

VIGNETTE

Dr. Beeawl, a senior professor at a large university, prided himself in his ability to be a resource to his graduate students in a variety of ways. Unfortunately, this resulted in his occasionally engaging in several concurrent professional roles with a particular student that were at odds with each other, all in the name of mentoring. One example of this was his willingness on occasion to provide psychotherapy to a graduate student who seemed to be in crisis, or depressed, with the belief that he could successfully maintain the professional boundaries between academia and the clinician's office. In spite of the fact that participating in these roles could, at times, be confusing to his students, Dr. Beeawl was unaware of the potential for any major conflict that might emerge, until he met Elise.

Elise was a doctoral student who had recently separated from her husband, and she began therapy with Dr. Beeawl about halfway through her graduate studies. With all the personal and financial stresses of her marital separation, she was having some difficulty completing her course work, particularly in the area of research, and she had resorted to some rather unorthodox methods. In therapy, she eventually disclosed to Dr. Beeawl that she felt guilty and anxious about having plagiarized parts of a research paper, yet at the same time she was being encouraged by her professor to submit it for publication. When Dr. Beeawl heard these revelations he quickly found himself in the dilemma of experiencing a professional role conflict: He was both a university professor, who is supposed to model and enforce ethical conduct among students, yet he also was Elise's psychotherapist, who is to accept virtually all patient disclosures in confidence and process this material in treatment.

The situation rapidly became further complicated when Elise decided that she wished to take Dr. Beeawl's advanced course in social psychology, as he was reputed to be the finest teacher in the department in that area. Her therapy was not yet complete, and Dr. Beeawl found himself in the uncomfortable position of teaching and evaluating the same individual for whom he was providing therapy. As a compassionate man, he found it increasingly difficult to maintain objectivity in evaluating Elise's classroom performance, in light of his awareness of all her personal difficulties. He began to wonder whether his diminished objectivity might afford Elise an unfair advantage over other students in his class whom he was also evaluating and giving grades. As time went on, he also noticed that he felt somewhat inhibited by having Elise in his class, because his style of lecturing normally included far more humor and self-disclosure than his interactions with her as a patient.

Dr. Beeawl had clearly bitten off more than he could chew! He wished that he had never allowed so many professional roles to develop with Elise, and it became progressively more uncomfortable for him to function competently in all of them simultaneously. He attempted to resolve this complex situation by giving Elise the option of either dropping the class that he was teaching without any penalty or selecting a different therapist. Elise initially felt coerced and frustrated by her mentor's "resolution" of this complicated situation. However, as time went on, she eventually appreciated the wisdom of it. She decided to retain him as her therapist and drop out of his class. Dr. Beeawl, for his part, had finally learned a painful and belated lesson about respecting the roles and boundaries of relationships as a psychologist in the complexities of an academic milieu. From that point on, he attempted to limit his roles with students so as to retain his objectivity and competence more effectively and provide even better mentoring by not attempting to be all things to all people. This ultimately resulted in better teaching and better therapy, as Dr. Beeawl learned to have clear boundaries in his professional work.

1. What might motivate someone like Dr. Beeawl to have such disregard for professional boundaries?
2. How would you deal with a depressed student in your class, clearly in need of psychotherapy, who says that she would like to begin psychotherapy with you, as you are the only person she trusts?
3. What would you say to a nonpsychologist friend who approached you for tips about dealing with his migraine headaches and the specific stresses that produce them?

3.05 (b)

If a psychologist finds that, due to unforeseen factors, a potentially harmful multiple relationship has arisen, the psychologist takes reasonable steps to resolve it with due regard for the best interests of the affected person and maximal compliance with the Ethics Code.

If you comply with Standard 3.05 (a) and nevertheless discover that you are caught up in a potentially harmful dual relationship, do what you can to get out of it or reduce the potential conflict of interests, keeping in mind the best interests of the recipient of your services and obeying the Ethics Code.

VIGNETTE

Dr. Yna Fix had been consulting with her new accountant for 5 months about the business aspects of her practice, including problems she had been encountering with the managed health care system. She had been considering closing her 35-year practice in a rural New England community and was exploring various retirement options, but she had not yet told any of her patients.

One day, the accountant informed her that he had just learned that his wife's brother, Joe, was Dr. Fix's patient. Joe was a middle-age man who was suicidally depressed and had been alcohol dependent for most of his life. He had begun therapy with Dr. Fix over 6 months ago and had a productive therapeutic relationship with her. Dr. Fix wondered whether her accountant would agree to keep their discussions confidential and refrain from revealing to Joe, just yet, her plans to retire. She feared that such a disclosure might increase the likelihood of Joe's binge drinking and attempts at suicide, given his current fragile state (although she did not disclose this to her accountant).

Dr. Fix certainly was aware that social coincidences frequently occur, particularly in small communities, and that one must be prepared for them. However, this particular scenario was something that she had never encountered before, and it called for a creative solution. In the interest of preserving the continuity of Joe's treatment, she considered changing accountants, despite the fact that she had paid his fees in advance and that she had a good business relationship with him. She also considered the possibility of referring Joe to a colleague, although the transition of starting therapy all over might constitute a hardship for him.

She decided to consult a senior colleague to help resolve this dilemma and arrived at a decision that attended to her patient's best interests. She requested that the accountant avoid disclosing to Joe anything about her retirement plans for a period of several weeks. The accountant agreed to keep her plans confidential for that period of time. At the end of 3 weeks, she planned to discuss her long-range retirement plans with Joe, while offering to remain his therapist until a time when they both felt that he could transfer to another therapist in the community.

1. If Dr. Fix were not planning to retire, would there still be some potential problem in continuing to treat Joe after she learned about the brother-in-law relationship?
2. According to the Health Insurance Portability and Accountability Act (HIPAA), would Dr. Fix have been required to tell Joe at the outset about the identity of her accountant, and would she have to have a signed contract with the accountant confirming that he was also HIPAA compliant?
3. How should Dr. Fix deal with disclosures from her accountant that Joe was getting worse, did not like the treatment he was receiving and, in fact, had begun binge drinking again?
4. What if, in the course of therapy, Joe happens to disclose to Dr. Fix that his brother-in-law is "crooked" and was found guilty of embezzlement from the accounting firm he used to work for several years before?

3.05 (c)

When psychologists are required by law, institutional policy, or extraordinary circumstances to serve in more than one role in judicial or administrative pro-

ceedings, at the outset they clarify role expectation and the extent of confidentiality and thereafter as changes occur. (See also Standards 3.04, Avoiding Harm, and 3.07, Third-Party Requests for Services.)

If you are compelled by law, the policy of your institution (university, hospital, clinic, etc.), or some unusual circumstance to participate in judicial or administrative proceedings (e.g., child custody assessment, divorce proceeding, litigation in which your client is either a plaintiff or a defendant), make sure that you clarify to your client or patient, and to relevant others, what your role will be and any changes in confidentiality that are to be expected.

VIGNETTE

Mrs. Susan Pine had suffered a lumbar vertebral fracture and ensuing back and leg pain for over 2 years from tripping backward over a plant at her office. As an adjunct to her medical treatment, she had been referred to Dr. Omni for training in biofeedback and cognitive–behavioral therapy for management of chronic pain. She also was experiencing major depression, and her marriage had been negatively affected as well. Dr. Omni decided to provide short-term marital therapy to her and her husband, for 2 months, concurrently with her individual therapy, in an attempt to reduce the intense stress in the marriage. He explained at the outset that the marital therapy would be primarily didactic in nature, focusing on the issues of chronic pain in a marital relationship; he also stated that it would be limited in time, so as to minimize his playing two roles at once and so that the focus would primarily be on Mrs. Pine's individual treatment.

After being declared permanent and stationary by her physician, meaning that her medical condition was unlikely to improve significantly, Mrs. Pine initiated a lawsuit against her employer, claiming that her injury had caused long-term suffering, depression, and, ultimately, the deterioration of her marriage. A key issue in this case was separating the sequelae of the back injury from other factors, such as a history of preexisting depression and marital dysfunction. During the course of litigation the defendant's attorneys selected their own psychological expert witness, Dr. Marion Ette, who was prepared to offer opinions about the likely interactions of Mrs. Pine's personality with chronic pain and her marriage. Dr. Ette was prepared to testify that, on the basis of the available evidence, Mrs. Pine could likely be diagnosed with borderline personality disorder, and thus the secondary gains of chronic pain would likely play a prominent role in her treatment. Such testimony might greatly lessen the vulnerability of the defendant, if it could be shown that the bulk of Mrs. Pine's symptoms were due to her own psychopathology and not to the physical injury sustained in her fall.

Mrs. Pine's attorney discussed the patient's diagnosis with Dr. Omni, seeking to invite testimony that would ultimately negate that of Dr. Ette.

Unfortunately, however, Dr. Omni had previously diagnosed Mrs. Pine as having borderline personality disorder as well; however, he was insistent that she was not malingering or deriving secondary gain from her injury. Mrs. Pine's attorney decided that the best strategy, although somewhat risky, would be to include Dr. Omni's testimony in the litigation and to invite him into the role of expert witness on the subject of borderline personality disorder.

Dr. Omni, for his part, found the trial testimony to be difficult as he attempted to play more than one professional role at a time. He found himself in the increasingly conflicting position of not only providing information about his patient's physical and emotional suffering, but also serving as an assessor of the patient's faltering marriage as well as attempting to be an expert witness on the diagnosis and treatment of borderline personality disorder. Dr. Omni did his best to present his opinions in response to the cross-examiner's questions about secondary gain for chronic-pain patients and the traits of patients who are diagnosed with borderline personality disorder. It finally dawned on him that he had created a dilemma for himself and his patient by attempting to play so many roles at once.

Unfortunately, when Mrs. Pine heard Dr. Omni's testimony, she felt quite hurt and angry that he had diagnosed her with borderline personality disorder, even though he testified that her symptoms were likely not based on secondary gain. This was the first she knew of his diagnostic impressions about her, as he had never taken the time to review these matters in therapy with her prior to the trial. She was also upset to learn, during the cross-examination phase, that much of her marital distress was likely due to her borderline diagnosis and not primarily attributable to her back injury and subsequent pain and dysfunction.

By agreeing to serve as an expert witness in the treatment of borderline personality disorder for his patient's attorney while also playing the role of the patient's therapist and former marital therapist, Dr. Omni significantly complicated the therapeutic relationship with his patient, ultimately adding to her distress. He would have been well advised originally not to provide marital therapy, given the complexity of her history, and to have informed the attorney that he could not serve as an expert witness about this particular Axis II disorder because it could place him in a position of a conflict of interest, reduce his objectivity, and impair his professional relationship with Mrs. Pine. He failed to clearly establish professional boundaries during the early treatment phase, and he compounded the problem when litigation began by refusing to restrict the roles he was expected to play to those that would not be in conflict with each other.

1. Could Dr. Omni have ethically refused to take on the role of expert witness on the subject of borderline personality disorder?

2. What might Dr. Omni have done, before the trial, when he realized the full significance and attendant conflicts of attempting to play several roles at once in this forensic drama?
3. What steps might Dr. Omni have taken to better prepare Mrs. Pine for his revelations about her during the trial?
4. After the trial was over, what risk of retaliation did Dr. Omni incur, for having played so many roles at once, at the hands of his angry former patient, Mrs. Pine?

3.06 CONFLICT OF INTEREST

Psychologists refrain from taking on a professional role when personal, scientific, professional, legal, financial, or other interests or relationships could reasonably be expected to (1) impair their objectivity, competence, or effectiveness in performing their functions as psychologists or (2) expose the person or organization with whom the professional relationship exists to harm or exploitation.

Never accept someone as a client, patient, supervisee, or in some other professional or scientific role when there is a good chance that other interests or relationships could (a) detract from your impartiality, proficiency, or efficacy in doing your job or (b) expose that person or organization to harm, mistreatment, or exploitation. Conflicting interests or relationships that you should consider include the following:

- personal (e.g., you already have a formal or social relationship with the potential recipient of your services, e.g., friend, family, coworker, or neighbor),
- scientific (e.g., you decide to carry out research on the efficacy of treatment vs. medication for major depression that is funded by the pharmaceutical company manufacturing the antidepressant in question),
- professional (e.g., your colleague on the hospital staff, with whom you attend regular staff meetings, now desires to consult you as her psychotherapist),
- legal (e.g., you are asked to serve as an expert witness in litigation involving your own patient, and it could either compromise your treatment of her or possibly weaken her case, as you could be seen as lacking impartiality in your expert testimony), and
- financial (e.g., the CEO of a large corporation hires you as a consultant at a lucrative fee and then casually asks if you would supervise his niece in your clinical practice, when you knew that she was unable to get a position because of her poor training and previous performance).

VIGNETTE 1: PSYCHOTHERAPY

The relationship boundaries in Dr. Goodboy's extended family became somewhat complicated when Blanche, his clinically depressed mother-in-law, sought him out "to talk over some important matters about the family." She insisted on meeting him in his office and actually paid him a small fee, because she valued his opinion and wanted to make it clear that she was consulting him "as a professional, not as a son-in-law." She was obviously depressed, refused to seek professional help with anyone else, and highly valued his professional opinion, and so Dr. Goodboy agreed to talk with her in his office. He also honored her request to keep the meetings a secret from his wife. However, this was a somewhat uncomfortable accommodation to make, because honesty very much was valued in his marriage.

After three meetings in 2 weeks, it slowly emerged that the cause of Blanche's depression was, in part, due to her daughter's marriage to Dr. Goodboy himself 2 years before. Dr. Goodboy had some personality traits that were similar to Blanche's older brother, with whom she had been in conflict for much of her life. As she became aware of the similarity, she became openly angry and blaming toward her son-in-law, demanding that he change his ways.

Dr. Goodboy began to see how difficult it was to continue in the role he had begun, and he began to wish that he had never agreed to provide counseling to his mother-in-law. His objectivity was certainly impaired in dealing with this depressed, now-hostile woman. He had only been trying to provide much-needed help to her, and he found himself trapped in a complex family web, which seemed to become tighter with every movement. He finally informed his mother-in-law that, for obvious reasons, he could no longer continue to discuss these matters with her, unless they consulted a third party, such as another therapist, or unless she began counseling with a separate therapist.

1. What steps might Dr. Goodboy have taken at the outset to avoid such a dual role from developing, when first contacted by Blanche?
2. What is a *folie à deux*, and how would it apply to this vignette?
3. Would you accept an extended family member into psychotherapy for depression if you knew very well that the cause had nothing to do with you or anyone else in the family?

VIGNETTE 2: RESEARCH

Dr. Kindly was carrying out research in a large university hospital on treatments for chronic pain involving biofeedback training, acupuncture, and hypnosis. As an inducement for research participants, she offered to provide some limited psychotherapeutic treatment at the conclusion of their involvement in the protocol. Although she generally did not accept colleagues as research participants, she made an exception for Dr. Spinnit, a colleague with chronic back pain and bronchitis. Dr. Kindly thought that offering this opportunity to her colleague, who had experienced such suffering over a long period of time, was a benevolent gesture on her part. However, the situation became complicated when she learned that Dr. Spinnit's pain probably also had a significant psychosomatic component, exacerbated by the stress of his upcoming tenure decision and resistance being offered by the psychology department chair, who happened to be the regular tennis partner of Dr. Kindly.

One day, Dr. Spinnit saw Dr. Kindly on the tennis court engaged in a lively match with the psychology chair and was quite dismayed that she was playing tennis with the very man whom he considered to be his nemesis. From that moment on, he felt such conflict that it seemed impossible for him to continue to be a research participant any further; neither did he feel comfortable in discussing the problems with the department chair, even though the stress contributed significantly to his back pain.

Dr. Spinnit also felt somewhat betrayed by Dr. Kindly because she had promised to be a therapeutic resource for him, and he had begun to count on her. Now, however, with the perceived conflict in roles, he felt he could not trust her as a therapeutic resource given her obvious close friendship with the department chair. For her part, Dr. Kindly felt incompetent to manage the situation, in either the research setting or the individual therapy that she had promised. She now understood that accepting a colleague as a research participant could be harmful to both the social and working relationship as well as to the research itself.

1. In the "gray area" of this scenario, would it be ethically acceptable for Dr. Kindly to have provided an additional measure of informed consent to Dr. Spinnit, so as to head off the problems that emerged early on? If so, what might she have told him?
2. Has Dr. Kindly acted in a way that is unethical or unprofessional?
3. Has anyone been harmed by the actions of Dr. Kindly?

VIGNETTE 3: DIFFERENCES IN REAL OR ASCRIBED SOCIAL POWER

Dr. Stone had been providing clinical supervision to Harmony, a 2nd-year student, for 3 months. One day, he asked Harmony to assist him with several research projects that he had started. Dr. Stone's research assistant had become ill with hepatitis, and his inability to complete his share of the work was holding up the projects. Specifically, Dr. Stone needed about 6 months' worth of clerical assistance coding responses and entering them into the computer and carrying out many telephone interviews as well. Although

Dr. Stone could offer only very meager financial compensation for this work, he reassured Harmony that it would be a useful learning experience in acquiring research methodology skills, even though it had no relevance to her own clinical work or supervision and was not a part of the original supervisory agreement.

Harmony reluctantly complied with Dr. Stone's request, even though her time was already in short supply because of two research projects that she was already working on with another professor. She could ill afford to devote the extra hours that these new projects required. However, being somewhat deferential by nature, she thought that she had little choice but to accept her clinical supervisor's request. He appeared to be quite needy and was rather insistent that she comply. She spent a large amount of time assisting him, to the detriment of progress on her own work. Harmony did not feel that she could even discuss the possibility of refusing to cooperate with Dr. Stone. She felt that doing so would negatively affect the clinical supervisory relationship, so she simply deferred to Dr. Stone's authority and agreed to work the long hours required.

Several months went by before Harmony was able to bring herself to discuss her objections to working such long hours for Dr. Stone. At that time, they came to a satisfactory agreement, but not before she had experienced significant distress as a result of overcommitting herself to his projects.

1. What options might Harmony have in dealing with her clinical supervisor's pressure to help with his research in the following settings: a large university, a small professional school of psychology, as a psychological assistant in a group private practice setting?
2. Was Harmony being harmed by Dr. Stone's coercion to assist in research?
3. How would it make a difference if Harmony suspected that her gender was a factor in the coercion?

3.07 THIRD-PARTY REQUESTS FOR SERVICES

When psychologists agree to provide services to a person or entity at the request of a third party, psychologists attempt to clarify at the outset of the service the nature of the relationship with all individuals or organizations involved. This clarification includes the role of the psychologist (e.g., therapist, consultant, diagnostician, or expert witness), an identification of who is the client, the probable uses of the services provided or the information obtained, and the fact that there may be limits to confidentiality. (See also Standards 3.05, Multiple Relationships, and 4.02, Discussing the Limits of Confidentiality.)

If you are asked to do psychological work (e.g., provide therapy, consulting, supervision, assessment, expert witness testimony, or some other psychological service) by a third party (e.g., a parent, teacher, training institution, referring physician, human resources office, court, commanding officer), first make sure that you and everyone else involved understands what, exactly, you will be doing. This means explaining

- what your role will be;
- who, exactly, will be the client or recipient of your services;
- how the service you provide or information you obtain will likely be used (as far as you know); and
- whether or how privacy and confidentiality will apply—where the information will go, what individuals or agencies will have access to it, and any other limitations to confidentiality that may exist.

Although not required by this standard, it may be wise to use printed handouts or correspondence that documents all of the above information as well as record it in client or patient records or in some other appropriate place.

VIGNETTE

Dr. Balm was contacted by an attorney who inquired about his willingness to provide court-ordered treatment for anger management to his violent male client, Mr. Biter. Mr. Biter had been found guilty of shoving and punching his wife during arguments over the previous year. The police had been called twice during this period of time, and there were many occasions when his wife had not called the police, but probably should have, because of the intensity of his rage.

Before accepting Mr. Biter as a patient, Dr. Balm considered some of the other options for treatment that might be helpful. For example, he was aware of several anger management classes that were conducted regularly at a nearby adult education center. He also knew of a university-sponsored "Forgiveness Seminar Series," from which several of his narcissistic and angry patients had benefited. Also, there was a men's ongoing psychotherapy group in the community, run by a psychologist and a clinical social worker, that had an excellent reputation for helping participants deal with negative emotions, particularly frustration and rage. He pointed out to the attorney that some combination of individual psychotherapy, a didactic group, and marital counseling would likely constitute an optimal treatment. He also informed him that he would prefer to meet with Mr. Biter to perform his own assessment and consider which, if any, of the group approaches might be useful adjuncts to treatment. As for his part, Mr. Biter was eager to "get on with things" and begin his mandated treatment. He was experiencing moderate depression and had recently increased his alcohol intake.

After several telephone conversations, Dr. Balm sent Mr. Biter and his attorney a brief letter summarizing the agreement. He would meet with Mr. Biter individually, for assessment, and with Mr. Biter's wife. After these evaluations, therapy would formally begin, as long as the match was satisfactory. Dr. Balm was careful to address the issue of confidentiality very clearly; per the requirements of the court, he agreed to provide, over a 1-year period, several very brief, periodic reports to the attorney regarding treatment compliance and general progress. He also provided information about his fee and expectations about payment. He also was clear about the scope of his authority during the course of treatment. He made it plain that adjunctive treatments, such as group therapy, treatment for alcohol dependence, marital therapy, psychopharmacological assessment for depression, or some other intervention, might be required. He stated in his letter that he would consider and recommend adjunctive interventions as appropriate; he also made it clear that Mr. Biter's compliance would be mandatory. If adequate progress had not been attained by the end of 1 year, then treatment would be extended, or some other rehabilitative course of action could be taken. Dr. Balm acknowledged his responsibility, as the treating therapist, to provide a brief letter or report at the conclusion of treatment regarding his patient's progress.

Each party to this agreement—Dr. Balm, the attorney, Mr. Biter, and Mr. Biter's wife—understood the role that he or she would be playing. There was little possibility for ambiguity or misunderstanding, because the salient aspects of the arrangement were thoroughly addressed in the telephone calls and then summarized in the letter. This was the simplest way to avoid misconceptions at the outset or disappointments later on in this potentially adversarial situation.

1. What might Dr. Balm have discovered in his assessment session of Mr. Biter that might dissuade him from accepting him as a patient?
2. What problems might develop if Dr. Balm attempted to offer both individual therapy to Mr. Biter and marital therapy concurrently?
3. What other aspects of informed consent must Dr. Balm provide Mr. Biter besides clarifying the role that he will be playing?

3.08 EXPLOITATIVE RELATIONSHIPS

Psychologists do not exploit persons over whom they have supervisory, evaluative, or other authority such as clients/patients, students, supervisees, research participants, and employees. (See also Standards 3.05, Multiple Relationships; 6.04, Fees and Financial Arrangements; 6.05, Barter With Clients/Patients;

7.07, Sexual Relationships With Students and Supervisees; 10.05, Sexual Intimacies With Current Therapy Clients/Patients; 10.06, Sexual Intimacies With Relatives or Significant Others of Current Therapy Clients/Patients; 10.07, Therapy With Former Sexual Partners; and 10.08, Sexual Intimacies With Former Therapy Clients/Patients.)

Never use your power or authority over someone else (e.g., client, patient, student, supervisee, research participant, employee, etc.) to your advantage. You provide a psychological service for which you get paid; you are not entitled to anything else from the other person, even though he or she may possibly be very willing to provide it. You can all too easily slip into exploitation or abuse by bartering for services, ignoring preexisting personal or professional relationships, considering friendship or romance with a consumer, and many other ways.

VIGNETTE

For over 10 years, Dr. Robert Guile had been teaching and chairing dissertation committees at a small university. Although he played a variety of professional roles, and was generally highly regarded by many people, he unfortunately was unclear about his professional boundaries and had a tendency to gratify his personal and professional needs primarily through his students. He prided himself on the good working relationships he felt he had with them, and he was genuinely willing to befriend them and their families. He frequently invited them to play tennis or to come to his house for dinner. As the relationship developed further, he would include them in family outings with his children, and sometimes he would ask them to care for his children when he and his wife would go out.

At his office, he assigned tasks to his students, such as bringing in coffee and croissants to clinical supervision sessions, or buying flowers or the morning newspaper—he even asked his teaching assistants to wash the windows of his office when they needed it. He also required some of his students to routinely peruse journals for articles of interest to him, regardless of their needs or interest, for no remuneration.

On occasion, he engaged in more serious exploitation, such as using data from his students' dissertations in his own publications, without citing his sources or obtaining students' permission in advance. On one occasion, he plagiarized part of a chapter from a student's master's thesis without citing it. When the student encountered Dr. Guile's article in print, 1 year later, and discovered the plagiarism, she brought her concern to Dr. Guile, who informed her coldly that if she wanted to ever receive her doctoral degree in this program, "or anywhere else, for that matter," she had better not pursue this any further. Besides, he reassured her, she should take it as a compliment that he was willing to use the part of her chapter that he did—this was really a tribute to the high quality of her work.

Finally, in his clinical practice, Dr. Guile disregarded professional boundaries by taking advantage of the expertise of his patients, if they had skills that might benefit him. When a lawyer consulted him for depression, Dr. Guile occasionally would use part of the hour to seek legal advice. For a period of time he was engaged in litigation with a neighbor over a house addition that he was building, and he would not hesitate to provide his lawyer–patient regular "updates" and wonder aloud about the wisdom of his own attorney's legal strategy. During one session, he spent over half the time discussing many details of his problems with the contractor and the architect, lamenting how long things were dragging out and how costly the project was becoming. On another occasion, when a stockbroker consulted him regarding panic attacks, and later in treatment volunteered some information about a "hot company" about to go public, Dr. Guile sought additional advice and acted on the tips that his patient provided.

Dr. Guile had little understanding of the concept of personal exploitation of students or clients. Neither did he appreciate the harm and confusion he brought into the lives of individuals whom he was supposedly mentoring or helping. He continued to use others to his own advantage, feeling entitled to do so, until several students brought grievances against him to the chair of the psychology department, their state ethics committee, and the state board of psychology after they no longer had any affiliation with the school. Dr. Guile was ultimately found to have violated this standard and many others. He received a formal reprimand from the state Ethics Committee and was required to undergo 1 year of monitoring of his clinical practice by the state licensing board.

1.   What steps can a graduate student take to deal with exploitation while still in the program?
2.   Where is the harm in discussing your own life problems with a patient, or with someone you are supervising? Would this not imply that you are simply treating him or her as a valued adult who has something to offer?
3.   Where do you draw the line, in an authoritarian relationship, between normal, friendly behavior and exploitation (as a patient, as a student, as a supervisee, as a teaching assistant, as an employee, etc.)?[3]

3.09 COOPERATION WITH OTHER PROFESSIONALS

When indicated and professionally appropriate, psychologists cooperate with other professionals in order to serve their clients/patients effectively and appropriately. (See also Standard 4.05, Disclosures.)

---

[3]The social power ascribed to individuals is important to consider in multiple-role relationships. The formal authority of one's rank or position within an institution may invoke compliance in another.

Cooperate with other therapists and health care professionals when treating or referring your clients and patients. This means returning telephone calls in a timely fashion, releasing records when requested (with a signed consent, of course), discussing your client or patient's individual treatment with a marital or group therapist if clinically indicated, following up when referring your patient to another health care provider if needed, and taking any other collaborative actions that promote the welfare of your patient.

VIGNETTE

Dr. Connie Sultan, a psychologist working in a behavioral medicine clinic, frequently treated patients who had both psychological symptoms and somatic complaints, such as chemotherapy and radiation side effects in cancer patients, migraine headaches, chronic pain from neck and back injuries, and sexual dysfunction. More often than not, she would find herself collaborating with primary-care physicians, oncologists, neurologists, gastroenterologists, pain management specialists, and physical therapists. The patients with whom she worked frequently experienced anxiety and depression concerning their physical status and required a different sort of care than the average psychotherapy patient with an Axis I disorder. At times, the telephone consultations, occasional correspondence, and occasional review of medical records took much time and effort; however, Dr. Sultan was well aware of the importance of collaborating with other providers with these difficult patients, and of how it affected the quality of her therapy with them, and she was fastidious about it.

When Dr. Sultan thought that an assessment for antidepressant medication would be helpful she generally referred the patient to a psychiatrist or other qualified health care provider knowledgeable about psychopharmacology. If a patient was already being medicated by a general medical practitioner or a pain doctor for anxiety or depression, but was experiencing little benefit, she would frequently suggest a consultation with a psychopharmacologist and would discuss this with the medicating physician. Usually, the physician was pleased and somewhat relieved to have a new resource "join the team," particularly one who was well versed in medications for mood disorders.

If Dr. Sultan learned of an ongoing patient's new physical complaint or pain, she would generally refer him or her for a medical assessment. Although she sometimes viewed the new symptom as likely functional in nature and

This vignette demonstrates how a power differential in an academic setting can result in coercion of the individual with less authority. Using, harming, or exploiting another person in a less powerful position can occur almost before you realize that it has happened, particularly if the other is overaccommodating, compliant, passive, or all three (*folie à deux*).

treatable within the context of her psychological interventions, she also knew the risks of assuming that a symptom was psychogenic when in fact it could very well have an organic basis. She was cautious, both ethically and clinically, to avoid straying from her area of competence as a psychologist by attempting to make medical diagnoses.

Sometimes, because of the perceived hopelessness of their situation or the intensity of their chronic pain, her patients threatened suicide. She always treated these disclosures with the gravity that they deserved, and she discussed hospitalization with the patient, or some other way to preserve their safety.

In keeping within the requirements of this standard, Dr. Sultan found it useful to view herself as part of a health care *team*, even though the other members of the team were often at separate hospitals, practices, and institutions. This physical separation required more time and effort to carry out effective collaboration, to be sure, and over the years she had encountered many physicians and mental health providers who took little initiative in coordinating treatment with each other. However, she found repeatedly that timely and effective collaboration contributed to a higher quality of therapy for her patients, and she considered it well worth the effort to initiate and respond to requests when the need was there.

1. Is collaborating with a chronic-pain patient's treating physician ethically required? Clinically wise? Legally mandated? Discuss your answers.
2. Is it ethical for Dr. Sultan to bill patients for the hours spent consulting with other specialists by phone or face to face, reading and writing correspondence, and so on?
3. What risks might be incurred if Dr. Sultan were too busy to respond to a physician's concerns about a mutual patient's abuse of painkillers?
4. If a patient were harmed by Dr. Sultan's failure to collaborate appropriately with another treating health care provider, and the patient later filed an ethics complaint, which sanction— a censure or a reprimand—might she likely be vulnerable to receive?

3.10 INFORMED CONSENT

(a) When psychologists conduct research or provide assessment, therapy, counseling, or consulting services in person or via electronic transmission or other forms of communication, they obtain the informed consent of the individual or individuals using language that is reasonably understandable to that person or persons except when conducting such activities without consent is mandated by law or governmental regulation or as otherwise provided in this Ethics Code.

(See also Standards 8.02, Informed Consent to Research; 9.03, Informed Consent in Assessments; and 10.01, Informed Consent to Therapy.)

Always obtain informed consent when conducting research or offering any psychological service, intervention, or consultation, whether face to face or via the Internet, videoconferencing, or some other form of electronic communication. This includes assessment and evaluation, all forms of treatment or therapy, and consulting services of any sort, to individuals, groups, or organizations. Convey to those with whom you work, in simple language, what they can expect before beginning the work. Research participants, patients and individual clients, organizational clients, and consultees should have a clear understanding of what to anticipate from you or the situation in advance. This does not apply to interventions mandated by law or governmental regulation, however, or to other exceptions provided by the Ethics Code. Remember—don't obfuscate; explain what you intend to do in simple language. (Many other standards are subsumed under Informed Consent as well. See also Standards 4.02, Discussing the Limits of Confidentiality; 4.03, Recording; 4.05, Disclosures; 6.02 (c), Maintenance, Dissemination, and Disposal of Confidential Records of Professional and Scientific Work; 6.04, Fees and Financial Arrangements; 7.05, Mandatory Individual or Group Therapy; 8.02, Informed Consent to Research; 8.03, Informed Consent for Recording Voices and Images in Research; 8.05, Dispensing With Informed Consent for Research; 8.06 (b), Offering Inducements for Research Participation; 8.07 (c), Deception in Research; 9.03, Informed Consent in Assessments; 9.09 (a), Test Scoring and Interpretation Services; 10.01, Informed Consent to Therapy; 10.02, Therapy Involving Couples or Families; 10.03, Group Therapy; and 10.04, Providing Therapy to Those Served by Others.)

VIGNETTE

Dr. Will Teller routinely informed his patients, clients, students, and supervisees what to expect in their professional interactions with him, and often he used printed handouts that further explained his services. He clearly described both the role he would play and the expectations he had of them. In discussing psychological testing, he did not exaggerate a test's usefulness or imply that it could yield information for which it had no validation. He provided feedback to clients about their performance on the Wechsler Adult Intelligence Scale—III (Wechsler, 1997), the Minnesota Multiphasic Personality Inventory—2 (Hathaway & McKinley, 1989), the Beck Depression Inventory—II (Beck, 1996), and other instruments of assessment in a simple, nontechnical way.

When discussing psychotherapy, Dr. Teller avoided giving guarantees about the outcome of treatment; instead, he generally provided information about the process of therapy. He discussed what therapy consisted of; what might be expected of the client; the approximate duration; the possible risks (e.g., the stressful aspects of treatment); and who could, with the client's permission, become involved in the treatment (e.g., specialists, a referring primary-care physician, spouse).

In carrying out clinical supervision, he was careful to inform his trainees about the frequency and duration of the supervisory meetings. He also told them what to expect from him and gave specifics about the format and content of the supervisory sessions, how these would be assessed, and other relevant details. He derived much value from supervising and providing informed consent to supervisees from routinely perusing the Web sites of the Association of Psychology and Postdoctoral Internship Centers (http://www.appic.org) and the Association for State and Provincial Psychology Boards (http://www.asppb.org) and publications from the National Register of Health Service Providers in Psychology.

Whenever Dr. Teller instructed recipients of his services about what to expect in their work with him, he generally was careful to invite their questions and gladly discussed any aspect of his work about which they were curious. Also, he usually solicited their feedback to verify their comprehension of the topic at hand.

1. What are the risks of failing to provide informed consent to research participants, patients, supervisees, and others to whom you provide psychological services?
2. What are the requirements of HIPAA as regards informed consent of patients, and must you ethically provide information in addition to HIPAA's requirements?
3. Does your institution, hospital, or group practice have any additional policies about which you are required to instruct patients at the outset?
4. How do you inform organizational clients about the services you intend to provide and any attendant risks or exceptions to confidentiality?
5. In providing supervision, what would you include in a letter or a contract at the outset describing the experience and responsibilities of each party?

3.10 (b)

For persons who are legally incapable of giving informed consent, psychologists nevertheless (1) provide an appropriate explanation, (2) seek the individual's assent, (3) consider such persons' preferences and best interests, and (4) obtain appropriate permission from a legally authorized person, if such substitute consent is permitted or required by law. When consent by a legally authorized person is not permitted or required by law, psychologists take reasonable steps to protect the individual's rights and welfare.

When conducting research with or providing services to children, people with mental disabilities, impaired elderly individuals, or others who cannot legally give consent, you must

- explain the research project or psychological intervention to them anyway, in a simple fashion;
- attempt to gain their assent—agreement to cooperate with you—even though they may not fully understand the research or intervention;
- give due consideration to their preferences and welfare; and
- obtain formal consent from a legally authorized person, such as a parent, caretaker, legal guardian, and so on, by fully disclosing in advance the research or psychological intervention that is intended (if such substitute consent is permitted or required by law).

When consent by a legally authorized person is not required by law, be sure to take steps to preserve the person's rights and his or her safety.

VIGNETTE

Dr. Anne Gram was interested in studying memory in 6- and 7-year-old children at various elementary schools. She was examining free and cued recall of events as influenced by interrogatory bias, coercive persuasion on the part of the examiner, various types of misinformation, and inherent suggestibility of the child.

Dr. Gram first sent a letter to all parents and then conducted a group meeting to discuss the details of her project. She informed them about the essence of the research; its goal, which was to examine the phenomena of distortion of memory of recent events, repression, and confabulation in young children; and the rationale for the research, which was to help assess the validity of the testimony of children who have been asked to provide details of their traumatic experiences in cases of child abuse allegations. She explained that there would be little or no risk, that participation was completely voluntary, and that the children could drop out of the project at any point.

After asking their own questions about the research and receiving answers to their satisfaction, most parents agreed to allow their children to participate in the research. Parents were also encouraged to ask additional questions or explore any other concerns that might arise during the course of the research. With that in mind, Dr. Gram also made herself accessible to any parent who might have reservations about continuing after the data gathering had begun; she provided several telephone numbers and e-mail addresses for her and her assistants, who would be readily available.

Before beginning the data-gathering phase, Dr. Gram also had a meeting with the children in which she discussed the study in general and informed them that she would be testing them for how well they remembered things. She told them that some of them would be allowed to play with toys, and others would watch television (videotapes), and then they would be asked some questions. This was done in a way to preserve their naivete for the tasks. They were also told that they would probably enjoy the experience but that they did not have to participate if they did not wish to. After hearing her brief introduction, one boy became tearful and began shoving his neighbor. An assistant took the boy aside and in the ensuing discussion learned that he did not wish to be in the study but was being forced by his father to participate. The boy was removed from the sample, because he clearly was not providing his assent, and it seemed to be in his best interest to avoid coercing cooperation, even though his father obviously consented. (As it turned out, the father did not even have legal custody of the child and could not have consented to his participation even if the child wanted to. The father had his own motives for the child's participation in the research: He was involved in a custody battle with his ex-wife, thinking she was abusive, and he was hoping that his son's participation in this research would verify him as a credible witness in the ongoing litigation—a long shot, by any standard!)

Although Dr. Gram knew that her protocol was not stressful or invasive, she was well aware of the ethical requirement to provide explanations to parents and children, to seek assent from the children and consent from their parents, and to consider the wishes of the children in following through with participation. By paying close attention to each phase of the informed-consent process, she ultimately obtained a higher quality of data (by excluding unwilling or problematical participants) while simultaneously protecting the rights and welfare of each child.

1. What sort of information would Dr. Gram be obliged to provide the parents?
2. In dealing with a linguistically and culturally diverse set of parents, how could Dr. Gram be certain that everyone comprehended her description of the research and any attendant risks and benefits?
3. Should Dr. Gram make an effort to verify the legal guardianship status of the consenting parents? If so, how?

3.10 (c)

When psychological services are court ordered or otherwise mandated, psychologists inform the individual of the nature of the anticipated services, includ-

ing whether the services are court ordered or mandated and any limits of confidentiality, before proceeding.

> If you are asked to perform therapy, assessment, or some other psychological service that is ordered by the court, or required by another third party (e.g., human resources office, commanding officer), be sure to inform your client at the outset about (a) the psychological service you intend to provide, including the fact that it is mandated, and (b) any limitations to confidentiality or privacy that might exist. Although not required by this standard, it may be wise to provide your client with a printed handout or advance correspondence that includes this information and, of course, to document all this information in the psychological record.

VIGNETTE

Dr. Sue Keen was contacted by an anxious, divorced father whose 15-year-old son, Bela, had just been ordered by the headmaster of his private school to have a psychological evaluation. It seems that Bela, in the course of writing a political science paper, had disclosed private feelings that raised concern in his teacher. The topic was terrorism, and Bela had written in support of violence as a viable means of implementing change; he had also mentioned vague threats about setting the school on fire and harming certain teachers as a means of "making a political statement." Bela's teacher met with him and learned of his depression concerning his parents' divorce and the resulting custody arrangement that he found so aversive. Although she could not believe that Bela was really capable of hurting anyone, she continued to be concerned about the boy's emotional state and his potential for violence.

A meeting with the school counselor (who knew Bela well) and the headmaster resulted in the unanimous decision to contact Bela's parents at once and require a full psychological assessment. This decision was submitted to the school board for review, with a strong emphasis on maintaining the privacy of Bela and his family. The board approved the decision unanimously, concerned about the safety and welfare of both students and teachers. Bela voiced his opposition to this plan: Psychologists "had only f*cked things up" in the past, he complained, and he "shouldn't have to bother with them now." In fact, it was a psychological evaluation of his parents that had contributed to the current custody arrangement. Nevertheless, the school administrators were adamant and quickly informed his mother (the custodial parent) that a psychological evaluation, a report to the headmaster, and treatment would be required as a contingency for Bela's continued matriculation at school. The names of two psychologists had been provided; Bela's father had learned about this, and he called each of them to learn about their qualifications. Although he did not have legal custody of Bela, he was concerned about Bela's welfare and wished to provide input about the choice of a therapist.

Dr. Keen scheduled an appointment with Bela and his father together at a mutually convenient time, that same week. However, after making the appointment, she learned from a colleague that she could not legally meet with Bela because of a state law requiring that consent for psychological services must be obtained from the legal guardian of a minor. Because Bela's mother had sole legal custody, she alone could authorize treatment. In her eagerness to be helpful, Dr. Keen had overlooked a state law that squarely placed the responsibility for authorizing treatment on the custodial parent. She telephoned Bela's father and informed him of the problem, making it clear that Bela's mother would have to either initiate the request for a meeting or at least document her agreement with it.

Even though she would not necessarily be providing services to Bela, Dr. Keen decided to address some of the broader issues of treatment, as the father had many questions about the process. Dr. Keen informed the father about the process of a psychological evaluation: what it consisted of, approximately how long it would take, and the fact that she would write a formal report. She explained further that the headmaster would be informed of the results of Bela's psychological assessment, as well as his overall progress in treatment, if she were to be his therapist. She told him about her policy of confidentiality with minors and discussed phone calls or other inquiries for details about the treatment from the parents or school officials. She further explained about record keeping and presented some of the patient rights and entitlements established by HIPAA. She also gave a balanced presentation about the advisability of joint sessions with one parent or the other and even offered a general opinion about the possible pros and cons of collaboration with the father's therapist, if he were willing to permit it.

Dr. Keen had several printed handouts on these topics, which she agreed to send to Bela's father after speaking with him on the telephone. In short, she began the process of providing thorough informed consent about psychotherapy with Bela, with an appreciation for the complexity of the family's needs. She attempted to clarify important issues in her conversation with the father concerning clinical, ethical, legal, and professional matters. However, she was careful to avoid offering professional advice or opinions about Bela, or his specific situation, and she avoided as well establishing a professional relationship with the father.

Nevertheless, when Bela's mother learned from her son that her ex-husband had contacted the psychologist before she had, and talked at length with her, she felt quite upset. She dashed off a quick letter of complaint to the American Psychological Association Ethics Office, faulting Dr. Keen for even speaking with Bela's father at all, because he had no legal rights to the boy. Over the course of several months, the Ethics Office thoroughly investigated her allegations and obtained sufficient information from Dr. Keen and the father to conclude that she had, in fact, violated no ethical standard and, to the contrary, had been careful to maintain her professional distance.

Providing psychological services of any sort that are mandated by a third party can be complicated enough. To do so in flagrant violation of state law and the Ethics Code would invite a grievance of some sort (ethics complaint, complaint to the state board of psychology, or a lawsuit). Dr. Keen was well aware of the potential intensity of each parents' passionate feelings in these matters and wisely took a course of action that protected the mother's rights, provided useful information to the father, and complied with all legal and ethical rules as well.

1. What are the possible negative consequences of providing psychological services to a minor when the custodial parent either does not know or finds out later and objects? Consider ethical, legal, and clinical consequences in your answer.
2. Would Dr. Keen have incurred a risk of becoming too involved in this case if she has advised the father over the phone, in a general way, about teenage violence and how to explore or deal with his son's violent thoughts? How would this differ from generic advice the father might obtain from a "pop psychology" book on the subject of parenting adolescents?
3. If Dr. Keen became Bela's therapist, and wished to collaborate with the father's psychotherapist, how would she go about seeking authorization to do so?
4. What steps should Dr. Keen take if she were told by the father that Bela had cut his wrists with a razor blade after learning of the decision to have a psychological assessment, and his mother did not know?

3.10 (d)

Psychologists appropriately document written or oral consent, permission, and assent. (See also Standards 8.02, Informed Consent to Research; 9.03, Informed Consent in Assessments; and 10.01, Informed Consent to Therapy.)

You must always keep a written record of any consent or acquiescence provided by anyone—research participant, client, individual or group therapy patient, corporate client—whether it was given to you orally or in writing. This will protect you in the future, if a question is ever raised about consent, and will clarify things for other individuals as well. If your practice or research is subject to the requirements of HIPAA, then make certain that your consent process and documents are compliant with this federal regulation.

A father who had recently remarried brought his 8-year-old son, Alan, to Dr. Wells for treatment. Alan was having difficulty forming friendships with the other students, was getting into fights on the playground, and had been caught stealing from teachers on several occasions. The boy's stepmother was often out of town on business trips and was unable to accompany them. Dr. Wells, who had spoken with Alan's father by phone, encouraged him to prepare his son for the meeting by telling him that he deserved to have someone special just to talk with by himself about anything that he wished. This person was to be his own special sort of coach or counselor who could meet with him in private each week.

The purpose of the first meeting was for all three to acquaint themselves with each other and for Dr. Wells to provide information to Alan and his father about what to expect in treatment. When Dr. Wells met with Alan alone, the boy made it clear that he did not wish to be there, that he "didn't need no more counselors to talk to!" After accepting Alan's remark, Dr. Wells took this opportunity to explain how they might spend their time talking, playing games, or even drawing pictures together. She also told him that she knew he had been having a hard time in school lately and that they could talk about that. She went on to say that she would give Alan a chance to tell her how he's feeling; what he's thinking about; and what he might be worried about, upset about, or even happy about. This was to be a special time each week to talk about those things just the two of them, and if he did not feel like talking, he could come anyway, and they could spend the time doing something else—Alan would help decide how to spend the time.

As part of informed consent, Dr. Wells also said that she might want to ask Alan's stepfather, mother, father, and stepmother to come in sometime (not all at once), but she made it clear that she would always discuss this with him first. She reviewed her policies on privacy and confidentiality, and the exceptions to these; she told him that he could let her know if there were something he wanted to keep secret, just between the two of them, or if there were something he specifically wanted her to tell his parents.

Dr. Wells also had a printed form that she gave to Alan's father explaining the nature of therapy in detail. It consisted of an introductory paragraph briefly describing some highlights of Dr. Wells's training and achievements, followed by brief paragraphs on each of the following topics: (a) confidentiality and its exceptions (according to the state law); (b) fees; (c) duration of therapy; (d) cancellations, missed sessions, and tardiness; (e) emergencies and telephone availability; (f) referral for medication assessment; (g) collaboration with other health care professionals; (h) vacations, absences, and coverage by another psychologist; and (i) untimely interruptions to treatment.

Dr. Wells had decided to comply with HIPAA regulations, because she routinely did electronic billing with Medicare and insurance companies, so she included a second section of the consent form entitled "Notice of Privacy Practices." As required by law, the first section informed patients about their rights regarding psychological information, including the following: (a) the right to inspect and obtain a copy of their psychological record, (b) the right to request a correction or add an addendum to their psychological record, (c) the right to an accounting of disclosures of their psychological information to third parties, (d) the right to request restriction on how their information is to be used, (e) the right to receive a notice of this "Notice of Privacy Practices," and (f) the right to file a complaint. A second section of the privacy notice described how Dr. Wells's office was entitled to use and disclose psychological information about patients, and it consisted of a list of brief paragraphs that covered the following topics: treatment, payment, health care operations, disclosures required by law, business associates (accountants, lawyers, etc.), and research. A final paragraph explained that there could be revisions to this notice from time to time and that clients and patients would be notified of such revisions as they occurred. The last page provided a space for the patient to sign, indicating that he or she had read the document and agreed to its terms.

Finally, as a part of informed consent, Dr. Wells displayed a small sign in her office describing how patients could bring a grievance to the state board of psychology against Dr. Wells, if they wished. Displaying such a sign was required by state law, and had been for many years, although many psychologists apparently were unaware of it and failed to comply.[4]

Dr. Wells had successfully provided and documented informed consent for Alan's father, according to the requirements of this Ethics Code as well as state and federal law. During this initial meeting, she also had honored her obligation to inform Alan about the nature of their contact and obtained his assent. His father agreed to keep Dr. Wells apprised of behavioral changes at home and at school. Whenever there was a need for change in the arrangement, such as a family meeting, Dr. Wells would first discuss this with Alan, as she had said she would. With clear communication about such fundamental issues, Alan felt secure enough to agree to a second meeting and, ultimately, many more over the course of the year.

1. How should Dr. Wells document informed consent (parental signature on the last page of her handout acknowledging compliance and understanding)? A note in the boy's psychological record? Some other way?

---

[4]Check with your state licensing board for regulations concerning displaying such a notice or providing information to clients and patients about the complaint process.

2. What risk might Dr. Wells incur in her authorization form for treatment by overstating her telephone availability, in case of an emergency?
3. How would you go about describing confidentiality rules to your preadolescent client? Young adolescent? Sixteen-year-old?
4. What are the laws in your state concerning providing and documenting consent for psychological services or research?
5. What steps might you take to create an authorization form for treatment, and whom would you ask to review it for ethical and legal compliance?

3.11 PSYCHOLOGICAL SERVICES DELIVERED TO OR THROUGH ORGANIZATIONS

(a) Psychologists delivering services to or through organizations provide information beforehand to clients and when appropriate those directly affected by the services about (1) the nature and objectives of the services, (2) the intended recipients, (3) which of the individuals are clients, (4) the relationship the psychologist will have with each person and the organization, (5) the probable uses of services provided and information obtained, (6) who will have access to the information, and (7) limits of confidentiality. As soon as feasible, they provide information about the results and conclusions of such services to appropriate persons.

As an independent consultant or member of a staff providing consultation to or through an organization, always provide information in advance to clients, both management and employees, who will be directly affected, and include the following information:

- details about the nature and objectives of your services,
- a clear statement about who the intended recipients are,
- a clear statement about who your clients are (e.g., the organization, various individuals—managers, leadership team, etc.),
- the type of relationship that you will have with each person or with the organization itself,
- the likely and intended use of your services and any information that will be obtained from clients in the process,
- the names of anyone else (individuals or organization) who will have access to any information that you will be acquiring about the clients, and
- any limits to privacy or confidentiality that might apply.

Also, as soon as practical, you must provide information about your results and conclusions to the proper parties.

VIGNETTE

🖐 Two privately held Silicon Valley computer software companies had agreed to a merger of equals, and the CEOs wished to optimize this complicated process by using the services of an organizational psychologist. They contacted Dr. Hugh Makepeace and made it clear that their goal was to balance the structure of the companies and capitalize on the unique competencies of the employees involved.

Dr. Makepeace met with the CEOs, the chief operating officer, and the vice president of human resources of each company and learned of their concerns, questions, general goals, and approximate timetable. After these meetings, Dr. Makepeace wrote a letter of understanding to each CEO clarifying the intended participants and presenting a general proposal of the intended services. This included a brief summary of the substance of the meetings to date and an outline of the next steps, including interviews with top managers in each company; a report summarizing these interviews; further recommendations involving interviewing additional layers of management and, possibly, using a measure to assess the corporate cultures of the two companies. This letter generally made clear the nature and objectives of the services to be provided; the fees to be charged; the type of relationship Dr. Makepeace would be having with each officer; and the names of any colleagues who would be participating in the process, either in face-to-face meetings with management or in helping process and evaluate data.

In the course of their work, Dr. Makepeace and his colleagues were intent on focusing on the strengths within each of the organizations and how these strengths contributed to the functioning of each company as a system. Specifically, they evaluated the process of setting goals, the decision-making process, who was involved in these activities, and leadership styles. After additional meetings, Dr. Makepeace and his colleagues drafted a more detailed report describing the nature of their intended intervention. This included, among other things, a focus on the leadership team of each company, how this team drove the organizational culture, and the best practices and utilization of key people. They summarized the topics that were raised at the preliminary meetings and presented important information about the consultation process itself, such as (a) the differing leadership models of each company and how that would affect the merger; (b) points of convergence and divergence and their impact on postmerger functioning; (c) a preliminary overview of the organizational cultures; (d) the nature of additional data to be gathered—interview data, testing, and observational data; (e) a statement about the confidentiality of all information that was to be gathered; (f) the approximate timeframe of the project; and (g) arrangements for the kickoff meetings with the groups of leadership teams. Dr. Makepeace further acknowledged that members of his immediate staff, including two psychology interns and several technical support staff members, would process the data that he collected. The clients were assured that privacy would be maintained about all proprietary and other kinds of information to be gathered and processed.

Over the next several weeks, Dr. Makepeace and his colleagues interviewed and assessed many members of the two companies. These included the CEOs, chief operating officers, chief financial officers, heads of human resources, directors of product development, vice presidents of sales, and various other vice presidents and managers who volunteered to be involved. They gathered a vast amount of information, from face-to-face interviews, observation, and several paper-and-pencil inventories used to assess leadership style and other variables of interest. They also discussed with the CEOs the best methods to provide feedback to the rest of the company; specifically, how they could help management formally communicate to the employees information about the upcoming changes and what specific information to present to management and employees at a planning meeting,

While interviewing the marketing director, Dr. Makepeace found her to be experiencing psychological depression secondary to a recent divorce and exacerbated by the stress of the merger. He maintained the focus on the task at hand, however, avoiding lapsing into the role of counselor or therapist during the course of their work. Because she indicated an interest in pursuing treatment, however, he did supply her with the names of several therapists in town.

After processing the data, Dr. Makepeace and his colleagues wrote a comprehensive report that addressed each of the areas in question—how much risk each contributed to the success of the planned merger and how to compensate for each. The report also provided specific recommendations and suggestions to assist in the transition process itself and for the subsequent management of the merged company. Dr. Makepeace and his associates accomplished this within the agreed-on timeframe, much to the satisfaction of the leadership in each company, and they made themselves available for further consultation in the future as the need arose.

1. How would Dr. Makepeace go about the task of ensuring that all involved employees he would be evaluating would be well informed of the fact in advance?
2. How would Dr. Makepeace deal with feedback while maintaining confidentiality on hearing critical or angry comments about management?
3. What course of action should Dr. Makepeace take if he discovered a disturbed employee, fearful of losing his job in the merger, who revealed indirectly that he might sabotage the computers?
4. What is Dr. Makepeace's ethical obligation if he learns that an important executive plans to leave the company in the very near future?

3.11 (b)

If psychologists will be precluded by law or by organizational roles from providing such information to particular individuals or groups, they so inform those individuals or groups at the outset of the service.

If you are not permitted, because of the law, your employment setting, or the formal role you play, to inform those whom you counsel, assess, or consult with about the nature of your work or its results, at least let them know this when you begin working with them.

VIGNETTE

Dr. Hirem worked in the human resources department of a large oil company, assessing candidates for employment. Company policy forbade him from giving individual feedback to applicants about their interview or testing results. He always informed applicants of this policy in advance, making it clear that he considered his client to be the company, not the applicant.

By scrupulously informing candidates about these restrictions inherent in his professional role, he was generally successful in preventing candidates from developing unrealistic expectations about receiving assessment results. Nevertheless, there were always some applicants who, when they failed to be hired by the company, expressed curiosity about the factors that had contributed to the decision. This sometimes resulted in telephone calls, letters, or e-mail messages to the human resources department requesting such information from Dr. Hirem. The policy of clearly informing candidates at the outset not only helped them understand the limits of his involvement with them but also reduced the likelihood that complaints would be raised by individuals who were disappointed at his failure to provide such results.

Working in a very different venue, his friend across town, Dr. Noetell, devoted much of her time carrying out forensic assessments in civil and criminal cases, using formal testing, clinical interviews, collateral interviews, and other means. She was frequently called on to assess families for litigation concerning child custody, perform mental competency examinations for defendants and death row inmates awaiting execution, and perform other psychological assessments in a broad range of cases.

Most of the time, Dr. Noetell was expected to write a psychological report describing the results of her assessments and then submit it directly either to the attorney who had retained her or to the court. On other occasions, her results would be communicated less formally to the attorney of the individual whom she had assessed. However, it was generally true that in her role as psychological evaluator she rarely had the opportunity to provide the individuals she examined with direct feedback about the results of any specific test or the general assessment itself. The adversarial nature of litigation and the rules of discovery and procedure in her state precluded, in most situations, any opportunity to disclose information directly to the defendant during ongoing litigation. Therefore, she considered it important to inform individuals clearly about this fact prior to assessing them. The individuals would generally learn of the results of the assessment from their attorney or from the report that would be presented in open court.

On some occasions, however, she would carry out an assessment when the results might never be reported during the course of the litigation; hence, the individual being assessed would not normally learn of her findings, either directly or indirectly. This might occur if she assessed someone pursuant to a motion of a party that was averse to the individual being evaluated, and who, under local court rules, enjoyed the option of using the psychologist's findings in support of his or her case. Should the party moving for the evaluation decide not to raise the issue of the assessed individual's mental status or psychological fitness (perhaps because the evaluation findings were not helpful for that strategy), he or she might be relieved of the legal duty to share the unused assessment with the person who was evaluated. The results of the psychological assessment would then be permitted to silently "disappear," almost as though it had never occurred. Whenever Dr. Noetell knew in advance that the results of the assessment might not become available to the person she was evaluating, for whatever reason, she so advised that person, in accordance with this ethical standard, even though she was not required to do so by law.

1. What problems might develop if Dr. Hirem decided to informally provide feedback to job applicants who were rejected, simply because he felt sympathetic toward them?
2. How should Dr. Hirem and Dr. Noetell provide and document informed consent to applicants who are being evaluated when results will not be provided? Orally? In writing? By making a note in the records?
3. How can you learn of requirements concerning revealing or withholding psychological assessment results in your company or organization? As defined by the laws of your state? As defined by the rules of discovery in your county?

3.12 INTERRUPTION OF PSYCHOLOGICAL SERVICES

Unless otherwise covered by contract, psychologists make reasonable efforts to plan for facilitating services in the event that psychological services are interrupted by factors such as the psychologist's illness, death, unavailability, relocation, or retirement or by the client's/patient's relocation or financial limita-

tions. (See also Standard 6.02c, Maintenance, Dissemination, and Disposal of Confidential Records of Professional and Scientific Work.)

Make plans in advance for your patient's ongoing care in the event of the following interruptions:

- an illness—physical or mental—that would interfere with or prohibit your continuing to work (chronic pain, mood disorder, etc.);
- a disabling accident or injury;
- your demise;
- your unavailability for any other reason (you go through a high-conflict divorce; you become overly involved in research or teaching activities; you travel a great deal);
- your client runs out of money (loses his or her job, uses up all the allocated visits from his or her health care plan, etc.); or
- your client moves away and desires treatment in a new location.

VIGNETTE

Dr. Planner, a psychology professor at a large university in New York, who also had a part-time clinical practice, sustained fatal injuries in an automobile accident. She was driving home late one night on the New York State Thruway when her car was struck from behind by an intoxicated driver. This tragic loss was keenly felt by her students, colleagues, and individual and group psychotherapy patients. A number of her patients experienced flashbacks to early traumas and abandonments and suffered panic attacks and depression. Some of her patients wondered secretly if her death were really a suicide, as she had seemed somewhat quiet and low in mood in recent months. Many of her patients were clearly quite needy at this time, having suffered a grave loss with her death.

Fortunately, Dr. Planner had left instructions with her secretary and on her computer about how to help patients with just such a transition as well as what to do with their records. Her secretary knew that she was to contact several psychologists and activate Dr. Planner's "transition team." Some of these individuals were among her closest friends, and some were simply competent colleagues whom she had previously selected and instructed about the role they were to play in the event of her death or disability. Specifically, each was to be immediately on call for any of Dr. Planner's patients who wanted to consult them. Furthermore, they were to accept her patients into therapy (time permitting) if the patient selected them as a new therapist or handle the referral process to another therapist if the match was not good.

Those psychologists who were Dr. Planner's closest friends were reminded that they should not take on this task; they obviously were coping with their own grief at her loss, and thus their ability to provide effective treatment for patients undergoing grieving and ambivalent feelings about Dr. Planner might be compromised. Indeed, two of her colleagues wisely opted to be helpful behind the scenes with office work and records because they realized that they could not cope with their friend's death and simultaneously attempt to offer therapy to her patients.

The transition team also took care to preserve the confidentiality of Dr. Planner's written records by asking patients to sign consent forms before their records were released to new therapists. In some cases, patients were curious about the contents of their records, so after releasing them to another psychologist, they had a chance to sit down and review them with that therapist. These steps were methodically, rapidly, and efficiently carried out as soon as the secretary made contact with the transition team and patients. Furthermore, over the course of the next several months, every patient who had consulted Dr. Planner during the previous year and had terminated therapy was notified by letter of her death. They were also referred to several other therapists in the event that they desired additional therapy.

1. In a managed health care setting, what alternatives could you offer a patient who has used up all his or her allocated sessions but obviously is in distress and requires further treatment?
2. What clinical, ethical, or legal problems might emerge for the therapist who was a close friend of Dr. Planner and who disregarded her advice against accepting her patients into treatment?
3. How would you go about referring a patient for continuing psychotherapy who moves to a city 1,000 miles away, where you have no direct knowledge of any therapist? Do you incur any ethical or legal risk in referring the patient to someone who turns out to be impaired and is ultimately harmful to the patient?
4. How would you execute the requirements described in this standard to provide for continuity of patient care in the event of your demise, as a private practitioner?
5. Some state psychological associations (e.g., Arizona) have begun to address this issue with specific printed forms and policies; does yours?

4

PRIVACY AND CONFIDENTIALITY

4.01 MAINTAINING CONFIDENTIALITY

Psychologists have a primary obligation and take reasonable precautions to protect confidential information obtained through or stored in any medium, recognizing that the extent and limits of confidentiality may be regulated by law or established by institutional rules or professional or scientific relationship. (See also Standard 2.05, Delegation of Work to Others.)

Carefully protect confidential information about clients and patients that you store in any medium or receive from others in any way—manually, electronically, or any other means. Be prudent about storing, maintaining, and accessing confidential information, whether you use pen and ink, computer, a handheld device, or any other technology or means of information storage. Never reveal identifying information about anyone, orally or in writing, to whom you have rendered a service, or even if that person has a professional relationship with you, without the person's written consent. Make sure that you understand state and federal laws pertaining to privacy and confidentiality (e.g., the Health Insurance Portability and Accountability Act [HIPAA]) as well as the confidentiality rules of your employment setting (e.g., Veterans Affairs hospital, university clinic, community mental health center, research setting) and how they affect you as a researcher, therapist, supervisor, consultant, and so on.

👍 Dr. Claire knew well the importance of keeping accurate records and preserving their confidentiality and had developed the habit of promptly entering her clinical notes on her laptop computer after every session. She logged every incoming and outgoing telephone call concerning her work with patients in the record as well, such as phone calls with them, their parents, teachers, collaborating psychiatrists, other therapists, or anyone else participating in their care. Her computer was always in her possession, and it could not be turned on without entering her password. She regularly backed up her hard drive on an external drive at home, and she backed up individual files as well—clinical records, billing, and so forth. To keep abreast of the latest technological advances in preserving the confidentiality of computer records, she scheduled occasional consultations with a computer technician. By taking these steps, she could easily track the details of her patients' treatment over time and the involvement of other health care providers in their care.

One day, Dr. Claire was contacted by Tony, a 17-year-old who was hearing threatening voices and reporting other psychoticlike symptoms. Tony was confused and fearful, and he was worried that he might not be able to complete his last year in high school. Before agreeing to meet with Tony, Dr. Claire asked to speak with one of his parents, because he was a minor, because it is important to obtain parental consent before beginning treatment, and because of the potential severity of Tony's symptoms. Tony gladly complied with her request. He also volunteered that at present his whole family was meeting with a family therapist on a weekly basis and that he wanted to stop going to the sessions. He revealed as well that his father was attending weekly Alcoholics Anonymous meetings and that he was wondering whether he should start attending, because he was consuming alcohol on a regular basis. He had heard much about its benefits and had observed the good effects on his father.

After several meetings with Tony, Dr. Claire decided to refer him to a psychiatrist for a medication assessment. She explained the reason for the referral to Tony and his parents and obtained both his and their signed consent permitting collaboration with the psychiatrist. She also told Tony that she would discuss the content of what was revealed to the psychiatrist to keep Tony apprised of those consultative sessions. She then sought the consent of Tony and his parents to contact the family therapist for the purpose of coordinating the two concurrent interventions. Tony and his parents understood the rationale for this request and agreed to sign the consent form. All consent forms were stored in Tony's file, along with other paper forms (health insurance claim forms, paper-and-pencil tests, etc.) that could not be stored on her computer.

With so many mental health professionals involved in treating these family members, some of whom were minors, maintaining confidentiality was a challenging task that required good boundaries and a working knowledge of relevant ethical rules and state laws. Dr. Claire appreciated the importance of collaborating regularly with certain therapists, when warranted, and Tony was in agreement with these contacts. However, she was also sensitive to his reluctance to include his parents in his therapy more than was absolutely necessary. She worked to maintain Tony's trust by clearly discussing the rules of confidentiality and how they applied in each situation.

When Tony's pediatrician telephoned Dr. Claire to report his concern about drug abuse, she did not reveal information about him to the pediatrician before first contacting Tony and obtaining his consent. The potential drug abuse was of significant concern, but Dr. Claire rightly judged that she would jeopardize her therapeutic relationship with Tony by discussing treatment with his pediatrician behind his back. She listened to what the pediatrician had to say regarding his concern about Tony's safety, but she disclosed little to him about her patient. She then promptly telephoned Tony and asked for his consent to her conversations with the pediatrician, again so that those health care providers immediately concerned with his care could coordinate their work effectively. Again Tony complied, revealing that he was the one who had told his pediatrician about his consultations with Dr. Claire in the first place and that he had no problem with them talking with each other. He emphasized, however, that there were some topics that he wished her to keep in the consulting room, between the two of them.

On one occasion, Tony's mother telephoned to ask if Tony had mentioned that his grandmother was very angry at him for being thoughtless and selfish the previous day. He had apparently driven her car without asking permission, and the grandmother's resulting agitation had aggravated her asthma. Dr. Claire refused to discuss this episode with his mother and suggested instead that the family therapy sessions might be a better forum, even though the next session wasn't for another 6 days. However, she was willing to schedule an extra appointment with Tony if he wished to see her sooner.

Tony was grateful that his therapist was attentive to confidentiality issues and, for the most part, informed him in advance about the nature of her disclosures to others. His trust in Dr. Claire grew, and he was comfortable remaining in treatment with her, confident that she would continue to protect his privacy in their work together. For her part, Dr. Claire was content to keep her clinical records and preserve their confidentiality as assiduously as she did. It helped her provide competent treatment for her patients and to obtain and maintain their trust.

1. What are the drawbacks and risks of keeping clinical records on a computer, and how can you protect yourself from them? Consider HIPAA regulations as well.
2. Why did Dr. Claire keep a record of telephone calls concerning her treatment with Tony?

3. How might you have handled the situation with Tony's grand-mother differently?
4. How should Dr. Claire handle a request from Tony's parents to view her clinical records of their son? Does your state law allow you to refuse a request from an adult patient to view his record?
5. Are you obliged to reveal to a patient, who is viewing his or her clinical record, a report that has been sent to you by another therapist?
6. If you are complying with the HIPAA requirements, how do you differentiate a clinical record from psychotherapy notes? Must you keep both?

4.02 DISCUSSING THE LIMITS OF CONFIDENTIALITY

(a) Psychologists discuss with persons (including, to the extent feasible, persons who are legally incapable of giving informed consent and their legal representatives) and organizations with whom they establish a scientific or professional relationship (1) the relevant limits of confidentiality and (2) the foreseeable uses of the information generated through their psychological activities. (See also Standard 3.10, Informed Consent.)

Inform patients and clients about confidentiality and its exceptions, even if you think they already know. This includes the patients themselves (even if they are children, developmentally disabled, elderly, or unable to fully comprehend) as well as their parents or caretakers. Be sure to tell them about any limitations on confidentiality in group work, child and adolescent therapy, marital and family therapy, organizational consulting, or any other setting. Also inform them about how any information they reveal to you might be used in the future, such as in research, your own teaching, by the courts, or in any other likely way.

VIGNETTE

Dr. Whispah, a clinician in independent practice, discussed confidentiality and privileged communication with Lori, a new adult patient with panic disorder, at the very beginning of their first session. He informed her that their conversations, her disclosures as a patient in therapy, and any records of them would remain confidential, unless certain conditions prevailed. He then gave Lori a handout describing, in simple language, all the exceptions to confidentiality. He made sure that Lori understood that the law required him to take certain steps, such as breaking confidentiality by notifying the police or the local psychiatric emergency team if she ever seriously threatened to commit suicide. He also explained what would happen if she ever communicated a serious threat of harm to another person—that state law required him to notify the intended victim and the police of the threat.[1]

Dr. Whispah also discussed with Lori the requirements for reporting child abuse, elder abuse, spouse abuse, and other situations in which confidentiality could be or was required to be broken, even though Lori had not indicated any problems in these areas. He also informed her about the kind of data that were typically requested for the managed health care provider's outpatient treatment reports and the frequency with which he had to file such reports over the course of their work.

Finally, he sought her compliance in a small research project that he and several colleagues were carrying out with patients diagnosed with anxiety disorder. This would involve the gathering of certain information, such as by means of paper-and-pencil tests and his clinical notes. Although Lori's name would not be shared with coinvestigators, her test data and other information would. Lori was clearly informed that her participation in the study was fully optional and that there would be absolutely no adverse consequences to her therapy if she refused to participate or if she participated and then chose to withdraw later on.

Lori manifested little concern about any of the exceptions to confidentiality or about participating in the research protocol. However, she was insistent that her consultations with Dr. Whispah remain a secret from her husband, who had little confidence in psychologists and had a punitive way of manifesting his disapproval when his wife did not comply with his wishes. Dr. Whispah assured Lori that even if her husband were to telephone him directly and ask him about his wife's consulting him for treatment, he was not legally or ethically permitted to answer his questions or disclose any information about this matter without her written consent.

Lori was pleased with his response, felt well informed about all aspects of confidentiality at the outset, and was secure about proceeding with treatment. Her previous therapist had never discussed confidentiality at all, and she had had no idea that there were so many "protections" built in to her disclosures to a psychologist.

1. What means could Dr. Whispah take to make sure that his new patient understood the exceptions to confidentiality, and how could he document this?
2. How can you find out the legal exceptions to confidentiality in your state?
3. How would Dr. Whispah handle a situation in which he decided to conduct clinical research with several anorectic pa-

---

[1]Check with the requirements of your state for disclosures and situations that would result in mandated reporting.

tients after having already begun their treatment? Could he engage their participation, or would this seem coercive to them?

4. What steps would Dr. Whispah take if his new patient's alcoholic husband telephoned and threatened to harm him if he continues to provide treatment to his wife? Does he have an obligation to continue seeing her in spite of this threat?

5. How would Dr. Whispah handle his new patient's disclosure that she had been sexually assaulted by her stepfather 22 years ago, when she was 14, and that, in her opinion, he still could be a threat to some of his grandchildren, who were living in the neighborhood?

4.02 (b)

Unless it is not feasible or is contraindicated, the discussion of confidentiality occurs at the outset of the relationship and thereafter as new circumstances may warrant.

Discuss confidentiality and its exceptions at the beginning of the professional contact, unless contraindicated, whether doing psychotherapy, supervision, organizational consulting, research, or any other psychological work. Also be ready to discuss confidentiality again as the situation may warrant later (e.g., new intervention, entry of other individuals into the treatment, forensic work).

VIGNETTE

Dr. Claire met with her new patient, a 49-year-old woman who was divorced and who complained of chronic depression and lethargy. After discussing confidentiality and its limitations with the woman Dr. Claire began psychotherapy on a weekly basis. A month later, the patient had a complete physical examination, and her primary-care physician diagnosed her with chronic fatigue syndrome.

At about the same time, Dr. Claire was considering referring the patient to a psychiatrist for evaluation for antidepressant medication. She was careful to discuss with her the importance of coordinating treatment with both her primary-care physician and the psychiatrist who would be assessing her for antidepressants. The patient asked several questions about the nature of the collaboration and wondered if everything that she discussed with Dr. Claire could be disclosed to the psychiatrist. Dr. Claire informed her that she would be happy to consider keeping her confidence about certain topics, if the patient "red-flagged" them, and that she would certainly honor her request if possible. She further revealed that it is a psychologist's ethical obligation to disclose the minimum amount of patient information possible to accomplish the desired task when consulting with other health care professionals (see Standard 4.06, Consultations). After this in-depth discussion of confidentiality and its exceptions, Dr. Claire asked the patient to sign consent forms releasing Dr. Claire to disclose information to both the primary-care physician and the psychiatrist.

The patient had also recently begun consultations with her endocrinologist about an enlarged thyroid gland and a possible diagnosis of Graves' disease. Because Dr. Claire was well aware of the research on mood changes in perimenopausal women and the complex interactions among thyroid hormone levels, fluctuating estrogen, and depression, she thought it was also important to at least have a preliminary discussion with the endocrinologist. She thoroughly discussed the rationale with her patient and obtained her written consent before contacting the endocrinologist.

In the interest of keeping all health care professionals informed and promoting coordinated treatment, Dr. Claire made consistent efforts to inform each physician about her work, in a general way, and the patient's progress in recovery from depression. Although this was time consuming, it was clearly in the patient's interest. Dr. Claire charged a reasonable fee for time expended on these professional consultations and had informed her patient of this policy at the outset. The patient, in turn, felt that her confidentiality was well protected by Dr. Claire and was pleased that her psychologist briefly reviewed her discussions with each physician with her during the therapy hour.

1. What kind of information might Dr. Claire's patient flag as confidential and not to be revealed to her primary-care physician, endocrinologist, or psychiatrist?
2. How could Dr. Claire address the topic of confidentiality in advance of the first session?
3. Should Dr. Claire use printed handouts about confidentiality and its exceptions, or should she present the information orally and then document it in the clinical record?
4. What can a therapist expect a patient to remember from an oral presentation about the complex topic of confidentiality, and how could his or her subsequent forgetfulness about the exceptions to confidentiality cause problems in his or her relationship with Dr. Claire?
5. How should Dr. Claire respond if the primary-care physician telephones and informs her that the patient has given her consent for him to speak with Dr. Claire and that he would like to ask her some questions about the patient (absent a signed consent)?

Psychologists who offer services, products, or information via electronic transmission inform clients/patients of the risks to privacy and limits of confidentiality.

If you use the Internet, a fax machine, or a telephone as a means of offering psychological services, products, or psychological information to patients and clients, make sure that you tell them about how their privacy might possibly be compromised and confidentiality might be breached. (Become knowledgeable about what might go wrong in using technology for handling sensitive information before it happens; consult with an expert information technology specialist or other mental health professionals who are experienced in these matters, so that you can better inform the public and minimize any risks.)

VIGNETTE

Dr. R. Ian Lyne had several patients who preferred to contact him by e-mail instead of the telephone for discussing therapeutic issues between sessions. This happened quite spontaneously and without prior discussion. In both cases, the patients simply used the e-mail address printed on Dr. Lyne's appointment card to send a question they had about the previous therapy session. Dr. Lyne checked his e-mail several times each day and easily had the time to respond to the topics raised by his patients. He actually came to prefer answering questions in this manner, instead of by telephone, as he could write a more thoughtful and comprehensive (and sometimes longer) reply than he could leave on a telephone answering machine, and he never had to worry about playing "telephone tag." He always kept a copy of the incoming and outgoing e-mails for the clinical record, and in the subsequent session he was careful to follow up with processing the content of the electronic communications.

This mode of communicating began gradually in his practice, with the patients' initiative, and seemed to imperceptibly grow and develop momentum on its own, eventually affecting the way he conducted therapy. The e-mails from his patients became longer, and increased in frequency, focusing on issues that the patients seemed to be avoiding in face-to-face contact. He was noticing that his replies similarly grew in length and complexity, as he attempted to be clear and precise about matters that could better be addressed in person. In general, however, Dr. Lyne enjoyed using technology, and he prided himself on rendering high-quality service in both a clinical and ethical sense.

However, he unfortunately was naïve about some of the things that could go wrong when a new medium, such as e-mail communication, is introduced into the therapy process. One day he responded to the e-mail of a Mr. Victor L., a 40-year-old man who had great ambivalence about his marriage to his young wife, Ilsa. Both Victor and Ilsa were recent immigrants to the United States. Victor had just finished visiting an online dating service for the first time. Dr. Lyne wrote a reply to Victor, commenting on this new behavior and how it was likely to affect his marriage. After viewing his reply, Victor left the room to answer a telephone call at the same moment that Ilsa arrived home from work. She promptly went in to switch on the computer, because she was late for her online chat group on health and diet. What she saw on the screen instead were her husband's revelations about his online dating visit and Dr. Lyne's reply. Although not entirely surprised, she felt hurt by this discovery, and she viewed Dr. Lyne's advice as entirely too lenient and permissive. She alternately pleaded with her husband and blamed him both for attempting to go "outside of the marriage" and for choosing a therapist who "doesn't have any religious values or morals." This accidental discovery clearly was damaging to an already-faltering relationship, and Dr. Lyne had possibly not taken adequate steps to protect against this scenario.

As if this were not enough, the next day, after meeting with six patients and dealing with one telephone emergency call, Dr. Lyne sat at his computer to write a response to an e-mail that he had received earlier that morning from a patient named Carol West. Carol was a 29-year-old obstetrics nurse who, by coincidence, worked at the same local hospital where Dr. Lyne had clinical privileges. She suffered from alcohol dependency and anxiety disorder, and she met many criteria for borderline personality disorder. She had written Dr. Lyne about a drinking binge she had been on for the previous 2 days, calling in sick to the hospital, and she felt too ashamed to face him at their next session. Dr. Lyne was rushing to write a reply before his final patient of the day walked into his office. Although he had deleted her e-mail, he began typing "Carol" into the address field of his screen, and immediately his computer filled in with four possible "Carol"s who were already on file. Regrettably, he clicked on the wrong Carol—the director of the human resources department at the hospital, with whom he had been corresponding recently. He was not aware of his mistake for another hour, when he received e-mail replies from the human resources department Carol, suggesting that he might have made a rather serious error, and from Carol West, wondering why he hadn't responded to her "all day long" and stating that she needed a drink to help handle her anxiety.

Dr. Lyne was flabbergasted that in the space of 2 days there could have been such serious problems with his confidential e-mail communications. He feared that a formal complaint against him might materialize, and he realized that he would have to consider making some changes in his use of technology with patients if he were to protect their privacy and his own good name.

About this same time, he received a letter from the hospital announcing the implementation of a new policy for all staff who had direct contact with patients concerning e-mail communications. Henceforth, each patient desiring e-mail communication with his or her health care provider would have to sign an authorization in advance and would be required to read a form explaining the risks to confidentiality inherent in this form of communication. In addition, health care providers were prohibited from giving in e-mails significant information, such as formal diagnoses, results of laboratory or psychological tests, health information that could be misinterpreted, or sensitive patient information of any sort. E-mails were most useful for confirming or changing appointment times or responding to questions that were simple and straightforward and not of an emergency or critical nature.

Dr. Lyne decided to investigate how to deal with the e-mail problem in his private practice. He consulted with colleagues who were more experienced in these matters to help create better patient informed consent up front. He sought the advice of an information technology specialist, to help with firewall and encryption matters in sending and receiving e-mail; a senior clinician, to discuss the risks of attempting therapy-by-correspondence, how to compensate for the missing nonverbal cues, and to help draw up an authorization form for e-mail; the ethics committee of his state psychological association, to solicit their input on these complex matters; the state licensing board; the department of psychiatry at a nearby hospital that had recently drawn up guidelines about the use of e-mail correspondence with patients; and an attorney who was familiar with mental health matters and sympathetic to the needs of psychologists, to review the authorization form he had created and to help with a disclaimer paragraph to accompany each e-mail, as well as faxes.

Dr. Lyne learned the hard way about venturing with little or no training into a new area of interacting with patients. Ultimately, Carol West broke off treatment with him and initiated an ethics complaint with the American Psychological Association and the state board of psychology. She claimed that Dr. Lyne had breached patient confidentiality by sending a private correspondence about the details of her drinking binge to the human resources department of the hospital where she worked, thus damaging her reputation and threatening the security of her job. Even though this breach was accidental, Dr. Lyne was sanctioned by the American Psychological Association, required to undergo supervision of his clinical practice for 1 year, and had to take formal training in ethics and the use of technology. After this judgment was made, Carol contacted an attorney to initiate a civil suit against Dr. Lyne for the damage he had caused her.

1. How would Dr. Lyne differentiate between offering information to his patient and conducting therapy-by-correspondence?
2. What are the clinical, ethical, and legal risks of interacting with patients between sessions by means of e-mail?

3. What are the ethical and legal risks of offering information to online surfers who view your Web site, which claims it specializes in "answering relationship questions"?
4. What if Victor had been an ongoing therapy patient of Dr. Lyne, and his wife Ilsa viewed the e-mail communication that led her to question Dr. Lyne's competence? Could Ilsa bring an action against Dr. Lyne, or at least make the attempt to do so (e.g., by means of an ethics complaint, complaint to the licensing board, letter to the editor of a local newspaper, etc.), alleging that he rendered incompetent therapy to her husband?
5. What elements would you consider to be essential to include in a patient authorization form allowing e-mail communication?

4.03 RECORDING

Before recording the voices or images of individuals to whom they provide services, psychologists obtain permission from all such persons or their legal representatives. (See also Standards 8.03, Informed Consent for Recording Voices and Images in Research; 8.05, Dispensing With Informed Consent for Research; and 8.07, Deception in Research.)

Always obtain permission to audiotape or videotape clients and patients in advance, and get a signed consent. With children or dependent adults, obtain the signed consent from their parents, caretakers, or legal guardians.

VIGNETTE

Dr. Saver informed his new marital therapy patients that it was his usual procedure to audiotape every session. He encouraged them to hear segments of the tape, or the entire session, at home, if they wished. He explained how this would give each of them a chance to hear how they communicated and suggested that studying their style of interaction could actually help accelerate the therapy process somewhat. He explained that no one else would ever have access to the tapes and that if there ever would be future research involving their use (as they were archived for a limited period of time) he would again seek the patients' formal consent, and they would be free to decline. He also informed them that they were not compelled to submit to audiotaping at this time, and it would not negatively affect the therapy in any way. Finally, he informed them that they could consent to audiotaping now and would have the right to withdraw their consent later on, for any reason, if they wished. Each of these terms of informed consent that he explained to them were also itemized in the written authorization form he asked them to sign.

Although husband and wife were both agreeable to the audiotaping and did not see the need to sign a consent form, they complied with Dr. Saver's request. By so doing, there were no misunderstandings about audiotaping, and all parties felt well informed about this aspect of the therapy process.

After 2 months of therapy sessions, Dr. Saver noticed that the husband manifested an array of nonverbal behaviors that were avoidant in nature and had the general effect of closing down communication with his wife. However, the man could not understand or appreciate the feedback that Dr. Saver provided about his avoidant style of communication. Consistent with his behavioral approach to treatment, Dr. Saver considered videotaping as a valuable addition to the marital therapy sessions at this particular stage, as he had found it to be quite useful with other couples in the past. Therefore, he discussed implementing videotaping for several sessions, as an adjunct to the therapy process, in much the same way that audiotaping had been used. The main difference was that videotaped segments would be reviewed during the session, from time to time, in addition to the opportunity for at-home viewing. Dr. Saver again reviewed the terms of the authorization form and then requested that the spouses sign the form acknowledging their permission to be videotaped. Again they complied. Each felt that they could freely refuse, if they wish, and each appreciated the steps that Dr. Saver took to protect their privacy and freedom of choice about participating in the taping.

1. From an ethical standpoint, how should Dr. Saver proceed if the wife willingly consented to taping but the husband refused?

2. What if Dr. Saver had a psychological assistant, or trainee, and wished to use the audio- and videotapes for training; what additional items should he include in the written consent form?

3. What if Dr. Saver hoped to use these videotapes in training graduate students in the future and wished to keep them on file for this purpose indefinitely? Would this be ethically acceptable, and how could he ever obtain informed consent from the couple if he could not identify the actual viewers of the video?

4. Are there any risks to recording and permitting the patients to keep the video- or audiotapes with a high-conflict couple who appears to be headed toward divorce?

5. Are there any additional risks to digitizing images of your patients, such as storing their audio or video information on your computer or digital video camera?

4.04 MINIMIZING INTRUSIONS ON PRIVACY

(a) Psychologists include in written and oral reports and consultations, only information germane to the purpose for which the communication is made.

> When creating a written or oral report, remain focused on the primary objectives and purpose of your work. Include only relevant information, facts, recommendations, and opinions that pertain directly to the process or task at hand. Omit anything that is gratuitous or superfluous, even though you might find it interesting.

VIGNETTE

Dr. Lew Szlips was the director and only psychologist in the human resources office of a police department in a small midwestern city. For too many years he had been involved in hiring, promoting, and terminating the employment of officers and helping to mediate disputes within the department. Unfortunately, his health had been gradually deteriorating, and his chronic neck pain had been increasing in intensity, and he simply did not have the energy to pursue continuing education the way he should have. He had not remained current about the ethical requirements of confidentiality and could no longer discriminate well between information that should remain private and that which could legitimately make its way out of the consulting room and into formal reports to supervisors and others.

On one occasion, a supervisor referred to Dr. Szlips a police officer who was experiencing panic attacks. In the consultation session, the officer revealed that he recently had learned that he was HIV positive, and he was gravely disturbed over this. He also discussed his homosexuality for the first time with Dr. Szlips. He reported that he was probably able to carry out his duties, but his mounting anxiety and depression were beginning to impair his concentration.

Dr. Szlips wisely referred him to an outside therapist for treatment; however, he unwisely revealed too much information to the referring supervisor. In a lengthy memo, in which he represented himself as the officer's advocate, Dr. Szlips accurately diagnosed the officer as experiencing panic attacks and depression. However, Dr. Szlips urged the supervisor to keep the officer on the job "in light of his recent discovery of his HIV status, because that would help provide some necessary structure in his life at a time when he may need it the most." The supervisor, who had no formal ethical duty to maintain confidentiality, casually discussed the officer's HIV status with several other individuals on the force. Soon most officers in the precinct knew that the officer was HIV positive much sooner than the officer would have wanted this information to become public.

The response to this news was mixed. Some officers reacted with sympathy and provided support and encouragement to their friend. Others, who previously had been unaware that the officer was gay, and were frankly homophobic, acted out their fearful and hostile feelings by avoiding and sometimes harassing him. His partner requested a transfer, and some people whom he had previously counted as his friends began to shun him.

The social climate eventually became unbearable, and the officer opted to stop working. At the very time when he indeed would have benefited from supportive relationships in his life, he found that they were slowly but surely eroding, primarily because of the confidentiality breach of the well-meaning but grossly unethical behavior of Dr. Szlips—behavior that was also in violation of the state's legal statutes concerning confidentiality. Seven months later, after enduring much psychological distress, the officer brought a formal ethics complaint and a civil suit against Dr. Szlips as compensation for his monetary losses and his significant emotional suffering at work caused by the breach of confidentiality.

As a result of these actions, the state psychology board later became involved and initiated its own investigation into the professional conduct of Dr. Szlips. To help in his defense with the board, the beleaguered psychologist hired his own attorney. He discovered, to his dismay, that his insurance carrier refused to pay for his defense in the board investigation; they would only supply an attorney to defend him in the civil lawsuit brought by the officer. The reason for this was simple: When Dr. Szlips had purchased his malpractice insurance years before, he had never bothered to add the rider that would have provided coverage for his own defense in a state licensing board investigation. The rider was quite inexpensive, yet it would have provided him with free representation by an attorney at a time when he badly needed it. He regretted his failure to consider this option; at the time, he had been convinced that he would never have to worry about someone complaining to the board about him.

1. How could Dr. Szlips have learned about the state laws concerning confidentiality and its exceptions, and how they specifically applied to his role, assuming that he considered it important?
2. As Dr. Szlips's health deteriorated, what steps could he have taken to avoid such failures in his professional competence?
3. How could Dr. Szlips have communicated in his memorandum to the supervisor his formal recommendations without breaching confidentiality?
4. What was Dr. Szlips's ethical duty concerning informing the police officer about confidentiality and its exceptions at the outset?

4.04 (b)

Psychologists discuss confidential information obtained in their work only for appropriate scientific or professional purposes and only with persons clearly concerned with such matters.

Never reveal or discuss any confidential information you've obtained while working as a therapist, consultant, supervisor, and so on, to anyone except those who have a scientific or professional interest in it (e.g., consultant, legal supervisor, collaborating therapist, coinvestigator, etc.). There should be no exceptions!

VIGNETTE

Dr. Lew Szlips occasionally discussed some of his more interesting police evaluation cases with his friends, who were neither psychologists nor police officers and who clearly had nothing to do with his work. He thought that, by hearing his anecdotes, his friends could learn something useful about human nature and the psychological stresses of carrying out such taxing work. Unfortunately, on several occasions, an officer's behavior had made headlines, and Dr. Szlips's friends found it easy to correctly guess the identity of the police officer involved in the case being discussed.

Dr. Szlips also taught a course on human resources at the local community college several nights each week. By way of making the lectures more appealing, he drew from his experience as a human relations consultant at the police department and presented many vignettes from his actual contacts with clients. Although he changed the details, he never bothered to tell his students this, and they believed that he was revealing factual information that had been told to him in confidence.

One student, who was engaged to be married to Officer O'Brien, felt certain that Dr. Szlips was talking about her fiancé during one class, even though this was not the case. Many of the details of the example seemed, coincidentally, to match his personality and behavior and, as mentioned, Dr. Szlips had made no disclaimer that these vignettes were altered in any way or, in some cases, entirely fictional. Thus, this student assumed that Dr. Szlips was, indeed, disclosing factual information about her fiancé. She felt upset and angry and, without even confronting her professor, took the radical step of bringing a complaint to the state psychological association ethics committee. This resulted in a formal investigation by that body, requiring over 6 months to process. Dr. Szlips learned from this painful experience that if one is going to draw from one's professional work with clients it is wise to first get the clients' consent, change the details enough so that they cannot be recognized, and inform the audience that the "case examples" are fictional.

1. What is the risk of discussing your clients and patients with your friends, if you provide no identifying information?
2. What steps should you take if you intend to use clinical material in didactic presentations?
3. Why would a student bring a complaint to a state ethics committee instead of discussing it with his or her professor first?

4.05 DISCLOSURES

(a) Psychologists may disclose confidential information with the appropriate consent of the organizational client, the individual client/patient, or another legally authorized person on behalf of the client/patient unless prohibited by law.

You may reveal information about your patient or organizational client as long as a valid authorization form has been signed. (Again, with minors, disabled adults, or elderly individuals, be sure to obtain consent from their legal guardians or caretakers.) Because *privileged communication* is often defined by state law, check with your state licensing board to determine what elements should be included in a valid release-of-information form. Also, learn about any federal laws pertaining to confidentiality, such as HIPAA (if your practice is HIPAA compliant) or policies of the Department of Veterans Affairs (if you work in a Veterans Affairs medical center), as they also provide rules and guidance on privacy and confidentiality and the authorization forms you should use.

VIGNETTE

Allison, a 29-year-old graduate student with suicidal thoughts, was seeking a psychotherapist. She had one consultation session with Dr. Sender, the owner of a small referral service. She wished to obtain the name of a female psychologist who specialized in boundary violations by psychologists. He referred her to Dr. Mae Bee and asked Allison to telephone him after several sessions to report her satisfaction with Dr. Bee.

Allison promptly made an appointment with Dr. Bee. In the first meeting, she learned of Dr. Bee's policy of contacting a patient's previous therapist to learn about that therapist's diagnostic impressions and course of treatment. Dr. Bee generally found this to be a valuable part of the history-gathering phase that was sometimes useful in validating her own diagnostic impressions. However, when asked, Allison refused to allow Dr. Bee to contact her previous therapist, whom she had seen for over 3 years. When pressed about this, Allison became somewhat agitated and indicated that she might grant permission in the future, but for right now she simply could not agree to it.

Dr. Bee deliberated over whether she should attempt to treat Allison under these circumstances, because they encouraged secrecy from the start and might convey the impression that it was acceptable to conceal information that she considered important to the therapy. With some misgivings, she decided she would forego her usual policy this time and delay contacting the previous therapist for a little while, because Allison appeared to genuinely desire treatment, and she obviously was gravely troubled about her previous therapy.

Allison was relieved that Dr. Bee was willing to see her under these circumstances and, after several weekly sessions, felt a growing trust developing toward her new therapist. However, Allison forgot to telephone Dr. Sender about her satisfaction with Dr. Bee, as he had requested. After 2 weeks, Dr. Sender himself contacted Dr. Bee to inquire whether Allison had begun treatment with her. He also wished to emphasize the urgency of her situation and discuss some of the history that Allison had related about her previous therapist. Without acknowledging whether Allison had consulted her, Dr. Bee abruptly interrupted Dr. Sender, asking him if Allison had signed a consent form allowing him to disclose information about her. He reported that she had not. However, he had not conducted any therapy with her and had been only a resource for the referral, so he felt that using a consent form was an unnecessary formality. Dr. Bee disagreed with his interpretation of the ethical standards concerning confidentiality and instructed Dr. Sender about his duty to avoid releasing any information about a recipient of his services to a third party unless he held a signed consent form from that person.

Allison greatly appreciated Dr. Bee's proactive stance in preserving her confidentiality. Within several weeks, when she felt comfortable broaching the topic, Allison was able to begin discussing the traumatic events of the previous 3 years. As it turned out, while she was working on her dissertation, she became quite depressed and began psychotherapy with one of her former professors, a very nurturing, senior faculty member. Their therapy relationship evolved rapidly, given their earlier relationship, and it was not very long before the boundaries among student, patient, friend, and budding romantic partner became unclear. Her therapist ultimately crossed the line and encouraged Allison to begin a sexual relationship. The affair lasted approximately 2 years, at which point Allison completed her dissertation and was preparing to start a postdoctoral fellowship. This is when her therapist–lover attempted to break off the relationship, expecting that Allison would leave the area very soon anyway. At this point Allison became quite depressed and angry and even made a halfhearted suicide attempt. She eventually was able to muster enough courage to begin therapy anew after this betrayal, by finding a female therapist, with Dr. Sender's assistance.

Dr. Bee was pleased that she had not insisted on having Allison sign a release-of-information form immediately; doing so may have delayed her beginning therapy that was urgently needed. She thought that it was vital to have provided some stern mentoring to Dr. Sender and thereby abort his unethical attempt to reveal her patient's history, because to have done so would have been premature and would have violated Allison's privacy.

1. What disclosures should be considered to be confidential in the first telephone call from a new patient? In the first exploratory meeting with that patient, even before a decision has been made to begin treatment?
2. How would Dr. Sender's disclosures to Dr. Bee about Allison's former therapy have affected the therapy?
3. Is Dr. Bee required to tell Allison about Dr. Sender's telephone call?
4. Should either Dr. Bee or Dr. Sender confront Allison's previous, transgressing therapist? How might this be handled, in light of ethical and clinical considerations?

4.05 (b)

Psychologists disclose confidential information without the consent of the individual only as mandated by law, or where permitted by law for a valid purpose such as to (1) provide needed professional services; (2) obtain appropriate professional consultations; (3) protect the client/patient, psychologist, or others from harm; or (4) obtain payment for services from a client/patient, in which instance disclosure is limited to the minimum that is necessary to achieve the purpose. (See also Standard 6.04e, Fees and Financial Arrangements.)

If your client or patient has not signed a consent form, never release any information about him or her unless you are required to by law (e.g., court order, threats of violence) or it is allowed by law for a valid reason, as described later in the chapter. Otherwise, do not reveal anything to anyone about the recipient of your services. The law may permit disclosures for well-founded reasons, with certain exceptions, such as the following:

- when the patient requires needed services;
- when you require consultation or supervision from another professional to provide competent service;
- when the patient requires emergency services or hospitalization to protect someone from getting hurt (e.g., suicidal, homicidal, or psychotic patients) or other needed services; or
- to collect fees for your services (billing, insurance, or collection agency), in which case you reveal the least amount of confidential information possible to get the job done.

VIGNETTE

Dr. Blunder's psychotherapy patient, Fred, signed a consent form for Dr. Blunder to obtain medical information on his chronic back pain from his physician, Dr. Lobax. After contacting Dr. Lobax, however, Dr. Blunder was informed that Dr. Heel, a podiatrist, had treated Fred for problems with his left foot. Dr. Heel had developed an orthotic device for Fred, which was helping with the back pain. Dr. Blunder thought that he should speak with the podiatrist directly, rather than hear about Fred's diagnosis and treatment from another health care provider, to learn whether additional podiatric treatment was being contemplated. Because he was in a rush to finish up his office work before leaving town for 1 week, Dr. Blunder took the shortcut of telephoning Dr. Heel without first obtaining any formal consent from Fred. During their conversation, he also discussed Fred's depression and possible Axis II diagnosis.

What Dr. Blunder did not know, however, was that Dr. Heel was Fred's next-door neighbor and a close friend of Fred's wife. Fred certainly would not have consented to Dr. Blunder's revealing details of his psychological profile to his neighbor, Dr. Heel. When he learned about the telephone consultation, he was shocked to discover that his psychologist had broken confidentiality by contacting his podiatrist without his permission, and he viewed this as a serious violation of his privacy. Fred understood the rationale for the consultation with Dr. Lobax, and he had consented to it, but he saw no reason to contact a doctor who had fashioned an orthotic device for him. Furthermore, Dr. Blunder never explained or discussed the basis for such an external consultation.

If Dr. Blunder had discussed the issue with Fred, Fred probably would have consented, with the proviso that his psychological diagnosis be excluded from the conversation. As it was, Fred felt betrayed and exposed by his therapist, and he decided to break off treatment. This situation could have easily been avoided had Dr. Blunder not acted unilaterally in contacting the podiatrist: There was no emergency, no imminent need, and no one was at risk of being harmed. He realized, too late, that a seemingly innocuous consultation with another health care provider can have unexpected and damaging consequences.

1. Why is it important to consult at times with your patient's treating physician?
2. Would Dr. Blunder have been violating any legal or ethical rules of confidentiality if he contacted Dr. Heel but revealed nothing about Fred's psychological profile or treatment?
3. Did Dr. Blunder's decision to reveal information to Dr. Heel meet any of the four criteria regarding disclosures to others?
4. What might you conclude, and how might treatment be altered, if Dr. Lobax informed you that Fred's X-rays and medical tests revealed no physiological explanation for his back pain?

4.06 CONSULTATIONS

When consulting with colleagues, (1) psychologists do not disclose confidential information that reasonably could lead to the identification of a client/patient, research participant, or other person or organization with whom they have a confidential relationship unless they have obtained the prior consent of the person or organization or the disclosure cannot be avoided, and (2) they disclose information only to the extent necessary to achieve the purposes of the consultation. (See also Standard 4.01, Maintaining Confidentiality.)

When consulting a colleague as a resource to assist you in carrying out your work, or for any other reason, always keep strict confidentiality:

- never reveal the names of either your individual patients or your organizational clients, directly or indirectly, or give information that could expose their identity without a signed consent; and
- never reveal any confidential information about your patient or client unless doing so is necessary for the purposes of the consultation.

VIGNETTE

Eight psychologists and psychiatrists routinely met every other week as a peer consultation group to discuss their clients. They were careful to avoid identifying patients by name, generally indicating only their gender, age, ethnic group (if relevant), career, marital status, and other demographic information that helped conceptualize the case. They generally would not reveal, for example, that a patient was the chair of the history department at the local university, or the chief financial officer of a local business, unless that fact was germane to the consultation.

Although not required by this standard, in the interest of informed consent, these therapists also had a policy of informing their patients and clients that they regularly participated in this consultation group. They also agreed that it was wise to inform their clients and patients about the identity of each member in the group. They did so to better protect their clients' and patients' privacy, on the premise that we all live in a potentially small world, regardless of the actual size of the community. If a patient happened to know a particular therapist who participated in the group consultation meeting in a different setting, such as at work, through a personal friendship, through participation in school board meetings, or as a next-door neighbor, they likely would refuse permission for their therapist to discuss their treatment in the group, because the chances of being identified would be much stronger.

One patient who ultimately greatly appreciated this policy was Wendy, a psychology intern who was about to complete her residency at the county mental health department. She had been consulting Dr. Silencio Shush for psychotherapy for nearly 2 years and found the therapy to be quite productive in her long battle with anorexia. As she was nearing the end of training, and her therapy, Wendy had been spending the past few months learning about and applying for both clinical and academic positions in universities and hospitals in the city. One position in which she was interested was at a small private hospital not very far from her apartment. As a part of preparing for her interview with the chief of psychology there, Wendy logged on the Web site of the hospital to view the faculty and programs that were offered. She was quite surprised to discover that she recognized the name of one of the psychiatrists in the eating disorders unit; he was also a member of her therapist's peer consultation group. It was certainly logical that he would be one of the persons Dr. Shush, as a member of the peer consultation group, had consulted in the course of treating Wendy, and she felt that she had probably benefited greatly, albeit indirectly, from those consultations. However, she never considered that the same therapist with whom her psychologist had consulted could some day be a potential colleague at her place of employment.

After carefully considering the situation, and the potential difficulty she would have in working closely with a therapist who likely would be able to identify her as Dr. Shush's patient, Wendy decided to refrain from seeking a position at that hospital. There were several other possible positions that interested her in the city, and none of them would have presented the potential for a dual-role relationship that the private hospital did. She felt fortunate, indeed, that her therapist had told her the names of the other group members at the outset, and even though she was well aware that her identity had never been revealed to the consultation group members, she rightly suspected that there was enough personal information, revealed over a 2-year period of meetings, that she could easily have been recognized by the psychiatrist in question.

For his part, Dr. Shush generally was careful to avoid using real first names of his patients in discussing patients in the group and would reveal information only as it was germane to the consultation. For example, this could include the statement that his patient was "in the process of completing her internship," or that his patient "was a therapist," but without indicating whether she was a psychologist, psychiatrist, or social worker. Nevertheless, long-running patients who were discussed in the group, who were in the mental health field themselves, did run some risk of possibly losing their anonymity, and this was more likely to be the case if group members would have collateral contact with them as colleagues. The members recognized this as such a sufficiently serious risk that they ultimately made the decision to exclude such cases from their meetings.

1. Would it have been possible for Dr. Shush to have masked Wendy's personal information sufficiently in the consultation

group so that she would not have been recognizable to the other psychiatrist colleague-to-be on staff at the hospital?

2. As a graduate student, how would you deal with an interdisciplinary clinical supervision group meeting (attended by psychiatrists, social workers, marriage and family therapists, etc.) in which the supervising psychiatrist freely provides the patients' names or other identifying information?

3. How do codes of ethics of other health care providers deal with this particular issue, and why is it important for you to know the answer to this if you work in an interdisciplinary setting?

4.07 USE OF CONFIDENTIAL INFORMATION FOR DIDACTIC OR OTHER PURPOSES

Psychologists do not disclose in their writings, lectures, or other public media, confidential, personally identifiable information concerning their clients/patients, students, research participants, organizational clients, or other recipients of their services that they obtained during the course of their work, unless (1) they take reasonable steps to disguise the person or organization, (2) the person or organization has consented in writing, or (3) there is legal authorization for doing so.

When writing articles or books, teaching courses, lecturing, presenting to the media, using the Internet, or discussing your work in public, avoid using real names or personal details that might lead others to identify your client, patient, student, supervisee, research participant, or anybody else to whom you render a professional service. (You would be surprised at how clever others can be at deciphering a thinly veiled vignette or accurately guessing the identity of the person you are using as an example in your presentation.) The best protection for you and others consists of the following:

- take careful steps to disguise the person or organization (e.g., alter the gender, age, ethnicity, geographic location, and other important variables of the scenario before presenting the information);
- obtain written consent from the person, couple, group, or organizational client to use information that has been revealed to you in the course of your work, before using it; and
- recognize that you are legally authorized to reveal such information if the information is already in the public domain, by virtue of litigation, the media (with appropriate prior authorization), or other situations that afford legal authorization.

VIGNETTE

Dr. Leaky drew on his experience as a group psychotherapist in teaching a seminar, for the first time, at a small school of professional psychology. He thought that it would be useful to describe actual narratives from his ongoing therapy group to students who were taking his group therapy course for credit. Because the therapy group was made up of both graduate students and laypeople from the community, he knew that there was always a risk that his classroom students could identify the people involved in his examples. Therefore, he was careful to change the names or not use names at all in his narratives.

Unfortunately, however, he usually did little or nothing in his classroom presentations to alter such important details as the subject matter discussed or to modify personal attributes such as gender, age, race, religion, or the physical disability status of the group member under discussion. His examples were sometimes transparent, and on several occasions a student was able to correctly guess the identity of the individual whose story Dr. Leaky was presenting in the classroom.

On one occasion, the example used to illustrate a particular aspect of group psychotherapy revealed the strong feelings of Clarke, a 35-year-old jazz musician, about his significant other, Lois, who, unbeknownst to Dr. Leaky, happened to be a student in his class. Dr. Leaky altered Clarke's name and age in presenting the vignette, but not his profession or any other personal attributes. He accurately portrayed Clarke's angry feelings and criticism about his girlfriend and the fact that Clarke had never before shared these feelings with her or anyone else. Lois was not prepared to hear the expression of these negative feelings in such a public place as a classroom, even though the group therapy member was supposedly anonymous. She experienced it as a public humiliation, because several of her friends also recognized the identities of those involved in the vignette. She felt confused, hurt, and ashamed, and she began to sob during the course of the lecture. She was too upset to discuss the matter with Dr. Leaky, and she quietly left the classroom before his lecture ended.

Dr. Leaky was careless and uninformed about the principle of confidentiality. His disregard for the privacy of others had resulted in harm to both a therapy group member and a student in his class. Although Lois was somewhat passive and fearful of complaining against Dr. Leaky, in light of his authority and seniority, Clarke felt no such constraints. Dr. Leaky listened to Clarke's objections about what had happened in the classroom, and he began to develop an appreciation for the damage he had done to two people who had placed their trust in him. Although neither Clarke nor Lois brought a formal ethics complaint against him, they felt that their message had gotten through to Dr. Leaky, as he expressed remorse that he had violated their trust.

1. How should Dr. Leaky have altered the information about Clarke when presenting the vignette to his class?
2. Should Dr. Leaky inform his class that the facts have been altered in the cases he is presenting? What purpose would it serve to do so?
3. Create a consent form that you might give to your therapy patients that would be acceptable for using their confidential information didactically. Then contact your state psychological association, an ethicist, or an attorney knowledgeable about mental health issues to review your document.

5

ADVERTISING AND OTHER
PUBLIC STATEMENTS

5.01 AVOIDANCE OF FALSE OR DECEPTIVE STATEMENTS

(a) Public statements include but are not limited to paid or unpaid advertising, product endorsements, grant applications, licensing applications, other credentialing applications, brochures, printed matter, directory listings, personal resumes or curricula vitae, or comments for use in media such as print or electronic transmission, statements in legal proceedings, lectures and public oral presentations, and published materials. Psychologists do not knowingly make public statements that are false, deceptive, or fraudulent concerning their research, practice, or other work activities or those of persons or organizations with which they are affiliated.

Public statements include everything that you say, write, publish, video- or audiotape, broadcast, send over the Internet, or communicate with others in any way. This includes advertisements for your services or products, endorsements of the services or products of others, grant applications, state license or other credential applications, brochures, various listings (information and referral services, directories for professional associations, etc.), résumés, interviews with journalists, legal testimony

131

VIGNETTE

One evening each month, Dr. Fluff gave a presentation at the Springfield Public Library on stress management for couples who were expecting their first child. As a part of the process of learning how to identify stress in their lives, the attendees filled out a short inventory he had created that culled items from the Beck Depression Inventory—2 (BDI–2; Beck, 1996) and the Symptom Checklist–90–R (SCL-90-R; Derogatis, 1993) into one brief questionnaire that he called the "Springfield Pregnancy Stress Inventory."

Although he lacked supporting research for his claims, but had some clinical experience on which to rely, Dr. Fluff routinely began each new lecture with the assertion that potential mothers or fathers who endorsed seven or more items in the inventory were "definitely at risk for developing a stress-related disorder, which would likely affect the development of the baby *in utero*, with lifelong negative consequences for his or her physical and mental health." He would make this utterance in as grave and authoritative a tone as he could muster, citing examples of adults who had chronic anxiety or depression and whose mothers had endured various sorts of stress during their pregnancies. At this point, there would usually be several couples who would be rather concerned or disturbed about these ominous statements and would raise questions about the difficulty of managing anxiety, depression, or the normal stresses of everyday life. Taking his cue, Dr. Fluff would then go on to assure them that he had a remedy that was pretty much guaranteed to reduce stress and enhance the parents' quality of life during these difficult months. He would then announce that his psychoeducational seminar would address both the stressors of concern to those present and the general topic of pregnancy stress prophylaxis. For everyone who was interested, the series of five 1-hour lectures would begin the following week for a total fee of $199.95 per couple.

By coincidence, Dr. Out, a psychologist, and his pregnant wife, Betta Watcher-Out, who happened to be an attorney, were attending the lecture. Dr. Out was well schooled in professional ethics and readily noticed Dr. Fluff's tendency to exaggerate claims about the validity of his questionnaire and his services, as well as his bent for misstating relevant research or ignoring it altogether. Dr. Out also easily recognized the test items from the SCL–90–R and the BDI–2, and his wife, Betta, remarked that plagiarizing test items from published materials without citation or permission violated the copyright law.

Indeed, Dr. Fluff's public statements to the audience at the Springfield library seemed to be in violation not only of this ethical standard but also of several others; specifically, Standards 2.04 (Bases for Scientific and Professional Judgments), 3.04 (Avoiding Harm), 3.10 (Informed Consent), 7.03 (Accuracy in Teaching), 9.02 (Use of Assessments), and 9.05 (Test Construction).

In his zeal to be enterprising and nourish his professional reputation—and, ultimately, his clinical practice—Dr. Fluff attempted to manipulate others, and in so doing disregarded important fundamental ethical standards and legal statutes. He also used scare tactics in making statements that were not founded on fact to individuals vulnerable to undue influence: couples expecting their first child. Dr. and Mrs. Watcher-Out confronted Dr. Fluff with his apparent oversights and urged him to consider these matters seriously in promoting his seminars and using instruments of assessment that were essentially plagiarized. Dr. Fluff took these admonitions to heart. He vowed to include more substance in his future presentations and to stop using a hodgepodge of plagiarized test items, hastily assembled into a semiplausible stress inventory. Somewhat skeptical, the Watcher-Outs continued to monitor Fluff's work, indirectly, through their friends who attended later seminars, and they were prepared to initiate a formal ethics complaint, if warranted.

1. How might Dr. Fluff have altered his presentation to couples so that it was in compliance with this ethical standard but retained their interest in participating?
2. Would anything be gained if Dr. and Mrs. Watcher-Out reported Dr. Fluff to the state licensing board or the American Psychological Association (APA) Ethics Committee, instead of talking with him directly and hoping that he would change his ways?
3. How will you answer questions of new clients or patients who are curious about your success rates with their type of presenting complaint?

5.01 (b)

Psychologists do not make false, deceptive, or fraudulent statements concerning (1) their training, experience, or competence; (2) their academic degrees; (3) their credentials; (4) their institutional or association affiliations; (5) their services; (6) the scientific or clinical basis for, or results or degree of success of, their services; (7) their fees; or (8) their publications or research findings.

Do not misinform, mislead, deceive, or hoodwink others by what you say or do not say concerning:

- your education, training, experience, skills, or areas of competence;
- your academic degrees (e.g., claiming to own a degree that you never earned and was not awarded; by the way, ABD—all but dissertation—is not a degree);
- your credentials, currently valid state license, certificates, diplomate status, and so on;
- your affiliation with hospitals, universities, professional associations, or other institutions or organizations;
- the psychological services that you offer;
- the scientific or clinical evidence of your effectiveness;
- what you will charge for your services; and
- your journal articles, books, or other publications, and your research findings, results, and implications.

VIGNETTE

When introducing herself to health care providers, such as physicians and dentists, and to new patients, Dr. Boaster, a recently licensed psychologist, made the following claims: She was affiliated with the local hospital, had been in professional practice for 5 years, and had a 75% success rate in treating anorectic patients.

Each of these statements was in some way an exaggeration or inaccurate. For example, Dr. Boaster had no formal staff affiliation with the hospital or its psychiatry department but merely knew some of the staff there and regularly attended weekly grand rounds presented by the department. It was true that she had applied for hospital admitting privileges there, but it would take approximately 6 more months to process her application and, for the present, she had no such privileges or formal connection.

Furthermore, Dr. Boaster had been licensed as a psychologist for only 1 year, not 5 years, as she implied. However, she felt entitled to insinuate that she had been licensed to practice as a psychologist for 5 years because she had, in fact, been treating patients as either a pre- or postdoctoral intern for 4 years prior to her actual licensure. Her supervisors had generally found her to be competent, although somewhat immature, but they had obviously supported her through her doctoral training and licensure.

Finally, Dr. Boaster had treated a total of only eight anorectic patients, three of whom were still in therapy with her. They were making progress in treatment, but they were far from terminating. Of the five others whom she had treated, two had dropped out of therapy, and three had remained relatively symptom free for 6 months. She had a wholly inadequate basis for making the claim of a 75% success rate with anorectic patients, given the small number of successfully terminated patients and inadequate follow-up data.

All of Dr. Boaster's introductory statements were misleading to both the public and her colleagues. However, she believed that she was engaging in reasonable ways of promoting herself in a highly competitive market and a lagging economy—that it was acceptable to put a slight spin on her experience and success rates, as long as it was not an outright lie. Her motivation was based on the assumption that patients would be far less likely to consult her for treatment, and health care providers less likely to give her referrals, if they knew of her relatively recent licensure and somewhat limited professional experience. Dr. Boaster unfortunately focused more on her own self-promotion than she did on accuracy and honesty in her public statements, misleading health care providers and potential consumers. By these actions she was directly violating this ethical standard and doing so in a way that placed her at significant risk of being easily discovered that she was in fact blatantly lying about her affiliation with the hospital.

1. What means could Dr. Boaster have used to promote her practice, in an ethical fashion, that would not involve exaggerating or misrepresenting the facts?
2. As a clinical supervisor, who viewed the young Dr. Boaster as immature and personally insecure, what training or other experiences might you suggest that could be helpful?
3. What would you do, as a colleague, if you discovered Dr. Boaster's misrepresentation about her hospital affiliation but had faith in her competence and had referred patients to her in the past?

5.01 (c)

Psychologists claim degrees as credentials for their health services only if those degrees (1) were earned from a regionally accredited educational institution or (2) were the basis for psychology licensure by the state in which they practice.

Do not use the title *Dr.*, or claim a PhD, PsyD, EdD, master's degree, or any other academic credential, if your degree was earned from a school that was not regionally accredited (i.e., a school that was not formally accredited by, e.g., the New England Association of Schools and Colleges, the North Central Association of Schools and Colleges, the Western Association of Schools and Colleges, or some other similar regional accrediting body), unless your degree qualified you to take the licensing examination and obtain your license to practice. (N.B.: If you move to a different state, and you have obtained your doctoral degree from an in-

VIGNETTE

Dr. Traveler earned his PhD from a school that was licensed by his home state but was not regionally accredited. After practicing for several years, he decided to move to a neighboring state with a stronger economy and attempt to establish an independent practice as a clinician and consultant.

To his surprise, the state licensing board there refused to acknowledge his PhD because he had not earned it from a regionally accredited school. Dr. Traveler argued that he had graduated from a professional school of psychology that was licensed by his home state, even though it was not regionally accredited. He added that he had achieved excellent grades during his academic career, worked under the formal supervision of a licensed psychologist for 1 year, taken the licensing examination and passed it on the first try, practiced independently as a psychologist for 2 years, and had three publications in refereed journals.

The licensing board was unmoved by Dr. Traveler's story, reiterating that, in spite of his other accomplishments, he had still failed to obtain his doctoral degree from a regionally accredited institution. Because the PhD he currently held clearly did not form the basis for licensure in the state, as it did not meet the criteria for training at the doctoral level there, he was not permitted to use the title *Dr.* Dr. Traveler thus quickly became Mr. Traveler; he could not even be a candidate to retake the psychology licensing examination, because the state licensing law required that every candidate must have a doctoral degree from a regionally accredited institution to take the examination.

Although discouraged, Mr. Traveler decided to formally appeal the licensing board's decision, on the basis of his experience, prior success on the licensing examination, innovative research and publications, and independent practice in his home state. If he failed to prevail in his appeal, then he would consider additional formal coursework and supervision, as the board of psychology might require, to eventually take the licensing examination and begin a practice in his new state.

1. How should Dr. Traveler have prepared in advance for his move to the new state, so that he would have known the problems he would encounter?
2. Could Dr. Traveler assume reciprocity of his licensure, when moving to another state, if his degree were from a regionally accredited university or professional school of psychology?

3. How does the Association of State and Provincial Psychology Boards' mobility program bear on psychologists attempting to relocate their practice in another state?

5.02 STATEMENTS BY OTHERS

(a) Psychologists who engage others to create or place public statements that promote their professional practice, products, or activities retain professional responsibility for such statements.

The buck stops with you in regard to the accuracy or suitability of any advertisements or public statements that you authorize about yourself, your products, or your services. You could be held responsible for how an advertising agency, public relations department, or anyone else portrays you or promotes your work.

VIGNETTE

Dr. Little's clientele had been diminishing over the years because of the fluctuating economy and, after exploring the benefits of advertising (newspapers, Yellow Pages, or other media), he decided to take a step that he had never thought would be necessary until now: formally advertising his practice. He contacted a small advertising agency in town, Huckster & Shootem, which had a good reputation for promoting the practices of plastic surgeons, dentists, and other health care specialists. He discussed with Mr. Huckster the general concepts he wanted to have described in the advertisement. He left the final details up to Mr. Huckster's discretion, because he was preoccupied with the final preparations for a workshop he was presenting at the state psychological association annual meeting out of town.

Huckster & Shootem designed a quarter-page advertisement to run in the local newspaper for 2 weeks. The advertisement ran before Dr. Little had a chance to preview it. It displayed his picture and included the following text:

> Do you drink a little too much just a little too often? Have you been noticing your weight inching upward, year by year? Does the boss get your goat a little more often than ever before? Do little things bother you much more than in previous years? You could be experiencing "midlife melancholy," a clinically proven syndrome that improves with treatment. I will show you a simple technique for making your life happier in only three therapy sessions. Results are guaranteed to improve your satisfaction and bring you happiness in these special years of life.

A psychologist in town read this advertisement and was disturbed about the hyperbolic and overly simplistic language. He telephoned Dr. Little and left a friendly but firm message on his voicemail to the effect that Dr. Little was probably not in a position to guarantee anything about outcomes in psychotherapy, and he wondered about "midlife melancholy" as a clinically proven syndrome. Certainly he had seen this term in the popular press, but never in the professional literature or listed as a diagnosis in the *Diagnostic and Statistical Manual of Mental Disorders* (4th ed., text revision; American Psychiatric Association, 2000). He questioned the practice of a mental health specialist using a phrase that was apparently coined by the media and promoting it as a psychological diagnosis that had a specific treatment.

After returning from his trip, Dr. Little heard the voicemail message and was chagrined to learn of his colleague's disapproval. However, after some reflection, and after reading the advertisement himself for the first time, he agreed that the language was indeed somewhat inappropriate. It was not scientifically based, it claimed a diagnostic entity that did not exist, and it made promises that could not necessarily be fulfilled. After all, the advertisement was broadly aimed at the public, and it had no disclaimers, creating the possibility that he would be guaranteeing favorable outcomes in only three sessions to people with major depression, chemical dependency, personality disorders, posttraumatic stress disorder, or other life situations or psychopathology that would normally require much longer treatment.

Dr. Little decided, reluctantly, that a significant rewording of his advertisement was in order. He knew that he was accountable for the content of his advertisement and that the inaccuracies appearing in the newspaper were his responsibility to correct. He immediately stopped the advertisement, although he was obligated to pay for the remainder of the days for which he had contracted.

Dr. Little significantly revised the text and even invited his colleague who had complained to review the final version before it went to press. He realized that having failed to preview the ad in its entirety, and leaving the final wording up to the enthusiastic and creative marketing efforts of Huckster & Shootem, constituted a lapse of judgment on his part.

1. Who is ultimately responsible for the actual wording of an advertisement in the print or electronic media: the psychologist, an advertising agency he or she has hired, or a consultant who has advised the psychologist?
2. If Dr. Little designed a promotional message for his psychological services and then turned it over to his editorial assistant or secretary for copyediting, before it went to the newspaper, would he still retain responsibility for the contents of the advertisement?
3. What if a psychologist hired a Web designer to publicize his or her services over the Internet (although not actually offer services online)? Are there any ethical or legal restrictions

about the use of photographs, special graphics, testimonials of satisfied clients or therapy patients, or video clips that are relevant?

4. How would you ethically promote your online tutorial on a topic of your choice (e.g., parenting skills in a second marriage, how to tolerate a difficult boss or manager, dealing with sexual addiction)?

5.02 (b)

Psychologists do not compensate employees of press, radio, television, or other communication media in return for publicity in a news item. (See also Standard 1.01, Misuse of Psychologists' Work.)

Never pay, give gifts to, or compensate a newspaper reporter, radio or TV reporter, Internet journalist, or any other journalist in the print or electronic media in return for an interview endorsing or promoting your work in a news story.

VIGNETTE

Dr. Seemee, a social psychologist, completed a small research project that he thought had important implications for society, and he wished very much for it to be disseminated to the professional and lay public. It involved analyzing anger and violent behavior in adolescent boys in inner-city schools and suggested ways of predicting and possibly forestalling the violence before it erupted. He decided to turn to the popular press, because every professional journal to which he had submitted his research article rejected it because of its poor statistical design, small sample size, and unwarranted conclusions. However, because he believed in its validity and wished to convey his message to the public, Dr. Seemee telephoned the science editor from a local newspaper and offered to pay $300 in exchange for an interview about his research.

By coincidence, the science editor, Dr. Halter, happened to be well educated in psychology and knew more about the APA Ethics Code than Dr. Seemee did. She declined the offer to interview him and reminded him that he would be violating his professional ethics if he ever paid a journalist for such a news item.

Undaunted, and ever creative, Dr. Seemee promptly withdrew the offer of money, acknowledging his ethical oversight, and instead pointed out that he had some knowledge of the daily stresses of individuals engaged in newspaper work and that he would be willing to make her a different sort of offer that might actually improve her health. He then presented her with the idea of providing six free biofeedback training sessions for stress and pain management if she would only agree to an interview and publish his story. Dr. Halter patiently pointed out, once again, that participating in such an exchange of psychological services for a news story might still constitute compensation being paid to a journalist (in the form of barter), a practice specifically prohibited by the Ethics Code. She added that furthermore, even if the APA Ethics Code did permit such an arrangement, the Canons of Journalism, as adopted by the American Society of Newspaper Editors, likely would not, under the principle called "Independence."

Realizing that he was making little progress, Dr. Seemee took a different tack, hoping to elicit sympathy from the hard-hearted Dr. Halter. He lamented that he had encountered a "minor problem" having his article published and explained how the article could be useful in light of the juvenile violence that had been in the news recently. He cited well-known examples in several cities of teenagers threatening violence and, on occasion, carrying it out by discharging firearms in school, sometimes with intentional targets and sometimes at random.

Dr. Halter agreed that the topic was timely and highly relevant to the American culture and its apparent appetite for violence but, nevertheless, she could not accept his offer for an interview. She observed that his research had already been reviewed by his peers and had been found lacking. She suggested that he would be better off to follow up on reviewers' critical comments in further investigating adolescent violence and improving his research design instead of attempting to publish it, as is, in the lay press. She did offer, however, to place his name on her list of mental health professionals to be interviewed in the future, should the need arise for a (gratis) interview.

1. Could Dr. Seemee have been found in violation of the Ethics Code if he were unaware of this standard and Dr. Halter accepted his offer of biofeedback training?
2. Would it be a violation of this standard if Dr. Halter had approached Dr. Seemee for a biofeedback interview, and Dr. Seemee offered to demonstrate the procedure on her in a free 25-minute session? Explain how this differs in substance from the previous question.
3. Given his responses in the vignette, do you think that Dr. Seemee is likely to learn from this interaction with the journalist to have a fuller appreciation of this ethical standard?
4. What steps would you take, as a colleague, if you read Dr. Seemee's interview in a newspaper, knowing that his research article had been rejected and the reasons why it had been rejected?

5.02 (c)

A paid advertisement relating to psychologists' activities must be identified or clearly recognizable as such.

When you intend to publicize your products or services by means of a paid advertisement, make sure that you clearly identify the message as such. Do not camouflage promotional messages as news stories or educational messages. However, if you write a regular newspaper or magazine column, or produce a presentation for the media, and you clearly are not creating an advertisement, then under this rule this would be acceptable (if the message is in compliance with all the other standards).

VIGNETTE

Dr. Slider wrote a weekly column entitled "What's Your Problem?" for the local newspaper on various topics of psychological interest: insomnia, weight control, sexual dysfunction, stress management, obsessive–compulsive disorders, and so on. However, promotional messages about the Slider Mental Health Centers, emphasizing innovative techniques, high success rates, low fees, and a broad range of services increasingly infiltrated the column's putative scientific message.

The true purpose of this thinly disguised informational column was to advertise the services of Dr. Slider's group practice, which consisted of nine psychologists and social workers at two different sites in the downtown area. By creating these columns, Dr. Slider hoped that readers would be encouraged to consider having a consultation as they learned about various psychological problems and the range of interventions offered at his clinics. Although not entirely obvious from the column's context, Dr. Slider's articles were essentially advertisements describing how treatment at his clinics would directly benefit consumers.

However, the column unfortunately was never labeled as a paid advertisement, as Dr. Slider felt justified that he was educating the public about various psychological problems and their remedies, not just promoting his practice. However, in discussing treatment alternatives, he rarely presented the full range of options according to the current standards of care and informed consent. Instead, he described only the options and interventions currently offered by him and his colleagues. As a result, a diabetic man experiencing erectile dysfunction due to peripheral neuropathy (not psychogenic causes) might read the column and reasonably conclude that Dr. Slider's approach to therapy was the only empirically validated one in town, and certainly the one with the highest success rate.

By creating a weekly column that reflected only the offerings of his own clinics, resulting in free publicity, Dr. Slider failed to discriminate accurately between psychoeducational and promotional activities, one being didactic and the other being essentially manipulative of readers, encouraging them to seek his professional services. By so doing, he did a poor job at both: Not only did he fail to educate the public in a broad way about psychological disorders and their remedies, as the column's title suggested, but he also failed to clearly present information about his staff, credentials, hours of operation, fees, or insurance practices, as one might expect to see in a paid advertisement. The unintended result of this column was that consumers who had never sought therapy before would initiate treatment at one of Dr. Slider's clinics, only to be frequently disappointed with poor results at significant expense.

1. Would Dr. Slider technically be in violation of this standard if, not having paid for any advertising message, he simply wrote a weekly column that, by its nature, seemed to promote his clinical practice?
2. Which standard would be relevant to the type of promotional messages Dr. Slider was embedding in his weekly articles?
3. How might this standard be applied to advertising messages over the Internet, or on psychologists' Web sites?
4. Create a disclaimer or an advertisement that you might use on your Web site if you were promoting innovative techniques for your specialty area.
5. Draft an advertisement that you might place in your local newspaper or Yellow Pages that is free of spin, hype, or exaggeration of any sort.

5.03 DESCRIPTIONS OF WORKSHOPS AND NON-DEGREE-GRANTING EDUCATIONAL PROGRAMS

To the degree to which they exercise control, psychologists responsible for announcements, catalogs, brochures, or advertisements describing workshops, seminars, or other non-degree-granting educational programs ensure that they accurately describe the audience for which the program is intended, the educational objectives, the presenters, and the fees involved.

If you are teaching in a nondegree program (e.g., continuing education, weekend workshop, ongoing seminar, presentation over the Internet), you must accurately describe the intended audience, educational objectives, presenters, and cost in brochures, catalogs, mailings, and advertisements of any kind. (If you do not have control over the publicity or advertising statements, at least make an effort to inform those who do about the requirements of this standard.)

VIGNETTE

👍   Three psychologists offered a 2-day seminar in neurofeedback training for migraine headache and temporomandibular joint pain. In the printed announcement, which appeared in professional journals for psychologists, psychiatrists, clinical social workers, and nurses, and which also was mailed out to health care professionals by means of a purchased mailing list, the psychologists stated the cost of the seminar and indicated that the workshop should be attended by licensed other health care practitioners whose legal scope of practice included the use of biofeedback and who were already trained in its basic applications.

In the announcement, the clinicians described the educational objectives of the seminar and the topic areas that would be included. They also outlined how much time would be allocated to each topic, whether the meetings were plenary sessions or smaller group presentations, and the degree to which instruction could be individualized. They further described how each participant would have some exposure to the more sophisticated biofeedback equipment, with some hands-on experience on the second day of training.

Finally, they made it clear that attendees could have follow-up supervision of their clinical work by any of the three presenters or other experienced practitioners. As a part of their participation in the seminar, they would be entitled to receive the names of supervising health care practitioners, experienced in biofeedback training, who were willing to provide consultation for them.

The teaching team took great care to develop a brochure and journal announcement that was accurate, comprehensive, and concise and that provided an excellent basis on which prospective trainees could make a decision about attending.

1. What additional information might have been described in the advertisement for this seminar?
2. What would you do if you were giving a presentation and you discovered that the publicity brochure describing your workshop had several mistakes in describing your experience and the focus of the workshop? How could you avoid this in the future?
3. Create an advertisement or a brochure describing a lecture or workshop that you might give on a particular area of interest.

5.04 MEDIA PRESENTATIONS

When psychologists provide public advice or comment via print, Internet, or other electronic transmission, they take precautions to ensure that statements

(1) are based on their professional knowledge, training, or experience in accord with appropriate psychological literature and practice; (2) are otherwise consistent with this Ethics Code; and (3) do not indicate that a professional relationship has been established with the recipient. (See also Standard 2.04, Bases for Scientific and Professional Judgments.)

When offering your advice, wisdom, commentary, reactions of any kind; or when giving a media presentation (e.g., radio, TV, newspaper, or magazine); or whenever addressing the public orally, in writing, or over the Internet, remember the following points:

- Always be able to support your statements with your knowledge, training, experience, or the psychological literature (you do not always have to cite your sources, or clinical studies, but occasional citations might be helpful).
- Make sure that you are in compliance with every other standard in the APA Ethics Code, not just the ones in this section.
- Do not attempt or encourage listeners, viewers, readers, or participants to assume that you have an individualized, professional relationship with them. The fact is, you actually know very little or nothing about them, the scope of their problems, their personal history, prior psychotherapy, involvement in litigation, and so on, and thus you should not offer them advice any more readily than you would if you had just met them for the very first time, in your office, to begin an initial consultation. General psychoeducational information is permissible, however, of the sort that they might read in a good educational publication.

VIGNETTE

Dr. Duhl was a psychologist who hosted a weekly 1-hour radio call-in show that regularly discussed topics concerning child development and parenting issues. She generally was careful to base her remarks on the current research in these areas, preferring to be accurate in the information she dispensed to callers. When asked a question that required a lengthy answer, she gave it the attention it deserved, sometimes speaking for 5 or 6 minutes at a time to provide a comprehensive reply. Each show was focused on a particular topic, such as dealing with one's angry teenager, school phobia in one's youngster, and age-appropriate sex education at home.

After several months on the air, the producer of the show and the director of programming were troubled by the show's slowly sinking ratings. They attempted to remedy the situation by discussing with Dr. Duhl their proposals for changing the format and content of the show in hopes of increasing the audience's interest level. They had analyzed callers' comments and concluded that many listeners were losing interest because of Dr. Duhl's tendency to focus on a single subject for each broadcast. They proposed a new format that would include brief presentations and call-in questions on several diverse topics per show instead of a focus on only one theme, as she had been doing.

They also had a number of other suggestions to spice up the show. They wanted Dr. Duhl to provide shorter answers than her usual lengthy, drawn-out replies. They asked that she keep her responses to under 1 minute to accommodate more callers and allow for greater audience participation. Dr. Duhl was uncertain about how to comply with this request because she feared that she would have to give superficial treatment to some topics that required greater elaboration than 1 minute of air time.

The producer and director also mentioned Dr. Duhl's tendency to use (appropriately) tentative language when addressing a caller's question rather than freely giving advice or suggestions. They viewed this as waffling and thought that it not only failed to meet the needs of less sophisticated listeners but also could be confusing. Listeners want to hear plain language, in simple English, and they do not like ambiguity, she was told. The director insisted that Dr. Duhl be less scholarly or dry in her presentation and not be so reluctant to suggest a course of action to callers. He and the producer thought that Dr. Duhl should simply tell them what to do to remedy a particular situation. Dr. Duhl had intentionally resisted this temptation because she was well aware that she did not know the details of a caller's history or his or her immediate situation, and she did not feel competent to give advice to a caller who presented a problem in 30 seconds or less.

Finally, Dr. Duhl's superiors thought that she could enliven the discussion and further pique the interest of listeners with stories and vignettes drawn from those of actual patients from her therapy practice. As long as she did not reveal the names of her patients, then there should be no problem, they believed. Dr. Duhl knew that there would indeed be many problems, and she strongly resisted this advice. She informed the director that such a presentation would violate the fundamental tenets of confidentiality, both according to her professional code of ethics and state law, and it could possibly reveal the identity of her patients, because she would be describing details of the treatment and patients that could be recognizable. She supposed there was a way that she could create fictional cases, however, on the basis of her aggregate experience with patients, but then she would be required to state that these were fabricated vignettes, not actual therapy cases. The director was willing to settle for that, although he would have preferred that she follow an actual case from beginning to end.

On reflection, Dr. Duhl felt that so many non-negotiable requests to change the format of her radio show might possibly result in wider appeal to the audience, but she did not think they were in compliance with this and other ethical standards. Neither would they have resulted in the kind of presentation that she had valued the most—more in depth and narrower in focus. She was concerned about maintaining a scientific approach to her presentations, being able to support her statements, preserving the confidentiality of her patients, avoiding giving advice in the absence of a defined professional relationship with an individual (e.g., client–therapist), and refraining from making suggestions about a specific course of action without adequate information about the caller's history and circumstances. In short, Dr. Duhl felt that she could not, in good faith, conduct a radio presentation in the style that was being requested without compromising her ethical standards. She considered carefully the wisdom of participating in a radio program that was geared more toward entertaining than informing and educating, and she eventually decided to exercise her option to withdraw from her contract with the station.

1. Was Dr. Duhl being too finicky about refusing to include actual case studies on her program? What effect might this have on ongoing patients who listen to her program, and how might it affect their treatment?
2. What if the programming consultant had asked Dr. Duhl to invite one of her current or former patients (anonymously) on the show? How might this constitute both a clinical and an ethical problem?
3. How can you determine whether the media presentation in which you have been invited to participate is primarily entertainment or primarily educational? How will this affect your decision to participate or the nature of your presentation?

5.05 TESTIMONIALS

Psychologists do not solicit testimonials from current therapy clients/patients or other persons who because of their particular circumstances are vulnerable to undue influence.

Do not ask your current therapy clients, patients, or others who are vulnerable to undue influence (i.e., those who might not have balanced judgment and would easily be persuaded by your request, because of their special relationship with you and their current life circumstances) for permission to quote them in advertisements for your services. This prohibition would include any medium in which you intend to advertise or promote your work: spoken word, Internet, and print media (newspapers, brochures, the Yellow Pages, etc.). It forbids you to ask your clients to be quoted about their success in, for example, your attention-deficit/hyperactivity disorder treatment program, anxiety and depression clinic, or other professional services you may offer.

VIGNETTE

Dr. Youzem offered a weight reduction program for individuals who also had been diagnosed with depression that consisted of participation in both individual psychotherapy and a group psychoeducational approach. His results had been quite good over several years, but recently he had moved to a new state, and he had relatively few patients. In an effort to expand his practice, Dr. Youzem asked 10 of his current patients who had maintained their goal weight for many months if they would be willing to make a few statements endorsing his program that he could quote in a brochure to be included in a broad mailing to physicians and mental health care practitioners.

Nearly every patient complied with his request, but they experienced a broad range of personal reactions. Some were happy to give testimonials; they were extremely pleased about the weight they had lost and felt proud to share their successful experience with others as an encouragement for them to lose weight. However, several patients provided testimonials only because they felt unable to refuse a request from Dr. Youzem, even though they would have preferred to quietly continue their work in treatment without having to participate in any promotional activities. These patients felt somewhat coerced and used, but none of them had the assertiveness to speak up to him about their feelings. Some patients who had initial success, and were happy to provide a testimonial, found themselves struggling with setbacks in their weight control plan several months later and had begun to gain weight; these patients felt as though they were unable to discuss their failures with Dr. Youzem because they had provided such positive statements for his promotional brochure about their success only a few months before.

Several patients experienced an exacerbation of their depression and a relapse in overeating, because they felt pressured to be successful in their weight loss plan and subsequently felt as though they had let their therapist down by dropping out of the program. Although they felt pressured by Dr. Youzem and thought he had taken advantage of his authority over them to obtain testimonials for advertising, they did not bring a complaint against him. One patient, however, wrote him a letter several months after termination indicating that she would gladly have provided a testimonial after she had completed all her therapeutic work with him but somehow, for her, to have done so while continuing to consult with him irrevocably altered their relationship and made it impossible for her to continue in treatment with him, as she had lost confidence in Dr. Youzem's commitment to her.

1. Would Dr. Youzem be entitled to use testimonials that were volunteered by current patients? What are the implications for clinical work if he were to do so?

2. What other ethical standard or standards would be relevant if a psychologist sought his or her patient's testimonial to present to the public, for his or her own gain?
3. After termination, is there any ethical or clinical problem with requesting a testimonial from a former patient? When is a patient not a patient?

5.06 IN-PERSON SOLICITATION

Psychologists do not engage, directly or through agents, in uninvited in-person solicitation of business from actual or potential therapy clients/patients or other persons who because of their particular circumstances are vulnerable to undue influence. However, this prohibition does not preclude (1) attempting to implement appropriate collateral contacts for the purpose of benefiting an already engaged therapy client/patient or (2) providing disaster or community outreach services.

Do not be an ambulance chaser or personally invite people to begin therapy with you at a time or in settings where their judgment may be clouded by their immediate circumstances (i.e., offering counseling to grieving family members at a mortuary). Keep in mind, however, that this standard does not rule out the following:

- inviting clients' family members or significant others into your office as an adjunct to their treatment;
- offering your services in a disaster (e.g., a terrorist attack, earthquake, etc.); or
- offering your services to the community in an organized outreach program (e.g., an enrichment program for underprivileged teenagers and parents at a high school).

VIGNETTE

Dr. Snarem was recently licensed and had learned everything she knew about practice building from her former supervisor, Dr. Freeman, an aggressive entrepreneur in the business aspects of mental health services with a poor understanding of many patient welfare issues. Following the lead of her mentor, Dr. Snarem had taken many business courses at her university while she was obtaining her doctoral degree in psychology. Being long on entrepreneurial creativity and somewhat short on her comprehension of psychological ethics, Dr. Snarem developed a plan to aggressively promote her services, hoping to make personal contact with people who were in immediate need of mental health services.

Dr. Snarem printed individualized brochures addressing individuals in the midst of major life transitions whom she thought might be likely candidates for therapy. Hence, she could be seen frequently distributing literature and business cards outside courtrooms where divorce and child custody litigation were going on, hospital emergency rooms, teenage after-school hangouts, retirement communities, assisted-living centers, and any other place she could think of where people who might need her services congregated.

Dr. Snarem rapidly built up a busy practice and even, much to her satisfaction, surpassed her mentor, Dr. Freeman. Unfortunately, however, many of her clients could have been better served had they interviewed several therapists first instead of beginning treatment with her. Some did not need therapy or counseling at all and would have recovered from their situational stress quite adequately with the passage of time. Others would have done far better to have had a therapist of a different theoretical orientation, or gender, or would have been better served by a group therapy intervention. However, because of the emotional intensity of their life transition and the unexpected face-to-face encounter with a nurturing therapist, their judgment about beginning therapy was somewhat clouded, resulting in an inviting shortcut to Dr. Snarem's door.

Many patients stopped therapy as abruptly as they began, once they fully understood the extent of the financial obligation. Others dropped out over a period of weeks in search of a different kind of therapist, one who was less manipulative and, in some cases, more competent and compassionate. After having paid too much money to Dr. Snarem for too long, these individuals felt exploited, as though she had taken advantage of their depression or panicky emotional state to initiate a therapeutic contract at a time when their objectivity and good judgment were at a minimum.

1. How could Dr. Snarem have made her services known to individuals in transition without confronting them face to face?
2. Would Dr. Snarem have an obligation to inform her new patients about alternative treatment options, according to the rules of the Health Insurance Portability and Accountability Act, or the state laws pertinent to mental health practice?
3. What would be an example of a community outreach service that would allow for in-person solicitation of business?

6

RECORD KEEPING AND FEES

6.01 DOCUMENTATION OF PROFESSIONAL AND SCIENTIFIC WORK AND MAINTENANCE OF RECORDS

Psychologists create, and to the extent the records are under their control, main-
tain, disseminate, store, retain, and dispose of records and data relating to their
professional and scientific work in order to (1) facilitate provision of services
later by them or by other professionals, (2) allow for replication of research
design and analyses, (3) meet institutional requirements, (4) ensure accuracy
of billing and payments, and (5) ensure compliance with law. (See also Stan-
dard 4.01, Maintaining Confidentiality.)

You must create a written record of your professional and scientific work,
keeping it safely stored, releasing it appropriately to others, and ultimately
destroying it, to the extent that records are under your personal control.
(If you work for an agency, hospital, university, group practice, etc., then
you likely will not have any control over the maintenance, release, or
timely destruction of your records.) Record keeping is for the benefit of
your patients, individual and organizational clients, trainees, research
participants, and for you (in the case of an ethics complaint, litigation,
or board of psychology investigation). Compliance with this rule:

- assists in providing psychological services at a later point in time, either by you or someone else;
- allows other researchers to replicate your design and data analyses;
- helps you meet the requirements of your university, hospital, mental health center, or other institution where you work;
- increases the accuracy of your bookkeeping for billing purposes; and
- ensures your compliance with the law, when record keeping is addressed by state or federal laws, such as Medicare, the Department of Veterans Affairs (VA), the Health Insurance Portability and Accountability Act (HIPAA), and so on.

Bear in mind that your secretary or other clerical staff members are not bound by this Ethics Code; you are the one who must train them.

VIGNETTE

Dr. Fussy worked in an outpatient clinic of a large VA hospital and had a small private practice several evenings per week. While at the clinic, she followed the record-keeping policies to the letter.

In her private practice she also was careful about record keeping, and she did so largely on her computer. She consulted occasionally with a computer technician who was knowledgeable about security matters such as firewalls, antivirus software, password protection, and backing up files on an external hard drive and who generally kept current on hardware and software developments that might have a bearing on her practice. Although the technician's services were not inexpensive, they were well worth the cost of avoiding such catastrophes as lost data due to corrupted files, problems with e-mail confidentiality, and related matters.

Dr. Fussy also kept her billing records on the computer and had purchased software to assist in this aspect of her practice. This greatly facilitated the printing of monthly invoices, with Current Procedural Terminology Codes and diagnostic codes, and provided a permanent record for the Internal Revenue Service (IRS) to view as well, if she were ever audited.

Since the advent of HIPAA in April 2003, Dr. Fussy had decided to comply with this new federal law, as she was on several insurance panels and had been doing electronic billing for some time. She had altered the way she kept records, for example, to comply with the HIPAA requirements, noting in her records not only the starting time but also the length of each session. For every patient she maintained the required *clinical record*, which includes the date, time, diagnosis, symptoms, relevant medical information, functional status, treatment plan, prognosis, and progress to date. For some patients, whom she felt presented with more complex symptoms or deeper psychopathology, she kept a second record, called *psychotherapy notes*, which included far more detailed and personal information, including such things as an analysis of the therapy session, verbatim patient quotes, names of family members or key figures, and so on. She kept these two records, separately, on her computer, as she interpreted the HIPAA requirements, and she was well aware that third-party payors would be entitled to view only the contents of the clinical record and would never have access to the psychotherapy notes.

Because Dr. Fussy had received little guidance, either from the American Psychological Association (APA) Ethics Code or from the state laws pertaining to mental health, in regard to how long to maintain her patient records, she had been abiding by the recommendations of the "Record-Keeping Guidelines" (APA, 1993b) and an older APA publication entitled *Specialty Guidelines for the Delivery of Services by Clinical Psychologists* (APA, 1981a). These documents required that psychologists maintain the complete patient record for a total of 3 years after terminating with the patient, and a summary of the records (or simply the entire record) for an additional 12 years, for a total of 15 years. She knew that counseling psychologists had a different recommendation, according to the *Specialty Guidelines*: maintaining the complete record for 4 years after termination and a summary (or the complete record) for an additional 3 years, for a total of 7 years before the file could be destroyed (APA, 1981a). After terminating with a patient, she normally would print out the entire record, place it in a folder, and then put the folder into a locked file cabinet, filed by termination date so that she could easily access them when the time was right to shred them.

On occasion, Dr. Fussy would carry out small clinical research projects, involving patients in her own clinical practice and those in the VA hospital as well. She generally submitted the resulting papers to APA journals for publication, and she was careful to maintain all her raw data for a period of 5 years. Although this was not necessarily convenient—and required, sometimes, that she rent locker space in which to place the many boxes of papers—she knew this came with the territory of being an ethical researcher, that is, maintaining raw data so that another psychologist would be able to reanalyze it, if he or she wished.

Dr. Fussy was very conscious of preserving natural resources and actually considered dumping obsolete records into a huge bin at the city's recycling center. However, her better judgment prevailed, and even though the probability might be remote that aging confidential files could be recovered from a recycling bin and lead to any tangible harm to a patient whom she had not seen for 15 years, she knew, at her obsessive best, that the odds might still be too great. She had purchased a high-quality shredder, and she put it to good use, twice a year, after gathering her obsolete files. For particularly large files, involving testing and other materials, she would use the services of a professional shredding company that specialized in the destruction of confidential materials.

Thanks to her close observance of the important details about record keeping, VA policies, ethical and legal rules, confidentiality, and the ultimate destruction of records, Dr. Fussy never had a problem in any aspect of record keeping. Although she knew that there was much information about which to remain current, given the changing state and federal laws and constantly evolving policies of APA, she followed these matters closely, by means of continuing education workshops, journals, and other means.

1. If Dr. Fussy were not compliant with HIPAA regulations, what exactly should she include in the records of her private patients?
2. What sort of records should be maintained for industrial or organizational consulting?
3. What measures might you take to protect the integrity of your records kept on your computer?
4. Does your state specify the length of time to maintain your records, or any other particulars about record keeping?

6.02 MAINTENANCE, DISSEMINATION, AND DISPOSAL OF CONFIDENTIAL RECORDS OF PROFESSIONAL AND SCIENTIFIC WORK

(a) Psychologists maintain confidentiality in creating, storing, accessing, transferring, and disposing of records under their control, whether these are written, automated, or in any other medium. (See also Standards 4.01, Maintaining Confidentiality, and 6.01, Documentation of Professional and Scientific Work and Maintenance of Records.)

Take steps to maintain the security and confidentiality of your records, whether they are written, typed, computerized, or stored in any other medium (e.g., clinical records, history sheets, raw test data, authorization forms, consent forms, inducements to cooperate in research, and any other documents that reflect your work). Be vigilant about confidentiality when creating, storing, accessing, transferring, moving, or interacting with your records in any way. If using a computer, be ever mindful of security and backup protocols to ensure confidentiality and reduce the odds that a computer crash will corrupt your files. Technology is fallible, and random corruptions or loss of text files can and do occur. And remember—never excuse faulty procedures on the part of your secretary or your institution; they are not bound by this Ethics Code, but you are.

VIGNETTE

Dr. Hush generally wrote her notes about a patient at the end of each therapy session rather than waiting hours or days, as she had done in the past.

She had learned several years before, after being deposed by a divorcing husband's attorney, that what she wrote about each therapy session and patient was crucial and was, in essence, a legal record. She knew that carelessness about records could come back to haunt her at a later time in the form of a deposition, subpoena, or a cross-examining attorney. She also felt that she was better able to maintain clinical continuity with patients by attending to this important task promptly and better able to capture the details and elements of change within the patient than if she delayed her notetaking.

Having read the APA (1993b) "Record-Keeping Guidelines" and examined other record-keeping forms, Dr. Hush had an accurate concept of record keeping that would facilitate the treatment process. She also knew that according to the law in her home state, patients were permitted access to their records and were entitled to receive a copy of their file if they wished, unless revealing such information would be damaging to them. Consequently, whenever she sat down to write her notes, she would engage in the following brief fantasy: Before making any entries, her best supervisor or senior colleague was looking over one shoulder; her patient was looking over the other; an aggressive attorney was sitting across from her; and, finally, 12 jurors were reading every word that she wrote.

Dr. Hush also kept scrupulous notes of each supervisory session with her psychological assistant, because she knew that she was legally and ethically responsible for the work he performed with each patient. She kept all records or summaries for 15 years, as recommended by the "Record-Keeping Guidelines" (APA, 1993b), and she filed them by termination date in a locked file cabinet so that they could easily be located and destroyed when the proper amount of time had elapsed.

Although Dr. Hush knew of colleagues who merely threw old records in the trash after tearing off the front pages with identifying information (and one environmentally minded individual who dumped them in the recycling bin downtown), she took a dim view of these practices. Even though the odds were against information that could be embarrassing or damaging to someone surfacing in a town dump or recycling bin, it could conceivably happen. Even one such event could have grave repercussions, for the patient, family members, and herself. Furthermore, such carelessness would imply to any disinterested party who might come across such casually discarded patient records that psychologists are negligent about confidentiality and that privacy is a sham. To avoid such problems, Dr. Hush was careful to shred or burn her obsolete files after the requisite period of time had gone by.

1. Aside from being sued for malpractice, under what circumstances might you be requested by the court to reveal your patient's records?
2. What are the risks of keeping records on your computer, or on an Internet server that allows you to store data?

3. What concerns about confidentiality might you have with faxing a patient's Minnesota Multiphasic Personality Inventory profile to another psychologist?
4. What are the risks of using an e-mail attachment for sending a patient's file to another health care professional?
5. Does the institution you work for have rules about using e-mail or fax machines to transmit patient data? If not, should it?

6.02 (b)

If confidential information concerning recipients of psychological services is entered into databases or systems of records available to persons whose access has not been consented to by the recipient, psychologists use coding or other techniques to avoid the inclusion of personal identifiers.

Remove all names and identifying information about your clients or patients whenever entering their data into databases to which others may have access, unless consent has been obtained. Use coding systems or some other means for maintaining anonymity and protecting their privacy.

VIGNETTE

Several psychology and clinical social workers on the staff of an infertility clinic were responsible for assessing couples who were attempting to conceive a child by means of a variety of medically assisted techniques. Much patient data had been accumulated over a 5-year period, including not only demographic information but also psychological testing, videotaped structured clinical interviews assessing parenting ability, the type of medical procedures used (e.g., *in vitro* fertilization with and without donor egg or sperm), and follow-up data about the couples' adjustment after successful or unsuccessful attempts to conceive.

A research team at a university hospital from another state was conducting a meta-study on the marital stability of couples who consult fertility clinics, regardless of whether they were successful in conceiving a child. The team made contact with the psychologists and social workers on the clinic staff by sending letters to all mental health professionals who were members of the American Society for Reproductive Medicine and requested access to their databases. Because the investigation would require releasing to a third party confidential information that had already been collected, the clinic staff consulted the in-house institutional review board about to how to proceed.

The institutional review board advised the staff that there were two ways of processing the request for data, depending on the type of data that had been collected. For all the psychological testing, structured clinical interviews, and other printed data that had been collected the staff had carefully removed all names and identifying information, and assigned code numbers instead. This material could readily be released to the requesting research team, with little concern for breaching patient confidentiality, as no identifying data were attached. However, the videotaped interviews, with clear images and voices, presented a different sort of problem. These would either have to be transcribed, with identifying names and information deleted, or else authorization to release the intact videotapes would have to be sought from the patient couples.

The research team was eager to have access to as much data as were available and therefore opted for seeking patient authorization. The team drafted a letter describing the investigation, and the clinic staff added an introductory paragraph inviting former patients' participation in this new study. The letter and consent forms were printed on clinic letterhead and sent to all patients who had consulted the clinic over the previous 5 years.

Only after receiving the signed consent forms by return mail did the clinic's research director proceed to release the videotapes to the external research team for analysis. Couples who declined to participate in the research either indicated their response on the form or simply did not return the form. In this way, all confidential information involved in the research was well protected, either by the use of coded entries or with the explicit authorization of the patient couples to rerelease the videotapes to the external research team.

1. How difficult would it be to transcribe a videotape and delete all identifying information so that it could safely by released to another researcher?
2. What would you do if your institution or clinic had no institutional review board to advise you on how to carry out research without harming participants? Whom could you consult about your protocol?
3. Would formal consent be required from former clients if their data had been archived in a clinic's database with all names and other identifying data removed?

6.02 (c)

Psychologists make plans in advance to facilitate the appropriate transfer and to protect the confidentiality of records and data in the event of psychologists' withdrawal from positions or practice. (See also Standards 3.12, Interruption of Psychological Services, and 10.09, Interruption of Therapy.)

> Protect your professional and scientific records and data, and plan ahead for unexpected changes in the future, such as your withdrawal from practice and even poor health, incapacitation, or death. Remember, your professional records and research data are uniquely valuable, and they must be securely maintained, or transferred to others, as dictated by your personal career path, retirement plans, or deteriorating physical health.

VIGNETTE

Dr. Gardit owned a small consulting firm that specialized in management consulting. He also occasionally taught in the business school of the local university, where he also, from time to time, engaged in research projects.

He was consistently quite scrupulous about preserving the professional records of his corporate clients. Some records he kept in password-protected files on his laptop computer, and he maintained other, paper files, in locked filing cabinets in his office.

To allow for the unpredictable, Dr. Gardit provided each new client the option of signing an authorization form allowing his two partners in the firm access to the confidential records in the event of his death or incapacitation. In this way, there could be a relatively smooth transition to another consultant, if it were ever necessary.

At the university, Dr. Gardit kept his research data under lock and key in the business school, with only one trusted departmental assistant having access to it. The data and information in his computer were password protected, so that no unauthorized access could occur. He also enlisted the help of a colleague in the school of psychology, who was well acquainted with the confidentiality requirements of the Ethics Code. This person was informed of his passwords and was apprised of the procedure for working with the departmental assistant in the event of Dr. Gardit's incapacitation or death. All clients and research participants were informed in writing of the measures that had been implemented at the outset of his work with them.

Fortunately, Dr. Gardit thrived for many years, consulting and teaching, with good attention to ethical practice. When the time came for him to retire, he devoted enough time to each corporate client to arrive at a sound decision about follow-up consultation. After many years of practice, he was acquainted with many colleagues in the field and thus was well equipped to help with the transfer of power, if the client so wished. In some cases, this included a series of meetings with the new consultant and appropriate written authorizations in advance. In all cases, however, there was an orderly and planful transfer of records and materials that would be useful to the new consultant, and confidentiality was well maintained at every turn.

1. Come up with several ways that you could arrange, in advance, for the orderly transfer of your professional records in the event of your untimely demise.
2. How would you handle your impending retirement from clinical practice as regards notifying current patients, notifying former patients, storing or destroying records, or any other details to attend to?
3. What would you do with any files or test data you may have about patients, separate from their clinical record (e.g., shadow files) if you leave a hospital clinic and relocate to a different part of the country?

6.03 WITHHOLDING RECORDS FOR NONPAYMENT

Psychologists may not withhold records under their control that are requested and needed for a client's/patient's emergency treatment solely because payment has not been received.

Don't hold records hostage just because your former patient has not paid you for services rendered. If the records are requested and needed for urgent treatment, you must release them (with proper consent, of course).

VIGNETTE

Dr. Penny Less had been providing treatment to Sal, a young cocaine-dependent jazz musician who had stopped using drugs for several months. The therapy went on for 7 weeks when Sal suddenly stopped showing up for his appointments. Attempts to reach Sal by phone were unsuccessful, and it was clear that, for some reason, treatment was being interrupted. Sal had made some partial payments but still owed Dr. Less about $700, and he had no insurance that included mental health benefits. After sending billing statements for 3 months, Dr. Less concluded that there probably would be no more money forthcoming, at least for the present, and that her former patient had most likely relapsed into his drug habit again.

One morning at around 7:30 a.m., her telephone answering service contacted her with an urgent call from a psychiatrist at the emergency room of the local county hospital. Sal had apparently overdosed on the narcotic Oxycontin and had been found unconscious in an apartment building several hours earlier. Although he had little identifying information with him, he was carrying an old appointment card of Dr. Less's. The psychiatrist on call took advantage of this information to contact Dr. Less and acquire any background information on Sal that he could, given his precarious state of health. Obviously, no consent form had been signed, but Dr. Less appreciated the urgency of the situation. She agreed to speak with the psychiatrist and provided the necessary background information about Sal and his treatment to date.

The next day, Sal was in stable condition at the hospital and had signed himself into the inpatient chemical dependency unit. The treating psychologist there contacted Dr. Less, requesting that she release some information about his course of treatment and the results of any psychological testing. By this time, the proper consent forms had been signed; in fact, Sal was pleased that Dr. Less would be providing information about their work together, although he felt guilty for having reneged on his payments. The consent form was faxed to Dr. Less's office while the original was being sent by conventional mail. Although Dr. Less was tempted to avoid any involvement with this patient because of his outstanding debt, she knew that she had an ethical obligation to release the information that was imminently needed for his treatment. Perhaps he could have been treated without this information being released, but clearly the staff at the hospital felt that treatment would be helped with input from the former therapist. Dr. Less decided to comply with the request and released the information that was requested.

1. What other steps might Dr. Less have taken to obtain payment?
2. Would payments by credit card have been a good idea at the outset? How would this be set up?
3. What if Sal had offered a barter arrangement, wherein his jazz ensemble would provide the music for an elaborate dinner party that Dr. Less was giving for her colleagues, at a much reduced rate? (See Standard 6.05.)
4. What if Sal refused to authorize the treating psychologist on his unit to speak with Dr. Less the next day, but he sought her input nevertheless, as he deemed it important for therapy? Should she disclose information about Sal and his treatment? Consider the clinical and ethical implications of her choice.

6.04 FEES AND FINANCIAL ARRANGEMENTS

(a) As early as is feasible in a professional or scientific relationship, psychologists and recipients of psychological services reach an agreement specifying compensation and billing arrangements.

Reach an agreement with your clients or patients about your fees and billing practices as early as practicable. It also may be wise, although not required, to use printed handouts or signed consent forms to reduce uncertainty about any aspect of financial obligations.

Before meeting with a new patient or client for the first time, Dr. Golding routinely sent out an informational brochure that clearly described his psychological services and his policies about fees and financial arrangements. In this brochure, he attempted to anticipate consumers' questions and clarify potential uncertainties or misunderstandings about the business aspects of his practice well before they could become problematic.

Dr. Golding had learned from experience that avoidance of discussing money matters—whether his own or that of his patients—could easily lead to erroneous assumptions that ultimately could result in lagging payments, a large debt owed, significant disappointment, and even disruptions in treatment at a future point in time. Indeed, he believed that it was best for the clinical relationship if business matters were cleared up at the outset. He would commonly review the basics of his fee structure over the telephone, in the initial contact. If Dr. Golding were to accept the caller as a patient, then he would mail out a brochure some time before the first appointment that covered the following:

- the fee structure for each psychological service (e.g., clinical services, varying lengths of sessions, telephone contacts, assessment, consultation);
- a statement requiring that fees and copayments be paid when the service is rendered, unless other provisions are made;
- a statement about the use of credit cards as a payment option;
- a description of his policy of sending out monthly itemized statements;
- a review of managed health care issues and obligations, and a list of the panels in which he participated;
- a statement about telephone and e-mail availability and fees for these services;
- his policy regarding missed appointments, canceling of appointments, and the time frame required to avoid being charged;
- a description of the range of fees for providing written reports and consultations to third parties; and
- a description of the range of fees for providing forensic services, court appearances, and the like.

When a patient arrived for his or her initial session, Dr. Golding would commonly review the above information in the office and explore any questions or misunderstandings that the patient might have. In many cases, some of the information, such as adjustments in fee or changes in the payment schedule, would already have been discussed on the phone. At other times, it was necessary to devote office time to negotiating these matters to reach an agreement that was acceptable to both parties. As a result of this policy of thorough informed consent about fees and financial arrangements, Dr. Golding rarely encountered a client who was surprised or dissatisfied with the business aspects of his practice.

1. Does this standard require that you inform patients about your fee structure in writing in advance of your first meeting?
2. Are you required to accommodate clients and patients with meager financial resources by providing a lower fee for your services?
3. What do you risk—ethically, clinically, legally, and professionally—by failing to inform clients and patients of your fee structure early on?
4. What is the benefit of having your fee and billing information printed, either as independent handouts, in the body of your authorization form for treatment (if you use one), in a brochure, or in some other form, instead of simply telling your patient of your rates and payment policies?

6.04 (b)

Psychologists' fee practices are consistent with law.

Comply with the terms of any contract you have signed or any policy or rule applying to fees and copayments relevant to your work setting, such as Medicare, other managed health care arrangements, mental health centers, hospitals, or group or individual practice, or else you could be guilty of insurance fraud, breach of contract, or some other violation.

VIGNETTE

When the state board of psychology received a complaint from a former patient against Dr. Billem for his unorthodox business practices, it discovered that he had been engaging in a number of illegal activities over a considerable period of time. The patient was not so unhappy with the financial arrangements but was very displeased with the type of treatment that Dr. Billem had provided. Feeling disappointed and betrayed by repeated carelessness on Dr. Billem's part, the patient complained to the board not only about his clinical competence but also, in an effort to vent his angry feelings and harm his former therapist in any way he could, about his fraudulent billing practices.

The patient knew that Dr. Billem had routinely billed his health insurance company for psychotherapy sessions that never took place. For example, when he had cancelled late, because of illness, and, on another occasion, failed to show up for an appointment because of car trouble, Dr. Billem had simply indicated on the health claim insurance form that the session had taken place, with the current date and corresponding CPT code number for a psychotherapy session. Evidently he felt entitled to take such measures because he had not received the requisite 24-hr notice of cancellation, according to his well-publicized policy. In this way, Dr. Billem would receive his fee for the missed session and the patient would not have to pay for it. Up to this point, no complaints had materialized, as patients had been spared having to pay for the missed session; those who read the insurance statements closely, however, could clearly see that money had been paid to Dr. Billem for the fictional consultations.

Dr. Billem engaged in additional fraudulent billing by claiming that a telephone consultation with a patient in crisis was really an office visit. Although telephone consultations are not covered by most managed-care policies, they constituted a significant part of Dr. Billem's work. He knew that patients would be less inclined to use this medium if the fee were charged to them instead of to the insurance company; therefore, he simply fabricated a face-to-face office visit for each phone consultation.

The psychology board's investigation also revealed Dr. Billem's practice of claiming that couple sessions or family sessions were really individual consultations whenever these were not reimbursable under managed-care contracts. Again, this necessitated writing inaccurate CPT codes on the billing statements, in clear violation of both the Ethics Code and state law. Finally, Dr. Billem frequently provided misinformation about certain procedures to guarantee payment under a particular managed-care contract. If an intervention such as biofeedback for pain management was not a service reimbursable under the terms of the contract, he simply relabeled it as "psychotherapy" and altered his clinical record accordingly.

Dr. Billem had engaged in systematic fraudulent business practices consisting of the erroneous reporting of diagnostic and procedural codes to increase his income from managed-care companies. Although he may have felt entitled to do so and knew that he was sparing his patients additional expense even when they had the resources to pay, he continuously violated the law, the terms of his contract with the managed-care companies, and many standards of this Ethics Code in the process.

1. Discuss the ethics and morality of Dr. Billem's philosophy about sparing patients needless expense and charging missed sessions and noncovered services to the large conglomerate managed health care companies instead. Is he a modern-day Robin Hood?
2. What kind of informed consent about his business practices, if any, could Dr. Billem have provided at the outset that would have allowed for legal reimbursement for missed sessions? How

would he know if this is consistent with expectancies of the managed-care company on whose panel he served?

3. How risky was Dr. Billem's behavior, and what are the implications for maintaining his license to practice, maintaining his membership in APA, and maintaining his malpractice insurance?

6.04 (c)

Psychologists do not misrepresent their fees.

Describe your fees accurately. Tell it like it is, without vagueness, ambiguity, or avoidance of questions about fees.

VIGNETTE

Dr. Golding, in contrast to Dr. Billem, always described his fee scale for patients orally and provided a printed informed consent document that included several paragraphs about fees. Patients knew approximately what would be required of them financially before beginning their consultations. He generally reviewed his expectations about payment at the first session and discussed any exceptions to his policies with those in financial need.

With students, lower income patients, or people on disability, he frequently lowered his fee when his personal finances could accommodate such a measure. He also made attempts to find other creative but ethical ways of managing the financial aspects of his practice when patients could not afford his regular fee. This might include such departures from his customary procedures as offering extended sessions for the same fee as his regular 50-min sessions, shorter sessions for a commensurably lower fee, less frequent meetings than his usual weekly therapy sessions, or cautiously considered barter for goods (see Standard 6.05). He might also suggest that a patient try supplementing less frequent individual sessions by participating in a lower cost or free group intervention (e.g., 12-step program, men's or women's support group).

Dr. Golding also addressed the use of e-mail, as occasionally this was an effective medium when he, or a patient, was out of town yet wished to maintain contact. He charged a prorated fee for the time he took to read the e-mail and write a response. He made it clear, however, that telephone consultations were generally more fruitful than e-mail exchanges, not only because of the additional vocal cues but also for confidentiality reasons. However, he acknowledged that there were times when phone contact was impractical, or impossible, and e-mail would suffice as a substitute.

He also informed patients at the outset about his policy of an annual fee increase that roughly paralleled the rate of inflation—unless, of course, such an increase would constitute a hardship for the patient. Dr. Golding went well beyond the mandates of this standard in attending to patients' welfare concerning fees and financial matters by carefully providing clear information and discussing any concerns about payment at the time of first contact, regardless of the patient's initiative.

1. Some therapists prefer to discuss fees in their office, face to face, instead of providing information in advance of the first session. Discuss this practice and its advantages and drawbacks.
2. Are you aware of lower fee therapists in your community, often recently licensed, to whom you could refer clients or patients with financial limitations?
3. What criteria would you use in deciding whether to refer a patient to another therapist who charged lower fees, as opposed to reducing the frequency of sessions to better accommodate the patient?

6.04 (d)

If limitations to services can be anticipated because of limitations in financing, this is discussed with the recipient of services as early as is feasible. (See also Standards 10.09, Interruption of Therapy, and 10.10, Terminating Therapy.)

If you must limit your services because of a client's or patient's inability to pay or other financial restrictions (e.g., managed health care, available funding), discuss this and the implications of these restrictions as early as is practical in the treatment. Do not wait until the patient has run out of money.

VIGNETTE

Ima Skaherdy was a 37-year-old woman experiencing paranoid thoughts, anxiety, and irritable bowel syndrome. She sought out Dr. Plannow for relief of her stressful psychological and physiological symptoms, specifically, relaxation training and any other treatment he thought best. The case manager of her managed health care program had preauthorized only five sessions, although there was a possibility that additional sessions could be approved if needed.

Dr. Plannow carefully discussed with Mrs. Skaherdy the problems of attempting to begin treatment of such a complex constellation of symptoms, consisting of an anxiety disorder, paranoid thoughts, and a diagnosed medical disorder, when only five sessions were currently allocated. He attempted to help her prioritize her goals for treatment and to examine the possible relationships, if any, among her presenting complaints. They discussed the overall goals of their sessions and reasonable expectations of what could be accomplished in the time allotted.

Together, they also reviewed the process of collaborating with the case manager, including the necessity of filing outpatient treatment progress reports at regular intervals and the losses in confidentiality entailed by such a practice. Dr. Plannow also informed Mrs. Skaherdy about the process of formally seeking additional sessions and the possibility that none would be forthcoming. They then discussed some alternate possibilities if, in fact, therapy was not funded beyond the initial five sessions.

Dr. Plannow was all too familiar with the constraints of being on a managed-care panel of providers, having often experienced resistance to allocating additional sessions when asked and having to terminate therapy at the end of the authorized number of sessions. He also was well acquainted with the formal process of seeking additional treatment sessions. He knew well the importance of at least making an attempt to formally appeal such a decision, even when the case manager was resistant to any further consideration of extending treatment.

When considering a treatment plan for Ms. Skaherdy, Dr. Plannow took into account the risk of failing to make such an appeal, when the time might come, and the patient's personal needs and changing status in treatment. If it were in the patient's best interest, it certainly was always wise to formally seek additional sessions and appeal a case manager's denial. If a patient felt that the therapist was not sufficiently proactive in seeking additional sessions and was prone to be litigious later on, then it was crucial to communicate to him or her that every reasonable step had been taken in the appeal process.

Dr. Plannow met Mrs. Skaherdy's expectations by discussing the implications of the likelihood that sufficient sessions would not be allocated to meet all of her goals. As therapy progressed, they occasionally referred back to this conversation and reevaluated their objectives, keeping in mind the extent of therapy authorized by the case manager.

1. How informed should you be about a patient's allocated number of sessions at the outset of treatment, to be in compliance with this standard?
2. If Mrs. Skaherdy's primary-care physician referred her to Dr. Plannow for psychological assistance with her irritable bowel syndrome, would more treatment sessions have been allocated from the start?
3. Do you know the steps to take with each managed-care panel in which you participate to challenge a case manager's limitations on therapy?

6.04 (e)

If the recipient of services does not pay for services as agreed, and if psychologists intend to use collection agencies or legal measures to collect the fees, psychologists first inform the person that such measures will be taken and provide that person an opportunity to make prompt payment. (See also Standards 4.05, Disclosures; 6.03, Withholding Records for Nonpayment; and 10.01, Informed Consent to Therapy.)

> If a former patient or client refuses to pay your bill and you are thinking of using a collection agency, attorney, or small-claims court to obtain compensation, make sure that you provide notification in writing well in advance of taking any additional action to collect the debt. Give laggards the benefit of the doubt many times (e.g., formal billings, letters, telephone calls if appropriate) before you start the machinery in motion to involve a third party. You might also consider the long-term benefits of accepting the loss instead of initiating an adversarial process that could drag on and ultimately result in negative publicity for you.

VIGNETTE

Dr. Thunder rarely provided billing or receipt statements to his patients, because he wished to minimize his clerical work. He did not employ a secretary, and he was simply too busy with challenging clinical work to print out statements every month, for every patient; he did so only for patients who requested statements to use for purposes of insurance reimbursement. He made this policy clear at the beginning of treatment, as he did with his policy that patients must pay in full at the time of the session or do so at the last session of each month.

On one occasion, Lester, a patient of Dr. Thunder's for 3 months who generally was conscientious about paying by the end of the month, informed his therapist that he must temporarily stop treatment and was unable to pay this month's balance. He had had a large unexpected expense for automobile repairs and was sending money to support his invalid sister in another state; he wished to stop treatment for several months and begin again when he was more financially solvent. His balance due at that time was $360.

Although surprised at the suddenness of this turn of events, Dr. Thunder understood, with compassion, and accepted Lester's plan, agreeing that the reasonable course of action was to allow payment to be deferred until he could again afford therapy. After 8 weeks went by and there was no communication from Lester, Dr. Thunder became concerned that his patient might simply be attempting to avoid paying his balance altogether. Because he was quite busy with other projects at work and did not wish to take the time to personally contact Lester, Dr. Thunder delegated that task to his attorney, Mr. I. Will Gogettum.

Mr. Gogettum eagerly sent a strongly worded letter with a menacing tone 8 weeks after Lester terminated with Dr. Thunder. This letter threatened civil action in small-claims court if full payment was not made within 3 weeks.

Lester was out of town when the letter arrived, having traveled a great distance to his home state to assist his aging father, who had just had a stroke. After returning and discovering the attorney's letter, he became distressed and felt somewhat betrayed by Dr. Thunder, who had been a good resource to him in the past. He considered himself an honorable man, and he had fully intended to pay his overdue bill in its entirety, but he was currently facing other, more urgent, unexpected expenses in addition to his automobile repair bills. He dutifully telephoned Dr. Thunder, explained the situation, and requested another extension. Dr. Thunder apologized for the letter from the attorney and quickly granted the extension. Unfortunately, however, Lester already had lost faith in his therapist, thinking that he was more concerned about money than providing a service. Lester never returned for treatment.

Such an outcome could have been avoided had Dr. Thunder simply attempted to contact Lester himself, instead of delegating the task to his attorney, and inquired about his welfare and financial circumstances. Consistent with the spirit of this ethical standard, he certainly bore an obligation to at least inform Lester that his policy was to use the services of a collection agency or an attorney if payment were not made in a timely fashion. Thus, he would be providing his patient the opportunity to make a payment or propose a payment plan before engaging the services of a third party for collection. Although he was familiar with the services that attorneys could provide, and relied on them for many tasks, he unfortunately had lost touch with the impact that a severely worded letter of warning could have on a patient. He regretted that he had been too busy to attend to this matter himself, resulting in an irrevocably broken relationship with his former patient.

1. What are the pros and cons of Dr. Thunder's agreeing to continue seeing Lester at a reduced fee, or for no fee, for a short time?
2. Draft a letter that you might write to Lester after 8 weeks, if you had not heard anything from him.
3. What restitution might Dr. Thunder offer Lester as an incentive to begin therapy once again?
4. How would you deal with a deadbeat former patient who threatens to go on a local radio talk show or write a letter to the local newspaper about your "incompetent therapy," in response to your repeated requests for payment?

6.05 BARTER WITH CLIENTS AND PATIENTS

Barter is the acceptance of goods, services, or other nonmonetary remuneration from clients/patients in return for psychological services. Psychologists may barter only if (1) it is not clinically contraindicated, and (2) the resulting arrangement is not exploitative. (See also Standards 3.05, Multiple Relationships, and 6.04, Fees and Financial Arrangements.)

Barter is the exchange of goods, services, special privileges, or any sort of payment in place of money, in return for your services. You may engage in barter if the arrangement with your client or patient satisfies the following two requirements:

1. It is not clinically contraindicated, and by engaging in barter you will not harm your patient or negatively affect the treatment (e.g., allowing your patient to provide child care for your 4-year-old child).
2. The arrangement is not exploitative of your patient (e.g., your patient is a house painter, with a rate so much lower than yours that he must work 10 hours to pay for each therapy session, resulting in a huge accumulation of hours owed, or your patient is a stockbroker, willing to engage in insider trading to pay his bill, putting himself, and you, at risk by breaking the law).

VIGNETTE

Dr. Rex Changer practiced in a small midwestern town and was accustomed to routinely engaging in bartering as a means for his lower income clients to pay for his psychological services. He was scrupulous about reporting bartered services and products as income, at a fair market value. At the end of each year, he filed his taxes using IRS Form 1099-B. He knew that bartering was the only way for poorer patients, particularly farming families who were frequently in financial distress, to obtain his services. He accepted chickens, sides of beef, cords of wood, and even, in some cases, machinery, in exchange for psychotherapy.

On the rare occasions when he bartered for a patient's services, such as gardening, he agreed to a reduction in the fee schedule. He knew that failure to reduce his fee would raise the likelihood that the gardener, who normally charged $18 per hour, would accumulate a huge debt over time while attempting to repay Dr. Changer at his customary rate of $95 per hour. This would effectively result in the gardener becoming an indentured servant of sorts long after the therapy ended.

One day, a young man with bipolar affective disorder contacted Dr. Changer for treatment. He was a roofer by trade but had little money and wished to exchange his roofing skills for treatment. Dr. Changer had needed a new tile roof for months and thought this would be opportune and beneficial for both doctor and patient. They struck an agreement, and within 1 week the treatment sessions began, along with the new construction on the roof.

Things proceeded well for several weeks, until an unfortunate event happened that might have been anticipated had Dr. Changer exercised more caution. While eagerly working on the roof one weekend, while Dr. Changer and his family were away, the patient entered a floridly manic state. He worked very rapidly, and far into the night, by moonlight, taking risks with his own safety. While climbing around the chimney, he slipped on a loose tile and slid down the steep roof, plunging into the doctor's flower garden far below, resulting in a broken shoulder and collarbone, and a severe back injury. The neighbors called an ambulance, and fortunately the roofer was rushed to the hospital in time.

This incident had strong negative repercussions for the therapist–patient relationship, resulting in much conflict and disappointment on both sides. The patient, who had been hospitalized for 1 week and was now in a cast, had negative feelings about Dr. Changer and his clinical judgment, and he decided to end treatment. He held Dr. Changer responsible for allowing him to put himself into a dangerous situation as a direct result of the bartering arrangement, particularly when he was in a manic state. Dr. Changer agreed that he had possibly used poor judgment in allowing someone diagnosed with bipolar disorder to work on his roof in exchange for treatment. Parenthetically, but also of importance, Dr. Changer noticed that the roofing work that his patient had accomplished before falling off the roof was of poor quality; he eventually had to hire another roofer to undo the shoddy workmanship before the job was completed.

The roofer was unaware of the ethical responsibilities of Dr. Changer, and because he was unsophisticated in legal matters no formal ethics complaint or civil suit resulted from this tragedy. However, the neighbors and some residents of this small town developed negative feelings about Dr. Changer as news of the incident spread, and they were reluctant to seek his services thereafter.

1. What are the relative risks of bartering for goods as opposed to bartering for services?
2. In engaging his patient in bartering for services, whereby the roofer came to his house and occasionally interacted with his family, did Dr. Changer alter the nature of their clinical work? If so, how?
3. If this patient were litigious, or had a litigious friend who advised him, what steps might he take against Dr. Changer?
4. Are you aware of state and national associations for barter and cooperatives that encourage health care providers to par-

ticipate, using a point system (debits and credits)? What are the implications of such an arrangement for confidentiality and informed consent?

5. Do you know how to obtain a copy of IRS Form 1099-B for reporting barter transactions when filing your income tax return?

6.06 ACCURACY IN REPORTS TO PAYORS AND FUNDING SOURCES

In their reports to payors for services or sources of research funding, psychologists take reasonable steps to ensure the accurate reporting of the nature of the service provided or research conducted, the fees, charges, or payments, and where applicable, the identity of the provider, the findings, and the diagnosis. (See also Standards 4.01, Maintaining Confidentiality; 4.04, Minimizing Intrusions on Privacy; and 4.05, Disclosures.)

Do not distort, exaggerate, or misrepresent information you provide to third-party payors and funding sources. Describe honestly and accurately the nature of your research or services provided, your fees, expenses, overhead, findings, diagnoses, *Diagnostic and Statistical Manual of Mental Disorders* (American Psychiatric Association, 2000) codes, interventions, CPT codes, the identity of the provider, and other information as requested.

VIGNETTE 1

Over the years that she had been participating in managed health care panels, Dr. Truesdale had observed a trend toward restricting available services to patients. This included allocating a lower number of sessions per year; a tendency to restrict sessions for Axis II disorders; and reduced or no reimbursement for certain services, such as marital and family therapy and hypnosis. She also noticed more invasiveness in the required treatment progress reports and negative responses on the part of case managers. In particular, there was a tendency by some case managers to suggest interventions or approaches that would supposedly expedite treatment, despite the lack of research data to support such approaches. However, Dr. Truesdale considered the welfare of her patients to be of paramount importance, and she resisted pressure from case managers to promote supposedly expeditious forms of treatment that were lacking in validation.

She was conscientious about her billing practices and was quick to adopt the most current technological advances in this regard; she had been using electronic billing to communicate with insurance companies almost since its inception, and she rarely made errors in her statements. On those occasions when a session was missed without formal cancellation, or when she conducted a telephone session, she always identified them as such in her billing statements, even though she knew that no reimbursement would be forthcoming from the managed-care company.

There were times, however, when Dr. Truesdale struggled with the temptation to file inaccurate reports to benefit her patients, such as exaggerating the suicide potential or dangerousness of an individual. She also wondered about reporting only a partial diagnosis, such as panic disorder or alcohol dependence, and omitting diagnoses for personality disorders, for which there would be less likelihood of allocating a sufficient number of sessions. Furthermore, she considered omitting the diagnosis of chronic pain (for which psychotherapy or hypnosis would not have been reimbursed under psychological services but would have been covered as a medical service if performed by a physician or psychiatrist). She weighed the benefits and risks of substituting a diagnosis that reflected an adjustment or mood disorder instead of chronic pain. In this way, her patient would have been able to afford treatment for chronic pain.

Ultimately, however, Dr. Truesdale decided to accurately report all diagnoses and treatment codes and to press for additional sessions, when needed, by using the formal procedures available to panel providers. She regularly discussed with case managers the ethical and clinical issues concerning disallowing treatment for certain clients and, when appropriate, would put her thoughts in writing and encourage patients to do likewise by way of formally appealing a decision.

Although carrying out these activities was time consuming, Dr. Truesdale considered it essential to adhere to a policy of accuracy and honesty in disclosures in conformance with this standard, thereby maintaining her professional integrity. She also thought that it was important to stir up interest among colleagues about challenging and changing a system that seemed to fail so frequently at meeting patient needs.

VIGNETTE 2

Far across town, on the other side of the tracks, was Dr. I. Pocket, a psychologist whose ethical competence and concern appeared to be far below that of Dr. Truesdale's. Dr. Pocket was in the process of developing an outreach program for preteens who belonged to a socioeconomic group at high risk for drug abuse. He was the director of a small nonprofit organization (IRS Category 501C3) and would routinely create grants to be submitted to large corporations and government agencies, including the National Institute of Mental Health. Over the years, his efforts resulted in funds for many projects, and he generally was regarded as quite successful at grantsmanship. What many did not know, however, was that he had a tendency to take occasional risks by engaging in fraudulent practices involving these grants. Because he was well aware that funding sources are more likely to award money requested when matching funds are also available, Dr. Pocket indicated on grant applications that such was the case, even though it was untrue. By so doing, he hoped to increase the odds that his project would be funded.

More egregiously, he attempted to acquire large sums of money for his personal use by covertly submitting the identical grant proposal for the same project to various corporations simultaneously, without indicating the existence of other possible funding sources on the proposals. Such double dipping into the resource pool required that he engage in elaborately fraudulent accounting procedures in case he had to respond to grant contract compliance requests at the conclusion of the funded project. By doing so, he was putting himself and the organization at grave risk.

Such unethical and illegal activities carry severe penalties, and with increased vigilance among funding sources to such abuses, the odds of getting caught are greater. However, Dr. Pocket enjoyed the risk and the remuneration that accompanied it. His grossly fraudulent practices in grantsmanship were discovered, and they resulted in civil and criminal penalties that significantly affected him and his institution. He was ultimately expelled from APA, sanctioned by the National Institute of Mental Health, and never again participated in grant writing as a psychologist.

1. What steps would you take if the clinic in which you worked endorsed a policy of routinely downgrading patients with Axis II disorders, to ensure remuneration by managed health care?
2. What are the ethical and legal liabilities of indicating, for the record, that you are the provider of services, when in fact you only provided supervision of an unlicensed trainee?
3. In treating a patient you suspect to have borderline personality disorder who has consulted you for her migraine headaches, are you obliged to note her borderline diagnosis on the managed health care form?
4. In addition to "double dipping," what are other examples of deliberately distorting or misrepresenting information to funding sources that should be avoided by those writing grant proposals?

6.07 REFERRALS AND FEES

When psychologists pay, receive payment from, or divide fees with another professional, other than in an employer–employee relationship, the payment to each is based on the services provided (clinical, consultative, administrative, or other) and is not based on the referral itself. (See also Standard 3.09, Cooperation With Other Professionals.)

> Never pay a professional (e.g., a psychologist, psychiatrist, other health care professional), or accept payment from them, for referring a client or patient for psychological services. You may pay another psychologist, however, for valid services rendered (e.g., consultation) or if you are in the role of employer or owner of a group practice or have received some valid service or product from another professional.

VIGNETTE

Dr. Bribermann had a multifaceted practice providing consultation to various electronic firms in the Boston suburbs and providing clinical services at his downtown office. He was eager to expand his clinical practice and thought that this goal would be well served by reimbursing each individual in his clients' firms who referred therapy patients to him from outside sources (i.e., friends or associates who were not connected to the firm). His practice was to send $100 to anyone who successfully referred patients to him for treatment; this included individuals such as the CEO, chief financial officer, managers, or anyone else in the firm who had consulted him and was aware of his clinical expertise and areas of interest.

Most of the referrals made in this fashion were limited to affluent individuals able to pay for psychological services directly, without relying on managed health care. Dr. Bribermann thought that his "rebate" policy was a small price to pay up front for rapidly generating a referral base that would allow him to avoid completely the managed health care system with all its limitations and reduced fees.

He was aware of the ethical rule that flatly prohibited the practice of providing payment to professionals for making referrals for his professional services, but because the referring individuals in this case were not health care professionals, he did not view this as a problem. This had been an ethical proscription for many years within APA, but Dr. Bribermann never knew about the rule or considered its implications for protecting consumers from potential harm. He also was unaware of the Massachusetts state law that similarly prohibited either giving or receiving commissions or rebates in exchange for referrals for psychological services.

Selecting a therapist may be a difficult task at best for most individuals, fraught with pitfalls of misinformation, persuasive advertising, and biased or bad advice. The process is made even more complex by therapists who covertly reinforce referral sources through monetary compensation to encourage a patient to seek treatment with a certain individual, regardless of that individual's competence. By asking those who consulted him at the electronics firms to refer patients and then offering them a kickback, Dr. Bribermann was engaging in a practice that encouraged consumers to seek his services without informing them of the incentive system that strongly encouraged the referral in the first place. It is likely that there were psychotherapists in the area who might have been better choices for certain consumers; they may have been more competent to treat certain disorders than Dr. Bribermann. However, potential consumers were unlikely to seek out other therapists because they were, in effect, being referred to the highest (and only) bidder while remaining unaware that any bidding was going on at all. This lack of informed consent for the referral process placed some patients at a distinct disadvantage. These patients required the services of a psychologist who was more competent than Dr. Bribermann but were told, instead, that Dr. Bribermann was skilled at treating all psychological disorders.

Dr. Bribermann's referral incentive resulted in substandard therapy for patients who might actually be harmed by his interventions or simply waste their money on fees for useless consultations. This serious breach of ethics was remedied one day when a potential patient discovered that a payment had been made for his referral from an offhand remark made by his friend who had given him Dr. Bribermann's name. That potential patient telephoned the Massachusetts Psychological Association to inquire about this practice and was informed of its unethicality. From this inquiry, a formal complaint was lodged against Dr. Bribermann, triggering an investigation and ultimately resulting in a sanction from the committee and the requirement that he end this harmful business practice.

1. What ethical means could Dr. Bribermann have used to expand his clinical practice?
2. Does this standard prohibit paying another psychologist by the hour for subletting her office to see your patients, some of whom she has referred to you?
3. Why would the Massachusetts Board of Psychology take a particularly strong interest in this case, as opposed to some other cases based on standards that did not involve legal infractions?

7

EDUCATION AND TRAINING

7.01 DESIGN OF EDUCATION AND TRAINING PROGRAMS

Psychologists responsible for education and training programs take reasonable steps to ensure that the programs are designed to provide the appropriate knowledge and proper experiences, and to meet the requirements for licensure, certification, or other goals for which claims are made by the program. (See also Standard 5.03, Descriptions of Workshops and Non-Degree-Granting Educational Programs.)

If you are responsible for teaching or training programs, plan your curriculum competently so that it will afford the right kind of knowledge, information, opportunities, and experiences for your students and trainees, given the nature and goals of the program. Provide experiences that meet the requirements for licensure, certification, or other goals claimed by your program. In essence, deliver what you promise.

VIGNETTE

Dr. Anne Lighten was the director of training in the psychology department of a small university, graduating about eight doctoral students per

177

year. Part of her responsibilities involved ensuring that students obtained the proper amount of practicum supervision while matriculating in the program and seeing that they had access to suitable internships. She routinely informed students in their last year about the various internship opportunities within the state and facilitated students' applications to them.

One year, an unfortunate situation was encountered by a recent PhD who was registered with the state as a psychological assistant under the supervision of a licensed psychologist within a large group practice. This particular supervisor, Dr. Cagey, actually had two psychological assistants in addition to his busy practice and administrative duties. He had little time to devote to proper supervision and frequently skimped on the requirement that psychologists spend at least 1 hr per week in face-to-face meetings with the supervisee. Sometimes he would meet his trainees over lunch at a busy restaurant, even though the distractions were many and the possibility for confidentiality breaches was great.

Dr. Lighten learned of these substandard supervisory practices from the psychological assistant. She judged that Dr. Cagey was effectively putting consumers at risk while providing a poor learning environment for trainees. This not only constituted poor mentoring but also was in violation of the state law mandating a minimum number of supervisory hours as a prerequisite for the state licensing examination.

Although the internship setting of Dr. Cagey's practice was not formally affiliated with the training program at her university, there had been sufficient informal connections for a long time to warrant concern by Dr. Lighten under this ethical standard. For over 12 years, she had been encouraging graduates to apply for Dr. Cagey's psychological assistantships and felt that he played an important role in the postgraduate training of her students. Now, as his practice grew, he seemingly was providing incompetent supervision and apparently could no longer make a significant contribution to the mentoring of the postdoctoral students.

Dr. Lighten felt she had no choice but to raise her concerns with Dr. Cagey, but he simply turned a deaf ear and refused to alter his supervision practices. He justified his conduct by informing her that by remaining under his supervision the interns were getting exposure to a broad and diverse patient population and were seeing how the real world operates in a busy private practice. Unmoved by his sophistry, and with reluctance, Dr. Lighten took the major step of deleting Cagey's name from her list of internship sites. Out of concern for his substandard supervisory practices and the ultimate impact on supervisees from other academic programs, she weighed the merits of either contacting the state psychological association's program for impaired psychologists, which did outreach work, or the state board of psychology regarding his formal status as a supervisor. In light of the potential for serious harm to patients who were consulting unlicensed and inadequately supervised therapists and because of Dr. Cagey's blatant resistance to her feedback, Dr. Lighten felt duty bound to notify the state licensing board. She also contacted the American Psychological Association Ethics Office to initiate a formal complaint.

1. In confronting Dr. Cagey, was Dr. Lighten overreacting to the experiences reported to her by the psychological assistants?
2. What harm would have been done—to the training program, to patients, to supervisees, and others—if Dr. Lighten simply overlooked the unethical and illegal conduct of Dr. Cagey?
3. What other reasons might prompt you to remove a supervisory site from your list?
4. If you were a professor or an administrator in a university or professional school that was not regionally accredited, what would you be obliged to inform prospective students about in advance?

7.02 DESCRIPTIONS OF EDUCATION AND TRAINING PROGRAMS

Psychologists responsible for education and training programs take reasonable step to ensure that there is a current and accurate description of the program content (including participation in required course- or program-related counseling, psychotherapy, experiential groups, consulting projects, or community service), training goals and objectives, stipends and benefits, and requirements that must be met for satisfactory completion of the program. This information must be made readily available to all interested parties.

If you are responsible for education or training programs, be sure to have an accurate and up-to-date description in the catalog or brochure of the following that is readily available to anyone who is interested:

- program content (including required courses, disclosure about mandatory counseling or psychotherapy, experiential groups, consulting projects, or community service),
- training goals and objectives (e.g., the purpose and focus of the program),
- stipends and benefits (e.g., available financial assistance), and
- requirements that must be completed.

VIGNETTE

Dr. Priscilla Punctillio chaired the psychology department at a large university. As a part of her responsibilities, she and several colleagues reviewed and edited all brochures, departmental publicity, and the annual course catalog that was made available to all prospective students. She was dedicated to promulgating a philosophy of the department that fully and accurately reflected its faculty, mission, and goals. She made a thorough attempt each year to modify the printed materials to accurately reflect the content areas of the department as well as its goals and objectives.

She was fastidious about ensuring that prerequisite academic experience and all requirements for the master's and doctoral programs were described comprehensively, with a clear explanation of the required core subjects within the program. For clinical and counseling psychology programs, the course catalog listed the faculty members, their specialty areas, and internship requirements. She provided careful guidance on the content of the descriptions to optimize students' understanding about a course offering prior to enrolling in it. Also, she and her colleagues made consistent attempts to review and update this information on an as-needed basis.

The requirement to participate in an experiential therapy group, with a licensed psychologist from the community, was clearly explained, with the sound rationale. The catalog also described the philosophy of the graduate school that encouraged and supported individual psychotherapy as an optional part of the curriculum. Students could select therapists from among a long list of community mental health professionals, none of whom taught or supervised in the university's psychology department.

Over all, Dr. Punctillio consistently upheld a high standard of providing clear, accurate, and comprehensive descriptions of the psychology department's mission, goals, and objectives. She and her assistants devoted much energy to this critical project each year by both personally reviewing the material submitted by professors and delegating and coordinating the efforts of other faculty members involved.

1. In your opinion, what might have been some events or complaints that would have contributed to the evolution of this standard?
2. Does such a requirement in an academic setting stifle creativity on the part of faculty members who are teaching courses or providing supervision?
3. Draft a description of some aspect of your supervisory or training responsibilities that could meet the requirements of this standard.

7.03 ACCURACY IN TEACHING

(a) Psychologists take reasonable steps to ensure that course syllabi are accurate regarding the subject matter to be covered, bases for evaluating progress,

and the nature of course experiences. This standard does not preclude an instructor from modifying course content or requirements when the instructor considers it pedagogically necessary or desirable, so long as students are made aware of these modifications in a manner that enables them to fulfill course requirements. (See also Standard 5.01, Avoidance of False or Deceptive Statements.)

Try to be as accurate as you can in creating your course syllabi and describing the courses that you teach. Inform students at the outset about the following:

- subject matter (primary content and focus of your course),
- bases for evaluating progress (system of grading or assessing learning), and
- nature of course experiences to be anticipated (lecture, discussion group, papers, examinations, experiential projects, etc.).

This standard does not prohibit you from creatively modifying course content or requirements, as long as students are informed of these changes, allowing them to meet your expectations.

VIGNETTE

Dr. Lernit taught the chemical dependency course at a nearby campus of her state's school of professional psychology and decided to include an experiential aspect she had never required before. She planned to require each student to attend three different Alcoholics Anonymous meetings, visit three unfamiliar bars, and walk or drive in the daytime through a part of town that was notorious for drug dealing. Unfortunately, she neglected to mention this new requirement in the school catalog or to indicate on the course syllabus that students would also be required to write about these experiences in a 10-page paper.

When Dr. Lernit gave this assignment, 2 months into the course, many students voiced their objections. Several female students were quite fearful of driving through the drug dealers' part of town because the area also had a reputation for violent crimes and carjackings. They objected on the grounds that it was excessively risky, stating that they never would have enrolled in this course had they known about the requirement at the outset. Several other students objected to the time it would take to visit the bars and also attend 12-step meetings, as this would involve considerable driving, in some cases to parts of town that were unfamiliar.

Many students objected to the assignment of processing their experiences in a 10-page paper. Although the paper was a reasonable component of the whole educational experience, the fact that it was added on instead of announced at the beginning of the course was seen as a hardship. Time was short for many students because they worked part time, and they struggled to find the extra hours to fit in this requirement, which had been given without advance notice. Another student had strong religious convictions prohibiting the use of alcohol and much apprehension about visiting bars.

Dr. Lernit began to see the problems she had created by springing this experiential assignment on the class without first having provided some description in the school catalog. She listened to her students' objections and, after much deliberation, and much to her students' relief, reluctantly decided to drop the requirement. Dr. Lernit was surprised to learn that there were a number of students who appreciated the possible benefits of such an assignment and decided to fulfill it anyway, for their own gratification.

After making appropriate modifications that reduced any substantial risk to her students, Dr. Lernit included the requirement in the next semester's course and made sure that she put a description of it in the school catalog. She had learned from experience that her ideas about enriching the course experience were fundamentally sound and only required some fine tuning and advance notice to become a solid part of the curriculum.

1. What steps could Dr. Lernit have taken in the planning stages that would have resulted in a more realistic and safe field experience assignment?
2. How could she have renegotiated the assignment with students instead of eliminating it altogether?
3. What experiences might you suggest for the student with strong religious convictions about alcohol use, to help with his or her overall training as a psychologist?

7.03 (b)

When engaged in teaching or training, psychologists present psychological information accurately. (See also Standard 2.03, Maintaining Competence.)

When teaching, training, or supervising, be sure to present psychological information accurately. Do not exaggerate, minimize, spin, or otherwise distort or bend the facts to suit your opinion or bias.

VIGNETTE

Dr. Leeda Strey, an assistant professor, who was well known for her preference for applying a narrow and oversimplified version of cognitive–behavioral principles to virtually every psychotherapy patient, was teaching a survey course to beginning graduate students that exposed them to various theories of psychotherapy. Over the course of the 12-week quarter, she covered nine different theoretical approaches to individual psychotherapy. However, she devoted well over half her lectures to the cognitive–behavioral approach because, as she put it, "This is really the only theory of therapy that students need to know to be competent, and it is mainstream in this country today."

The rest of the theories of psychotherapy were compressed into the remaining few weeks of the quarter. In teaching object-relations theory, interpersonal psychotherapy, ego psychology, psychoanalysis, Adlerian therapy, and other theories, Dr. Strey's style changed considerably. She tended to sarcastically belittle the exponents of these theories and, more important, would present only a cursory and often one-sided and inaccurate exposition of the basic theories and strategies. Her examples of treatment and outcomes were not very detailed, and she presented inadequate data to support her claims.

However, when teaching the cognitive–behavioral model, Dr. Strey would regale her students with fascinating case histories drawn from her clinical work and did not hesitate to point out how her own expertise and creativity within this theoretical framework were critical factors in these successful outcomes. Dr. Strey, unfortunately, did not use scientific principles in assessing her own clinical work and often drew unwarranted conclusions from her patient outcomes. As an example, she presented the history of a patient she was treating who was in remission from breast cancer for 11 months after comprehensive treatment at a local hospital. The woman had consulted Dr. Strey for depression 5 months before and had indeed experienced substantial elevation in her mood that resulted in more active engagement with her family and friends. Dr. Strey correctly inferred that the elevation in her mood was due chiefly to the work in cognitive–behavioral therapy; however, she also stated that the patient's cancer remission was likely a reflection of cognitive–behavioral therapy as well, rather than her medical treatment.

Using such a case as an example of the profound efficacy of cognitive–behavioral psychotherapy in her graduate seminar exemplified this professor's bias and poor judgment as well as her blatant disregard for the empirical basis on which psychologists must rely in their work. It was also potentially dangerous to imply in a training setting that a psychotherapeutic intervention alone was preferable to medical intervention for an illness as significant as breast cancer. Some naïve students were indeed impressed by Dr. Strey's lectures, whereas others were disappointed and frustrated that they had selected a survey course and were receiving what essentially amounted to a crash course on one theoretical school of thought.

1. How could Dr. Strey have changed her teaching style while holding her convictions about cognitive–behavioral psychotherapy?

2. Does this standard require that you be comprehensive and objective in your teaching?
3. What steps might you take, as a student in Dr. Strey's class, to help alter the classroom experience?

7.04 STUDENT DISCLOSURE OF PERSONAL INFORMATION

Psychologists do not require students or supervisees to disclose personal information in course- or program-related activities, either orally or in writing, regarding sexual history, history of abuse and neglect, psychological treatment, and relationships with parents, peers, and spouses or significant others except if (1) the program or training facility has clearly identified this requirement in its admissions and program materials or (2) the information is necessary to evaluate or obtain assistance for students whose personal problems could reasonably be judged to be preventing them from performing their training- or professionally related activities in a competent manner or posing a threat to the students or others.

Protect the privacy of your students and supervisees. Never inquire about, or expect them to reveal, orally or in writing, personal information about the following topics as a part of a course or training program:

- their sexual experiences, preferences, gender identity, and so on;
- their history of childhood abuse or neglect or any adult abusive experiences;
- their own psychological treatment, past or present;
- their family of origin—details of relationships with their parents, siblings, peers, and so on;
- their current personal or love relationships—friends, partners, significant others, spouse, marital status, and so on.

In two words: Don't snoop. However, you may inquire about such personal information, and other information as well, under the following circumstances:

- if the training program or facility has frankly described this requirement in its admissions and program materials in advance;
- if the information is required to evaluate or help troubled students or those with personal problems who are struggling with their training or professionally related activities, and seem to be impaired and unable to perform their duties; and
- if the student or trainee poses a threat to fellow students or others.

VIGNETTE

Dr. Holter had recently joined the clinical faculty of a university, and his major responsibility was to provide supervision for postdoctoral trainees. His first supervisee at his new position was Dr. Gale Grey, an older student in her mid-40s, who had changed careers several years before, after many years of being a parole officer. She had earned her doctoral degree from a small school of professional psychology with a mediocre reputation that was not regionally accredited.

At the first meeting with Gale, Dr. Holter discussed the experience of supervision, including such things as the frequency and duration of meetings, the type of clientele she would most likely encounter, audio- and video-taping, record keeping, confidentiality within the clinic, and the process of good client-informed consent for treatment. In the early weeks of supervision Gale appeared to be a model supervisee, highly motivated and clinically competent, performing capably with her clinic patients and responding well to supervision. As time passed, however, she appeared to become withdrawn and somewhat sullen. Dr. Holter noticed that she had fewer new patients than most of the other postdoctoral trainees; on inquiring about this, he discovered from the appointment secretary that Gale had requested, covertly, that she not be assigned any new patients, as she was having some personal problems. He also discovered that she had failed to show up for one appointment with a patient yet had never informed him of this lapse; the secretary had covered for her.

Dr. Holter confronted Gale with her behavior, and she tearfully acknowledged that she had made some poor decisions recently. She volunteered that her mood had been quite low lately, due primarily to the fact that her lesbian partner had suddenly moved out of her apartment, breaking off an 8-year relationship. She felt bereft and simply could not concentrate on her work at the clinic.

Dr. Holter supported Gale at this critical time while attempting to remain in his role as her clinical supervisor. He had known about her lesbian lifestyle, as she was quite open about this, but he had never sought any information other than that which might bear on her work as a clinician. Gale wept about her painful loss and began to reveal a great deal more about her private life than she had ever discussed with him before. Dr. Holter listened for awhile and then gently interrupted her, suggesting that she might wish to consult a therapist who was available at a low fee to the postdoctoral students. She could then remain the supervisee of Dr. Holter while she was in therapy, if she wanted, and possibly could continue her work at the clinic, if she were able.

Gale valued the gentle but firm approach of her supervisor, who was able to validate her suffering and yet maintain their professional boundaries at the same time. Indeed, on reflection, she decided that she did prefer to retain the supervisor–supervisee relationship, if possible, and begin therapy as had been suggested.

For his part, Dr. Holter knew that he could have listened to Gale for an hour or two but that this would likely have irrevocably changed their professional roles. Although he considered supervision to be therapeutic, he knew that it could never be a substitute for therapy. Exercising his clinical judgment that Gale would very likely be able to return to work quite soon, even while continuing in her own psychotherapy, he encouraged her to seek treatment with someone else while he remained her supervisor.

1. Should Dr. Holter monitor Gale's compliance with his recommendation to follow up with a referral to a psychotherapist?
2. Should Dr. Holter simply have allowed himself to shift roles, into becoming Gale's therapist (as they had a good relationship), or attempted to play both roles —therapist and supervisor—simultaneously?
3. What ethical and legal liability would Dr. Holter incur if he allowed Gale to see patients while, by her own admission, she was impaired?

7.05 MANDATORY INDIVIDUAL OR GROUP THERAPY

(a) When individual or group therapy is a program or course requirement, psychologists responsible for that program allow students in undergraduate and graduate programs the option of selecting such therapy from practitioners unaffiliated with the program. (See also standard 7.02, Descriptions of Education and Training Programs.)

When your students are required to have individual or group therapy as a part of their education or training, they must always have the choice of a therapist who is not on the faculty or associated with the program in any way. This avoids the complications of a dual role in which the same professor could be teaching a student and simultaneously serving as his or her psychotherapist.

VIGNETTE

For many years, Dr. Joe Friday had chaired a psychology department in a large midwestern university. He and most of his colleagues were well acquainted with some of the personal problems that some psychology graduate students tend to experience and knew well the research reporting significant rates of alcoholism, child abuse, and childhood sexual abuse in therapists' families of origin. To optimize the overall graduate level training for incoming students, some of whom undoubtedly emerged from abusive or impaired families, Dr. Friday implemented a policy of compulsory individual psychotherapy as an integral part of graduate training.

Each student was required to have an experience in individual psychotherapy provided by a psychiatrist, psychologist, or clinical social worker who was not a faculty member of the university. A list of therapists and a brief description of their theoretical orientation was provided students at the beginning of the year. Some of the therapists taught in the university's school of social work, and some were medical school faculty, but, consistent with this ethical standard, no therapist was from the psychology graduate program. If a student wished to consult a therapist who taught in the program, he or she would have that option as well, as long as a dual-role relationship did not exist.

This policy was well explained in the psychology graduate school catalog, so that there was no ambiguity about its compulsory nature or its implementation. Students who already had had individual therapy were still required to have some therapeutic experience during their period of matriculation. They would have the choice of selecting a therapist with a theoretical orientation different from that of their former therapist, or they might opt for group therapy or some other intervention to fulfill the requirement. Each student felt well prepared in advance about this required experience as an adjunct to the didactic portion of graduate school. There were no surprises; the facts were clear. Although some felt that it was unnecessary for them, or felt some anxiety at the prospect of beginning treatment, they all knew that it was part and parcel of the doctoral program and accepted it as such.

1. How would Dr. Friday decide on a satisfactory way of assessing the adequacy of the students' treatment? Length of therapy? Students' self-report? Therapist's report, with consent?
2. How would you induce therapists in the community to participate in providing psychotherapy at a reduced fee for students? Is it an ethical mandate? Aspiration?
3. How might you deal with the student who enters the program claiming to be in treatment with a Christian counselor or a master's-level therapist who is not licensed by the state?

7.05 (b)

Faculty who are or are likely to be responsible for evaluating students' academic performance do not themselves provide that therapy. (See also Standard 3.05, Multiple Relationships.)

> If you teach a course, serve on students' dissertation committees, or otherwise evaluate or mentor them, do not also offer individual or group therapy to those same individuals.

VIGNETTE

Dr. Janus taught several graduate-level courses in a medium-sized university located in a rural area. Over the past year, the psychology faculty had reached a consensus about requiring every graduate student to have an individual or group psychotherapy experience as a part of their training. Therapists were to be selected from the community or from other departments within the university, such as the Departments of Clinical Social Work, Psychiatry, and Marriage and Family Therapy.

This policy was well known to Dr. Janus when he was approached by Andy, a 1st-year doctoral student, after a lecture on anxiety disorders. Andy confided in Dr. Janus that he had suffered from panic attacks for approximately 1 year, and he felt that Dr. Janus could serve as a resource. He was not necessarily seeking therapy but was hoping that some reading might assist him in coping with his disorder. Dr. Janus agreed to speak with him at some length in his consulting office and suggested that he purchase two self-help books on the subject; these were standards in the field and ones that he had often recommended to patients in his clinical practice.

The following week Andy again sought out Dr. Janus, having had two more panic attacks, and asked for another consultation in his office. Dr. Janus saw no harm in this and proceeded to give more instruction in how to weather panic attacks: what to do, and what to avoid. Andy was grateful and felt a growing dependence on his psychology professor. The next day, following yet another panic attack, Andy telephoned Dr. Janus and asked if he could begin seeing him for short-term therapy; after all, it was a requirement of the department, there was a need, and Dr. Janus was the expert. Furthermore, every other therapist at the university had a waiting list, and the therapists in the community were too expensive.

With some misgivings, Dr. Janus agreed to be Andy's therapist, as long as they both agreed that the consulting office was separate and distinct from the classroom. He justified his decision on the basis of Andy's need, the fact that they already had developed a friendly and professional relationship, and that there apparently were no other therapists available. Treatment proceeded on a weekly basis for 1 month, with Andy's anxiety and depression appearing to subside somewhat. When it came time for the final examination in the class, however, Andy was unable to concentrate well enough and, unbeknownst to Dr. Janus, had begun to rely on alcohol and marijuana for relief. He did poorly on the examination and Dr. Janus reluctantly had given him a low grade for the semester.

Andy was disappointed in his own performance but even more disappointed that Dr. Janus could have given him such a low grade, in light of their supposedly "good" therapeutic relationship. He confronted Dr. Janus about his consternation and feelings of betrayal; it raised an obstacle in treatment, he felt, that would be impossible to circumvent.

Dr. Janus could appreciate Andy's disappointment, and he attempted to explain how the roles of professor and therapist really were separate and distinct, as they had agreed. Andy was inconsolable, however, and felt that his therapist had betrayed his trust just the way his alcoholic father had, years before. Andy broke off treatment and avoided Dr. Janus for the duration of the year.

Dr. Janus experienced firsthand the problems of entering into a dual-role relationship, and he regretted that he had ever accepted a student as a patient in his practice. There were alternatives, if only he had taken the time to seek them out. The university health center was always an option, and there were therapists in neighboring towns that were also available, although less convenient. With the time pressure of his various professional responsibilities and his overly strong desire to be helpful to someone in need, Dr. Janus made a decision that ultimately resulted in harming a student and potentially himself, as well, by risking an ethics complaint.

1. When did Dr. Janus cross the line between instructor and therapist?
2. How might Dr. Janus have handled Andy's second request for an office consultation that would have precluded any possibility of his becoming a patient?
3. Could Dr. Janus ethically accept Andy as a patient if he were not his instructor but would be teaching a statistics course next year that Andy was required to take?

7.06 ASSESSING STUDENT AND SUPERVISEE PERFORMANCE

(a) In academic and supervisory relationships, psychologists establish a timely and specific process for providing feedback to students and supervisees. Information regarding the process is provided to the student at the beginning of supervision.

As an instructor or supervisor, always have a well-defined and timely process for providing feedback and constructive criticism to your charges. Be sure to inform them about this at the outset.

VIGNETTE

On the first day of class, Dr. E. Lucy Date would take the time to carefully inform students about course requirements and grading criteria. She discussed the details of written assignments and specified the due dates for each. She made her expectancies clear about carrying out research as a part of the course and whether it should involve the use of psychology journals, Internet databases, personal interviews with psychology faculty, or some other means. She also informed students that class participation would be an important part of the grading process because it was a means of informally assessing students' understanding of various aspects of the material. She expected each student to engage in class discussion, by posing or answering queries on a fairly regular basis. She gave the date of the midterm and final examinations and described the nature of the tests, including whether they involved multiple choice, essay writing, or some other type of performance.

Dr. Date kept regular office hours several days each week, and she informed students that they could make appointments to consult with her or drop by for a nonscheduled chat. She gave out her e-mail address and office telephone number, to encourage dialogue with students, although she made it clear that shorter messages were appreciated, as she had a very full schedule. She also informed students that they were required to meet with her individually at least once during the second half of the semester to discuss their progress and performance to date.

Students had a clear notion from the beginning of the class about how to meet their professor's expectations, and those who needed additional support or structure were able to discuss their needs with her. There were rarely any major disappointments about grades at the end of the semester, as students felt that they received adequate feedback, either formally or informally, about the ongoing quality of their work.

1. How would you go about providing information to your clinical supervisees about the process of evaluating their performance, progress, and competence during the course of supervision?
2. How would you document your discussion with supervisees concerning informed consent about the supervision process? In your supervisory notes? In a formal letter to the supervisee? Some other way?
3. What ethical and legal issues apply to a clinical supervisor but not to a classroom professor concerning informed consent, liability, and so on?

7.06 (b)

Psychologists evaluate students and supervisees on the basis of their actual performance on relevant and established program requirements.

> Base grades and evaluations on how a student or supervisee actually performs, according to program requirements or criteria, not on extraneous but compelling factors such as friendliness, physical appearance, personal feelings about the trainee, and so on.

VIGNETTE

In keeping with the temporary (but unspoken) policy of a new, small professional school of psychology, once students were accepted into the doctoral program, they would most certainly graduate, regardless of the quality of their academic performance. The financial growth of the institution was to be held at a higher priority than academic excellence, according to the president, Dr. Pete Cuniare, until such time as fiscal security was no longer an issue, and because student tuition constituted the major share of the school's income, it was important to maintain a full complement of enrollees at all times. This policy enabled the rapid hiring of additional faculty and development of the library and other resources for student use.

As a result, most faculty members were overly lenient in grading, overlooking substandard work and allowing students to matriculate who clearly did not belong. Students who put forth a great amount of effort and were especially competent generally earned As. However, students who struggled with the work and seemed, in the long run, unqualified to continue in the program earned Bs as long as they supplemented their academic work with research and clerical activities in the department (data entry, typing, minding phones, etc.).

These B students who were strung along eventually experienced significant problems in their academic careers, including poor performance in clinical internships; personal problems that had never been attended to earlier; or inability to pass the state licensing examination, even with repeated attempts. They would likely have fared better had they been weeded out sooner and encouraged to pursue other career paths.

One senior faculty member, Dr. Neverbend, tended to resist the school's unspoken rules and base student evaluations on academic performance instead of extraneous factors. Because of her values and educational philosophy, she gave some students low passing or even failing grades at times in various core courses, thus threatening their academic status at the school. Over time, Dr. Neverbend was pressured by the administration to comply with the temporary grading policy of her peers and to bear in mind that her salary was being paid by those very students who were about to fail out of the program.

Unwilling to yield to the social pressure, Dr. Neverbend ultimately left the professional school, because the prevailing climate was antithetical to her values. On her departure, she brought formal ethics complaints against

President Cuniare, the dean, and several faculty members for their pervasive and persistent ethical violations concerning student evaluation practices. These individuals were clearly violating this ethical standard on a daily basis, and they were ultimately harming students who should have been given timely and honest feedback about the mediocre quality of their work and their dubious potential as budding psychologists.

1. Could Dr. Neverbend have taken other, less drastic steps instead of resigning from the professional school?
2. Were faculty members putting themselves at risk of an ethics complaint, later on, from students who should have been weeded out, but were not, and who eventually realized that their education at the professional school was essentially a sham?
3. What are some other (unethical) bases for awarding grades that have nothing to do with a student's competence yet prevail in academia nevertheless?

7.07 SEXUAL RELATIONSHIPS WITH STUDENTS AND SUPERVISEES

Psychologists do not engage in sexual relationships with students or supervisees who are in their department, agency, or training center or over whom psychologists have or are likely to have evaluative authority. (See also Standard 3.05, Multiple Relationships.)

Do not sexualize relationships with your current students, supervisees, interns, psychological assistants, or anybody else whom you mentor, teach, manage, or evaluate directly. This means avoiding all sexual contact, even if it is the other one who believes he or she cannot live without you. You must be wise and do the thinking for both of you.

VIGNETTE

Dr. I. Neader was a middle-aged psychologist who tragically lost his wife of 25 years to uterine cancer, a little over 1 year before. He had participated in group therapy for widows and widowers and felt that he was making good progress in his recovery. As a part of his new life, he decided to assume some new professional responsibilities and to begin supervising psychological assistants within his private practice. He was well connected in the community, had plenty of patients, and would welcome the chance to meet some new people and do something different besides his usual clinical duties.

Over the course of several months, Dr. Neader notified colleagues who were teaching in the psychology departments of nearby universities of his interest in supervising, and soon he found himself with two competent and well-trained supervisees ready to see patients. He began weekly supervision and found that he enjoyed it immensely, both professionally and personally.

After several weeks of supervision, he began to notice a certain chemistry between him and one of his charges, Veronica. She was older than the average postdoctoral student, was more mature, had a warm and engaging manner, and had more life experience than the other students. He found himself thinking about her increasingly, and eventually daydreaming about her almost constantly. During clinical supervision he found himself probing the marital and sexual aspects of her patients' treatment more than might have been appropriate. Veronica, for her part, felt attracted to her mentor as well; she made it clear that she too would like to see Dr. Neader after hours. Soon, pleasantries, sexual innuendoes, and friendly touches opened the door to an intense and fully intimate relationship.

This was Dr. Neader's first time in several respects: It was his first love affair since his wife's death and the first time that an affair of the heart had emerged from a professional relationship. Dr. Neader felt confused. First, he was Veronica's supervisor and thus had an ethical and legal responsibility for each person whom she treated. Second, he was in love with her, and felt her compassion and warmth filling his life more with each passing day. He never noticed his own diminished objectivity; neither did he consider that his intense feelings about Veronica would preclude his providing a competent supervisory experience for her. He was consumed by his own emotional needs and mistakenly believed that he could continue the intimate relationship while remaining sufficiently objective to continue supervising. Unfortunately, as it turned out, both relationships appeared to suffer. Certainly, he was too forgiving (read: "loving") to notice and confront her occasional clinical incompetence, and he failed to teach her the way he should have when she was working with challenging patients.

As the supervisory year began to wind down, so did Dr. Neader's passion. To be sure, he had learned to love once again, with Veronica's help, but he knew that this twosome would not work in the long run; Veronica did have life experience, but she still was too immature for him. He was no longer interested in continuing the relationship, and he informed her thus shortly after their last supervisory session. He told Veronica that he would be happy to supply her with excellent letters of reference, however, and to be of assistance to her in locating a professional position.

Veronica felt rejected, hurt, and depressed by this turn of events, having invested much of herself in this passionate love affair with a man whom she admired as a mentor and who indeed held real power over her as a supervisor. As the months passed, and Veronica continued trying to regain his affections, she eventually lost hope of ever reconstituting the relationship again. She ultimately came to view the entire episode as an abuse of power and to see herself as a victim of a needy and overly dependent man's emotional and sexual exploitation. Although this may have been a somewhat less than accurate rendering of the course of events, and exploitation may not necessarily have been a conscious motive of Dr. Neader, one nevertheless could readily make an argument to support Veronica's genuine feelings about his conduct.

1. Which other ethical standards would be relevant to Dr. Neader's "falling in love" with Veronica?
2. What might have been some of Dr. Neader's options in providing for Veronica's supervisory needs if he were aware of his own diminished objectivity and competence yet wished to continue the personal relationship with her?
3. How great would Dr. Neader's legal liability have been if one of Veronica's borderline patients had committed suicide, or harmed a third party?
4. What steps might Dr. Neader and Veronica take to normalize the power differential, after supervision terminated, if they still wished to be together?
5. If Dr. Neader were your colleague, how could you approach him and have a friendly discussion about the risks of his conduct, to himself and others?

8

RESEARCH AND PUBLICATION

8.01 INSTITUTIONAL APPROVAL

When institutional approval is required, psychologists provide accurate information about their research proposals and obtain approval prior to conducting the research. They conduct the research in accordance with the approved research protocol.

Obtain permission from the institution before you begin your research there. This means obtaining formal consent from hospitals (research involving patients or health care providers), schools or colleges (research involving teachers or students), factories or places of business (research involving employees or managers), police departments (research involving police officers or detainees), and so on, before you actually approach individuals and begin collecting data. Be accurate and truthful in disclosing the details of your research proposal (e.g., goals, design, confidentiality issues, informed-consent issues, possible benefits and risk to participants, possible benefits and risks to the institution, and any other matters that would affect their cooperation). Do not make significant changes after your proposal has been approved without again submitting them to the institution for review.

VIGNETTE

A research team consisting of two child psychologists and several computer software engineers developed a protocol for researching the impact of a carefully designed sequence of video games on aggressive behavior in junior high school boys. They contacted the superintendent's office in an inner-city school district to present their research rationale and methodology. After being referred to the assistant superintendent for curriculum and the human research committee of the school district, they proceeded to discuss their project.

They informed the district officials that participating in the study could benefit students whose behavior was provocative or aggressive and, thereby, indirectly benefit the school, by reducing the frequency of such behaviors. They explained that students would be told that they were being asked to evaluate a series of new video games emphasizing ingenuity instead of power and violence and that their feedback could be useful to the developers of the games. This was essentially true because the games were, in fact, designed to expose participants in the experimental group to a sequence of social conflict situations in which cleverness, intellectual creativity, and negotiation were reinforced but the use of brute force was not. The researchers explained to the school officials that their mild deception—presenting games to be evaluated instead of inviting the cooperation of participants—was an acceptable means of increasing student participation in the project.

The researchers went on to explain that the entire project would span approximately 5 months, with three 45-min game sessions each week at the end of the school day and occasional discussion groups. Pre- and posttesting would be carried out by using a computer-administered instrument to assess aggressiveness and self-esteem. Confidentiality would be managed by allowing students to select their own password and fictitious names, so the students' true identity would never be tracked by the computer. Informed consent would be addressed by means of signed parental and student consent forms. Debriefing at the end of the study, after the data had been analyzed, would consist of presenting the pre- and posttesting results to students and their parents and the students' performance on various simulations that reinforced nonviolent behavior.

After learning about all the details of the proposal, the assistant superintendent and the human research committee consulted with the three junior high school principals in the district, each of whom had an opportunity to raise questions and concerns of the researchers. The administrators were invited to ask about any aspect of the research that was unclear or problematical. The researchers, in kind, responded to queries in a clear and comprehensive fashion, always encouraging an open and scholarly discussion of the details of the research and their implications. The dialogue was thorough, the school officials were satisfied that they had been given a sufficient chance to scrutinize the research protocol so they could make a sound decision as to its suitability, and each agreed to allow the study to take place in their school.

1. With an interdisciplinary research team such as this one, how important is it for all team members to be present when presenting the research project to the school administrators?
2. If psychiatrists or social workers are involved as coinvestigators with you, which ethical standards pertinent to research activities are binding on whom?
3. How much exaggeration or spin is permissible in describing the possible benefits to the institution that might accrue from the research?
4. Is it important to discuss changes in the protocols with the school administrators, after the research has begun?
5. Try role playing an attempt to obtain permission to carry out research in a school or other institution, where administrators are skeptical or resistant.

8.02 INFORMED CONSENT TO RESEARCH

(a) When obtaining informed consent as required in Standard 3.10, Informed Consent, psychologists inform participants about (1) the purpose of the research, expected duration, and procedures; (2) their right to decline to participate and to withdraw from the research once participation has begun; (3) the foreseeable consequences of declining or withdrawing; (4) reasonably foreseeable factors that may be expected to influence their willingness to participate such as potential risks, discomfort, or adverse effects; (5) any prospective research benefits; (6) limits of confidentiality; (7) incentives for participation; and (8) whom to contact for questions about the research and research participants' rights. They provide opportunity for the prospective participants to ask questions and receive answers. (See also Standards 8.03, Informed Consent for Recording Voices and Images in Research; 8.05, Dispensing With Informed Consent for Research; and 8.07, Deception in Research.)

Create a thorough informed-consent document, written in relatively simple language, that educates research participants about the following:

- the purpose of the research, the expected length of time required of participants, and specific procedures;
- their right to refuse to participate or to drop out of the research after it has begun;
- any consequences of declining or withdrawing from the research;
- any factors or details that would likely influence their willingness to participate, such as possible risks, danger, discomfort, unpleasant effects, or other possible negative consequences of participating;

- any potential benefits that may result from the research, to them, other individuals or groups, society at large, and so on;
- any threats to confidentiality or privacy (e.g., releasing data to third parties);
- incentives for participation (e.g., money, psychological services, other benefits); and
- how to contact you or your coinvestigators for further questions about the research and their rights as participants.

Finally, be sure to answer questions raised by prospective participants forthrightly and accurately (without compromising their naivete, as necessary). Although not mandated by this standard, it is also important to comply with additional requirements by institutional review boards (IRBs) or other relevant professional or regulatory agencies when creating an informed-consent form (e.g., Health Insurance Portability and Accountability Act [HIPAA] requirements, National Institutes of Health, ethics codes of professional associations other than those of the American Psychological Association [APA] or the American Psychological Society).

An informed-consent form should include the following elements:

1. *Description of the research.* Describe the nature of the research and what will be expected of participants. What is the subject of the investigation? Why is it important? What will be expected of the participants in terms of their effort? Will there be compensation of some sort?
2. *Time involvement.* Inform participants about the time requirements. Is there any flexibility in scheduling?
3. *Confidentiality and privacy.* Inform potential participants about any threats to confidentiality. If video- or audiotaping will be done, what will become of the tapes in the future? Will they be shown at scientific meetings, used in training or education, and so on? Will participants' health care information be accessed or used in any way and, if so, who will see it? If the research involves the use of the Internet, how secure is the server, and what are the risks of leaks to uninvolved parties?
4. *Voluntary participation and consequences of dropping out.* Inform potential participants that their involvement is completely voluntary and that they may drop out of the project at any time without being penalized or discriminated against in any way. Make certain there is no subtle pressure to participate, such as gaining the favor (and grade bonus) of a professor.

   Inform participants if there will be any consequences of declining to participate or withdrawing from the project once it is under way. For example, if a student enrolled in Psychology 101 refuses to participate, will he or she be required to complete another project instead, such as a paper or presentation, to get comparable credit? Is there the potential for adverse effects to withdrawing, such as losing out on the opportunity for debriefing, if desired? Will dropouts forfeit their entitlement to receiving compensation or inducements for participating that were offered at the outset (e.g., money, psychological products or services)? Will participants who withdraw still be entitled to receive a copy of the results of research, if they wish? Describe the procedure for withdrawing from the research.

5. *Risks and benefits*. Inform potential participants about foreseeable risks and benefits of participation. What would likely affect their willingness to participate in the research? Are there any physical or psychological risks, discomfort, or adverse effects? Will they experience stress, medication effects, unpleasant emotional or physical sensations, pain, sleep deprivation, sexual arousal, or any other negative effects? Will there be unpleasant psychosocial effects or experiences that might be offensive to one's gender, ethnic roots, religious beliefs, or other fundamental traits or values that one holds dear? Are there any limitations on confidentiality or privacy, such as the use of videotaping? Reveal anything that would likely make a difference in their willingness to participate. However, you don't have to compromise prospective participants' naivete if it is essential for the research.

Are there benefits to participation, such as educational experiences, training, or some useful skill or mental health benefit?

6. *Compensation*. Inform potential participants about what they will be paid. Will there be other compensation, in the form of applying their participation toward course credit or fulfilling some academic requirement? If so, how will this be arranged?

7. *Minors*. Parental permission must be obtained if minors are participating in research. In some cases, such as classroom activities and minimal-risk situations, a partial waiver of parental consent may be acceptable. However, full parental consent should be strongly considered when the research involves any of the following topics: parental political affiliations or beliefs; mental or psychological problems; sexual behavior or attitudes; illegal, antisocial, or self-incriminating behavior; appraisals of other individuals with whom the minor has a familial relationship; a relationship legally recognized as privileged (e.g., lawyers, doctors, clergy); and religious affiliations or beliefs ("Stanford University Sample Consent Form, Human Subjects in Medical Research," 2003).

8. *Whom to contact*. Inform potential participants about whom they can contact for additional information. Provide necessary contact information for you, your coinvestigators, or both.

9. *Questions about participants' rights*. Some institutions may require investigators to supply participants with names and telephone numbers of administrators who can respond to complaints or ques-

tions about participants' rights that may have been abridged during the course of the study. Know your institution's requirements in this area, and be sure to comply.

10. *Responding to questions at the outset.* In addition to the preceding, it is always important to fully answer questions raised by participants when discussing their potential participation in the study. Answer questions as candidly and clearly as you can without distorting, minimizing, exaggerating, or omitting important information. Remember, potential participants do not always know which questions to ask; they don't know *what they don't know* about the research under way. How can you allay participants' concerns without giving false reassurances? How can you be sure that a potential participant, particularly children, elderly individuals, or people with developmental disabilities or who are impaired in some other way, fully understand your answers? Are your responses framed in simple language that can be easily understood by people with less education or who speak English as a second language? When is an individual sufficiently informed, in your opinion, to make a sound decision about whether to participate in your study? How much is enough?

1. Why is informed consent such an important concept in psychological research?

2. What is the Belmont Report, implemented in 1979, and how has it influenced the evolution of informed consent in research (National Commission for the Protection of Human Subjects of Biomedical and Behavioral Research, 1979)?

3. How would you go about having your research protocol reviewed if you were not attached to a university, hospital, or similar institution that had an IRB?

4. How do HIPAA requirements affect the kind of consent you must provide to your prospective participants?

8.02 (b)

Psychologists conducting intervention research involving the use of experimental treatments clarify to participants at the outset of the research (1) the experimental nature of the treatment; (2) the services that will or will not be available to the control group(s) if appropriate; (3) the means by which assignment to treatment and control groups will be made; (4) available treatment alternatives if an individual does not wish to participate in the research or wishes to withdraw once a study has begun; and (5) compensation for or monetary costs of participating including, if appropriate, whether reimbursement from the participant or a third-party payor will be sought. (See also Standard 8.02a, Informed Consent to Research.)

If you work in a clinic or other setting where innovative research with patients is carried out, be sure to inform them of the following points at the outset:

- that the treatment they are about to receive is experimental;
- that if they are assigned to a control group, certain services or interventions will be available, whereas other services or interventions will not, if this is appropriate;
- the method of assigning them to experimental and control groups;
- what other intervention or treatment is available, if the patient refuses to participate, or decides to drop out of the research; and
- how the patient will be compensated, or what the costs will be, for receiving the experimental intervention, and whether insurance will be billed for the services.

VIGNETTE

Faculty in a large department of psychiatry with a focus on integrative medicine were conducting research on the efficacy of various group interventions for anxiety and depression. The interventions included group psychotherapy, meditation, relaxation training, group didactic instruction with videotapes and self-led discussion, massage therapy in a group setting, and a control group with assigned readings of self-help books. Participants had to meet the criteria for either panic disorder, general anxiety disorder, or dysthymic disorder.

The psychologists and psychiatrists involved drew up a participant's informed-consent form and submitted it to their IRB for approval. After implementing all the formal recommendations by the IRB, the investigators began the task of recruiting participants. They advertised in local newspapers, over the Internet, over the university's FM radio station, on bulletin boards, and by contacting local therapists who had a waiting list of clients and patients.

As the investigators began receiving responses, they met with potential candidates to provide informed consent about participation and then formally assess them for suitability. The assessment consisted of a variety of clinical instruments and a structured clinical interview. Because this was intervention research, the investigators were careful to include specific elements in the consent form that reflected ethical concern for the welfare and safety of participants, in addition to the customary disclosures concerning the purpose of the research, individuals' right to decline and withdraw, confidentiality, and so on. Specifically, the following elements were included and discussed with participants:

- *The experimental nature of the treatment.* Participants were informed that they were about to take part in research for the amelioration of panic, anxiety, or depression with interventions that were experimental, lacking in research validation, had the potential for either improving or exacerbating symptoms, or had the potential for making no difference in their symptoms.

- *Services that will or will not be available for the control group.* Participants assigned to the control group would not have access to any of the other modalities; neither would they be able to initiate individual psychotherapy on their own. In the event of a significant worsening of symptoms, they could contact one of the research assistants for advice regarding remaining in the study or withdrawing and receiving a referral for treatment, if desired.
- *How participants will be assigned to treatment and control groups.* Participants would be randomly assigned to each of the seven groups, with an attempt to achieve a balance by gender.
- *Treatment alternatives for those refusing or withdrawing from the research.* Any potential participant who opted out at the beginning, or withdrew after participating in the group sessions, would have the choice of receiving referrals for individual psychotherapy or consultation with a psychiatrist for medication assessment if he or she wished. This option would extend for a period of 6 months if the person dropped out at the outset (at any stage of the formal assessment) or 1 year after his or her withdrawal from the assigned group.
- *Compensation for participation.* The participants would be paid nothing; neither would they be charged a fee for their involvement with the study. If they withdrew from the study and sought therapy within the university, then normal fees would apply, including reimbursement from third-party payors, as appropriate.

After reading the consent form and asking questions of the investigators, potential participants felt reassured about the potential benefits and risks of becoming involved. Although some of the elements seemed unnecessary, or redundant, the senior researchers knew from experience that it was better to anticipate every worst-case scenario possible than to hold assumptions that were optimistic but unwarranted.

1. Why does intervention research, as opposed to other kinds of psychological research, require additional elements in the standard consent form?
2. How would HIPAA rules for research influence the elements of your consent form?
3. What additional steps would you take if your intervention research involved children or individuals who were mentally retarded?

8.03 INFORMED CONSENT FOR RECORDING
VOICES AND IMAGES IN RESEARCH

Psychologists obtain informed consent from research participants prior to recording their voices or images for data collection unless (1) the research consists solely of naturalistic observations in public places, and it is not anticipated that the recording will be used in a manner that could cause personal identification or harm, or (2) the research design includes deception, and consent for the use of the recording is obtained during debriefing. (See also Standard 8.07, Deception in Research.)

Always obtain research participants' informed consent before audio- or videotaping, because people may be identified by their voice or image. You do not need their consent, however, in the following situations:

- when doing naturalistic research in public places (e.g., observing the reactions of window shoppers to various displays of electronic products) the recordings of which will not be used in a way that would reveal identities or could otherwise harm people; and
- if deception is a necessary part of the design and you acquire the person's consent to use the recording afterward, during the debriefing session.

VIGNETTE

Dr. Philmore, who was teaching a course in group psychotherapy for advanced doctoral students, was planning to videotape a colleague's group therapy sessions for both didactic and research purposes. He was investigating nonverbal communication, both facial and postural, and measurable changes in these behaviors over the duration of the group. For this purpose, he had trained five doctoral students to serve as raters who would view videotaped segments and record their observations.

Dr. Philmore was aware of the ethical standard requiring informed consent by research participants when videotaping and was careful to seek their consent in advance. Unfortunately, however, he provided a rather narrow informed consent, neglecting to describe the intended audience of the videotape or provide the general rationale for taping. He also neglected to mention that trained raters would be viewing the tape later. He gave a printed consent form to the group therapy members to sign and offered them a chance to ask questions about the taping. When several group members raised questions about who would see the tape, it became clear to Dr. Philmore that he had forgotten to include important elements of the consent. He quickly provided the names of all the raters and discovered, to his surprise, that an unanticipated problem immediately surfaced. By coincidence, two of the group therapy clients lived in the same large graduate student housing complex as one of the raters. Although not friends, the rater was known to both of them, and neither person wished to expose himself to this particular individual by means of participating in the videotaped segments.

The two group therapy clients were troubled that the so-called "informed consent" had neglected to reveal such an important fact as the identity of the raters, and they confronted their feelings of betrayal to the group therapist. The group therapist, in turn, relayed this information to Dr. Philmore, who realized that not only was his consent form flawed but also his plan to videotape a therapy group and show segments to students might be flawed because of the possibility that students in his seminar might recognize other students on the tape. He considered revealing the names of his doctoral students to the therapy group members, so as to provide them with a concrete idea of who would view the tape. However, he quickly rejected this idea when it became obvious that facial recognition and name recognition were not necessarily equivalent and that the community was simply too small to presume anonymity in research such as this. After gaining an appreciation of the potential risks to confidentiality by engaging in such a practice, he elected to refrain from pursuing this project any further.

Coincidences happen all too often, even in larger communities, and the most unlikely circumstances can sometimes pose real risks to individuals' privacy and confidentiality. Dr. Philmore promptly took measures to guard against any further omissions in his consent form with a careful revision that provided much better protection to future patients and research participants. He would have done well to consult with the university's IRB first, so as to avoid the very problems he nearly created.

1. How might Dr. Philmore have altered his design to allow raters to view videotaped segments of individuals in public places?
2. Would an audiotape or printed transcript of group therapy sessions have been acceptable as an alternative to videotaping?
3. Dr. Philmore's research protocol appears to be poorly designed and missing essential elements regarding informed consent of potential participants. If you were the group therapist, what steps would you take to raise Dr. Philmore's awareness of the risks he had generated for others and himself?

8.04 CLIENT/PATIENT, STUDENT, AND SUBORDINATE RESEARCH PARTICIPANTS

(a) When psychologists conduct research with client/patients, students, or subordinates as participants, psychologists take steps to protect the prospec-

tive participants from adverse consequences of declining or withdrawing from participation.

> When conducting research with people who have less social power than yourself (real or perceived), such as clients, patients, students, or subordinates in any other sense, be sure that you shield them from any punitive consequences for refusing to participate in your research or from withdrawing from it. You might urgently need to gather data for your study, but always remember that participation in research must be voluntary. This not only protects others but also may improve the quality of your data.

VIGNETTE

Dr. Will Smite was an untenured assistant professor engaged in full-time teaching and research who, with his tenure decision fast approaching, was feeling much pressure to publish. He dipped into the usual participant pool of undergraduate and graduate students, but this year he had developed a rather creative but unorthodox system of incentives: In return for students' participation, he would invite them to monthly dinners at his home and afternoon social events at his office on campus. It was well known among psychology students that refusal to participate in his research meant that one would suffer certain minor penalties—no more monthly dinners and office parties.

More important, Dr. Smite was well connected in the psychological community and was able to be of great assistance to graduate students in their quest for desirable internship settings and other postdoctoral professional opportunities. Of some ethical concern however, were his recent tendencies to be less cooperative with trainees who declined to serve as participants in his research; on the contrary, he seemed to base his assistance primarily on the extent to which students had met his professional goals in research—that is, he helped place students in the best internships who were eager to serve as participants repeatedly in different investigations, regardless of their academic competence as compared with other students in competition for a limited number of openings. His letters of reference seemed to be influenced by these same factors, namely, how extensively students had offered to be a research participant or help his projects in other ways, not their actual strengths or appropriateness for the internship.

Dr. Smite was clearly engaging in punitive tactics for students who declined to participate or who dropped out of his research projects. Some students felt disadvantaged by such a system of incentives, but they failed to complain, concerned that even greater retribution by Dr. Smite might be forthcoming. After graduating, however, two students who felt they had evidence of his punitive strategies over the previous year brought a grievance against Dr. Smite to the department chair. This complaint was echoed by several other postgraduates a few months later, when they heard about the grievance from others. One student contacted the APA Ethics Office to inquire whether this conduct, if validated, would meet the threshold of an ethics violation. When informed that it very likely would (although this could not be determined with certainty), she decided to initiate a formal ethics complaint.

Dr. Smite was smitten, and he spent much time and energy over the next year dealing with both the departmental investigation of the grievance and the APA Ethics Committee's interrogatories. Not only had he failed to protect students from adverse consequences of declining or withdrawing from participation in his research, as the standard required, but also he had added a few adverse consequences of his own. As the year dragged on, complaints continued to surface. All this took its toll on Dr. Smite's mood and productivity, and ultimately he failed to achieve tenure. In addition, he received a formal sanction by the APA Ethics Committee and was required to attend three ethics workshops relevant to research issues and be monitored by a senior colleague for a period of 1 year. Dr. Smite learned a painful but valued lesson about applying the ethical principles of justice, beneficence, and nonmaleficence in addition to the specifics of this particular ethical standard.

1. Was it unethical, unwise, unprofessional, or just plain petty for Dr. Smite to disinvite students for dinner and to his office parties if they refused to participate in his research?
2. How might students have dealt with his manipulative behavior about letters of reference and postgraduate opportunities even while they remained at the university?
3. If Dr. Smite were not a member of APA, could he have been investigated by its Ethics Committee nevertheless?
4. Would the state board of psychology take an interest in this case, even though Dr. Smite was not a licensed psychologist?

8.04 (b)

When research participation is a course requirement or an opportunity for extra credit, the prospective participant is given the choice of equitable alternative activities.

When students are required to participate in psychological research as a part of a course, or may do so for extra credit, they must always be permitted to decline and be given a choice of an equitable substitute project (e.g., research paper, presentation, participation in a different research project).

☞   Dr. Will Badger, an instructor carrying out research that required a large sample, recruited students from one of his introductory psychology classes. His consent form stated that the time required would not exceed 3 hours and that students would receive credit toward their final grade for participation in the study. He offered an alternative to students who did not wish to participate but, hoping to improve their motivation, he required every nonparticipating student to write a 15-page paper on a topic related to his research.

Several students complained about this alternative, arguing that they felt it was too long and essentially punitive. They claimed that writing a good research paper of that length would require considerably longer than the 3 hours expected of the research participants. Furthermore, the effort in writing such a paper involved very different skills and was far more demanding intellectually than merely participating in a research project.

One student, who already bore negative feelings about Dr. Badger, saw the research paper assignment as self-serving. He summed up the prevailing sentiments of some fellow students by declaring that he would "be damned" if he was going to write a paper that would "contribute to Dr. Badger's review of the literature section for his most recent journal article." He thought that it was unreasonable and exploitative, particularly in view of the time that would be required to write a high-quality 15-page paper.

It was true that Dr. Badger had not given adequate thought to the equitable-alternative aspect of this ethical standard in assigning the research paper. After listening to the objections of his students, he conceded that he had possibly given an assignment that was not a reasonable alternative and that he would accept papers that were shorter, or even a different project altogether that took approximately 3 hours to complete. By so doing, he demonstrated both a responsiveness to student feedback and a willingness to examine his own conduct in light of the current Ethics Code.

1. What are some equitable alternatives that you might assign students who decline to serve as research participants?
2. Do you welcome or solicit student feedback about your teaching or assignments?
3. Is Dr. Badger required to honor this ethical standard if he is not a member of APA or his state psychological association?

8.05 DISPENSING WITH INFORMED CONSENT FOR RESEARCH

Psychologists may dispense with informed consent only (1) where research would not reasonably be assumed to create distress or harm and involves (a) the study of normal educational practices, curricula, or classroom management methods conducted in educational settings; (b) only anonymous questionnaires, naturalistic observations, or archival research for which disclosure of responses would not place participants at risk of criminal or civil liability or damage their financial standing, employability, or reputation, and confidentiality is protected; or (c) the study of factors related to job or organization effectiveness conducted in organizational settings for which there is no risk to participants' employability, and confidentiality is protected or (2) where otherwise permitted by law or federal or institutional regulations.

You do not need to obtain informed consent from prospective research participants under the following conditions:
- when the research is not likely to cause distress or harm and it involves:
  - investigating normal educational practices, curricula, or classroom management methods in schools and other educational settings; or
  - using anonymous questionnaires, naturalistic observations, or archival research in which participants' responses, if revealed, would not place them at risk of criminal or civil liability or jeopardize their financial standing, employability, reputation, or their confidentiality; or
  - investigating factors related to work or organizational effectiveness conducted in organizational settings where participants' employability and confidentiality are not jeopardized; or
- when the research is permitted by law or federal or institutional regulations (e.g., blanket consent has already been obtained by a research assistant for all participating patients in the hospital, and you need not, again, obtain consent when you carry out your role in the research project).

VIGNETTE

Dr. Seeker was investigating the psychological effects on partners who had survived the AIDS-related death of a loved one. Some of the independent variables he was exploring were length of time the patient had been HIV positive, course of AIDS-related symptoms, duration of the relationship, financial stability, and family-of-origin support. Dr. Seeker developed a questionnaire that addressed these issues and planned to distribute it in a random fashion at various locations throughout San Francisco. He thought that it was not necessary to seek respondents' informed consent, because their participation consisted merely of completing an anonymous questionnaire, and he did not view this as interventional research or see it as posing any significant risk to anyone who volunteered to participate.

However, after discussing his research design and questionnaire at length with a gay male colleague who had personal experience in losing his partner, Dr. Seeker began to appreciate the potential for creating distress or suffering in others by simply exposing them to certain questions. It was likely that for some survivors, the experience of responding to the questionnaire would enhance insight, understanding, resolution, or peace of mind or even stimulate them to consult a counselor to further explore the unfinished grieving process. However, for survivors who had made little progress in resolving their grief, guilt, anger, and other dysphoric feelings, the mere act of responding to probing questions about thoughts, feelings, and behavior concerning a highly stressful and protracted period of suffering and loss could likely rekindle feelings of profound pain. It could exacerbate negative feelings, contribute to depression, and interfere with the individual's (possibly) fragile psychological defenses and functioning, depending on his or her mental health at the time he or she completed the questionnaire. One could not necessarily assume that respondents would necessarily engage in an intelligent self-selection process of participation, and it was necessary to anticipate a worst-case scenario.

Dr. Seeker began to understand that he could not necessarily accurately predict the range of effects that responding to the questionnaire items could have on various individuals. Therefore, in response to advice from his friend and colleague, he created an informed-consent sheet on which he described the nature of the questionnaire items and the range of possible effects that participating in this research might have on respondents. This might include activating feelings of guilt, anxiety, depression, anger, or other negative mood-altering emotions. It might induce the recurrence of unwanted thoughts or memories or interfere with cognitive functioning in minor ways. It could also interfere with sleep, appetite, or other vegetative functions.

Dr. Seeker's colleague previewed the consent form and agreed that an individual could now freely make a well-informed decision at the outset about whether to participate in the research. It was of critical importance not only that potential respondents had some understanding of the nature of the questionnaire but also that they appreciated the range of possible adverse effects that their participation might invite.

1. What other means might Dr. Seeker have used to further enhance his informed-consent form in addition to discussing it with his colleague?
2. What would be an example of ethically dispensing with informed consent in carrying out research in a high school?
3. As an industrial–organizational psychologist, what type of research might you carry out that would not require informed consent of participants?
4. As an employee of a veterans' hospital, how would you decide when to omit informed consent with outpatients?

8.06 OFFERING INDUCEMENTS FOR RESEARCH PARTICIPATION

(a) Psychologists make reasonable efforts to avoid offering excessive or inappropriate financial or other inducements for research participation when such inducements are likely to coerce participation.

When offering financial or other kinds of incentives to prospective research participants, make sure that the incentives are not excessive (e.g., offering too much money) or inappropriate (e.g., creating a dual relationship with you, or violating an institutional rule or policy), as this would tend to coerce cooperation from those who otherwise would have no interest (and, in some cases, such coercion could have a compromising effect on your research data).

VIGNETTE

Dr. Aufermuch taught at a small university in a rural setting and was having difficulty obtaining a sufficient number of students to volunteer for his research projects. Because he was rapidly approaching the publication deadline for a chapter in a book, he felt that he had to be quite creative in inducing students to come forth so that he could complete his research. He designed several strategies that he thought would significantly increase students' motivation to participate in two of his research projects that required approximately 4 hr of their time.

First, he waived the final examination in a course he was teaching and awarded the equivalent of an automatic A on the test to students enrolled in his course if they volunteered for both projects. Second, for other students in the school who were not enrolled in his course, he offered money drawn from grant funds for a different project that had not been expended. He paid each student $45 per project (over $20/hr) for being a research participant. This was several times over the hourly minimum wage for his state.

Finally, he offered a 1-night stay in his timeshare condominium in Lake Tahoe to those who volunteered to be in both projects and provided help in serving as raters and scorers of the data. Dr. Aufermuch had little understanding of this ethical standard, which prohibits researchers from offering excessively large inducements to research participants. By so doing, he risked the possibility of a conflict of interest, placing research participants more in the role of employee or partner than volunteer for a scientific study. By offering inducements that were so overwhelmingly attractive to a graduate student population, he may have also compromised the validity of his data by essentially buying research participants who would have an interest in attempting to help prove his research hypothesis as they understood it.

1. Could Dr. Aufermuch's actions be considered in violation of the law, in addition to being ethically questionable?

2. What risk might he incur by offering students who like to party and are heavy drinkers the opportunity to stay, unsupervised, in his Lake Tahoe condominium?
3. Rather than increasing the speed of his research efforts, how might he have negotiated with the book editor for additional time?

8.06 (b)

When offering professional services as an inducement for research participation, psychologists clarify the nature of the services, as well as the risks, obligations, and limitations. (See also Standard 6.05, Barter With Clients/Patients).

When providing incentives to prospective research participants by offering professional services (e.g., receiving limited counseling or tutoring services, or having test results interpreted), make sure that you are straightforward in describing the services, including risks, obligations, and limitations.

- *Risks* includes the possibility that one might feel anxious or stressed after learning of his or her scores or performance on some aspect of the research.
- *Obligations* means that you must clearly state your intended responsibilities, such as providing a specific service, number of counseling sessions, and so on.
- *Limitations* refers to the extent or scope of services that are being offered. Providing counseling or tutoring is not a long-term, cost-free intervention, and individuals should be told at the outset about what to expect.

VIGNETTE

Dr. Sue Nami was beginning a study on the effects of a variety of individual and group interventions for obese individuals extending over a 6-month period. As an inducement to participate, she offered each participant the opportunity to have individual consultations at the conclusion of the series of group meetings. The design specified three randomized groups: (a) didactic, (b) therapeutic, and (c) pharmacological interventions. The rationale for the inducement of private consultations was that, for some people, the group experiences could elicit strong feelings, including depression and anxiety, and these might be best remedied by individual sessions at the conclusion of the study.

There were initially 30 men and women in each of the four groups (three experimental groups and one control group) and, predictably, some did experience dysphoric feelings over the course of the investigation. In fact, for a few, the promise of individual consultations at the end was the main reason they continued their participation.

At the conclusion of the study, Dr. Nami attempted to make good on her promise but was dismayed to find that out of a total of 105 participants who completed the study, more than 25 wished to follow up with individual consultations. Furthermore, some of them had made it clear that they wished to have an ongoing series of meetings or individual psychotherapy, because the consent form had clearly stated that "the researcher and her assistants will be available for individual consultations following the conclusion of the study to help group members resolve any distressing feelings resulting from participation in the project." The consent form had failed to give a limit on time or the number of individual consultations. Such a vague and open-ended statement was an invitation for some group members to feel entitled to seek support by having many sessions (essentially beginning a course of short-term psychotherapy) rather than a single debriefing session, as Dr. Nami had hoped. She was beginning to feel like she was drowning in this virtual tidal wave of participants flooding her and her coinvestigators' every available hour.

The research team ultimately spent many more hours providing support and therapy than they had ever intended and found that they were obligated to make several referrals for individual psychotherapy to comply with providing the inducement promised in the informed-consent document. It was also necessary to enlist the help of friendly colleagues—other psychologists, clinical social workers, and psychiatrists—who were willing to donate some time for this project, which had gone out of control.

1. How should Dr. Nami have changed the inducement section of her informed-consent form?
2. How might she have been better informed about the likely needs of her participants?
3. What screening methodologies might have been useful in decreasing the likelihood of such demands by participants at the conclusion of the study?

8.07 DECEPTION IN RESEARCH

(a) Psychologists do not conduct a study involving deception unless they have determined that the use of deceptive techniques is justified by the study's significant prospective scientific, educational, or applied value and that effective nondeceptive alternative procedures are not feasible.

Never deceive your research participants unless the investigation warrants it and there is no other way to obtain the results. Do not mislead, lie, fool, or use any deceptive techniques as a part of your research, unless you judge that the future value of your research results is worth it, on the basis of one or more of the following criteria:

- scientific (e.g., it is an important and significant contribution to the knowledge base);
- educational (e.g., it has significant potential benefit to individuals or society); or
- applied (e.g., it has significant application to industrial and organizational settings, environmental psychology, or direct implications for the ways in which psychologists intervene in the lives of others).

VIGNETTE

Dr. Nares had received a large grant from a pharmaceutical company interested in investigating the efficacy of a new fast-acting, antianxiety medication that could be self-administered through a nose spray. His goal was to compare the effect of the new medication with a placebo in a randomized, double-blind study, involving women who had no premorbid history. To fairly evaluate the drug's potential, he developed a research design that depended on deception as a fundamental concept.

Participants were to be informed that they were part of an experiment intended to measure perceptual acuity and cognitive ability as a function of aging; they were required to fill out a health history questionnaire, take a psychological inventory, have a structured clinical interview, and undergo a brief medical examination. Physiological measures, blood chemistry, and subjective reports would yield the data on state anxiety and any changes therein. After being accepted into the study, and carrying out each of the preliminary assessment activities mentioned previously, the participants were then examined by a physician to obtain the requisite physiological measures. It was at this point that deception entered the process: Each participant was then to be falsely informed that he or she had an irregular heartbeat, slightly elevated blood pressure, and other potential indicators of a mild vascular or neurological disorder. Those participants who developed significant anxiety would then be offered either the new nose spray or placebo, with the recommendation that this was a new drug, recently introduced, that had an excellent track record in reducing anxiety.

The IRB that evaluated Dr. Nares's protocol quickly rejected it on the grounds that the prospective scientific value of the research did not merit deceiving participants about such a significant matter as their own current medical status or risk of disease. Furthermore, the IRB argued that there were alternate ways to investigate this anxiety-alleviating product without putting individuals at risk. One way to test the medication might be to seek individuals who already experienced symptoms of anxiety and freely volunteered for the research.

Indeed, it might require more effort and ingenuity on the part of Dr. Nares and his team to select a particular setting that would yield cooperative and anxious participants. However, by so doing it would not require needlessly deceiving possibly at-risk individuals and increasing the likelihood that they would suffer resulting intense emotional and physiological reactions.

1. What adverse effects might have affected some research participants if the IRB had permitted Dr. Nares to proceed with his research project?
2. Consider additional settings or designs that Dr. Nares might use to test the new drug that would not require such deception.
3. What means would you use to assess the prospective value of some proposed research of yours that necessitates deception?

8.07 (b)

Psychologists do not deceive prospective participants about research that is reasonably expected to cause physical pain or severe emotional stress.

Never deceive potential research participants about research that would likely cause them to experience physical pain or suffering or severely disturbing feelings. Such deception would amount to fraudulent behavior on your part and not only harm others but also could put you at risk of a professional sanction or lawsuit.

VIGNETTE

Dr. Parshall was a health psychologist who worked in a small group of independent practitioners. He was interested in carrying out research with two groups of healthy men—former smokers and those who had never smoked—to assess the effects of physical exercise on a variety of psychological measures and interventions. Participants were offered no monetary compensation for completing the 3-month study; however, the health benefits would likely be considerable, and they would be provided much personal health information along the way. Dr. Parshall informed participants who responded to his advertisement that they would be required to visit the laboratory facility regularly to achieve a consistent amount of exertion. He also informed them that they might be assigned to experimental groups in which biofeedback training or "other interventions" might be used as independent variables, necessitating that meetings take place at certain times of the day.

Unfortunately, however, he failed to inform participants about two key factors. First, he neglected to state that one of the "other variables" was hypnosis; second, he underestimated the total amount of time that would be required of participants. They were informed that the amount of exercise would be easily tolerated by most people on a regular basis. However, the protocol called for participants to spend anywhere from 35 to 75 min on alternating days performing fairly rigorous exercise.

Because he failed to disclose these important details about the research requirements, Dr. Parshall lost many prospective participants after they learned what was expected of them. Many did not wish to visit the facility so often, for such long periods of exercise, and viewed this obligation as a major inconvenience. Some had philosophical or religious objections to the use of hypnosis or did not wish to participate in what they viewed as "mind control" experiments. Of that subgroup, some had previous aversive experiences with hypnosis in therapy settings, such as lingering posthypnotic effects of unpleasant sensations or memories from early life events, and, understandably, did not wish to risk reexperiencing them in this project.

The participants who withdrew from the study regretted that they had wasted nearly an hour of their time, with no monetary compensation, before learning of the specific requirements for physical exercise and hypnosis. They felt that they should have been informed of the expectations for their participation at the outset, because the study requirements obviously affected their willingness to participate and could easily have been disclosed in the newspaper advertisement without compromising their naivete as participants.

1. How much information should Dr. Parshall have disclosed in the newspaper solicitation or the initial telephone contact?
2. It is obvious that this study had never been approved by an IRB, as Dr. Parshall was not affiliated with any institution. How might Dr. Parshall have nevertheless received feedback from an IRB before proceeding with his study?
3. What ethical, legal, and professional risks would Dr. Parshall incur by exposing research participants to an intervention (hypnosis) about which they had not been informed in advance?
4. What steps would you take if a research participant informed you that he or she wished to withdraw from your study?

8.07 (c)

Psychologists explain any deception that is an integral feature of the design and conduct of an experiment to participants as early as is feasible, preferably at the conclusion of their participation, but no later than at the conclusion of the data collection, and permit participants to withdraw their data. (See also Standard 8.08, Debriefing.)

If you have used deception in your research, make sure that you debrief participants as early as possible, and give them the choice of withdrawing their data at any time. This must be done at the end of their involvement in the research, or it could be delayed until all the data have been collected from every participant.

VIGNETTE

Two researchers were studying how negative or positive mood states might affect potential jurors engaged in the task of meting out punishment to individuals who had been convicted of committing a serious crime. The study hypothesis was that participants writing about a personal experience that had a specific negative mood state would likely dole out a more harsh sentence than those writing about a positive mood related event. Participants were deceived about the purpose of the research, however, and were told instead that it was an investigation of how memories of mildly unpleasant events are coded (sensory inputs) and how exposure to new information further affects mood. They were provided informed consent about what would be expected of them concerning the nature of their participation, time requirements, any potential risks, their right to withdraw at any time, monetary incentives, and whom to contact for further information about the study.

The methodology included the following three parts: Participants were randomized into four groups and asked to write down a memory that was associated with the following feelings: anger, fear, pride, or gratefulness. They were given 20 min to write, using computers in the psychology laboratory, and were then instructed to rate the vividness of the memory on a number of sensory dimensions both at the time of the event and now. Finally, they were asked to read actual excerpts from a court transcript of a defendant who had been convicted of a felony and to act as a juror in assigning a sentence to the individual from a range of choices.

Immediately after completing the sentencing, each participant was ushered into another room, where a research assistant explained the nature of the deception. The participant was then given a chance to ask questions about any aspect of the study, or his or her role in it, before he or she exited the psychology laboratory. Participants were provided with a handout containing the contact information of the principal investigators in case they had any delayed reactions, such as negative feelings or a desire to withdraw their data, or other questions about their participation. Finally, they were asked to refrain from disclosing details about the research to preserve the naivete of future participants.

Several participants chose to drop out after writing of the fearful memory. They found that the feelings that were evoked brought a surprising amount of intensity, and they did not wish to continue. They withdrew from the study, were paid for their time (as was agreed in the informed consent), and were interviewed by a research assistant to ascertain whether they felt a need for any further consultation with a psychologist to process their reactions.

Participants were treated respectfully at all times and were informed in advance of aspects of the research that might affect their willingness to become involved (i.e., the fact that they were being asked to recall an autobiographical memory). They were never subject to coercion at any time, and they were permitted to freely withdraw from the study, with close attention to assessing their frame of mind, mood, strong negative feelings, tearfulness, or other dysphoric reactions. Even those who chose to withdraw felt that their needs were well attended to, and they had no negative feedback to provide the investigators about their experience. Debriefing about the deception and the research hypotheses of the study occurred in a timely fashion, at the end of the session, and participants felt that they were treated in a professional and appropriate manner at all times.

1. Does this standard require that you debrief participants about even very minor deceptions?
2. Does this standard imply that the debriefing should consist of a personal explanation by a research assistant, or would a printed handout suffice? What are the benefits and limitations of each?
3. How might the coinvestigators deal with a situation in which a participant telephoned a day later, reporting that she had a nightmare and intrusive thoughts related to her remembered experience?

8.08 DEBRIEFING

(a) Psychologists provide a prompt opportunity for participants to obtain appropriate information about the nature, results, and conclusions of the research, and they take reasonable steps to correct any misconceptions that participants may have of which the psychologists are aware.

When you have completed your investigation, make sure that you promptly give research participants an opportunity to learn about the nature, results, and conclusions of your study after they have completed their role, and always correct any remaining participant misconceptions of which you are aware.

VIGNETTE

Dr. Dee Briefer and her associates had carried out research involving the rating of videotapes of mindfulness meditative training sessions. She was well aware of the importance of providing participants with information about the study at the conclusion and was attentive to this final aspect of the project.

After the final round of data gathering, Dr. Briefer presented the participants with information about her study. She described the research hypothesis: that there would be significant changes in pre- and postinterviews in verbal behavior (volume, pitch, pace, inflection, etc.) and nonverbal behavior (facial expression, body posture, muscle tension, etc.) as a function of participation in 12 sessions of mindfulness meditation training groups; she also told them that she used a control group with no meditation. She was careful to describe her hypothesis in straightforward language, so that participants could readily understand the nature of the investigation. Dr. Briefer also made herself available for individual consultations with any participants who had specific questions about the research. She wanted to be certain that she had communicated her ideas clearly and that there were no misconceptions in the minds of participants about the research or their role in it.

Several participants had questions that went beyond the research; specifically, they sought information about their own individual ratings and what their nonverbal behavior in the interviews might signify. Dr. Briefer was unwilling to review the videotapes or individual ratings with those participants, because that would have constituted a major time commitment and was beyond the scope of her assurance to provide information about the study. However, she did agree to spend some time educating them about basic principles of nonverbal communication and providing some generic information that seemed to meet their needs.

Much later, after all the data were analyzed, all the videotapes rated, the statistical analyses completed, and the journal article was in its nearly final form, Dr. Briefer's assistant sent the abstract to all interested participants—either by conventional mail or e-mail, if they preferred. Every participant who was interested had an opportunity to learn about the study and its outcome, and they each had questions answered to their satisfaction.

1. How might Dr. Briefer be aware of misconceptions on the part of her research participants that would need to be promptly addressed?
2. Are Dr. Briefer and her coinvestigators responsible for addressing misconceptions that are never brought to their attention but may nevertheless have a negative effect on participants? How would they learn of such misconceptions?
3. How soon after the data are collected should a researcher provide information to participants about the study?

8.08 (b)

If scientific or humane values justify delaying or withholding this information, psychologists take reasonable measures to reduce the risk of harm.

If there is a good reason to delay informing participants about your study (e.g., preserving the naivete of future participants) or avoid debriefing them altogether (e.g., out of sensitivity to their feelings, e.g., with a moribund population) you may do so, but be sure to always minimize any possible harm to them if you opt to delay or avoid debriefing.

VIGNETTE

Dr. Kara Forr planned to investigate psychosocial variables that might affect the longevity of terminally ill patients. Her sample included HIV patients who were experiencing advanced clinical symptoms and cancer patients who had particularly aggressive forms of the disease. Her independent variables were the amount of love and emotional support available from a partner, family of origin, friends, and caretakers. She used objective measures and brief personal interviews to assess the quantity and quality of social support present (e.g., frequency and length of visits, topics discussed in depth, physical and sexual contact).

Some earlier research supported the importance of these variables in prolonging and improving the patient's quality of life. Dr. Forr hypothesized that patients who had little or no social support might be at greater risk for dying sooner. She reasoned that little purpose would be served by revealing the true nature and goals of this research to dying patients. In fact, she thought that there was a reasonable risk of some patients becoming further depressed on learning of the possibility of a further shortened life span. She decided to avoid providing direct information about the study to the patients themselves. Patients and others were simply told at the outset that the project focused on individuals who had a chronic illness and the methods they used to cope with pain, isolation, and other dysphoric feelings.

When patients died, Dr. Forr provided their families or those who had legal responsibility for them additional information about the research. Care was taken to avoid blaming or inducing feelings of guilt or wrongdoing in those family members and helpers who had been able to offer only limited social support. By preserving the naivete of dying patients, Dr. Forr avoided inflicting additional pain and suffering on some of them but was able to obtain important data that might have significant implications for others diagnosed with serious diseases.

1. Was Dr. Forr's rationale for withholding information about her research from moribund patients justified?
2. How might a hospital ethics committee respond to Dr. Forr's intended research if the patient were hospitalized for a long period of time?
3. Can you think of any other way to carry out this type of research without affecting the integrity of the study?

8.08 (c)

When psychologists become aware that research procedures have harmed a participant, they take reasonable steps to minimize the harm.

> If you learn that someone has been harmed by participating in your research, do what you can to minimize the damage and rectify the situation (i.e., arrange for counseling or therapy, assist in referral to a health care provider for treatment or medication, etc.).

VIGNETTE

Dr. Nicholas Katean was studying the effectiveness of a new intervention for stopping smoking. It was a synthesis of a behavioral approach and meditation, examining various emotions that cued a smoking impulse in the individual. The methodology included, in part, asking participants to briefly write about a stressful event or an emotional state that would usually cause them to feel like smoking. Then they were asked to close their eyes, reflect on the feeling, and, using a particular meditative technique, attempt to diminish the feeling and the intensity of the impulse as well.

To minimize the chances of harm to participants, the investigators screened out those who had a mood disorder, personality disorder, were taking psychotropic medication, had a history of suicidality, were currently consulting a psychotherapist for treatment, or had recently terminated treatment. They also had several therapists on call during the data-gathering phase to help with any potential adverse reactions. As it turned out, it was fortunate that they had taken these precautions, because one research participant had a surprisingly strong response.

Audrey Billows was a drama major who had experienced a major trauma between the time of her original screening and her participation in data gathering 3 weeks later. Her drug-using boyfriend became violent one night and struck her in the face. Audrey went to the campus health center for treatment and was released, but over the next few days she decided to end this relationship, which had been becoming more abusive recently. Also, several days before the data gathering in the psychology laboratory she failed an important examination in her set design class, and she also came down with the flu.

Nevertheless, she wished to take part in the research and receive the promised payment of $30, and she showed up at the appointed time to fulfill her role as a participant. At the first meeting, she was feeling slightly feverish and had a moderate level of depression. When asked to describe the stressful event that made her want to smoke, her mood began to deteriorate. All she could think about was the traumatic episode of being punched by her boyfriend a week earlier, and as she began to write about it, the tears began to flow. She continued writing, as she had been assigned; however, her thoughts began to shift to a much older episode that she had not thought about for many years. When she was 8 years old, she was suddenly awakened one night but did not know why. She rushed out of her bedroom, only to see her parents arguing loudly and her intoxicated father slap her mother hard in the face. Her mother fell down, knocking her forehead on a radiator, and lost consciousness on the floor. As Audrey began to relive some of the intense fear from this scene, experiencing some dissociation, she began to have panicky feelings, shortness of breath, and nausea. She could not continue; she gasped, stood up, and walked rapidly out of the room.

One of the research assistants, Joseph, who had been closely monitoring the group, immediately rushed out of the room and caught up with Audrey. In spite of her sobbing and gasping for air, she was able to communicate in a general way about her panicky feelings and that she needed to "get away." Joseph walked outside with her and continued listening and talking to her supportively. Soon Audrey's panic subsided, and feelings of sadness, fatigue, and shame became more predominant. Joseph used his cellular phone to notify Dr. Katean about what had happened. Dr. Katean told Joseph to offer Audrey an opportunity to speak with one of the on-call therapists and to give her the handout with the names and telephone numbers of all the on-call therapists, as well as a 24-hr telephone hotline number. Audrey thought this over, thanked him for the names, and decided that she would call her old therapist instead. She felt confident that he could talk with her by phone and that she could probably have a session within a few days, if she needed one.

The cascade of losses and distressing experiences over a 3-week period had taken its toll on Audrey, and she realized that it would be beneficial for her to return to psychotherapy. She had never discussed the childhood event of viewing her mother being abused by her father, and she had never had such a vivid memory of it before she began to write about her own trauma of the past few weeks with her boyfriend. She felt comforted by Joseph's quick and gentle response and his willingness to remain with her as long as she needed; she was able to recover from her panic more quickly because of it. She realized that she never should have participated in this research project but that, once again, she had bitten off more than she could chew, an old behavior pattern of hers.

Audrey felt that she had been well informed by Dr. Katean and his associates at the outset, and she appreciated their professionalism and caring. She did not blame them in any way for her reaction and, in fact, was ultimately grateful that she had an experience that resulted in her return to psychotherapy to process these important childhood events.

Dr. Katean followed up with a telephone call during the next few days to see if Audrey was feeling better and whether she had contacted her therapist. When he heard Audrey confirm that she had indeed spoken with her therapist and had made an appointment with him for later that week, Dr. Katean resolved that they had taken every reasonable step to rectify the situation. He documented this call in his telephone log.

1. What additional steps might the researchers have taken in screening participants to reduce the likelihood of adverse reactions, such as the one experienced by Audrey?
2. What training might you provide your research assistants to maximize their effectiveness with participants who might have overly intense negative memories or other adverse reactions?
3. As an investigator, how would you maximize your protection, and reduce your ethical or legal liability, from a participant who felt harmed and had an adverse reaction as a result of his or her involvement in your investigation?

8.09 HUMANE CARE AND USE OF ANIMALS IN RESEARCH

(a) Psychologists acquire, care for, use, and dispose of animals in compliance with current federal, state, and local laws and regulations, and with professional standards.

If you conduct animal research, be sure to abide by relevant federal, state, and local laws and regulations as well as the standards of any other professional associations to which you belong concerning obtaining, caring for, using, and disposing of animals.

VIGNETTE

Dr. Snatcher usually purchased animals through his university's Research Animals Resource Unit, which had well-established business relationships with animal dealers across the country. He was aware of the Guide for the Care and Use of Laboratory Animals (Institute of Laboratory Animal Resources, Commission on Life Sciences [National Research Council], 1996) and the regulations of the U.S. Department of Agriculture (USDA). However, he routinely engaged in some practices that were not in compliance with all the regulations, thinking that they were creative and harmless ways of dealing with some of the common problems encountered by animal researchers.

For example, at the conclusion of research with mice, rats, and pigeons, when there was no further planned use for the animals, he would commonly release them into a nearby woods. He thought that the animals would fare better in a natural setting than by remaining cooped up in their cages for long periods of time. However, by releasing the animals in this way he was exposing them to greater risk; they had been born and raised in captivity and had no experience fending for themselves in the wild. In spite of his benevolent intentions, Dr. Snatcher was actually increasing the risk that the animals would be harmed by predators, extreme weather conditions, infection, and disease. It would have been more humane to have them euthanized appropriately, according to the standards of the American Veterinary Association, or, if consistent with institutional policies, to make arrangements with other researchers to make use of the animals.

Over the past year, Dr. Snatcher also had begun acquiring animals in rather unorthodox ways, using a variety of sources instead of licensed vendors. For example, he had a good friend who owned several animal petting zoos in nearby cities. This resulted in a regular supply of rabbits, marmosets, and capuchins for his research; he could regularly be seen driving his modified pickup truck with the young animals in the back. He also occasionally carried his pet dogs and cats in the same truck, and sometimes he transported raccoons, opossums, and other garden nuisances to remote places for dropoff. Unfortunately he did not disinfect the truck cages adequately, and the resulting contamination placed the animals to be used for research at a high risk of infection. On occasion, these animals also brought diseases from the petting zoo into the existing colonies of Dr. Snatcher's laboratory, causing illness in other animals that sometimes resulted in death. This had obvious implications for the research, because animals that are in poor health tend to behave differently, thus compromising the integrity of the research data.

When he consulted his friends who sat on the university's Institutional Animal Care and Use Committee about the recurring problem of illness among his animals, Dr. Snatcher was told that the problem was probably because of his unusual way of procuring and transporting the new animals. Several committee members were concerned about his methods and informed him that they were contrary to the university's guidelines as well as USDA regulations. The committee as a whole realized after the fact just how lax they had been in enforcing its federally mandated duties. However, when Dr Snatcher approached the members directly, in obvious need of guidance, they provided it and resolved to arrange better oversight of animal procurement in the institution from that point on.

1. Does this ethical standard require any specific behavior of animal researchers other than to know and comply with the existing law and other regulations and professional standards for dealing with animal subjects?
2. What steps might you take, as a junior member on the Institutional Animal Care and Use Committee, if you observed lax enforcement of ethical or federal standards because of cronyism, indifference, or some other reason?

3. What formal action should the Institutional Animal Care and Use Committee have taken when the committee learned of Dr. Snatcher's unorthodox practices?

8.09 (b)

Psychologists trained in research methods and experienced in the care of laboratory animals supervise all procedures involving animals and are responsible for ensuring appropriate consideration of their comfort, health, and humane treatment.

Oversee every procedure involving your animal subjects to ensure competent and humane treatment by assistants and caretakers. Attention should be paid to the animals' comfort, health, medical care, and other basic physiological and psychological needs.

VIGNETTE

Dr. Hugh Mayne and his colleagues were investigating whether an electric current administered by means of an implanted electrode in the spinal cord altered the reactivity to different types of pain in rats. The rats were derived from the Holtzman Company stock and were bred at the university's Research Animals Resource Unit. Because his research involved the administering of different kinds of potentially painful stimuli to his animal subjects, Dr. Mayne was particularly fastidious about closely adhering to all ethical and federal standards and knew that his university's Institutional Animal Care and Use Committee would take a particular interest in closely scrutinizing every aspect of his protocol. His research would have major implications for the treatment of chronic pain in humans who were disabled by their suffering and unable to obtain sustained relief by any other means.

Dr. Mayne took great care in teaching his graduate students and research assistants exactly how to use each piece of equipment and handle the animals according to currently held principles (Iversen & Lattal, 1991). He first trained them in the handling of rats and thoroughly supervised their desensitization to the animals. The assistants were then carefully shown how to prepare the rats for the experiment, which included placing them into a Plexiglas restraint box.

He carefully instructed his assistants in the use of computer software that controlled the amperage to be administered through the implanted electrodes to guarantee standardization in treatment. He also scrupulously reviewed the various aversive stimuli to use in the research, such as chemical, thermal, or electrical, and the methodology of delivering the stimuli to the rats. Finally, he took great care in teaching his assistants observational methods for assessing pain reactivity in the rats, including tail flicks and other motor reactivity.

In supervising his research assistants, Dr. Mayne was methodical, comprehensive, and compassionate. He encouraged his collaborators and assistants to ask for guidance when needed rather than risk harming animals or compromising the data collection. He even requested that they telephone him at home if they had any questions that needed immediate attention. He would randomly monitor their activities and had well-established procedures for being contacted if problems developed. In this way of teaching and supervising in an ongoing way, he maximized the chances that the rats would be well attended, the data gathering would be standardized, and the assistants would be well qualified to carry out their duties. The meticulous way in which Dr. Mayne conducted his research resulted in an extensive contribution to the field that did not have to be repeated and that required less suffering for the animals and less financial cost in the long run.

1. What degree of ethical and legal responsibility does Dr. Mayne hold for the behavior of his research assistants, on a federally funded project, regardless of whether they are psychologists?
2. What means should Dr. Mayne take to remain well informed about humane treatment of his laboratory animals?
3. Who is ultimately responsible if Dr. Mayne delegates the supervision of a new research assistant to an experienced coinvestigator who is not a psychologist?

8.09 (c)

Psychologists ensure that all individuals under their supervision who are using animals have received instruction in research methods and in the care, maintenance, and handling of the species being used, to the extent appropriate to their role. (See also Standard 2.05, Delegation of Work to Others.)

Make sure that assistants under your supervision receive thorough training in research methods and in the care, maintenance, and handling of the kind of animal being used, according to their role in the laboratory.

VIGNETTE

Dr. Hatta Skip was conducting a behavioral pharmacological study on rats that required repetitive blood sampling. While she was in the middle of training her postdoctoral fellows, she had a family crisis that necessitated her leaving town for a short while. Unfortunately, this resulted in inadequate instruction on techniques for drawing blood and how to handle the animals during the procedures. Dr. Skip also failed to educate her assistants adequately about the importance of maintaining proper antiseptic procedures, including the use of proper restraint procedures and inhalational anesthetics.

Fortunately, most of the postdoctoral fellows were already competent in these procedures because they had had much previous experience with research on rats. However, one assistant, Kermit, had virtually no experience in drawing blood from rats. He made many errors, such as disregarding the importance of antiseptic procedures and reusing needles, resulting in the spread of infection to some of the animals. Because he lacked knowledge in proper handling of the rats, he was bitten and ended up dropping or even throwing the rats at times, in frustration.

Kermit's incompetence did not come to the attention of Dr. Skip until several weeks had gone by, when two other postdoctoral fellows felt compelled to bring his woeful inadequacy to her attention. As it turned out, Kermit had misrepresented his experience to Dr. Skip when he originally interviewed for the position and neglected to inform Dr. Skip about how green he really was in handling laboratory animals. Furthermore, he had a long history of addiction to opiates, for severe chronic pain because of a back injury, and his primary motivation for working in an animal laboratory was to gain access to a variety of drugs. Dr. Skip discovered, much to her chagrin, that a significant amount of opiates was missing from the laboratory stock. After she questioned Kermit about this, he acknowledged that he had been diverting drugs from the laboratory stock for his own personal use.

Because Dr. Skip mistakenly assumed competence in all her assistants and had failed to properly train and supervise them in the application of standardized techniques, she lost five animals to infection. Thus, she lost time and accumulated data that were essentially unusable, necessitating restarting some of the animals in the experimental conditions. Kermit had also subjected many animals to needless suffering because of improper techniques that resulted in pain and infection. Because the assistant was incompetent, and Dr. Skip had provided him inadequate training at the outset, the animals, the assistant, and, ultimately, the research project itself, were harmed.

1. What recourse did Dr. Skip have in taking remedial or punitive action against Kermit (a graduate student and thus not a full member of APA) for stealing opiates from the laboratory?
2. Under normal circumstances, how would you determine the competence and limitations of your research assistants in handling and caring for various species of animals under their control?
3. What preventive steps might Dr. Skip have taken to minimize problems while she was called out of town?

8.09 (d)

Psychologists make reasonable efforts to minimize the discomfort, infection, illness, and pain of animal subjects.

Attend compassionately to your animal subjects' medical needs, illness, and suffering. Always take steps to reduce their discomfort or pain and promptly treat any infection or illness.

VIGNETTE

In a long research project using macaque monkeys, Dr. Rex Emplery was fastidious in his care for and supervision of the animals, going great lengths to attend to any discomfort, illness, and suffering. He thoroughly reviewed pertinent sections of the USDA regulations pertaining to the Animal Welfare Act (Title 9, 1992) and the Guide for the Care and Use of Laboratory Animals (Institute of Laboratory Animal Resources, Commission on Life Sciences [National Research Council], 1996) with his assistants and animal care workers. These documents describe in detail the standards for indoor and outdoor housing facilities; mobile housing facilities; environment enhancement to promote psychological well-being; transportation requirements; and, of course, such basics as feeding, watering, and sanitation requirements.

Because Dr. Emplery housed the animals in facilities that were under his authority, as approved by the Institutional Animal Care and Use Committee, he was well aware of his responsibility to meet the standards of the code of federal regulations. Although he knew that his assistants and animal care workers were somewhat experienced, he still felt an obligation to review some of the standards with them to maximize the chances that the monkeys would remain healthy and robust for the duration of his research and would not suffer needlessly.

In particular, he was concerned about temperature control and ventilation of the cages, because the university was having significant problems in these areas. He found it necessary to closely monitor these conditions and, at times, to be in regular contact with the maintenance staff during summer and winter. There had also been problems with the automatic light timers in the past and some laxness in replacing light bulbs when they burned out. Such illumination variability could possibly affect the performance of the monkeys, and Dr. Emplery wanted to take no chances in increasing threats to the validity of his data.

He also was concerned about the general cleanliness of the cages, feeding and watering on a strict schedule, and control of disease. If the cages were not cleaned on a regular schedule and the bedding changed as needed, which occasionally happened over extended weekends or during vacations while the regular staff was away, he was quick to see that these lapses were corrected. He also exhorted his staff to be vigilant about unusual behavior or symptoms that might signify illness in the animals. By seeing to it that skin and other diseases were promptly diagnosed and treated, Dr. Emplery minimized the likelihood of contagion within the colony and, ultimately, any negative impact on his data collection.

Indeed, Dr. Emplery was a model of concern for the health and welfare of his animals. Some might say he was excessive in his attention to some of the minor aspects of animal care. However, because of his vigilance and ongoing supervision of others responsible for the monkeys, he was able to complete his research in a timely fashion with healthy animals and valid data.

1. How would you operationally define *discomfort, illness, infection,* and *pain* in ways that maximize understanding and compliance by your research assistants?
2. What were Dr. Emplery's primary resources for remaining current in animal care techniques? Primary source documents? Internet Web sites? Continuing education opportunities?
3. What variables might contribute to the decision to either treat or euthanize an animal subject?

8.09 (e)

Psychologists use a procedure subjecting animals to pain, stress, or privation only when an alternative procedure is unavailable and the goal is justified by its prospective scientific, educational, or applied value.

Never conduct research that exposes animals to pain, stress, trauma, or privation, unless there are no alternative procedures that address the same research question and the goal is justified by the following:

- prospective *scientific* value (e.g., it is a significant contribution to the knowledge base);
- prospective *educational* value (e.g., it is of significant benefit to individuals or society); or
- prospective *applied* value (e.g., it has significant application to industrial and organizational settings, environmental psychology, or direct implications for the ways in which psychologists intervene in the lives of others).

VIGNETTE

A child psychologist, child psychiatrist, endocrine neurologist, and several geneticists were engaged in planning a large research project focusing on the long-term cognitive and behavioral effects on dogs of repeated exposure to aversive stimuli during early developmental stages. The study was intended to be an animal analogue for child abuse, namely, its effects on various physiological systems (e.g., endocrine, neurological) and implications for long-term psychopharmacological treatment once the animal reached maturity.

The investigators used dogs of various ages, from 1 month to 3 years, and measured stress hormones, such as adrenocorticotropic hormone, prolactin, and plasma catecholamines, as a means of quantifying the animals' stress reactions. At various stages of their growth, and then at maturity, the dogs in the experimental groups received two new medications; one increased the availability of certain neurotransmitters (e.g., serotonin, dopamine), and the other was a genetically engineered drug directly affecting the DNA of several sympathetic nervous system target organs, somewhat reducing their reactivity to adrenalin. The results of this investigation would have major implications for decisions about long-term medication of adults who had been severely abused as children.

It was of prime consideration to ascertain the minimal threshold values of current intensity and duration that would evoke a stress reaction of sufficient magnitude to produce hormonal changes but not so aversive as to inflict needless suffering on the animals for no additional return on the data. A major consideration of the hospital's Institutional Animal Care and Use Committee was that the animals not be exposed to unnecessary pain. The researchers presented the rationale that using a carefully titrated electric current was the simplest and most precise way to obtain the hormonal and neurological changes necessary for testing the research hypotheses: A carefully controlled electric shock in the developing dogs would constitute an approximate physiological equivalent of recurring severe abuse in a child by evoking similar arousal of the organism's sympathetic nervous system and its target organs (e.g., heart, gastrointestinal system). The ultimate prospective value of the research was its potential contribution to the psychopharmacological treatment of adults who had suffered severe child abuse at various developmental stages and were at risk for a lifetime of increased anxiety, depression, physiological disorders, and suicidality.

To ascertain the optimal range of electric current stimuli, the team had relied largely on their earlier research and those of other investigators that assessed the changes in stress hormone output as a function of varying amperage with dogs of different ages. They also carried out additional research for this particular study to establish the optimal amount of electric shock for each animal by age and weight. It was critically important that optimal current values be achieved for obtaining useful data without inflicting unnecessary pain or discomfort on the animals. Too little current would simply be uncomfortable but would not elevate hormone levels sufficiently, and too much shock would cause unnecessary suffering in the animals.

The team members were hopeful that their protocol would be approved by the medical center's Institutional Animal Care and Use Committee and the IRB, because its prospective applied value was significant. They felt that there was no other way to obtain this data, and they had taken great care to minimize the suffering of the animals.

1. How would the primary investigators justify taking such extreme measures in their research with animal subjects?
2. Are there other ways this research team might have gathered comparable data without actually exposing the animals to trauma?
3. How would you respond to an overly assertive television news reporter who takes the position that such animal research is immoral, unethical, and cruel and ought never to occur?

8.09 (f)

Psychologists perform surgical procedures under appropriate anesthesia and follow techniques to avoid infection and minimize pain during and after surgery.

When performing surgery on an animal, use current methods for anesthesia and analgesia, including postoperative pain management, that are appropriate for the species. Take steps to prevent infections by performing the surgery under aseptic conditions and with the use of antibiotics, as needed.

VIGNETTE

Dr. Crest had a good reputation for maintaining high standards in her laboratory, in conformance with the Guide for the Care and Use of Laboratory Animals (Institute of Laboratory Animal Resources, Commission on Life Sciences [National Research Council], 1996). Unannounced visits to her research facility by inspectors from the USDA never revealed any violations or improper procedures. It was her habit to provide comprehensive instruction to her research assistants, and she was particularly scrupulous in supervising them during invasive procedures, such as implanting electrodes, collecting body fluids, or surgery.

Her laboratory personnel consistently observed standard anesthetic and aseptic procedures, and as a result the animals had a very low infection rate and recovered quickly from invasive procedures with a minimum of discomfort or suffering. Dr. Crest also encouraged her staff to be vigilant about preoperative care, postoperative pain, and the proper use of analgesics. She sought consultations with the veterinary staff on an as-needed basis and encouraged her assistants to do likewise. In this way, she was able to remain current about the proper type and dose of analgesics and tranquilizers consistent with the species being used and the research objectives.

Because of Dr. Crest's firm convictions and scrupulous observance of animal research standards, her university enjoyed full accreditation by the Council on Accreditation of the American Association for the Accreditation of Laboratory Animal Care. Over the years, many generations of research assistants learned from Dr. Crest's deeply held and well-informed philosophy of humane treatment of animal subjects.

1. What are some reasons that proper anesthetic and antiseptic procedures are not implemented in animal research?
2. What are the signs and symptoms that various species of laboratory animals with which you work with are experiencing pain and suffering?
3. What are the various options, and your reasons for selecting them, in dealing with a fellow animal researcher who repeatedly fails to comply with this standard, resulting in pain and infection? Directly confront? Report to the IRB of your institution? Report to APA Ethics Committee or state psychological association ethics committee? Notify the funding source? Other options?

8.09 (g)

When it is appropriate that an animal's life be terminated, psychologists proceed rapidly, with an effort to minimize pain and in accordance with accepted procedures.

If you must terminate an animal's life, comply with existing standards and procedures so as to accomplish this task rapidly, minimizing pain and suffering.

VIGNETTE

In research requiring the ultimate sacrificing of rats to examine brain tissue, Dr. G. Reaper was considering the options to select a method that was quick and painless. In keeping with the protocol, however, it was essential to euthanize the animals without significant risk of damaging brain tissue. As a part of providing mentoring on the topic of euthanizing animals to his postdoctoral fellow, Arthur, Dr. Reaper asked him to formally study the variety of techniques available. Specifically, he asked Arthur to research and justify the various methods of euthanasia to increase his understanding of the procedures and rationales from the ground up rather than simply blindly following what others have done.

Arthur was already well aware of the regulations of his university's Institutional Animal Care and Use Committee, and he knew that the committee would have to approve any methods of terminating an animal's life because this was a federally funded project. He was also aware of the National Institutes of Health's standards concerning the broad array of euthanizing agents. He found the American Veterinary Medical Association's (AVMA's) "Report of the AVMA Panel on Euthanasia" (1986), which provided a thorough review of the subject, most useful in his considerations. This document reviews in depth the characteristics and relative merits of using each of the three major methods of euthanizing animals: (a) hypoxic agents (e.g., carbon monoxide, curariform drugs, nitrogen inhalation), (b) direct neuron-depressing agents (e.g., anesthetic gases, barbiturates, chloral hydrate), and (c) physical agents (e.g., decapitation, exsanguination, rapid freezing). To minimize the animals' suffering, Arthur learned that the most preferable method was one that would induce a rapid loss of consciousness prior to death, lest the rats be incapacitated and conscious and increasingly anxious and distressed. He learned that drugs such as curare or succinylcholine used in isolation were prohibited because they paralyzed the animal, including respiratory muscles; thus, the animal could experience pain and panic while it suffocated. He also learned that agents that blocked apprehension and pain perception first, such as chloroform or barbiturates, were preferable because they brought death rapidly following a quick loss of consciousness. There were many factors to be considered in this final phase of the project that were new to Arthur and required knowledge of the effects of various methods and consideration of the animal species involved.

After reviewing the results of Arthur's research, Dr. Reaper asked him to participate in consultations on the merits of several different methods with a veterinarian and with another psychologist to be certain that their knowledge was current. Dr. Reaper and Arthur finally agreed on a method of euthanizing the rats that was quick and painless, posed little risk to brain tissue for analysis, was relatively safe to administer, and was aesthetically acceptable to laboratory personnel. They were satisfied that they had devoted ample time and energy to this important aspect of the protocol, lest the animals suffer unnecessarily at the conclusion of the research.

1. How rapidly would you attend to the task of euthanizing an animal after all data have been collected?
2. What responsibility does Dr. Reaper bear in ascertaining that the animals were, in fact, euthanized in the appropriate manner?
3. Although not stated in this standard, what are Dr. Reaper's responsibilities for monitoring the psychological reactions of

his research assistants who carry out euthanasia and see that they have access to debriefing or counseling if necessary?

8.10 REPORTING RESEARCH RESULTS

(a) Psychologists do not fabricate data. (See also Standard 5.01a, Avoidance of False or Deceptive Statements.)

> Never fabricate, alter, adjust, amend, improve, modify, massage, transform, transmogrify, tweak, or otherwise fool with data when carrying out research. The numbers are what they are, and your scientific contribution will stand as it is. Besides, the risk of getting caught is real, and the consequences are severe—professionally, financially, and in many other ways. Don't even think about it!

VIGNETTE

Dr. Will Alter and a colleague were investigating changes in positron emission tomography brain scans of young children while viewing violent cartoons and playing certain types of online video games. This was a timely and important study. However, for Dr. Alter there was some urgency, because this was his tenure decision year, and he badly needed additional publications in refereed journals if he were to remain on the faculty. Furthermore, his mortgage expenses had increased recently, and his wife's income had been declining.

For the first time in his professional life he dabbled with the idea of committing research fraud. He thought that the publication of his results would have more impact if his data revealed greater statistical significance than was actually the case. Thus, unbeknownst to his coinvestigator, he altered the positron emission tomography scan data of several children to yield such an increase. Fortunately, Dr. Alter's coinvestigator, Dr. Gnoyieu Dohnt, was reviewing the data one night and discovered the anomalies, much to his surprise and disappointment. He confronted his colleague about the erroneous data, and after a discussion that went long into the night, he prevailed on Dr. Alter to abandon his plan and maintain the integrity of the study, even though it might have less of an impact on the scientific community. At least it would be veridical; would not corrupt the psychology knowledge base; and would likely spawn other studies, which might lead to even more significant findings.

This painful confrontation and its sequelae strained the professional and personal relationship of the two scientists. For many days, Dr. Dohnt wondered if he should report his coinvestigator to an ethics committee, because altering data was such a fundamental abrogation of the responsibilities of a researcher and a violation to the science of psychology. Although Dr. Alter had never modified data or distorted results in any previous research, his judgment for the present was obviously impaired, and possibly he would require monitoring in the future. Dr. Dohnt wondered if he could ever trust his friend again, as a coinvestigator, and he continued to engage in dialogue about the matter with him. The beleaguered Dr. Alter realized in the course of these discussions that for many months he had been suffering significant depression that was extensively clouding his judgment. He admitted to his friend that he had had suicidal thoughts of late and feared that his career would take a major turn for the worse if he were not granted tenure.

As a result of this crisis and Dr. Dohnt's compassionate confrontation and concern about his friend, Dr. Alter finally decided to begin consultations with a psychotherapist and address his depression. Because it was obvious to Dr. Dohnt that Dr. Alter was deeply troubled by his own uncharacteristic behavior and was taking active steps to remedy the situation by consulting a therapist, he considered it unnecessary to bring a formal complaint to any ethics committee. In arriving at this decision, however, he carefully reviewed Standards 8.04 and 8.05 of the Ethics Code.

1. What might the full consequences have been if Dr. Alter had successfully published his results with the false data and conclusions and this fact was discovered, several years later, when another researcher asked to review his data for reanalysis?

2. How would you approach a colleague whom you suspect of manipulating research data? As the "ethics police"? As a sympathetic colleague? As "thy brother's keeper" and someone who has suffered a similar temptation in the past?

3. What steps might you take if you discovered intentional distortion of data by a university colleague, and he was not a member of APA or the state psychological association and hence not under the jurisdiction of this Ethics Code?

8.10 (b)

If psychologists discover significant errors in their published data, they take reasonable steps to correct such errors in a correction, retraction, erratum, or other appropriate publication means.

If you find significant mistakes in your published research, make a good-faith effort to correct them, such as by contacting the publisher and printing a retraction, correction, erratum, or some other formal means of notifying readers of the error. The onus is on you to take action, not to wait for others to initiate it.

VIGNETTE

Dr. Rhea Tell had recently concluded a 10-year study on weight loss with moderately obese adults. She presented her results at the APA Annual Convention and was pleased with the attention accorded her research by colleagues and the mass media. She was rather dismayed, however, to read the sensationalistic claims presented by a newspaper reporter who attended her presentation. Significant exaggerations were printed in the newspaper, and all the disclaimers and qualifications that were an important part of her presentation concerning demographics of the participants and details of the interventions had been omitted.

Dr. Tell phoned the newspaper the next day with her complaint and was met with reluctance on the part of the reporter to make any changes. She persisted in her argument that the newspaper was essentially printing erroneous information, and the reporter finally agreed to print a correction on the following day. Because an abbreviated form of the newspaper was also published on the Internet each day, it too had to be corrected.

Unfortunately, Dr. Tell had less success attempting to correct errors in a short television interview that she had also conducted the same day. The journalist conducting the interview, Ms. Kitten Paste, misstated the conclusions of the study and deleted much of what Dr. Tell said in the service of adhering to the station's policy of relying primarily on brief sound bites. Many of Dr. Tell's statements were taken out of context and juxtaposed, presenting a significant distortion of her basic research. Although Dr. Tell was able to eventually contact Ms. Paste, she could not convince her to include more of the interview or present a more balanced view of the research, thus correcting the apparent misstatements. Ms. Paste justified her refusal by saying that there was simply too much news breaking on that day, with world events being what they were and all, to accommodate her request. Attempts to contact Ms. Paste's supervisor to remedy the situation were equally unsuccessful. Although disappointed that she had little control over the actual broadcast, Dr. Tell was satisfied that she at least had made a persistent effort at attempting to correct the situation, as ethically required. Much to her surprise, the newspaper reporter called back a day later informing her that she had made appropriate changes on the newspaper's Web site; apparently, Dr. Tell's efforts were not entirely in vain, after all.

Another error occurred when Dr. Tell's study was published in an APA journal 1 year later. The statistics as printed in a table were inaccurate, because several decimal points had been misplaced, and two lines of text were missing in one paragraph. She had been too busy to personally review the proofs of the article sent to her prior to publication and had delegated that task to her trusted secretary, who failed to catch the errors. She promptly contacted the editor to inform him of the omissions; an erratum correcting these errors was printed in the very next issue. Dr. Tell learned the important lesson that some tasks are too important to delegate to others, no matter how busy one might be.

1. What comparative control does Dr. Tell have over a video-taped interview that is to be broadcast at a later time, and altered to fit a time slot, compared with a live panel discussion or an interview broadcast in real time?
2. Does the Ethics Code require that one be 100% successful in remedying situations over which one may not have full control, or does it require one to simply make a serious attempt? How would one determine how much effort to invest in making such an attempt?
3. Would you choose to delegate a review of the galley proofs of your journal article to someone, so as to minimize the possibility of error? If so, whom?

8.11 PLAGIARISM

Psychologists do not present portions of another's work or data as their own, even if the other work or data source is cited occasionally.

Never characterize another person's ideas, concepts, data, text, or work product as your own, whether in print, in presentations, in the media, over the Internet, or anywhere else. Always cite your sources, as accurately as you can.

VIGNETTE

Dr. Cribwell routinely performed psychological assessments for a group of physicians specializing in chronic disorders, such as chronic fatigue syndrome, myofascial pain syndrome, and autoimmune disorders. He relied on several standard objective instruments and generally sent them to automated scoring services to obtain profiles and a printed narrative report. When writing psychological reports to be included in patients' medical records, he would typically use entire paragraphs verbatim from the computerized narrative that he received back from the scoring service, but it never occurred to him to cite the source. He paid no attention to the bold print at the bottom of the printout stating that the narrative report was copyrighted material. By integrating it into his psychological report and claiming authorship, Dr. Cribwell was violating both the APA ethical standard about plagiarism and copyright laws as well.

Dr. Cribwell also occasionally conducted research in his area of specialty and relied heavily on Internet resources, such as several electronic journals. When he used information and data from these journals in his writings, he usually failed to ascribe authorship because he assumed that anything available on the Internet was in the public domain and thus freely available to subscribers to use as they pleased, without attribution. He did not realize that the obligation to cite one's sources includes online journals as well.

Fortunately, a colleague contacted Dr. Cribwell and informed him about his obligation to honor the ethical standards concerning plagiarism and suggested he review the laws concerning intellectual property, too. He also referred his colleague to sections of the APA *Publication Manual* (APA, 2001a) that address plagiarism. He further reminded him that the rights to scholarly work generally belonged to the author or the publisher, regardless of the medium in which it was published (e.g., journal, book, Internet), even though, admittedly, there was still some uncertainty concerning the ownership of material that was electronically published. In any case, the ethical standards prevail, and one should never claim authorship of material that was written by another.

1. How might Dr. Cribwell have continued to use excerpted paragraphs from the computerized assessment narratives in his psychological reports without risking plagiarism?
2. Who might prove to be a good source of information about plagiarism and intellectual property issues? Within APA? Your institution? Your professional community?
3. Is it acceptable to use very small portions of another's text without citing the source?

8.12 PUBLICATION CREDIT

(a) Psychologists take responsibility and credit, including authorship credit, only for work they have actually performed or to which they have substantially contributed. (See also Standard 8.12b, Publication Credit.)

Claim responsibility and credit only for work that you actually did or to which you substantially contributed. This includes authorship credit, such as journal articles, chapters, books, monographs, and the like, as well as presentations disseminated over the Internet and in the print or electronic media.

VIGNETTE

Dr. Shadow was the owner of an employee assistance program and had a long-standing practice of publishing a monthly newsletter that was sent to all contracting employees who had access to psychological services. Although her name appeared as the author of such articles as "Burnout in the Workplace" and "Getting Along With Your Supervisor," she never actually contributed any text to the newsletter. Instead, she had delegated that responsibility to several of her staff members and was so busy with administrative responsibilities that she often did not have a chance to review a draft of the newsletter before it went to print. She would usually scan the column that appeared under her own name, but she never wrote any material for it.

Sometimes she would submit a column from the newsletter to the local daily newspaper. Again, her name would appear as the author when in fact she had written none of the text. More egregiously, she sometimes used ghostwriters on her staff to create articles for publication in electronic journals on the Internet. She commissioned several colleagues to investigate topics relating to clinical services in a managed health care setting, but aside from specifying the focus of the research she did not participate in any other aspects. She was listed as sole author, and the writers on her staff who performed the research and did the writing were not credited at all. They did receive monetary compensation for their efforts, however.

Everyone involved was content with the business arrangement, even though Dr. Shadow was consistently violating an important ethical standard. When another psychologist in the office became aware of her apparent disregard for the requirements of the publication standard, she called her attention to it. Dr. Shadow was surprised to learn that her practices were considered unethical. After much deliberation, she took the appropriate steps to comply with this standard by ceasing to falsely claim publication credit for work that was clearly not her own. This was not difficult to do but simply required a certain paradigm shift in her thinking as to how she chose to interact publicly with the business and professional world.

1. What actual harm is there in Dr. Shadow's policy of using ghostwriters for the newsletter, newspaper, and online publication?
2. Is this standard, at times, more typical of a deontologically based rule than a teleological one (if no one feels harmed)?
3. How would the psychologist who confronted Dr. Shadow decide whether to take her complaint directly to her or to an ethics committee?

8.12 (b)

Principal authorship and other publication credits accurately reflect the relative scientific or professional contributions of the individuals involved, regardless of their relative status. Mere possession of an institutional position, such as department chair, does not justify authorship credit. Minor contributions to the research or to the writing for publications are acknowledged appropriately, such as in footnotes or in an introductory statement.

> Only claim publication credit that reflects what you actually contributed to the final product. Just because you may chair the department, run the laboratory, contribute to research funding, or obtain research participants does not mean that you are automatically entitled to be listed as an author. However, if you made a minor but important contribution, you should be credited, by means of a footnote or in some other way.[1]

VIGNETTE

Dr. I. M. Sun chaired the psychology department at a nearby university but seemed to have little familiarity with the current standards concerning authorship credit. He was involved in conducting interdisciplinary research involving opiate dependence among amputee patients suffering phantom limb pain in collaboration with several physicians on staff at the neurology clinic of a local hospital. In his methodology, he relied heavily on the wisdom and experience of two widely published junior colleagues in the psychology department, namely, a statistician and a specialist in chronic pain. He also spent many hours conferring with the director of the hospital's chemical dependency unit in addition to the two physicians on the pain clinic staff. Each of these individuals played a key role, in one way or another, in helping shape the research design, formulate hypotheses, select instruments of assessment, obtain research participants, and analyze the data. Each of them also contributed text to the journal article; without their cooperation, the project would not have happened.

Each participant considered him- or herself to be a coinvestigator, even though there was no formal agreement in advance about the listing of authorship credit. Dr. Sun, however, had his own ideas about how to share publication credit. Because he chaired the department, conceived the study, and felt that he did most of the work, he listed himself as principal author, with the two physicians as his junior authors. The psychology colleagues and director of the chemical dependency unit were relegated to a 5-line footnote of acknowledgment.

When they reviewed the proofs of the article and discovered that they were not listed as authors, these three individuals were understandably quite

---

[1]The reader may recall two lawsuits against two former members of the Beatles, George Harrison and John Lennon. George Harrison's song "My Sweet Lord" was said to have been plagiarized from an earlier song: "He's So Fine," by the Chiffons. The charge was based on identical progressions of notes for the chorus (not lyrics). Also, in John Lennon's song "Come Together," the very first line is a close approximation of a line in Chuck Berry's song "You Can't Catch Me." Berry's original line was "Up come a flattop/He was movin' up with me"; Lennon's line was "Here come old Flattop/He come groovin' up slowly." Obviously, the alleged imitation does not have to be an exact copy for a plagiarism accusation to stick. Neither does it have to be deliberate, as Harrison was ruled to have unconsciously plagiarized the Chiffons' song (Rothschild, 2002).

disgruntled. They confronted Dr. Sun about his lack of fairness in failing to list them as coauthors. Dr. Sun, however, responded that they had no claim to joint authorship because they played a comparatively small role in the project and had no part in authoring the grant that funded the project. It took the consultation of two senior faculty members, combined with an in-house grievance and the threat of a formal ethics complaint, to bring about a partial eclipse of Dr. Sun and to convince him to share authorship credit among all contributors to the project.

1. If it was unclear at the outset how publication credit would be distributed, at what point should a discussion have taken place to clarify this important matter?
2. How might you document principal and second authorship at the time it is decided? By a contract? By e-mail correspondence? By a letter?
3. How would you go about modifying an authorship agreement if, months later, it becomes obvious that the second author has made more of a contribution and likely will continue to do so?
4. How would you, as a coauthor, track the origin of a seminal idea or the relative contributions you and your cohorts have made, over the course of time, to determine the order of authorship?

8.12 (c)

Except under exceptional circumstances, a student is listed as principal author on any multiple-authored article that is substantially based on the student's doctoral dissertation. Faculty advisors discuss publication credit with students as early as feasible and throughout the research and publication process as appropriate. (See also Standard 8.12b, Publication Credit.)

Principal authorship is usually reserved for a student in a multiple-authored publication based mainly on his or her doctoral dissertation. If you as the faculty member think there is a good reason for departing from this tradition, discuss this with the student as early on as possible, or during the course of the research and publication process, if it becomes apparent that your contributions may merit principal authorship.

VIGNETTE

Dr. Meefurst had chaired many dissertation committees over the course of his academic career and had a long list of multiple-authored publications after his name. In general, he would assist the student in publishing research results based on his or her dissertation and would provide a great deal of practical guidance about which journals to consider for publication. Dr. Meefurst also made his secretarial staff available for editing and revising a student's articles, as needed, and often he would be willing to provide extensive collaboration with the student in formulating an article for publication that was basically an outgrowth of the student's dissertation.

In return for all these efforts, Dr. Meefurst felt entitled to list himself as the primary author of the articles, even though they were based primarily on his students' dissertations. If a student were to raise a question about this practice, he or she would be met with Dr. Meefurst's characteristic rebuff: that it had always been his custom to list himself as the primary author, which had been a perfectly acceptable practice in academia "forever." In response to further questioning, Dr. Meefurst would remind the student that without all of his support and clerical assistance—which, in fact, had greatly promoted the student's work—it never would have reached the publishable stage in such a short period of time. Any additional resistance offered by the student would be met with not-so-subtle reminders that a student has limited power within an academic setting and may be vulnerable to losing out on important professional opportunities in the future. Because of this perception of powerlessness, few students ever objected or raised a formal complaint.

One particularly assertive student, Dr. Katherine Fermly, who was inappropriately listed as a second author by Dr. Meefurst, her former dissertation chair, had studied the 1992 and 2002 editions of the Ethics Code thoroughly and was well aware that his assumption of primary authorship had been open to question for many years. Although she was grateful for the help he had provided in the course of writing her dissertation, she felt that she should have been listed as the primary investigator on the paper submitted for publication. She waited until all her work at the university was completed, her degree was awarded, and she was well established in her postdoctoral internship. She also reviewed the rules and procedures of the APA Ethics Committee and knew that the statute of limitations allowed her 5 years from the time the alleged misconduct occurred until the complaint was received (APA, 2001b). Finally, with some uncharacteristic ambivalence and even some guilty feelings, Dr Fermly formally initiated a complaint against the man who had formerly chaired her dissertation committee and for years provided much support for her work. By so doing, she not only began a process of formal scrutiny of Dr. Meefurst's conduct but also set an example for other graduate students who were being discriminated against by being robbed of due principal-authorship credit.

Thus began a 9-month process of correspondence back and forth, from the Ethics Committee, to Dr. Meefurst, to other members of the faculty, to Dr. Fermly, and so on. Dr. Meefurst ultimately was issued a cease-and-desist directive by the Ethics Committee, requiring that he stop the practice of listing himself as first author in a paper that is based on a student's dissertation. He was also ordered to attend over the following year an ethics workshop that covered research and publication practices. (As a conciliatory gesture, however, and in deference to the good research that he had contributed to the field, the Ethics Committee reached a consensus in not requiring Dr. Meefurst to do something about his perplexing surname.)

1. Under what circumstances might faculty members rightly list themselves as a first author in collaborating with a student on a journal article that was originally based on the student's dissertation?
2. Who should be more aware of the requirements of this ethical standard and be prepared to comfortably discuss coauthorship in faculty–student collaborative efforts: the professor or the student? Why?
3. If the balance of responsibility for writing or contributing to the article seems to change, over time, how and when should this be addressed by the coauthors?

8.13 DUPLICATE PUBLICATION OF DATA

Psychologists do not publish, as original data, data that have been previously published. This does not preclude republishing data when they are accompanied by proper acknowledgment.

Only publish your original data as original one time (i.e., do not publish seminal research or original data in different journals as though each is a novel and unique publication). When referring to your findings in subsequent writings, you must cite the original publication, even though it is your own work.

VIGNETTE

In 2002, Dr. Overanover published a seminal article about his well-designed inventory for assessing psychological distress and physical pain as distinct entities in patients coping with chronic illness. He introduced normative data with samples representing excellent diversity in gender, age, ethnicity, and other variables. This proved to be a useful tool for psychologists and physicians alike specializing in this population. So optimistic was he that had begun contacting publishers to begin the introductory steps of creating an assessment package for health care professionals consisting of the instrument itself, scoring templates, a manual, and other materials.

In his enthusiasm to promulgate his research results to an even wider audience, Dr. Overanover submitted another article for publication to a non-APA journal that relied heavily on the already-published data about his inventory. He had made a few modifications to the items of the inventory, but unfortunately he neglected to cite the original 2002 article. Thus, he introduced his instrument of assessment again, in 2003, for the "first time" with the second article that was published.

By failing to cite the original source (i.e., his own 2002 publication), Dr. Overanover gave the false impression that the inventory was new. It would have been simple enough to cite his earlier work; however, Dr. Overanover thought it was unnecessary to do so. Because these were his own data, he thought that he bore no responsibility to cite the earlier publication; it was impossible to plagiarize from oneself, or so he thought.

This practice made it difficult for other researchers to track the natural evolution of the inventory or to know which version they were using in attempting to carry out further clinical research. If Dr. Overanover had simply complied with the ethical standard that forbids duplicate publication of data, he would have cleared up all potential confusion for readers.

1. How does Dr. Overanover's penchant for duplicate publication of his research harm the database or interfere with carrying out accurate research?
2. If Dr. Overanover had made substantial changes in his second publication, would he still have been obliged to cite the original 2002 article?

8.14 SHARING RESEARCH DATA FOR VERIFICATION

(a) After research results are published, psychologists do not withhold the data on which their conclusions are based from other competent professionals who seek to verify the substantive claims through reanalysis and who intend to use such data only for that purpose, provided that the confidentiality of the participants can be protected and unless legal rights concerning proprietary data preclude their release. This does not preclude psychologists from requiring that such individuals or groups be responsible for costs associated with the provision of such information.

After publishing your research, be prepared to provide any raw data that are requested to other investigators who wish to verify your claims. You need not release your raw data, however, if you have concerns about confidentiality of the participants or if legal rights exist with reference to proprietary data. Also, you may pass on the costs of accessing and producing your raw data to the individuals or groups seeking it. (N.B.: APA journals require you to keep your data for reanalysis for 5 years; APA, 2001a.)

VIGNETTE

A psychologist who was acting as a consultant to a major telephone company was asked to carry out research on the subject of consumers' abilities and preference for accessing e-mail, Internet, and certain databases through cordless and cellular phones. She completed a comprehensive study involving questionnaires, personal interviews, and use of hardware prototypes. Because her work had implications beyond the research and development needs of the telephone company with which she had contracted, she decided to publish her results in a professional journal also.

Within a few months of publication, Dr. Doobius, a psychologist, contacted her for the purpose of reviewing her data and statistical analysis. He questioned her methodology and did not find her claims to be credible concerning the pervasiveness of computer avoidance, particularly by women; members of older age groups; and people who were disabled in some way, such as with a chronic illness or hearing impairment.

The consulting psychologist would gladly have released her data as requested by Dr. Doobius, but her research was essentially owned by the telephone company, who legally held the proprietary rights. By contracting with the company in the first place, she had agreed to keep her data in-house. She could present or publish her general results and conclusions, as she did with permission from the phone company, but she was not permitted to reveal the raw data in their entirety or the protocols developed for the research. As indicated in this standard, her ethical obligation to retain her data and yield it for reanalysis was secondary to her legal obligation to honor the contract she had with the phone company.

1. If the telephone company had released the consulting psychologist from the agreement, would she then be required to turn over her data to Dr. Doobius?
2. Who would pay for the cost of accessing the data, removing identifying information, and duplicating it?
3. What might be the consequences of releasing data for reanalysis when you do not hold the intellectual property rights yourself?
4. Have you violated the Ethics Code if your reanalyzed data reveal a mistake?
5. What is your obligation if errors are found in your published results?

8.14 (b)

Psychologists who request data from other psychologists to verify the substantive claims through reanalysis may use shared data only for the declared pur-

pose. Requesting psychologists obtain prior written agreement for all other uses of the data.

> If you request data from another researcher for reanalysis, to verify and corroborate, you may use the data only for that purpose. If you would like to use the data for any other purpose, you must obtain the consent of the primary investigator in advance, in writing.

VIGNETTE

Three psychologists and two physicians were investigating the use of cannabis in patients with chronic pain from AIDS, cancer, and severe neck and back injuries. This was a large study, involving an experimental group of more than 500 individuals who had been legally purchasing and using marijuana over a 2-year period and a carefully matched control group. It required careful tracking of long-term users' names and addresses because the data were useful only if the participants of the study could be assessed for psychological and physiological changes attributable to cannabis use throughout the whole time span. There was also a possibility that the researchers would extend this longitudinal study even further and gather additional follow-up data from these same participants after many more years had elapsed; therefore, their whereabouts had to be carefully tracked after the initial data gathering was over.

One year after the researchers completed and published their work, they received requests from several psychologists who wished to reanalyze their data. They believed that one of the statistical procedures had been improperly applied and suspected that there might be some arithmetic errors as well, because the results did not seem consistent with their own studies of long-term cannabis use. Fortunately, the psychologists on the team had retained the original data, consistent with the 5-year postpublication retention rule for APA journals (APA, 2001a). They knew of their obligation to make raw data available for reanalysis (although the physicians on the team had no such ethical responsibility), but they also were obliged to maintain confidentiality.

Unfortunately, the research participants' personally identifying information was accessible along with raw scores because of the way the data had been gathered, and there was no easy way to extricate it. Therefore, the group found it necessary to invest clerical time to extract names, addresses, and other identifying information from the raw data before releasing it to the requesting psychologists. This took several days of secretarial time, but it was critical to protect the privacy of the participants. The cost of coding and extricating the requested data was passed on to the requesting psychologists.

After reviewing the vast amount of raw data, the requesting psychologists found no significant errors; however, they did develop some new hypotheses, along their lines of research, that could readily be tested by the data. They sought permission from the research team to carry out new research, and it was granted. A formal permissions document was drafted and signed by all parties, specifying the transfer of data and the details of the agreement for carrying out the new analyses.

The research team learned from this experience the importance of designing methods for collecting and coding their data from the outset so as to avoid such time and money expenditures in the future. They could easily have done so, and they had considered it, but they estimated the risk of their data being sought to be quite small and thus not worth the additional work of deleting identifying information.

1. Although not required for non-APA journals, why might it be desirable to retain your raw data for a period of time after you have published your results?
2. What costs are you entitled to pass on to the requesting scientists for accessing your raw data?
3. Might it be useful to use the services of an editor or an attorney in drawing up an agreement to release your data for uses other than to verify your substantive claims?

8.15 REVIEWERS

Psychologists who review material submitted for presentation, publication, grant, or research proposal review respect the confidentiality of and the proprietary rights in such information of those who submitted it.

If you review or screen the work of others, resist the temptation to use the newly submitted information for any purpose whatsoever. This includes papers to be presented or published; grant and research proposals; media presentations; and lectures to be presented in any forum—academic, to the lay public, over the Internet, and so on. The material is to be evaluated by you and then essentially treated as if it did not exist until it is published in a professional journal or otherwise freely available to the public.

VIGNETTE

Dr. Will Uzit was asked to review a paper submitted for publication in a non-APA hypnosis journal. Because he was an expert in the application of hypnosis as an adjunctive technique for some patients in the treatment of posttraumatic stress disorder, and the paper explored the validity of repressed memory for traumatic events, he seemed to be a logical choice as one of the three reviewers. While reading the paper, Dr. Uzit became interested in the authors' area of research, namely, the use of EEG data for assessing the accuracy of long-term memory for traumatic episodes, regardless of the patient's subjective belief that a particular trauma did in fact occur. Although much additional research remained to be done, the preliminary data were promising.

Dr. Uzit reviewed this well-written manuscript and suggested some minor editorial changes only. In his evaluation, the paper successfully met the journal's criteria for outstanding and scientific professional merit: The topic was timely and appropriate for the journal, it was written in a highly scholarly fashion, the review of the literature was comprehensive, and the design and statistical analyses were exemplary.

About 2 weeks after reviewing the paper, Dr. Uzit was invited to participate on a small panel for a major cable TV presentation entitled "Child Abuse and Repressed Memory: What Can You Believe?" During the taping of the 2-hour show, the discussion became heated, including *ad hominem* attacks by the panel members. Dr. Uzit became somewhat flustered and, in the heat of debate, attempted to defend his strong views on the subject by citing the study that he had recently reviewed for publication. He referred to "new and important research involving brain scans that yields hard scientific data validating that patients do, in fact, remember exactly what happened to them in the past." Not only did he disregard the confidentiality and proprietary rights of the author in citing this study, but he also misstated the results, leaving out qualifying and cautionary comments.

After the show aired, two journalists from major newspapers telephoned Dr. Uzit for interviews. By this time, he had recovered his objectivity and declined their requests, realizing the error he had made on the air by citing a study that was not yet published. He knew that in his eagerness to take a shortcut in educating the public and championing his cause, he had violated the important property rights of another psychologist and, with his show of poor judgment, diminished his own credibility among his peers.

As it happened, the authors of the paper had seen the broadcast and wondered whether Dr. Uzit was citing their work, even though it had not yet been published. They rightly guessed that he most likely was one of the reviewers for the refereed journal and had improperly referred to their research on the air. They considered initiating a formal ethics complaint against him for his transgression. They ultimately decided against it, as the revelations on the television show were somewhat vague and no authorship or journal was cited. They did decide to contact Dr. Uzit, however, and issue a personal reprimand of their own—if, in fact, he would acknowledge his unethical conduct.

1. Were there sufficient grounds for the authors to have proceeded with an ethics complaint, if they wished?

2. Are there any corrective actions that Dr. Uzit could take with the cable TV company, even after the show has aired one time, to at least minimize the potential for future damage?

9

ASSESSMENT

9.01 BASES FOR ASSESSMENTS

(a) Psychologists base the opinions contained in their recommendations, reports, and diagnostic or evaluative statements, including forensic testimony, on information and techniques sufficient to substantiate their findings. (See also Standard 2.04, Bases for Scientific and Professional Judgments.)

When writing psychological reports or recommendations, making diagnostic or evaluative statements of any kind, or providing forensic testimony, be sure to base your comments on facts and verifiable information (e.g., formal assessments, test results, personal interviews, the professional literature, your own valid research, relevant documents, and other such materials). Do not rely on unverified or third-party reports, idle talk, so-called common knowledge, or ill-founded hunches.

VIGNETTE

Dr. Mittelsperson was asked to perform a child custody assessment by Mrs. Ethel Scarlett, a divorcing mother of two who was a frequent marijuana user. Her estranged husband was the chief financial officer of a steel manufacturing company and regularly worked over 100 hr per week. Dr. Mittelsperson had assessed several other families in her brief forensic career, with the mentoring of a former supervisor, but she was not accustomed to the intensity and acrimony of this high-conflict divorce proceeding or the array of problems it presented.

It seems that Mr. Scarlett had suddenly moved out of the house several months before, and recently he had threatened to harm his wife and kidnap the children if things did not go his way. He had been stepping up his attempts to gain legal and physical custody of the children. Fearful of her husband's threats, Mrs. Scarlett had called the police for support on more than one occasion, and she was considering seeking a restraining order to maximize the safety of her and the children.

Under these circumstances, Dr. Mittelsperson did her very best to formally evaluate the individuals involved, using proper instruments of assessment and personal interviews. However, Mr. Scarlett was nearly impossible to contact, because of his frequent business traveling and his hostile interpersonal style, so she never had a face-to-face structured interview with him as part of the total assessment. In her written report to the court presenting her assessment of Mr. and Mrs. Scarlett and their children, she provided the summarized results and conclusions from psychological testing, collateral information from other sources (neighbors, teachers, etc.), and personal interviewing that she had carried out. However, she failed to reveal in her report that she had not personally evaluated Mr. Scarlett. It was not until the cross-examination, when Mr. Scarlett's attorney raised the issue of Dr. Mittelsperson's glaring omission and the resulting prejudicial assessment and recommendations in favor of the wife, that the problem of the inadequate assessment came out into the open.

Dr. Mittelsperson appreciated the seriousness of her lapse in judgment in dispensing with a face-to-face interview with a difficult individual and agreed that the assessment was not comprehensive and had not been competently performed. Because she had not performed a personal evaluation of Mr. Scarlett, she should not have made any statements about his parenting skills, or about the relative parenting capabilities of Mr. and Mrs. Scarlett. She also realized, belatedly, that she should have informed the court during her direct examination about her failure to have assessed Mr. Scarlett personally instead of waiting until the cross-examination brought it to light.

1. What steps might Dr. Mittelsperson have taken to remedy the problems in attempting to personally evaluate Mr. Scarlett?
2. How seriously compromised are Dr. Mittelsperson's report and testimony as they currently stand?
3. How would you go about disclosing an opinion in a psychological report that is not clearly supported by your assessment of the individual but nevertheless may be an astute observa-

tion worth reporting, in your view? How would you substantiate verbalizing such an opinion if challenged by an attorney for the other side?

9.01 (b)

Except as noted in 9.01c, psychologists provide opinions of the psychological characteristics of individuals only after they have conducted an examination of the individuals adequate to support their statements or conclusions. When, despite reasonable efforts, such an examination is not practical, psychologists document the efforts they made and the result of those efforts, clarify the probable impact of their limited information on the reliability and validity of their opinions, and appropriately limit the nature and extent of their conclusions or recommendations. (See also Standards 2.01, Boundaries of Competence, and 9.06, Interpreting Assessment Results.)

Only provide your opinions about a person's psychological traits if you have carried out a formal assessment sufficient to support your statements, conclusions, recommendations, and so on. If circumstances prevent you from personally examining an individual, do the following:

- document your efforts to carry out the personal assessment or evaluation and the results of these efforts (e.g., what repeated efforts did you make to actually contact the individual, and what was the result?);
- clarify how the limited information will affect the validity, reliability, and relevance of your comments (e.g., is the accuracy or dependability of your statements degraded by your not having carried out a personal examination of the individual?); and
- limit the nature and scope of your conclusions and recommendations accordingly, and never make statements that go beyond the data about the person or situation.

VIGNETTE

In a child custody case, Dr. Noah Spin initially was intent on personally assessing every family member and not relying on the statements of others or a blind review of psychological testing in forming his opinions. In this unusual case, Tess and Abby, two lesbian women raising a 6-year-old boy, were in the process of separating. They had been together for 9 years, and each wanted to retain full physical and legal custody of the child.

Dr. Spin was able to meet with Tess, but he found it impossible to arrange a face-to-face meeting with Abby to have an interview and administer psychological tests. In fact, unbeknownst to Dr. Spin, Abby's attorney had recommended that his client avoid the psychological assessment in any way she could, because she was actively alcoholic, and he feared Dr. Spin's assessment might adversely affect Abby's chances of obtaining custody. Besides, he had retained his own expert witness, Dr. Overschoot, to assess Abby, and he was pleased that Dr. Overschoot's psychological report failed to mention Abby's alcohol dependence or any other factors that might weaken her case. The only data about Abby that Dr. Spin was successful in obtaining were interviews with those who knew her and a parenting abilities checklist, which he had administered over the telephone. Unfortunately, little or no standardization data existed for lesbian parents with this particular instrument.

When it came time for Dr. Spin to testify, he responded conservatively to questions about Abby. He made clear that (a) he had never met the woman; (b) he had not performed a comprehensive assessment; (c) his only sources of information about Abby were Tess, two teachers from her son's school, and two workers at the day-care center; and (d) the data from the parenting abilities checklist, which probably had questionable validity given the lack of norms for gay populations and the fact that he had administered it to Abby over the telephone. He made these points clear in his psychological report, his deposition, and his court testimony. He also raised the question about Abby's failure to cooperate in the process of a court-ordered assessment, and he recommended that the court find a means of proceeding with a psychological evaluation of her before attempting to resolve the case.

When asked pointed questions about Abby, Dr. Spin was cautious in responding, usually replying that he lacked sufficient data to answer. Although the attorneys strongly encouraged him to reach conclusions about Abby's parenting ability, on the basis of the data that were available, Dr. Spin was steadfast in his resolve to avoid the temptation to offer opinions or conclusions that could not be substantiated by the data. He wisely reigned himself in, refusing to provide corroborative information about Abby in response to pointed questions by the attorney, or even to speak in general terms about his impressions of her. This left very little of substance that he could present about the woman, on the basis of his own assessment, but at least he had kept his statements accurate and remained within his area of competence.

Finally, Dr. Spin informed the court about the asymmetry of this evaluation process and the inherent problems therein; specifically, a complete psychological assessment of Tess would tend to reveal both her strengths and weaknesses as a potential single parent, and provide much information for examination and cross-examination, whereas a partial assessment of Abby would necessarily produce a skewed picture, with possibly muted weaknesses and amplified strong points, yielding far fewer data to analyze. Therefore, it would be much more difficult for the court to make a valid and fair judgment about which woman should have physical and legal custody.

1. How are psychological evaluators or expert witnesses invited to compromise their ethical standards by the legal system?
2. If Dr. Spin had heard from every source with whom he spoke that Tess was a heavy drinker, should he include this as a part of his report or testimony?
3. What are Dr. Spin's alternative courses of action that might have allowed him to carry out the court-ordered psychological assessment of Abby, in spite of her efforts to avoid it?

9.01 (c)

When psychologists conduct a record review or provide consultation or supervision and an individual examination is not warranted or necessary for the opinion, psychologists explain this and the sources of information on which they based their conclusions and recommendations.

If you are conducting a record review, providing consultation, or supervising another individual, and a personal assessment of the individual is not warranted or needed, be sure to explain this fully. Also be sure to disclose the sources of information that formed the basis of your opinions, conclusions, or recommendations.

VIGNETTE

Mr. Levitt was a 55-year-old in-house accountant for a large food-processing company who was recovering from the effects of treatment for his prostate cancer. He had recently completed a course of hormonal treatment, followed by implanted radioactive beads and external beam radiation therapy. Although his prognosis was fairly good, during the course of diagnosis and treatment Mr. Levitt began to exhibit symptoms of depression. His employer needed him back on the job, as he had already taken quite a bit of time off, and it was nearly the end of the fiscal year, a time when the workload was the heaviest. To prove that he was incapacitated by depression, and truly unable to work and at the request of his manager, Mr. Levitt had a clinical interview with a psychologist, Dr. Marion Ette, who was on the staff of the employee assistance program (EAP) contracting with the company. At the beginning of the interview, Mr. Levitt signed an authorization form releasing the interview results to his company, thinking this would benefit his plea. In her report, Dr. Ette suggested that, on the basis of this cursory examination, which included the Beck Depression Inventory and a brief clinical interview, she believed Mr. Levitt was not depressed but malingering and was quite capable of returning to work.

Mr. Levitt was surprised to learn of Dr. Ette's conclusions when he discussed the matter with his manager by phone the next day. His manager reaffirmed that Mr. Levitt was needed at work and that the psychological report of his malingering might possibly constitute a threat to the security of his position, unless he could be back on the job soon. He also mentioned, offhandedly, that Mr. Levitt was entitled to have a thorough assessment by one of the psychologists from the EAP, if he wished.

Mr. Levitt promptly scheduled an appointment with an EAP psychologist, Dr. Moira Thorrow, and was evaluated the following week. Dr. Thorrow used a lengthy structured clinical interview, as well as the Minnesota Multiphasic Personality Inventory (MMPI), the Rorschach, the Hamilton Depression Inventory and Anxiety Scales, and interviews with Dr. Levitt's treating oncologists. Dr. Thorrow concluded that Mr. Levitt was indeed experiencing a major depressive disorder, secondary to his significant health problems and medical interventions over the past year. Furthermore, she felt there was no evidence to suspect that Mr. Levitt was malingering or being noncompliant with his medical treatment.

Although Dr. Thorrow's diagnostic assessment appeared to be comprehensive and valid, it dramatically contradicted that of Dr. Ette, who happened to be a personal friend of Mr. Levitt's manager and quite persuasive in that role. Therefore, Mr. Levitt soon discovered that he was still under pressure to return to work at once, or face the prospect of eventually losing his job.

As a last resort, Mr. Levitt consulted an attorney to advise him on a course of action that would help protect the security of his job. The attorney advised Mr. Levitt to contact the human resources department of his company and to contract with a psychologist to review the records of both Dr. Ette and Dr. Thorrow and write a final report.

With assistance from the human resources office, Mr. Levitt and his manager agreed on the choice of a psychologist who would conduct a record review of the two assessments and then write a report of the findings. The psychologist, Dr. Anne O'Tate, asked to see all the test data, clinical interview records, and any other notes and formal records of the psychiatric and psychological consultations. After carefully reviewing all the data, Dr. O'Tate wrote a report in which she clearly stated its purpose, its substantive bases, and her findings. Dr. O'Tate's report clearly stated that she had not examined Mr. Levitt and that her impressions were wholly based on her interpretations of Mr. Levitt's past performance records, his medical records, and a review of the two psychological assessments (performed by Drs. Ette and Thorrow). Dr. O'Tate concluded that Mr. Levitt was experiencing a major depressive episode, that there was no evidence of malingering, and that he was eager to return to work as soon as he was able. She recommended that Mr. Levitt begin individual psychotherapy and consider scheduling an appointment with a psychopharmacologist to assess his need for antidepressant medication. Her recommendations were ultimately accepted by the human resources department, which was mediating this dispute. Although Dr. O'Tate never personally assessed Mr. Levitt, she performed an important service by reviewing the records of his previous evaluations and writing a report on the basis of her findings.

1. Is it ethical for Dr. O'Tate to perform this kind of review, without ever having seen the patient? How valid and meaningful would her report be?
2. How can a psychologist maintain ethical integrity when asked to be the arbitrator between two conflicting psychological reports?
3. What are the ethical obligations of a consulting psychologist on a work-dispute case?
4. What are the ethical ways of handling a case like this one if, when reviewing the records, you discover that you are friends with one of the report authors? What if one of them is a colleague with whom you have a collaborative working relationship?

9.02 USE OF ASSESSMENTS

(a) Psychologists administer, adapt, score, interpret, or use assessment techniques, interviews, tests, or instruments in a manner and for purposes that are appropriate in light of the research on or evidence of the usefulness and proper application of the techniques.

Whenever you do assessment work—administer tests, adapt or modify instruments for special use, perform assessment interviews, score tests by hand or computer, interpret results, and so on—be sure to use proper and orthodox methods. This means selecting the right test for the task at hand and using it in the approved manner, with knowledge of the current research or evidence of its usefulness. Do not take shortcuts when performing psychological assessments; do things by the book.

VIGNETTE

Dr. Loevalid, a young therapist with minimal grounding in test construction, developed an instrument that he titled the "Marital Distress Syndrome Inventory" (MDSI), which he used to assess and treat married couples who had repeatedly sought counseling or crisis management over the course of their marriage.

The items Dr. Loevalid created were drawn primarily from his own clinical experience, which consisted of providing counseling to approximately 10 couples over a period of 1 year. He had never carried out a pilot study or formally assessed a sufficient number of couples to establish the instrument's reliability or validity, but he had already begun to use it routinely as a basis for making judgments about the long-term viability of couples' marriages. In presenting the instrument to his new clients he failed to inform them of its experimental nature and its utter lack of established validity. He thought this was unnecessary because he had much faith in the instrument, on the basis of his clinical experience, so he relied on it routinely as an important tool in treating couples. At times, he would recommend to the husband and wife that they experiment with a trial separation, based primarily on their scores on the MDSI.

One day, a senior colleague questioned Dr. Loevalid about his application of the MDSI. This colleague was seeking reliability and validity data, as he was considering using the instrument in his own practice. However, Dr. Loevalid could supply no information other than his clinical intuition and experience. The colleague then discussed the ethical and clinical issues of Dr. Loevalid's continued use of an unvalidated instrument and the possibility of harming clients by failing to provide informed consent in advance concerning the experimental nature of the assessment.

Dr. Loevalid considered seriously his colleague's friendly confrontation and began to reflect on the actual risks of continuing to use the MDSI as well as the possibility of harming others. He reviewed his therapy records for the previous 8 months and discovered that a majority of couples had scored in such a way so as to warrant a recommendation of trial separation. As it turned out, only one out of five couples took Dr. Loevalid's advice to separate—at great financial expense and significant disruption for them, their children, and their extended family members. The majority of couples strongly considered his advice but ultimately rejected it, with some losing faith in therapy and ending treatment.

Dr. Loevalid began to understand that his unscientific application of assessment principles had the potential for serious negative effects on the lives of his clients, causing unnecessary hardship at times already characterized by great stress. He decided to stop using the MDSI as a diagnostic tool and began to use it as a concise means of gathering data for marital therapy instead. He also began to formally instruct every couple about its experimental nature and told them that the results of this assessment would not necessarily be predictive of compatibility or therapy outcome. Dr. Loevalid had finally gained the beginnings of an appreciation for the necessity of adhering to scientific principles in constructing and using instruments of assessment. It was not until he took several continuing education workshops on assessment, which provided far better instruction than he had received in graduate school, that he was able to feel more confident about the formal use of assessment instruments both with couples and individuals.

1. What damage could Dr. Loevalid's test practices do to individuals?
2. If a couple were to complain, to which entity would they turn, and why? The state licensing board? The state association's ethics committee (if it still adjudicates ethics complaints)? The American Psychological Association (APA) Ethics Committee? A lawyer?
3. What steps might Dr. Loevalid's benevolent colleague take to further mentor and assist him (rather than simply to complain about his conduct to a third party)?
4. What recourse might a colleague have if Dr. Loevalid refused to change his ways?

9.02 (b)

Psychologists use assessment instruments whose validity and reliability have been established for use with members of the population tested. When such validity or reliability has not been established, psychologists describe the strengths and limitations of test results and interpretation.

Use psychological instruments of assessment that have established validity and reliability with populations for which they have been normed. If for some reason validity or reliability has not been established (e.g., a very new instrument, or an older instrument that you are using with an unusual population) make sure to state this in your report, along with any other restrictions or possible distortions on results and interpretation.

VIGNETTE

Dr. Nouveau was a White psychologist who had just joined the staff of an outpatient clinic in a large, understaffed county hospital with many African American patients. Unfortunately, the director of the clinic recently had heart surgery and was unable to be on the job for most of the early months of Dr. Nouveau's new appointment. Although lacking much guidance about some of his professional duties, Dr. Nouveau did his best; he understood that a major part of his responsibilities would include the initial screening of new patients and diagnosing and treating individuals with a broad range of Axis I and Axis II disorders.

As is common for many psychologists, Dr. Nouveau relied on the instruments of assessment with which he was most familiar—his old favorites. He used, among others, a nearly obsolete objective instrument that had been standardized many years before on young White men and women. He had used this aging instrument in his doctoral research 4 years before, and he planned to use it in the clinic for assessing depression, anxiety, personality disorders, organicity, and many other mental disorders. Unfortunately, however, it constituted a poor choice for use with a predominantly African American population, and it had little validity or established diagnostic use in this clinical setting.

A particularly complicated case involved a 39-year-old man who was currently divorcing his wife. He had been experiencing chronic back pain for 3 years and was diagnosed as having a significant amount of psychopathology on the basis of Dr. Nouveau's test results. Dr. Nouveau relied on this test even though it had never been standardized for African American clinical populations and there were virtually no norms available for chronic-pain patients.

One year later, the results of this assessment found their way into a forensic setting when the divorced couple was attempting to negotiate custody of their three children. The man's mental health was raised as a consideration in his parenting abilities, and Dr. Nouveau, who was subpoenaed to testify as the man's former therapist, was placed in the position of having to defend and interpret the results of testing that were essentially invalid. It was clear that Dr. Nouveau's incompetence in selecting an appropriate instrument the previous year had resulted in questionable test results that had the potential for adversely affecting these former patients. The stakes were high, and the long-term consequences, particularly in a child custody assessment, were serious, affecting the lives of many individuals and extended family members.

After Dr. Nouveau's court appearance, an opposing expert witness in marital assessment and therapy successfully challenged his conclusions and invalidated his testimony. When the litigation was over, this woman initiated an ethics complaint against Dr. Nouveau for violating several ethical standards regarding competence in assessment. Adjudication of this complex complaint required the careful review of many hundreds of pages of testimony and took well over a year for the APA Ethics Committee to complete.

1. Dr. Nouveau was not well trained in assessment and had some blind spots as well; as a colleague in the clinic, what might you have recommended to this new staff member that would help in his responsibilities and reduce the risk of harm to others?
2. Is there ever value in using a nonvalidated protocol of your own design for clinical use?
3. Is there a way that Dr. Nouveau could have used and documented results of psychological testing in the clinical record

with a nonvalidated instrument to maximize its effectiveness and minimize risk to his patients (and to himself)?

9.02 (c)

Psychologists use assessment methods that are appropriate to an individual's language preference and competence, unless the use of an alternative language is relevant to the assessment issues.

When carrying out assessments, be sure to adapt to the patient's or client's native language or linguistic skill level, if necessary, unless using a different language is part of the assessment itself. This may mean administering the test or performing the interview in a language the client may better understand (i.e., the client's native language), explaining instructions in English that is simpler than the printed text, using the services of an interpreter if you do not speak or are not proficient in the client's language, or some other appropriate way of modifying the testing procedure that would not significantly affect the assessment itself.

VIGNETTE

Mr. Flores, a Latino migrant worker in his late 30s, was referred by his physician for assessment for suitability for a heart transplant. A clinical social worker on the cardiac transplant team briefly interviewed Mr. Flores and found him to be quite anxious and depressed; he recommended that Mr. Flores be formally evaluated by a psychologist for transplant suitability.

Dr. Lexi Kahn, a clinical psychologist, formally assessed Mr. Flores by means of a lengthy clinical interview. She found that he had a high degree of anxiety and depression, with psychotic symptoms that included significant somatic delusions. Given the extremity of his psychological state, she recommended that the patient be declined for cardiac transplantation at the present time, with the recommendation that he obtain psychological treatment at once.

The physician who referred Mr. Flores found Dr. Kahn's recommendation to be unacceptable. As Mr. Flores's primary-care physician, he had treated him for over 1 year for a variety of symptoms, and he had never seen evidence of psychosis or even significant anxiety during that time. Suspecting that cultural factors may be at work, he requested a second evaluation of his patient with a psychologist who was fluent in Spanish.

The cardiac transplant team consented to a second evaluation and contacted a Latino psychologist, Dr. Gomez, from the hospital's psychiatry department, to perform it. Dr. Gomez was methodical in carrying out his assessment and, unlike Dr. Kahn in the first assessment, did so entirely in the patient's native language. He used different clinical measures in evaluating Mr. Flores than Dr. Kahn had, ones that were consistent with cultural factors and values. More important, by virtue of understanding the client's culture, Dr. Gomez was capable of making adequate interpretations of Mr. Flores's somatic displays of fear and emotional distress. Consequently, his results and conclusions were quite different from those of Dr. Kahn. He found that the major share of Mr. Flores's psychological symptoms were because of the cardiac disease itself and considerable anxiety about the psychological examination process. The supposedly psychotic symptoms with somatic themes were little more than a display of culturally sanctioned reactions commonly seen in Latino clients in response to a foreign and highly anxiety-evoking setting—in this case, the hospital and the intimidating interview process, which Mr. Flores saw as getting in the way of obtaining a new heart. There was also an element of culturally appropriate paranoia commonly seen in medical settings in which minority patients are in a dependent position and fears of discrimination or memories of past mistreatment color their perceptions of authority figures. Dr. Gomez advised the cardiac transplant team that Mr. Flores and his family be referred to a bilingual social worker for short-term supportive therapy. He saw nothing in the patient's dynamics that would prohibit his successful candidacy for a heart transplant, as long as appropriate social supports were in place in advance.

Dr. Kahn learned an important lesson in following up with this patient and obtaining feedback from her bilingual colleague: It is not always language alone that is the issue in making an accurate diagnosis of a patient from another country. She realized that the ability to speak the client's language, albeit helpful, is not enough to achieve an accurate diagnosis. Equally important, if not more important, is having adequate knowledge of the culturally appropriate ways of expressing anxiety and distress in the client's culture, as well as clinically relevant knowledge of the client's cultural values and customs.

1. What criteria might you use in deciding about the ethicality and advisability of formally assessing a patient from another culture?
2. How would you decide about the necessity of actually speaking the same language of your patient, for whom English is a second language, to carry out an accurate assessment?
3. Are you aware of the research regarding misdiagnosis of psychological disorders when interviewing bilingual clients in English?
4. What should you do if you are referred a client whose language you do not speak and, even if an interpreter is available, whose culture you do not understand?

5. What are the ethical and clinical issues associated with using the client's family members as translators when you do not speak the client's language?

9.03 INFORMED CONSENT IN ASSESSMENTS

(a) Psychologists obtain informed consent for assessments, evaluations, or diagnostic services, as described in Standard 3.10, Informed Consent, except when (1) testing is mandated by law or governmental regulations; (2) informed consent is implied because testing is conducted as a routine educational, institutional, or organizational activity (e.g., when participants voluntarily agree to assessment when applying for a job); or (3) one purpose of the testing is to evaluate decisional capacity. Informed consent includes an explanation of the nature and purpose of the assessment, fees, involvement of third parties, and limits of confidentiality and sufficient opportunity for the client/patient to ask questions and receive answers.

You must obtain informed consent when doing assessments, evaluations, or diagnostic services, except under the following circumstances:

- when the assessment is required by law or governmental regulations (e.g., court-ordered psychological assessment in child custody evaluations, mental competency evaluation to stand trial);
- when informed consent is implied as a part of a customary educational, institutional, or organizational activity (e.g., group aptitude testing for high school students, employment evaluations, or job applications); or
- when one purpose of the testing is to evaluate decisional capacity (e.g., with a moribund patient to help with decisions about end-of-life interventions).

VIGNETTE

Mr. Kling, a high school French teacher, had recently been observed to be argumentative and sometimes belligerent with students, with little provocation. Also, his usually well-developed organizational skills had shown such deterioration in the past few weeks that his department chair saw fit to have a formal discussion with him. It was well known that Mr. Kling had had a skiing accident the previous month, slamming into a tree and losing consciousness, but because he returned to his teaching job within 2 weeks, his colleagues assumed that he had made a full recovery. Aside from headaches and neck pain, Mr. Kling was indeed able to carry out most of his professional responsibilities. What his colleagues did not know, however, was that after being admitted to the emergency room of a small hospital, and being held overnight, he left the hospital the next day, against medical advice, and avoided any further medical treatment. He had had a quick temper ever since, and he noticed that it took him longer to prepare his lesson plans and correct papers than before. After discussing these matters with his department chair, Mr. Kling agreed to contact his primary-care physician for a follow-up assessment.

Mr. Kling met with his internist who, after examining him, decided to refer him to a neuropsychologist, Dr. Nauggin, to assess him for changes in his memory and mood resulting from his head injury on the ski slope. Despite his trepidations at dealing with doctors of any sort, the following week Mr. Kling mustered enough courage to keep his appointment with Dr. Nauggin to begin the psychological assessment.

Dr. Nauggin noticed Mr. Kling's anticipatory anxiety and did what she could to allay his fears about the assessment process. She explained to him that a head injury could result in changes to certain parts of his brain, particularly those influencing his moodiness as well as his memory. The purpose of neuropsychological testing, she explained, was to determine whether there was neuropsychological evidence of difficulty in areas that could affect his teaching. If so, she could recommend strategies that might help him to compensate for these changes in his ability to teach French as well as his everyday functioning. She explained that she would be giving him tasks to do that would assess different functions of the brain and told him approximately how long the testing sessions would last, and over how many days. She informed him that she would allow him to take breaks, when needed, and to stop if he had any headache or neck pain that interfered significantly with his concentration.

Dr. Nauggin also discussed with Mr. Kling her fees and the necessary paperwork to be completed for insurance reimbursement. She informed him that she would review the results of testing with him and release a copy of her report to his referring physician, with his signed consent. She discussed the confidentiality of testing, and she underscored that no one would gain access to the results unless (consistent with state and federal law) Mr. Kling formally agreed and gave his written authorization. She patiently answered all of his questions and even prompted him with a few of which he had not thought. Mr. Kling felt relieved and was satisfied with this introduction to the assessment process. He agreed to proceed with the testing and even looked forward to obtaining the results.

After scoring all the instruments and analyzing the results, Dr. Nauggin carefully reviewed the results with Mr. Kling. She then discussed his performance over the phone with his physician, informing the physician that the patient's auditory memory appeared to be excellent but that his visual memory ability was quite low. Furthermore, she explained that he had significant problems in monitoring his own behavior—something that Mr. Kling had some difficulty understanding when she explained it to him.

Dr. Nauggin's formal recommendations focused on capitalizing on the abilities that were intact, such as Mr. Kling's superior auditory memory. She encouraged him to use the strategy of reading out loud and verbalizing all his written material, such as his daily agenda, instead of relying on visual input, as had been his custom. Learning to monitor his own behavior to avoid out-bursts was more problematic, however. She referred him to another neuropsychologist who specialized with this particular aspect of rehabilitation.

Dr. Nauggin had answered Mr. Kling's questions and helped him to accept the difficult facts about his changed mental functioning, which necessitated daily accommodation. Mr. Kling was grateful for her gentle but hardheaded style and found her to have been consistent in her approach: She did what she said she was going to, in their introductory meeting, and she prepared him adequately for each step of the process along the way.

1. What authorization forms should Dr. Nauggin make available to Mr. Kling for him to sign in advance?
2. According to the rules of the Health Insurance Portability and Accountability Act (HIPAA), what must Dr. Nauggin inform Mr. Kling about regarding his right to view the test data after the assessment?
3. What information would be helpful for Dr. Nauggin to share with her client's physician?
4. Several months after the testing, Mr. Kling's brother visited him and, noticing a change in his functioning, telephoned Dr. Nauggin, requesting information. What should she reveal to him?
5. If Dr. Nauggin suspects that Mr. Kling might decide to sue the ski resort for the injuries he sustained, what might she anticipate about being deposed or being asked to testify in court?
6. How would Dr. Nauggin deal with a request from an attorney, 8 months later, seeking copies of all testing data for his client, Mr. Kling?

9.03 (b)

Psychologists inform persons with questionable capacity to consent or for whom testing is mandated by law or governmental regulations about the nature and purpose of the proposed assessment services, using language that is reasonably understandable to the person being assessed.

If you are about to assess someone who might be unable to give his or her consent (e.g., a young child, a developmentally disabled individual, an elderly person with some degree of dementia) or someone who is required by law to undergo psychological assessment (e.g., court-ordered child custody assessment, evaluation of mental competency to stand trial), you must still do the following:

- inform clients about the kind of testing you are about to do;
- tell them the reason why you are assessing them at this time; and
- always use language that they can understand—avoid technical or psychological jargon or vocabulary that is beyond them either because of their educational level, cognitive impairment, or lack of familiarity with the English language. Use an interpreter, if necessary.

VIGNETTE

Mr. Dinesh Patel was 72 years old and had been living with his wife, Veena, near his son's family in San Francisco for 13 years. Recently, he had been manifesting some signs of possible dementia. He gave away his Social Security and MasterCard numbers to an unknown caller on the telephone, which presumably was an incident of identity theft, and he wandered out of the house on several nights "to walk back home to Bombay." Most recently, he gave $450 in cash to a "nice young couple" he encountered at the mall, who claimed that they would invest it and quickly triple his money for him. His wife became increasingly worried about him and the security of their assets. She expressed her concerns to her husband's primary-care physician at his last examination, and the physician referred Mr. Patel to Dr. Altmann, a neuropsychologist in his same office building, for assessment.

Mrs. Patel discussed the matter with Dr. Altmann, who invited the couple and their son into his office to explain the nature and purpose of psychological testing. Dr. Altmann gently explained to Mr. Patel, in the presence of his family, that his wife and son were concerned about him and his safety and were especially worried about his lapses in memory and judgment. Mr. Patel denied that there was anything wrong with his judgment but did acknowledge that he had gotten lost while at the mall on several occasions, wandering around for a long time. He also acknowledged his possible mistake in getting caught up in the scam at the mall and giving away $450 to total strangers. Dr. Altmann then patiently explained, in very simple language, that it was important for Mr. Patel to keep his money secure, so that he would never be poor, and how wise it was to preserve his financial assets for the future, in the case of health problems or other emergencies.

Dr. Altmann gradually gained Mr. Patel's confidence and then began describing the nature of the tests that he might administer. He informed him that the tests helped measure how his memory functioned and different aspects of cognitive functioning. He further told him that the tests consisted of many different types of questions—some that he could easily answer and some that would be very difficult for anyone to answer. He explained that over the course of the morning Mr. Patel would be taking several different tests and that there would be plenty of breaks when necessary. Finally, he explained that he would go over the results of testing afterward and that he would be discussing the test results with Mr. Patel's physician; for that, he would obtain his client's formal consent at a later time. He encouraged Mr. Patel and his family to ask any questions about the testing that they wished.

After this lengthy meeting, Dr. Altmann made an appointment to administer some tests designed to measure dementia. After he scored the tests, he discussed the findings with Mr. Patel's primary-care physician. After considering various options for presenting the test results to the family, the two agreed that the primary-care physician would be the one to do it, as he had a long-standing relationship with Mr. Patel.

At this meeting, the degree of Mr. Patel's dementia was reviewed, and it became clear that Mrs. Patel would be wise to become his conservator. This would allow for future decisions to be made regarding Mr. Patel's health care and any changes in his living situation that might be necessary, in light of his likely decline. Mr. and Mrs. Patel eventually consulted an attorney who specialized in the affairs of senior citizens, and the attorney implemented the steps to place Mr. Patel under his wife's conservatorship.[1]

1. How would your knowledge of ethnic values and customs be important in considering the provision of informed consent about psychological testing with a potential client, such as Mr. Patel, who is unable to provide legal consent?
2. How would Dr. Altmann answer a question from Mr. Patel about the possibility that others might be making decisions for him if the testing revealed certain deficiencies?
3. How would Dr. Altmann ascertain the possible need for using an interpreter, or referring Mr. Patel to an Indian psychologist for assessment?

9.03 (c)

Psychologists using the services of an interpreter obtain informed consent from the client/patient to use that interpreter, ensure that confidentiality of test results and test security are maintained, and include in their recommendations, reports, and diagnostic or evaluative statements, including forensic testimony,

---

[1] It is important to be familiar with laws and regulations concerning guardianship or conservatorship, because they may vary by state.

discussion of any limitations on the data obtained. (See also Standards 2.05, Delegation of Work to Others; 4.01, Maintaining Confidentiality; 9.01, Bases for Assessments; 9.06, Interpreting Assessment Results; and 9.07, Assessment by Unqualified Persons.)

If you use an interpreter in carrying out psychological assessment with someone, make sure that you do the following:

- obtain the client's or patient's consent to use an interpreter, and explain how the interpreter would interface between you and the client or patient;
- make sure that you maintain the client's privacy concerning his or her test results by obtaining the interpreter's commitment to maintain confidentiality;
- make certain that the test security is not compromised by making an agreement with the interpreter to refrain from divulging test contents to others or taking test materials or notes with him or her afterward; and
- determine how the assessment data might be compromised, limited, or distorted because of the interpreter and state this clearly in any reports, formal recommendations, diagnostic or evaluative statements, or forensic testimony.

VIGNETTE

As recent immigrants from Russia, Mr. Nikolay and Tatiana Fyodorov and their three small children had been attempting to adapt to American life, with variable degrees of success. Tatiana spoke no English and was about 15 years younger than her husband. After a few months of unemployment, Nikolay found work in a meat packing plant. During the months since they immigrated, Nikolay had developed clinical symptoms of depression and had sharply increased his use of alcohol, often arriving home late and intoxicated. One night, as he came home from work, Nikolay found his wife talking in the hallway of their apartment building with a young man in the neighboring unit. The door of the young man's apartment was open, and Tatiana was standing at the threshold. Suspecting the worst, Nikolay rudely interrupted the conversation, grabbed his wife by the arm, and pushed her inside the apartment, slamming the door behind them. The neighbor could hear Nikolay yelling loudly at Tatiana in jealousy and the children crying. Worried about the safety of Tatiana and the children, a woman living in the adjacent unit called 911, and the police quickly responded to this apparent domestic violence incident.

Nikolay was arrested and initially taken to the local police precinct. There, one of the officers who spoke some Russian overheard him make comments regarding wanting to die. Because of his level of intoxication, his inconsolable crying, and the fact that at times he would hit his head with his fists, as well as reports of the neighbors regarding possible depression, Nikolay was transferred to the psychiatric unit of the county hospital and placed on suicide watch. The next day, a clinical interpreter fluent in Russian who had a contract with the hospital was brought in, because Nikolay's English was insufficient for a valid assessment to take place.

Before beginning the evaluation, Dr. Smith, Nikolay's physician at the county hospital, introduced himself to the interpreter and raised the issue of confidentiality, explaining that the interpreter was ethically, contractually, and legally bound to maintain the patient's privacy by not disclosing anything to others that had been revealed during the course of the assessment. Toward that end, she would not be permitted to bring any written materials from the room, including any copies of the tests that were being used.

Dr. Smith described the process of the assessment by asking the interpreter to translate into Russian exactly what he would ask or say, with any necessary pauses, listen to the patient's reply, and then translate the reply back into English, again as literally as possible. Dr. Smith made it clear to the interpreter that she was not to make any interpretations of the patient's language or responses at first. If any cultural interpretations were necessary, they could be added on after the literal translation of the language occurred.

The interpreter introduced herself and Dr. Smith to Nikolay, and the interview began. Dr. Smith informed Nikolay, via the interpreter, that he had been requested by the state to formally assess him and conduct an investigation of the complaint against him caused by the events of the night before and allegations of similar events in the past made by neighbors. Nikolay agreed but wondered what the examination would consist of. Dr. Smith described what the assessment would involve as well as the overall goal of the evaluation. He also reassured Nikolay that he would discuss the test results, as well as their implications, with him.

The assessment included a structured clinical interview and additional questions about the reasons for his arrest. The Hamilton Depression Inventory and Anxiety Scales were also administered orally, by means of translation. With the assistance of the interpreter, Dr Smith concluded that Nikolay was likely experiencing severe alcohol abuse and an adjustment disorder, with depressed mood. In regard to the earlier reports of suicidal ideation and some self-destructive behavior (i.e., hitting his head), the interpreter helped clarify that Nikolay's statements and actions were culturally appropriate displays of shame and distress and not completely inappropriate under the present circumstances. Nevertheless, Nikolay emphatically denied any suicidal ideation or plans. Later that day, Dr Smith had the opportunity to interview Tatiana, again with the assistance of the interpreter. Tatiana admitted that her husband had a drinking problem and was often loud, but she denied that he had ever been physically abusive toward her or the children. Furthermore, she reported that when he was not drinking he was usually pleasant and happy.

After the assessment, Dr. Smith scored the tests and wrote a report of his findings, which were to be forwarded to the police, the district attorney, and the family court. He was careful to include a statement on the limitations of this sort of assessment, where such linguistic and cultural differences existed, such as the following: (a) There were no Russian norms for the Hamilton Depression Inventory and Anxiety Scales, and hence the scores may be less valid; (b) the patient might have felt uncomfortable with the interpreter's presence and, at times, provided inaccurate and more socially acceptable answers; (c) although the interpreter was Russian, she had been living in the United States for 30 years and was thoroughly acculturated, resulting in the possible imposing of her own views on the patient's replies and, at times, inaccurate judgment calls; (d) the interpreter might miss important culture-specific nonverbal cues; (e) the interpreter might have condensed and summarized the patient's replies at times, in spite of the initial instructions, resulting in significant omission of data, or she might have minimized or negated clinically useful information; and (f) the interpreter may have identified with Nikolay and projected or transferred some of her feelings and judgment into the case.

In spite of the possibility for distortion, Dr. Smith's psychological report was accepted by the investigators and deemed useful in determining how to follow up with Nikolay's legal case. Dr. Smith had carefully adhered to his ethical standards as well as the hospital's clearly articulated policies for dealing with non-English-speaking patients. Although the assessment took much longer than usual, and entailed additional administrative requirements, he was satisfied that the patient had been well served under these difficult circumstances.

1. How might the gender of the interpreter affect the interview process?
2. How important is it for the interpreter to be of the same culture as the patient, or at least understand it, not just speak the language, and how would this affect the results of the evaluation?
3. Is it necessary to actually state the limitations or threats to validity of the assessment if (a) you are being deposed, (b) you are testifying in court, (c) you write a report to a third party, or (d) you make entries into a clinical record (hospital, clinic, your own, etc.)?
4. How could you ensure the confidentiality of the evaluation process and records when using an interpreter?
5. What are the most common errors made by poorly trained or lay interpreters, or how could you find this out?

6. How would you go about contracting with an interpreter if you were in independent practice and not affiliated with a hospital or institution?

9.04 RELEASE OF TEST DATA

(a) The term test data *refers to raw and scaled scores, client/patient responses to test questions or stimuli, and psychologists' notes and recordings concerning client/patient statements and behavior during an examination. Those portions of test materials that include client/patient responses are included in the definition of* test data. *Pursuant to a client/patient release, psychologists provide test data to the client/patient or other persons identified in the release. Psychologists may refrain from releasing test data to protect a client/patient or others from substantial harm or misuse or misrepresentation of the data or the test, recognizing that in many instances release of confidential information under these circumstances is regulated by law. (See also Standard 9.11, Maintaining Test Security.)*

Test data includes the following:

- the examinee's raw and scaled scores;
- the examinee's actual answers and responses to test questions and stimuli; and
- all of your notations and records about the examinee's statements and behavior during the assessment.

Please note that everything that the examinee actually writes or draws on answer sheets or preprinted forms (e.g., his or her actual responses) is included in the concept of *test data*.

If clients or patients give their consent, you may release test data to them or to anyone whom they designate in the authorization form. However, you may refuse to reveal test data to them or others if you think that it might result in substantial harm to them or someone else. You may also refuse if you think that it might result in misuse, mishandling, falsification, or misrepresenting the data or the test itself. Also, it is wise to learn and be up to date about the ever-changing state and federal laws as they pertain to release of patient information and test data.[2]

---

[2]The relationship among Standard 9.04, Release of Test Data, state laws regulating such disclosures, and federal regulations (most notably, HIPAA) is complicated. Standard 9.04 requires that test data be released pursuant to a client's consent, and HIPAA and many state laws require or support a release of test data when a client has requested the release. However, it is also important to note that Standard 9.04, HIPAA, and certain states have exceptions to the disclosure requirements. For this reason, psychologists should be knowledgeable not only about the APA Ethics Code but also about their state's laws and HIPAA's requirements regarding the release of test data, especially when they decide to withhold test data after receiving a client's formal request and authorization.

VIGNETTE

Dr. White, a neuropsychologist, was contacted by Mr. Brinkman, an attorney representing a 44-year-old San Quentin prisoner who had been on death row for 12 years. Mr. Brinkman had been retained by the prisoner's family to reexamine his medical history for information that might account for his impulsivity and poor judgment, resulting in the two murders for which he had been convicted. After briefly presenting an overview and some details of the case, Mr. Brinkman inquired whether psychological testing might reveal information about a brain injury that the patient might have experienced as a result of being struck by an automobile when he was 11 years old. Dr. White acknowledged that neuropsychological testing might confirm deficits in brain functioning that could be consistent with the medical record of his boyhood injury and possibly account for his homicidal behavior. Dr. White stated that she had had experience testifying in criminal court before, was experienced with similar cases, and described the approach she would take as an expert witness in this case. She also informed Mr. Brinkman her fee for carrying out testing, reviewing court records, providing deposition and courtroom testimony, and other professional activities. In response to his request, she e-mailed him a copy of her curriculum vitae.

An agreement was reached, after several phone calls, and soon Dr. White initiated her professional responsibilities. Her duties would involve the following: (a) reviewing all depositions, documents, and court records relevant to the case thus far; (b) carrying out a neuropsychological assessment of the prisoner; and (c) reviewing the prisoner's primary and secondary school academic records and transcripts of interviews with his teachers and other adults who knew him as a youth.

An appointment was made for testing to be done over the course of several days. Dr. White asked to see and retain the release that the prisoner had already signed authorizing her to reveal to Mr. Brinkman the testing results intended to be used in court as a part of the prisoner's appeal process. She discussed privately with Mr. Brinkman the prisoner's right to know the test results, if the prisoner wished to be informed, as well as the prisoner's likely reactions if those results disclosed things about him that he would otherwise be reluctant to share even with his attorney, let alone be placed on the public record. However, disclosure to the prisoner would ensure that he knew exactly what he was consenting to be shared with Mr. Brinkman. It also reduced the likelihood of his dissatisfaction or resentment, later on, if he were to discover in open court, for the first time, how Dr. White viewed him.

Dr. White was well aware of the ethical requirements to release test data as it applied in this case and the likelihood, if she were called to testify as an expert, that cross-examination would result in her disclosing to the court the details of the prisoner's responses in the psychological testing. However, she was also aware of her obligation to attempt to preserve the security of testing materials by not revealing protocols, test manuals, or copyrighted forms, as required by Standard 9.11, Maintaining Test Security. To comply with these seemingly contradictory standards, Dr. White took special measures that would allow her specifically to reveal the examinee's test data without simultaneously compromising test materials. For example, she created a separate answer sheet for the Wechsler Memory Scale, so that none of the test questions would be revealed to the attorneys or the court at any time. She was aware, however, that, once in court, a cross-examiner might argue to the judge that the answers alone were unintelligible and that the questions might have to be revealed to support the expert's diagnosis. In that case, Dr. White would be prepared to provide the various rationales for maintaining test security. However, it was possible that a judge might direct her to reveal the questions nevertheless. This she would be required to do; however, at least she would have complied with the ethical rule requiring her to make reasonable efforts at maintaining test security.

Several weeks later, after the psychological testing and a thorough review of the medical records, Dr. White discussed her findings and conclusions with Mr. Brinkman. She specifically was concerned with the details of the prisoner's injury he sustained when he was 11 and had been struck by an automobile while riding his bicycle. The CT scan done at a local hospital at the time showed damage to the frontal lobe, and Dr. White explained that in the course of neuropsychological testing she observed behaviors that, 33 years later, were consistent with that injury. She affirmed that it would be reasonable to assume that such an injury would contribute to a decrement in judgment and impulse control as well as the potential for a significant increase in aggressive behavior.

Dr. White wrote a lengthy report describing her conclusions and their bases in neuropsychological testing as well as her review of the patient's medical records, early academic records, and interviews with relevant others. The court was ultimately persuaded by the attorney's arguments, and the sentence was commuted to life imprisonment. Dr. White was satisfied that the steps she took enabled her to play the role of psychological examiner, with the expected disclosures of test data in open court, while at the same time maintaining the security of the tests themselves.

1. If your practice is a covered entity of HIPAA, what obligations do you have about releasing test data to your psychotherapy patients, on request, and how might these obligations conflict with this standard?
2. What steps might you take to maintain test security while at the same time complying with your obligation to release test data to a client or patient who makes such a request?
3. What sort of harm might justify your refusal to release test data to a current or former client or patient?

4. What does the law in your state permit or require of you concerning the release of test data to clients or patients requesting you to do so?

9.04 (b)

In the absence of a client/patient release, psychologists provide test data only as required by law or court order.

> Never release your client's or patient's test data, as defined above, except in either of the following cases:
>
> - your client or patient has signed a valid release form authorizing the release, and specifying to whom and for what purpose, consistent with state, federal (HIPAA, if appropriate), or institutional regulations about release forms, as they may apply); or
> - you are required by law (e.g., you are carrying out a court-ordered psychological assessment) or have been presented with a court order requiring you to release the data (this is not the same as a subpoena).

VIGNETTE

Dr. Thomas Grimm received a subpoena *duces tecum* ordering him to appear for a deposition and bring all psychological records in his possession about one of his clients, a defendant in a civil case. He was aware that his patient was a party to an employment discrimination lawsuit; the patient was suing a potential employer for failure to hire her because of her psychological history, and the arrival of a subpoena was not unanticipated. Nevertheless, he first attempted to determine whether the subpoena was valid, as he had learned at a recent forensics lecture that sometimes they are not. He noted that his office was within the jurisdiction of the court where the litigation was pending and that it had been hand delivered to his office by the same company contracting with attorneys who had delivered valid subpoenas to him in the past.

Although he believed the subpoena to be valid, Dr. Grimm was still reluctant to release his patient's entire psychological record. It not only contained all of his consultation notes but also raw test scores of all the assessments he had performed to date, including the MMPI–2, the Beck Depression Inventory—2, the Millon Clinical Multiaxial Inventory—III, and Rorschach test results. He reasoned that the record contained data and details about his patient that would not be relevant to the issue before the court, might be embarrassing to his patient, damaging to her relationships with others, and even harmful to the patient and the therapy itself. Furthermore, he believed that the data could be misinterpreted and misused by the defendant's attorney to bias the court in this case. He telephoned his patient to discuss the case and invited her to come into the office to view her clinical record and then sign a consent form authorizing compliance with the subpoena, if she wished, allowing him to release the record. However, she declined, instead referring Dr. Grimm to her lawyer to discuss the pros and cons of releasing her psychological record. This was a wise decision, as the attorney, in consultation with his or her client, not the psychologist, is the one who usually spearheads the strategy for proceeding ahead in litigation.

The attorney explained that an argument could fairly easily be made that would result in quashing the subpoena, based on the reasons that Dr. Grimm had mentioned, summarized in Standard 9.04a. He further explained, however, that it was possible that the defendant's attorney could then seek to compel the release of the records and test data by means of a court order. A court order, he explained, derives its authority from a sitting judge who has listened to arguments from both sides (usually) for and against justifying the order. It adds this judicial support to the legal enforceability of a subpoena that might otherwise be challengeable. A psychologist would thus have to comply with the demand that a patient's clinical record be released, test data and all, if the judge ruled in favor of the defendant's attorney, even without the patient's consent.

Much to Dr. Grimm's surprise, his patient and the attorney decided on compliance with the subpoena; it suited the strategy of the lawsuit to reveal her psychological records, with one exception: No assessment records would be released to the attorney, as this would be in violation of ethical standards protecting patient privacy and the security of test materials. Instead, after entering into dialogue with the defendant's attorney, he and Dr. Grimm arrived at a compromise: All test data would be released to another licensed psychologist, who would interpret the assessment results to the court.

Dr. Grimm was satisfied that he had proceeded slowly and deliberately in this case, instead of making assumptions about his patient's preferences or automatically reacting to the subpoena, whose austere language and legalistic format appeared highly coercive and unambiguous at the outset. He knew that he had choices in his response, however, and he recognized the difference between a subpoena and a court order. Moreover, he made a consistent effort to include his patient on each step that was taken. In addition to a continuing education workshop that he had taken, he derived much benefit from an article authored by APA's Committee on Legal Issues, which had appeared several years before in a professional journal (American Psychological Association, 1996).

1. How might Dr. Grimm give useful input to the attorney and his client about the advisability of releasing the clinical record?

2. What is the difference between a subpoena and a court order, and what entity is the source of each?
3. Would Dr. Grimm have been wise to simply write a letter to the defendant's attorney refusing to comply with the subpoena, citing ethical Standards 9.04a and 9.11 (Maintaining Test Security)?
4. How would you handle a situation in which your client authorized the release of her test data but was ill informed or having difficulty comprehending why this was a poor choice?

9.05 TEST CONSTRUCTION

Psychologists who develop tests and other assessment techniques use appropriate psychometric procedures and current scientific or professional knowledge for test design, standardization, validation, reduction or elimination of bias, and recommendations for use.

If you plan to develop tests, questionnaires, inventories, and other formal assessment techniques, be sure to use the proper psychometric procedures as well as relevant and up-to-date scientific and professional knowledge of test design, standardization, validation, reduction or eradication of bias, and recommendations for use.

VIGNETTE

Dr. Goodvale and several colleagues had worked for many years at a university clinic in a large city in the Midwest. They were currently engaged in developing a paper-and-pencil test that would measure an individual's hypnotic capability. With such an instrument, a new client wishing to be hypnotized could be rapidly assessed and then confidently referred for treatment to the proper therapist on the staff. In some cases, the use of hypnosis would likely increase the efficiency of the therapy, an important consideration with the restrictions on treatment imposed by the managed-care system.

In carrying out each phase of the work, the research team adhered to well-established scientific standards of test construction. They reviewed carefully the *Standards for Educational and Psychological Testing* (American Educational Research Association, American Psychological Association, & National Council on Measurement in Education, 1999) before beginning their work. Each psychologist was experienced in both the applications of hypnosis and various hypnotizability measures. The team members began by reviewing many of the hypnosis assessment instruments that had been developed over the years, such as the Harvard Group Scale of Hypnotic Suscepti-bility (Shor & Orne, 1962), the Stanford Hypnotic Susceptibility Scales (Weitzenhoffer & Hilgard, 1962), the Dissociative Experiences Scale (Bernstein & Putnam, 1986), the Tellegen Absorption Scale (Tellegen & Atkinson, 1974), and the Hypnotic Induction Profile (Spiegel & Spiegel, 1978) to name a few. This valuable step—reviewing the subject areas and items from other scales—was helpful in generating a content grid with rows and columns representing different areas to be filled in the course of develop-ing the new instrument.

As the work continued, groups of items periodically were pilot tested with small samples of individuals. The researchers attempted to determine whether the individuals taking the test understood the language of the test items and what the item response characteristics were. High numbers of people answering a particular item in the same way would detract from that item's discriminatory value and make it less useful for inclusion on the test.

Establishing validity and reliability and carrying out the necessary ad-ministrations for standardizing the instrument with people of different gen-ders, ages, and ethnicities required many months of testing, data gathering, and careful analysis. The final version of the instrument was validated by using criterion-related validity. This was accomplished by establishing corre-lations between an individual's performance on the instrument and his or her hypnotic capability as measured by both an individual induction proce-dure and performance on several other measures of hypnotic susceptibility, including the Hypnotic Induction Profile (Spiegel & Spiegel, 1978).

Retest reliability measures for the instrument were obtained by readministering the test to the same individuals after a lapse of several months and computing correlation coefficients between the first and second testing. The team members also decided to compute *homogeneity reliability*, or interitem correlations, because they considered hypnotic capability to be a construct (although there were different opinions on this subject held by other re-searchers). Dr. Goodvale and her team were highly diligent and painstaking in their work and ultimately successfully met their goal of creating a paper-and-pencil instrument that was useful in assessing hypnotic capability.

1. What harm could result from developing and promulgating an assessment instrument with inadequate concern for valid-ity and reliability factors?
2. How could harm occur to litigants in child custody assess-ment if you used an instrument of your own design that was not properly normed or was defective in some other way?
3. How might this standard also pertain to inventories or ques-tionnaires that you have developed for use in your clinical or management consulting practice?

9.06 INTERPRETING ASSESSMENT RESULTS

When interpreting assessment results, including automated interpretations, psychologists take into account the purpose of the assessment as well as the various test factors, test-taking abilities, and other characteristics of the person being assessed, such as situational, personal, linguistic, and cultural differences, that might affect psychologists' judgments or reduce the accuracy of their interpretations. They indicate any significant limitations of their interpretations. (See also Standards 2.01b and c, Boundaries of Competence, and 3.01, Unfair Discrimination.)

When you interpret assessment results to someone, or use computer-generated narratives and profiles as a part of the interpretation, always remember to address any limitations on the accuracy or meaning of your statements. Also, be sure to take into account the following when providing test interpretations:

- the purpose and goal of the psychological assessment;
- the various test factors (e.g., its construction, the meaning of subtest scatter, knowledge of norms and standard scores);
- the person's test-taking abilities (e.g., reading or attentional difficulties, education level); and
- any attributes of the person that might impair the accuracy of your interpretations of his or her test data, such as (a) situational (the person was highly anxious, had some other intensity of mood, or was fatigued), (b) personal (the person's level of education or mental disorder), (c) linguistic (English is a foreign language for the person) and (d) cultural (the person's race, ethnic roots, beliefs, or country of origin somehow affected his or her performance during the assessment).

Also be sure to make known any reservations you may have about limitations of your interpretations when providing results or creating a report.

VIGNETTE

Dr. Offset had contracted with the research-and-development section of a manufacturing company of office supplies and computer accessories. He was expected to select employees to participate in focus groups that would help determine new products and services to be offered by the company. Toward this end, he used a computer-administered experimental assessment instrument to measure, among other things, all interested employees' social aptitude, intellectual fluency, and collaborative and competitive traits.

However, the test had norms only for White participants and had never been standardized on a population that reflected the cultural diversity of the company's employees, which included a sizable percentage of Asian Americans and African Americans. Furthermore, some employees experienced apprehension about taking a test that was administered by means of a computer; some had reading difficulties in addition to their poor familiarity with English; and for others fatigue, mood, and cultural values likely had an impact on their range of scores. Thus, Dr. Offset was reluctant to rely exclusively on the results of testing for the selection process. He appropriately discussed his reservations with various managers throughout the company; however, he recommended that the test might be able to make a partial contribution to the selection process nevertheless.

To help compensate for deficiencies in the screening process Dr. Offset determined that he would offer each employee who tested below a cutoff score an opportunity for a structured interview with him or his associates, if he or she desired, as an aid assessing eligibility for the focus groups. Even this additional measure did not necessarily provide adequate compensation, however, because some low-scoring employees might have felt undeserving to participate, and others may not have been assertive enough to request an opportunity for the structured interview. At least providing such an interview opportunity clearly communicated the message that instruments of assessment would not be relied on exclusively when they had never been normed on the populations for which they were being used.

In general, Dr. Offset was successful about informing employees and management of the somewhat experimental nature of his selection process. He did this in his personal discussions with them and also documented the process via e-mail correspondence and a formal descriptive letter of agreement. Likewise, he took the reasonable step of encouraging employees from the various ethnic and racial groups to help compensate for the biased testing by providing an individual interview. At the end of this selection process, he followed up by soliciting feedback from employees by means of a questionnaire. He then reviewed the results and outcome of the entire process with several Asian American and African American psychologist colleagues who had agreed to serve as consultants. The purpose of these consultations was partly to assess the validity of Dr. Offset's selection process and partly to formulate ideas for improving his methodology for the next time around.

1. How would you assess the usefulness of the structured interview that Dr. Offset offered to low-scoring employees as a means of compensating for using a culturally biased instrument?
2. Does Dr. Offset bear an ethical responsibility to provide test results and an explanation of the meaning of their score to every employee who was tested?
3. Given that this was a voluntary assessment process, comment on the adequacy of Dr. Offset's compliance with this ethical standard.

9.07 ASSESSMENT BY UNQUALIFIED PERSONS

Psychologists do not promote the use of psychological assessment techniques by unqualified persons, except when such use is conducted for training purposes with appropriate supervision. (See also Standard 2.05, Delegation of Work to Others.)

> Do not endorse the use of tests or assessment techniques by unqualified people unless they are trainees or supervisees under proper supervision (e.g., supervised by someone who is competent and licensed to use the assessment techniques themselves).

VIGNETTE

Dr. Watcher was the clinical supervisor of Dr. Saul Lidd, a new PhD who was not yet licensed to practice independently. Because Dr. Watcher was well aware of supervisors' responsibility for all patients—clinically, legally, and ethically—he was careful to clarify all of his expectancies to his supervisee. This was done in writing (a letter), at the beginning of the supervisory year, as was his custom.

Dr. Watcher planned to delegate to his supervisee the administration, scoring, and, when appropriate, report writing, for patients requiring diagnostic testing. This included the MMPI–2; various anxiety and depression inventories; and the Wechsler Adult Intelligence Scale—III, when appropriate; as well as tests to assess individuals with chronic pain, attention-deficit disorder, and other psychological disorders. Dr. Watcher intended to scrupulously review Dr. Lidd's scored tests, psychological reports, and other written work. He expected his supervisee to submit each one for review and cosigning in a timely fashion. This was a critical aspect of the supervisory process that had strong implications for the instruction of supervisees as well as maintaining integrity of the clinical services for patients.

Furthermore, Dr. Watcher expected Dr. Lidd to carry out structured clinical interviews for some patients presenting possible symptoms of eating disorders and some Axis II disorders as well. Some of these activities were to be audio- or videotaped, with patients' awareness and consent, of course. Dr. Watcher would view excerpts of the videotapes during some supervisory sessions.

It is a supervisor's duty to be knowledgeable about his or her supervisee's strengths and weaknesses, thought Dr. Watcher, and to be well informed about the supervisee's background, training, blind spots, and unique professional attributes as well.

As a result, when necessary, Dr. Watcher encouraged additional training, such as workshops and seminars, and he took the time to nurture Dr.

Lidd's professional growth and development in many different ways. It was clear that he took a responsible interest in his mentoring role and spent much time and energy providing a good learning environment that was well paced to the needs of his supervisee. Above all, he was careful to limit Dr. Lidd's duties to his areas of expertise and provide close supervision in new areas, as needed.

1. What is the value in describing the goals of supervision in written form (either in correspondence, a contract, or some other documentation)?
2. As a clinical supervisor in a busy practice, how can you be certain that you have achieved a balance between your own needs to meet the demands of patients and those of your supervisee?
3. What is the extent of your liability and responsibility for the assessment work that is carried out by your supervisee?

9.08 OBSOLETE TESTS AND OUTDATED TEST RESULTS

Psychologists do not base their assessment or intervention decisions or recommendations on data or test results that are outdated for the current purpose.

Do not use obsolete data or test results as a basis for your current assessments, decisions about interventions, treatment plans, or recommendations.

VIGNETTE

Dr. Race, an overworked school psychologist, was asked to assess Steven, a 14-year-old boy who was referred by his teacher. Steven had been experiencing great difficulty with reading over the last 6 months, had recently gotten into a fight with two other students, and was being insolent with teachers. As a part of her assessment, Dr. Race relied heavily on teachers' comments from the previous 2 years. She also reviewed test data on reading aptitude and personal problems that were several years old, and she deemed unnecessary any additional testing or formal assessment.

Dr. Race remembered Steven from an interview she had had with him 7 months before and did not think that she required any additional information about his current status. Besides, she was quite involved assessing and working with boys and girls who had what she considered to be more serious behavior problems involving drug use or extremely violent and aggressive behavior. She failed to interview Steven again or refer him for counseling;

instead, she referred him to a remedial reading group and agreed to review his case again in 6 months.

Dr. Race's recommendations, which were based on obsolete data and outmoded information, failed to adequately address the situation. By failing to interview Steven again, or gain any current information, she never learned that his mother had recently been diagnosed with cancer. Neither did she learn that the mother's chemotherapy and resulting fatigue, nausea, and depression were having a strong impact on the entire family. By failing to update her knowledge of Steven with appropriate and current instruments of assessment or having a face-to-face evaluation with him, she made a formal recommendation that failed to address the cause of his recent pattern of misbehavior and was not only unlikely to be helpful to him but also could possibly exacerbate the situation.

1. If Dr. Race considers herself to be responsible for too many students in the school system to competently assess them, what steps might she take to remedy the situation?
2. If Dr. Race fails to at least attempt to address the excessive workload placed on her by the expectations of her school system, does she run an increased risk of being found in violation of an ethics complaint, if one were brought against her?
3. Do the ethical standards require that you succeed in changing a professional work setting that is untenable, or merely that you make a good-faith effort?

9.08 (b)

Psychologists do not base such decisions or recommendations on tests and measures that are obsolete and not useful for the current purpose.

Do not use obsolete tests as a basis for your assessments, decisions about interventions, treatment plans, or recommendations. Be sure that you have the latest available edition of a given assessment instrument, unless there is a valid reason why you should use an older version.

VIGNETTE

Dr. Yawn, a school psychologist, had been providing services to the same two secondary schools in an ethnically diverse rural school system for 27 years, and much of her time was spent doing psychological assessments of students who had special needs. Over the years, she had accumulated quite a large library of individual tests.

In recent times, Dr. Yawn had become less attentive to obtaining current editions of recently revised tests, and she refused to purchase revisions of intelligence, reading, and personality tests, even though she was aware that newer editions had been published. She justified the use of obsolete tests in relation to her impending retirement; because she was planning on leaving the district in 3 years, she thought that she should not be expected to purchase and become familiar with the newer instruments. Tests were costly, and the learning curve required for some of the revisions appeared to be too steep for her. Even though she was confident that the school district would have been able to afford some new versions of certain tests, she refused to requisition them because she did not wish to spend time and energy learning the new procedures. She rationalized that she was saving the school money that could be better spent elsewhere, particularly in these days of tight budgets.

Dr. Yawn's refusal to use current versions of tests over an extended period of time proved to be harmful to certain students. Those particularly affected were boys and girls for whom English was a second language, the very individuals who were highly represented in this part of the state, where there were many first- and second-generation Asian and Latino families. These students would have been more accurately assessed with the revised editions of tests that were more culturally sensitive, or at least somewhat more fair to test takers for whom English was not a native language, than the older editions.

Dr. Yawn felt secure in her ability to compensate for these deficiencies in the older instruments and believed she had a wealth of personal data and a "feel" about students' characteristic performance on them that helped in her judgments and recommendations. However, she placed her students at a disadvantage by relying exclusively on these outdated instruments. By systematically using obsolete instruments of assessment, she occasionally made incorrect decisions about her students' educational and mental health needs, resulting in inappropriate intervention recommendations with significant negative long-term consequences.

1. What are some of the serious clinical implications for consumers of different ages of using obsolete tests on a regular basis?
2. What else does this ethical standard prohibit besides basing decisions on the results of using obsolete tests?
3. How could a psychologist explain or support his or her practice of using obsolete tests or measures in a child custody case or some other litigation where the stakes are high and the opposing counsel makes liberal use of psychologist expert witnesses?

9.09 TEST SCORING AND INTERPRETATION SERVICES

(a) Psychologists who offer assessment or scoring services to other professionals accurately describe the purpose, norms, validity, reliability, and applications of the procedures and any special qualifications applicable to their use.

> Be truthful and accurate in promoting and describing your assessment or scoring services. Do not embellish or make exaggerated claims about the purpose, norms, validity, reliability, applications of the procedures, or any limitations or restrictions that may apply to their use.

VIGNETTE

Dr. Van Slyck was a psychologist with an aggressive business style who was attempting to develop his assessment and test-scoring company. His concern about ethical compliance was inconsistent, at times, and he would promote his services in an exaggerated way. For example, he advertised that his company had a quick turnaround time for scoring tests, with a 24-hr maximum wait time, through the extensive use of fax machines and e-mail correspondence. However, his low-paid clerical staff often varied in their competence level and were not especially efficient in the use of the technology or customer relations. In addition to being slow, at times they mixed up answer sheets and computer printouts, thus sending the wrong client's test results to a particular psychologist.

Furthermore, Dr. Van Slyck was careless about matters pertaining to test security. For example, he would fail to restrict access to psychological instruments to people who were not competently trained and experienced in using them. In his promotional materials and ordering forms, he and his staff did not always require a state license number from the individual wishing to order test materials; neither did he routinely seek other credentials or evidence of a customer's competence in the area of assessment. When he or his staff did request a consumer's psychology license number, they never made an attempt to verify it.

Another aspect of Dr. Van Slyck's business plan included developing instruments that could be of use in various forensic settings. One such instrument was the Slyck Parenting Competence Assessment Inventory, a relatively short instrument with inadequate empirical validation and few of the usual safeguards against motivational distortion. Dr. Van Slyck promoted this test by advertising widely in legal and psychological journals; the advertisements exaggerated the instrument's usefulness, applicability, and validity. It was his hope to encourage attorneys representing litigants in divorce proceedings and psychologists to rely on it, and he touted it as being suitable for a broad range of individuals, regardless of gender, age, socioeconomic status, religion, or ethnic origin.

To facilitate administration and scoring—and, he hoped, to increase its desirability—Dr. Van Slyck made the Slyck Parenting Competence Assessment Inventory available over the Internet as well, so that the scoring turnaround time was virtually instantaneous. Psychologists could administer the test to individuals online, if they wanted to; it would be scored immediately, and narrative reports could then be sent to the psychologist by e-mail. Unfortunately, however, because of his company's lax procedures in marketing—selling to all buyers—the test materials, by being made available online, were accessible by nonpsychologists as well as professional psychologists. With such careless procedures, there was no way to verify the true identity of the test taker or to control for lapses in confidentiality at various stages of the process. As a result, parents engaged in child custody litigation and their attorneys could readily acquire advance copies of the test items themselves to assist in the litigation.

After only 3 months of offering services to the professional community, Dr. Van Slyck had accumulated several complaints: two to the state ethics committee and one to the state licensing board. No complaint was made to the APA Ethics Committee, because he was not a member. These complaints materialized because Dr. Van Slyck's careless and unethical practices had indirectly contributed to a litigation process that resulted in a poor child custody decision, in which three children at probable risk were placed with their new custodial parent. In another case, a parent who had been adversely affected was preparing to initiate a civil suit as well, for damages he felt he had sustained, partly because of Dr. Van Slyck's practices.

It took little time for the licensing board and the ethics committee, independently, to determine that Dr. Van Slyck had promoted his scoring services unfairly and inaccurately and also had developed assessment instruments in an idiosyncratic fashion, without proper statistical and standardization procedures. He had also jeopardized test security by making the test available over the Internet with little concern for the professional credentials of the test user. He had failed to honor ethical principles that have evolved over the course of many years to safeguard both the public and the science of psychology. These adjudicative bodies found that Dr. Van Slyck had violated not only Standard 9.09, Test Scoring and Interpretation Services, but that he had also demonstrated a consistent pattern of flagrant disregard for many other ethical standards as well, including Standard 2.01, Boundaries of Competence; 2.03, Maintaining Competence; 3.04, Avoiding Harm; 4.02, Discussing the Limits of Confidentiality; 5.01, Avoidance of False or Deceptive Statements; and virtually every standard in the Assessment section except for 9.08, Obsolete Tests and Outdated Test Results. He was expelled from membership in the state psychological association, and his case is still pending before the state board of psychology. To date, his attorney's fees in his defense in the board investigation have amounted to nearly one fourth of his annual income. These fees were paid out of pocket, because malpractice insurance covers only one's defense in a lawsuit; it does not reimburse for attorney fees in a board of psychology investigation (unless the psychologist had added that particular insurance rider when paying the annual premium).

1. What steps should Dr. Van Slyck have taken when he became aware of his false advertising—quick turnaround times, inaccurate information, about validity and norms, and so on?
2. What are some of the significant clinical, ethical, and legal risks to making any assessment instrument available over the Internet?
3. If you were an expert witness for the opposing side in a child custody case, how would you fault the use of Dr. Van Slyck's parenting inventory, and with what might you compare it?
4. What defense could Dr. Van Slyck offer for his flagrant disregard for many ethical standards?

9.09 (b)

Psychologists select scoring and interpretation services (including automated services) on the basis of evidence of the validity of the program and procedures as well as on other appropriate considerations. (See also Standard 2.01b and c, Boundaries of Competence.)

> Be well informed when choosing a test scoring and interpretation service; base your selection on important factors, such as the validity of the scoring program and procedures, turnaround time, and other factors that might affect your decision. Select your test-scoring services wisely, because the results could have important clinical or forensic implications that you might not be able to predict.

VIGNETTE

Dr. Askem was the owner of an EAP that provided a full range of psychological services to several large corporations. Dr. Askem's many responsibilities included decisions regarding using scoring services for results of various instruments of assessment, including the MMPI–2, the Millon Clinical Multiaxial Inventory—III, the 16-Personality Factor Questionnaire, and the Symptom Checklist–90–R. For some of these instruments he had the option of purchasing software that would score answer sheets and produce narrative reports. For others, he would select scoring services that processed mailed or faxed answer sheets and were most cost-effective for his needs and those of his corporate clients.

Because most of the tests his employees used were produced by different publishers, Dr. Askem was faced with the task of comparing different services on a variety of criteria. In some cases, there was only one scoring service available. However, where there was a choice, he sought documentation about the validity of computer-generated narratives and the bases for any extra scales or interpretations provided. He carefully reviewed the sample narrative reports, when available. He noted that in some cases the reports contained confusing, ambiguous, or even contradictory language. In others, the statements were overly strong, lacking qualifiers or disclaimers, and seemed to present an exaggerated trait or profile of an individual. When he observed these problems, he sought information from the test-scoring service about the additional scales or accompanying narratives, such as software algorithms or configurable rules for creating computerized text, even though the services were not always cooperative in fulfilling his requests because they considered the information to be proprietary or simply lacked the manpower to comply with his request.

Dr. Askem also considered other factors in selecting a test scoring service: the availability of telephone consultation support; the use of fax machines for sending answer sheets and receiving results; cost; availability of electronic billing; and the service company's willingness to provide references, bibliographies, or research information about specialized assessment needs. Although Dr. Askem's comprehensive approach to evaluating and selecting test-scoring services was time consuming, in the end it proved invaluable and yielded final selections that provided competent and scientifically sound services addressing the specific needs of his clients.

1. What are the relative merits of using a test-scoring service as opposed to purchasing software to process answer sheets yourself?
2. Is being uninformed about choosing a test-scoring service an ethical violation? Is it unwise clinically? Potentially costly in several ways?
3. How much time might you be willing to devote to learning about the various strengths of test-scoring services?
4. To what extent can you rely on advertisements in journals or other professional publications about test-scoring services?

9.09 (c)

Psychologists retain responsibility for the appropriate application, interpretation, and use of assessment instruments, whether they score and interpret such tests themselves or use automated or other services.

> The buck stops with you when doing psychological testing, whether you score the test yourself or send it out to a scoring service. You must have a sound rationale for your choice of a test with a particular client or patient, use the test properly, and be able to support all the evaluative statements that you make about a person.

VIGNETTE

Dr. Newelby, a recently licensed psychologist, worked in the human relations department at city hall. When performing psychological assessments for job candidates and writing her reports, she frequently used verbatim paragraphs from the computer-generated report from a well-known scoring service. However, she usually deleted the qualifying phrases and disclaimers so that her report would read more smoothly and definitively, without the characteristically tentative language that is normally included in narratives. Lacking these qualifiers, the report seemed to make diagnostic and predictive statements that went far beyond the established validity of the assessment instrument and provided a distorted or exaggerated picture of the candidate examined. This not only resulted in an inaccurate psychological report but also adversely affected the employment opportunities for certain candidates who were being depicted in a far more negative way than they should have been.

On one occasion, Dr. Newelby noticed some significant differences between the computer-generated report from the scoring service and her own clinical assessment of a particular candidate. There were major diagnostic discrepancies, with strong implications about the candidate's potential for employment. However, she decided to rely on the computerized report without question because she was relatively naive about using and integrating narrative reports from scoring services. Little did she know that a new employee at the scoring service had made a serious error, interchanging the printout of Dr. Newelby's client with that of a young man indicted for check forgery. By an unfortunate coincidence, the identification code numbers on the reports were almost identical, and each was mailed to the wrong party. The employee at the scoring service never detected the mistake; neither did Dr. Newelby. It was never corrected, and her psychological report reflected the error, eventually contributing to a poor endorsement of the candidate and his failure to be hired for the managerial position for which he had applied.

Dr. Newelby should have been alert to the ever-present possibility of a scoring or clerical error. She should have taken appropriate measures when her clinical judgment yielded such a radically different assessment of the candidate than the one from the computer-generated report received from the scoring service. Also, she should have refrained from altering the language of the text so significantly, because the tentative language and disclaimers reflect the inherent uncertainty of the assessment process and should always be retained.

1. Would it be unethical for Dr. Newelby to select a test for a certain purpose that had lower validity than another instrument that was widely available?
2. What steps might Dr. Newelby have taken when she discovered that the narrative report on her patient did not jibe with her clinical assessment?
3. How significant is Dr. Newelby's alteration of the narrative report, in the manner indicated, and what would be the potential impact in the following settings: (a) clinical, with a worker's compensation case; (b) clinical, with a chronic-pain case; (c) forensic, with a mental competency assessment; (d) organizational consulting; or (e) in the human resources office of a large corporation?

9.10 EXPLAINING ASSESSMENT RESULTS

Regardless of whether the scoring and interpretation are done by psychologists, by employees or assistants, or by automated or other outside services, psychologists take reasonable steps to ensure that explanations of results are given to the individual or designated representative unless the nature of the relationship precludes provision of an explanation of results (such as in some organizational consulting, preemployment or security screenings, and forensic evaluations), and this fact has been clearly explained to the person being assessed in advance.

No matter who does the scoring and interpretation—psychologists, your employees or assistants, or an automated (or other contracted) service—you must make sure that clients and patients receive some explanation of their assessment results, either from you or someone you designate. The only exceptions to this rule are when the nature of your professional relationship with the person you are evaluating precludes giving him or her the results, such as in the following situations:

- organizational consulting, when the individuals being assessed are informed in advance that results will not be provided;
- preemployment or security screenings (e.g., testing carried out to assist in hiring or assessing security risk); and
- forensic evaluations of your formal assessments (e.g., mental competency examinations).

In these cases, be sure that you tell the person in advance that you will not be giving him or her any results or interpretations.

☞ Cary, a 26-year-old man who had been using cocaine and other drugs for about 3 years, was brought to a chemical dependency center by Tina, his exasperated girlfriend. He had been raised in the projects of Chicago's South Side and had not graduated from high school, had never held a full-time job, and showed little interest in making constructive changes. The only consistency of focus in his adult life appeared to be maintaining his relationship with Tina.

The psychologist who assessed Cary, Dr. Sharper, was familiar with the type of problems Cary was experiencing, on a personal level. He, too, had been born and raised on the South Side, and he had also struggled with drug addiction during his young adult life. Even though his rapport with Cary was excellent, given their similar backgrounds and personality style, he resisted the temptation to abbreviate his usual manner of assessing new patients. Therefore, over the next few weeks, in addition to clinical consultations, Dr. Sharper administered several objective tests and inventories that helped develop his clinical impression of Cary and the course of treatment that would ensue.

When the assessment phase was finished, Dr. Sharper explained the results of the diagnostic testing in everyday language and gave the young man some printed handouts that helped him understand the test interpretations. Given Cary's level of education, it was important for Dr. Sharper to interpret the results for him in simple language and clear concepts, lest they be misunderstood. As it turned out, Cary was interested in learning the results and had many questions about the feedback he received. Some of the information piqued his curiosity and provoked more of an interest in participating in therapy.

Dr. Sharper further developed an initially good patient–therapist match by adhering to his standard operating procedures and providing direct feedback about the assessment results to his new patient. With such good communication at the outset, Dr. Sharper established a strong working alliance with Cary that boded well for the treatment to come.

1. How might Dr. Sharper proceed if Cary did not wish to receive feedback about some of the tests that he took?
2. Does this ethical standard state that psychologists should normally use psychological tests as a part of the assessment process?
3. How would you handle a request from a candidate whom you had screened for employment, was rejected, and wished to know how his test results had influenced the decision against him?

9.11 MAINTAINING TEST SECURITY

The term test materials *refers to manuals, instruments, protocols, and test questions or stimuli and does not include* test data *as defined in Standard 9.04, Release of Test Data. Psychologists make reasonable efforts to maintain the integrity and security of test materials and other assessment techniques consistent with law and contractual obligations, and in a manner that permits adherence to this Ethics Code.*

Maintain the integrity and security of tests and assessment techniques by keeping them away from the eyes of individuals who are not trained to use them. This includes the tests themselves, manuals, protocols, and actual test items or stimuli. It does *not* include test data as described in Standard 9.04 (raw data, scaled scores, responses to questions and stimulus items, or your notes about the client's statements and behavior during the assessment). You must also be aware of and abide by any state or federal law pertaining to test security; any agreements or contracts that may be relevant; and, of course, the various standards of this Ethics Code that address test security.

VIGNETTE

Dr. Eve Madison was being interviewed for a television talk show on the subject of mental competency assessments for prisoners on death row. Before she went on the air, she requested a chance to speak with the host of the show, Mr. Gladmouth, to discuss her presentation and to inform him briefly about the testing materials she routinely used in carrying out assessments with prisoners. During this meeting, in her zeal to contribute to the success of this day's talk show, she showed Mr. Gladmouth a copy of the MMPI–2 and the other instruments she used, to enhance his understanding of just how comprehensive and complex a process the assessment was. It was her hope that educating him about some of the finer points of the assessment might help him frame his questions in a more appropriate manner. She said nothing to Mr. Gladmouth about test security but trusted that he would know that these were copyrighted materials and that he would also be aware of her ethical duty to withhold them from the lay public.

Little did Dr. Madison suspect the risk that she was taking in giving Mr. Gladmouth an actual copy of the tests; she neither gave much thought to, nor had much experience with, the ethics or judgment of talk show hosts. As it happened, when the live interview aired, Mr. Gladmouth had his engineer display many of the MMPI–2 test items crawling along the screen while he interviewed Dr. Madison; he did this in the interest of "public awareness." He was planning also to place all the test batteries, including several Rorschach cards, on his talk show's Web site so that viewers could see them and use e-mail to provide audience feedback; he did this in the interest of stimulating audience interest and increasing his television show's ratings.

Dr. Madison was distressed by Mr. Gladmouth's opportunistic style and obvious disregard for protecting test security. When she found out from one of the show's producers about his intention to place the protocols on the Web site, she strongly voiced her opposition. She confronted Mr. Gladmouth about the ethical and legal aspects of protecting these materials, which were to be used by licensed practitioners only. She described the potential for harm to numerous individuals (potential future patients and clients) by compromising their naivete concerning the test items and the threat to future diagnostic testing if test items were revealed in such a manner that the public had an opportunity to study them. She also acknowledged her mistake in giving him copies of the instruments, in her attempt to make a good faith effort at collaboration in this joint venture.

Fortunately, Dr. Madison was successful in prevailing on Mr. Gladmouth to refrain from placing the tests on the Internet. She also succeeded in having him delete the test items shown on the screen from subsequent rebroadcasts of the interview. As a result of these exchanges Mr. Gladmouth became intrigued with the topic of test security, the public's right to know, and psychologists who he thought were obsessed with secrecy about these materials. He decided to invite Dr. Madison back for a provocative interview on this topic the following week. She discussed the conditions under which she would be willing to return for another interview and scheduled a second interview when he agreed to her terms in writing. Wisely, however, she left all copies of tests at her office this time.

1. Explain Dr. Madison's zeal to contribute to an interesting talk show program and how she might have unwittingly entered a secondary role, besides that of psychologist?
2. What risk might Dr. Madison have incurred if Mr. Gladmouth had already placed the test items in question on his Web site, while the show was in progress?
3. Would Dr. Madison have any options about restricting further publicizing of the test items, once the materials were in Mr. Gladmouth's hands?
4. Whom should Dr. Madison consult, and what efforts should she make, if she were unable to retrieve the test materials from Mr. Gladmouth?
5. Is Mr. Gladmouth bound by any code of ethics?

10

THERAPY

10.01 INFORMED CONSENT TO THERAPY

(a) When obtaining informed consent to therapy as required in Standard 3.10, Informed Consent, psychologists inform clients/patients as early as is feasible in the therapeutic relationship about the nature and anticipated course of therapy, fees, involvement of third parties, and limits of confidentiality and provide sufficient opportunity for the client/patient to ask questions and receive answers. (See also Standards 4.02, Discussing the Limits of Confidentiality, and 6.04, Fees and Financial Arrangements.)

Always obtain informed consent before beginning therapy, as is required by the four subsections in Standard 3.10. Tell your clients and patients, as early in treatment as is practicable, something about the nature of treatment and how it is likely to proceed. Also be sure to discuss financial arrangements (e.g., your fees, insurance or worker's compensation reimbursement, or expected limits of these payments), any participation by third parties (e.g., previous therapists, primary-care physician, family members), and confidentiality rules and exceptions (e.g., state and federal laws pertaining to confidentiality and its exceptions, mandated child abuse reporting, Tarasoff reporting, suicidality, and other exceptions). Consider telling them what you might want a good friend to know about

291

VIGNETTE

Rosemary, a 38-year-old woman, was experiencing postpartum depression and chronic pain in her lower back as a result of a 2-year-old injury. She also had concern about her infant, who was experiencing several unusual health problems, causing much worry for her and her husband. She contacted Dr. Tellem for psychotherapy and nonmedical interventions for her pain. She had somewhat magical beliefs about therapy, based partly on misconceptions disseminated by the news media and on the experiences of her close friend, who seemed to be making remarkably fast progress in her work with a therapist. She was hoping for substantial relief from her back pain with one hypnotic session, and she welcomed the thought of rapid gains in her low mood as well.

Dr. Tellem explained to Rosemary in their first telephone conversation that treatment would likely take more time than she anticipated, consisting of history taking, possible psychological testing, relaxation training, biofeedback or self-hypnotic training, psychotherapy, and perhaps other interventions as well. He explained the importance of each of these phases of the process and how they contributed to maximizing the overall treatment. Other therapists might proceed differently, Dr. Tellem explained, but his treatment was based on many years of experience working with chronic pain and depression, and he generally obtained good results with patients.

In response to Rosemary's question about his theoretical orientation, Dr. Tellem explained that it was primarily based on cognitive–behavioral principles, a well-researched intervention for assisting with the treatment of pain disorders and associated symptoms. He also discussed the importance of coordinating treatment with her physician and (possibly) specialists, and he explained the necessity of signing consent forms to permit these exchanges.

Rosemary feared that the expense of such treatment might exceed her insurance benefits. Dr. Tellem informed her about the costs, as best as he could estimate. He indicated that because he was not listed as a provider on her managed health care plan, he would be considered an out-of-system provider, and thus it was possible that partial payments could be made by the insurer. The patient, however, would be expected to make a copayment, the exact amount of which could be determined with a telephone call to the managed health care case manager. He urged Rosemary to contact her insurer before beginning treatment, to clarify any misconceptions about the cost and reimbursements of treatment.

Rosemary was quite surprised to learn of both the anticipated duration of therapy and the expense, as she had previously spoken with another psychologist who virtually assured her that she would achieve significant pain relief in two or three sessions. However, after this enlightening conversation with Dr. Tellem she felt quite well informed about the salient issues. He had taken the time to encourage and answer her questions thoroughly, at no cost; after thinking it over, Rosemary decided to consult him for treatment and was ultimately well pleased with the results.

When she arrived for her first session, Dr. Tellem gave her a printed handout describing other aspects of informed consent in detail, such as confidentiality and its exceptions; financial matters (fee structure, third-party reimbursement, credit cards, etc.); duration of therapy; cancellations and missed sessions; telephone availability and emergencies; collaboration with psychopharmacologists, for medication, and with other health care professionals; consultation with other psychologists; and interruptions to treatment, such as vacations and business trips. Because Dr. Tellem's practice was also compliant with the requirements of the Health Insurance Portability and Accountability Act (HIPAA), and he routinely did electronic billing, he gave Rosemary a second handout describing her rights and other relevant information, as required by law.

1. How can Dr. Tellem provide preliminary informed consent over the telephone without having met or assessed the patient?
2. If your practice is not compliant with HIPAA, is there a need to have a printed consent form?
3. How can you have confidence that your patients have understood your informed-consent form, even if they have signed it at the bottom? What difference might it make—ethically, clinically, and legally—that they have a good understanding of the terms?
4. If you do not choose to use printed forms providing informed consent in your practice, how, specifically, must you document in the patient's clinical record the elements of informed consent that took place?
5. Describe your obligation to provide informed consent yet again as the therapy changes over time. What would be an example?

10.01 (b)

When obtaining informed consent for treatment for which generally recognized techniques and procedures have not been established, psychologists inform their clients/patients of the developing nature of the treatment, the potential risks

involved, alternative treatments that may be available, and the voluntary na-
ture of their participation. (See also Standards 2.01e, Boundaries of Compe-
tence, and 3.10, Informed Consent.)

Be sure to inform your clients and patients about therapy that is based on techniques, interventions, strategies, or procedures for which there is little or no supporting research or that are not generally accepted by the mental health community as being valid or successful. Good informed consent about this sort of treatment includes the following:

- inform patients about the experimental or developing nature of your treatment (e.g., that you may have achieved good results with patients, if that is true, but that it has yet to endure the scrutiny of scientific research);
- tell them of any risks that might apply (e.g., the treatment might not be successful, their symptoms might increase, new symptoms or side effects could develop);
- educate them about alternative treatments that are available for their presenting complaints, regardless of whether you can provide them; and
- remind them that their participation in treatment is completely voluntary and that they may withdraw at any time.

VIGNETTE

Dr. Evan Garde had developed a new protocol for overweight patients for which there was little supporting research in the literature. It relied on current computer technology and required the daily logging of food intake and other information as well as daily communication between client and therapist. The informed consent provided at the outset described the protocol clearly, and this information was again presented and explained in the very first consultation.

Specifically, Dr. Garde asked participating clients who were consulting him for weight loss to fulfill the following for a period of 4 weeks:

- make log entries daily, including (a) total food consumption, (b) the corresponding times of the food consumption, (c) exercise amount, (d) mood assessment, (e) length of workday, (f) gratifying or fun activities, and (g) amount of sleep. These entries were to be made either manually; on a personal digital assistant; or on a computer, according to a specific template created for the treatment;
- send an e-mail each evening to Dr. Garde of the daily log after the last food item has been eaten;
- read one return e-mail each morning from Dr. Garde providing feedback;

- log on Dr. Garde's Web site once each day for a period of approximately 20 minutes to read and answer questions on a programmed text module about eating behavior, health, and related matters;
- talk briefly with one family member or friend every other day about some aspect of the weight loss program and how it is proceeding, and note it in the log;
- discuss food and its meaning within the family, with parents or siblings, including rituals, habit patterns on weekdays and weekends, holiday celebrations, and related matters, at least once each week for a minimum of 30 minutes over a 2-month period. Specific topics were to be included; and
- have a complete physical examination at the outset of therapy (if the patient had not had one recently) and comply completely with any medical or health-related recommendations that predated the weight loss treatment program.

Dr. Garde informed his clients that common risks of this protocol included a possible increase in stressful reactions among family members precipitated by the weekly discussions. Another risk involved a possible temporary increase in anxiety, depression, or other dysphoric feelings as food became less available as an emotional resource. Finally, it was possible that there would be no permanent weight loss even if the client complied fully with treatment, as this protocol was yet too new to yield significant data or provide long-term results.

Dr. Garde also reviewed the array of weight loss programs that were currently available in the area, both with professional therapists and community resources (e.g., Weight Watchers, Overeaters Anonymous, etc.). He made it clear, both in the printed informed consent form and in the very first face-to-face session, that client participation was wholly voluntary and that they could withdraw at any time. However, if they withdrew from the new protocol, they could no longer continue in their weight loss program with Dr. Garde, as he currently was working only in this modality. He would, however, refer any patient who withdrew to three other therapists in the community who used other methods.

With such a thorough presentation at the outset, both with printed handouts and a comprehensive explanation, allowing for ample questions and answers, patients felt that they were well informed about the requirements of participating in this novel approach. There were few disappointments, and few dropouts, as Dr. Garde had anticipated most of the problems to be encountered in advance, from his experience with earlier patients.

1. How might Dr. Garde go about providing good informed consent with the very first clients he ever worked with on his developing protocol? On what might he rely?

2. Does this standard require that you provide printed handouts to clients and patients about your novel techniques? If not, how would you document that informed consent had in fact occurred?
3. How would you determine whether a creative approach of yours crosses the line and requires a specific informed consent discussion with your patient, at any point in therapy?

10.01 (c)

When the therapist is a trainee and the legal responsibility for the treatment provided resides with the supervisor, the client/patient, as part of the informed consent procedure, is informed that the therapist is in training and is being supervised and is given the name of the supervisor.

Patients and clients must always be informed at the outset if their therapist is in training and someone else is legally responsible for the treatment, such as in the case of a pre- or postdoctoral intern, fellow, practicum student, and so on. Also, recipients of services must be informed of the identity of the supervisor, as it reduces the risk that the client or patient might have a prior relationship with him or her (this is particularly important in cases where the patient is also a mental health provider or student; we live in a very small world!). Although not necessarily required, it is best to do this in writing, in the form of handouts, correspondence, or in some other fashion, and not just orally.

VIGNETTE

Dr. Rhea Veel had just received her PsyD and was beginning to accrue postdoctoral supervisory hours for licensure by working in a group private practice in a small midwestern town. She worked under the clinical supervision of the owner of the practice, Dr. Tellem. One of Dr. Tellem's procedures was to require each of his supervisees and employees to give new patients a handout describing the fiduciary relationships of consumer, therapist, and supervisor and other information about the psychological services offered. In this way, patients were well informed how the process of therapy and supervision worked in this group practice.

Dr. Veel understood her ethical obligation to inform clients clearly that she was being supervised by Dr. Tellem and to make sure that they understood the implications of the handout that she provided. She took the time to answer their questions and present any information she thought might be helpful to their decision-making process about treatment. This included the fact that therapy sessions would be audiorecorded (with patient signed consent, of course); that only Dr. Tellem would be privy to the tapes and discussions of the session content; and that if a different supervisor or colleague were ever consulted, Dr. Veel would clear this with the patient in advance.

On several occasions, new clients declined to begin therapy with Dr. Veel because they were acquainted with Dr. Tellem in various social contexts and did not want him to know about their therapy disclosures. They liked him as a friend or colleague but felt that the relationship would change considerably if he were supervising their therapy. Had Dr. Veel failed to inform them about the identity of her supervisor, they would have begun treatment and later on would have been exposed to a potentially embarrassing and even harmful situation. Dr. Tellem would, of course, have known the identity of the patient from the outset but might not have known his or her preferences about participating in treatment under his supervision; he might have felt accepting of the situation, whereas the patient might reject it.

1. If you have a supervisor who is careless about complying with this standard, what steps should you take?
2. How would you go about documenting this aspect of informed consent?
3. In which settings would this standard have particular importance, and why? Small rural area? Metropolitan setting? University counseling center? Employee assistance program providing services to city officials?

10.02 THERAPY INVOLVING COUPLES OR FAMILIES

(a) When psychologists agree to provide services to several persons who have a relationship (such as spouses, significant others, or parents and children), they take reasonable steps to clarify at the outset (1) which of the individuals are clients/patients and (2) the relationship the psychologist will have with each person. This clarification includes the psychologist's role and the probable uses of the services provided or the information obtained. (See also Standard 4.02, Discussing the Limits of Confidentiality.)

Whenever you treat more than one person simultaneously, such as spouses, family, roommates, and so on, make the following as clear at the beginning of treatment as is practicable: (a) which person is actually your client or patient and (b) what type of relationship you will have with each person. Also, clarify what role you intend to play and how your interventions and services can best be used, as well as how you intend to use personal or historical information that the patient or patients will be providing.

VIGNETTE

Mr. and Mrs. Crandall began couples therapy with Dr. Sole after many months of conflict. Mrs. Crandall had become increasingly depressed and agitated, with periods of apparent dissociation. Mr. Crandall had been work-ing long hours; avoiding his wife; and beginning to use alcohol on a regular basis, with increasing incidents of intoxication. Dr. Sole saw the potential need for individual psychotherapy for each of them but felt an obligation to first address the immediacy of their couples work.

Dr. Sole informed the Crandalls that he saw his role primarily as a re-source to them by focusing on their marital relationship as the main part of their work. He went on to explain that even though other therapists might work differently, he primarily would be meeting with them as a couple. He informed them that if there were a need for individual psychotherapy then he would explore the options of continuing couples sessions with him or changing the format of therapy in some way.

After four meetings, Mrs. Crandall informed Dr. Sole that she wished to meet with him individually, to obtain relief from her dissociative episodes and depression, while continuing couples sessions. He informed her that al-though in some cases this was possible, he thought it would pose a conflict for him because he could not function simultaneously as her individual psy-chotherapist and as a marital therapist for her and her husband. Further-more, the nature of her dissociation was such that she would likely require long-term individual psychotherapy, with a therapist experienced with her symptoms (which he was not). He explained that he was willing to have occasional individual sessions with her if she wished, for focusing on anxiety or depression management, but his theoretical framework did not permit the extensive therapeutic intervention that she was requesting and that was ap-parently warranted. He referred her to another psychologist in the commu-nity and obtained her consent to consult with him at regular intervals to coordinate treatment.

Shortly thereafter, Mr. Crandall asked Dr. Sole if he would also meet with their 16-year-old son, who had increasingly been using marijuana and alcohol and failing in school. Again, Dr. Sole was willing to discuss some possibilities, such as having a single meeting with the boy or referring him to another therapist, but he was unwilling to simultaneously attempt to counsel the son and provide marital therapy to the parents. He informed Mr. and Mrs. Crandall that therapists from other theoretical schools might agree to family therapy in conjunction with collateral treatment with another family member; however, Dr. Sole had long ago found that for his style of therapy it was essential to keep the therapeutic contract clear and simple and keep the boundaries clear. He saw potential harm, and no lasting benefit, in attempt-ing to provide individual treatment to family members while carrying out marital therapy. He explained that their son would likely establish a stronger relationship with another therapist and make more rapid progress than if Dr. Sole were to attempt to treat him. He persistently restated the role he would play, as a referral source for the boy, and he provided several names of indi-vidual and group therapists.

Although initially finding his resistance to their requests frustrating, the Crandalls were ultimately grateful that Dr. Sole was straightforward about his role and its boundaries. They opted to continue regular weekly sessions with him while Mrs. Crandall remained in individual treatment elsewhere. Mr. Crandall eventually began individual therapy with another therapist too, stopped drinking, joined Alcoholics Anonymous (AA), and continued in marital counseling with Dr. Sole.

1. What are the risks—clinically, ethically, and legally—of carrying out concurrent individual therapy with a husband or wife whom you are treating in marital therapy?
2. Was Dr. Sole being overly cautious in refusing to meet with Mrs. Crandall for individual therapy for treating her dissociation? How would you handle such a request given your theoretical orientation?
3. How would you document that you have provided informed consent to treatment in this situation?

10.02 (b)

If it becomes apparent that psychologists may be called on to perform potentially conflicting roles (such as family therapist and then witness for one party in divorce proceedings), psychologists take reasonable steps to clarify and modify, or withdraw from, roles appropriately. (See also Standard 3.05c, Multiple Relationships.)

Play only one role with your patients at a time, unless circumstances unfold that make this impossible. If it becomes obvious that your couple is moving toward divorce, and you might be asked to testify or reveal information about the husband or wife in court, be aware that your forensic role could conflict mightily with your role as a therapist to this troubled couple. Whenever possible, simplify the nature of your professional role with your clients and patients by refusing requests to participate in a secondary role with them, providing additional explanations or withdrawing from a preexisting role. Refer them to someone else, if needed. You don't have to do it all yourself!

VIGNETTE

Dr. Summa Ubermacher, a newly licensed psychologist, had recently joined the staff of a busy community mental health center. Eager to demonstrate her competence and establish her reputation in the county, she considered accepting various members of the same family for a variety of presenting complaints. The mother first brought in her 11-year-old son for problems in school that involved difficulty with reading and studying. Within 3 weeks, the mother asked Dr. Ubermacher to see her 9-year-old twins, who were having difficulty sleeping through the night and seemed to have some symptoms of hyperactivity. Soon after that, she wanted to discuss with Dr. Ubermacher her own sexual dysfunction because her relationship with her husband had started to deteriorate.

Within 1 month, the woman's husband telephoned Dr. Ubermacher to ask if she would be willing to consult with him on an "important professional matter." He was the CEO of a large architectural firm and was seeking her assistance in coping with some interpersonal stress in the workplace. He was beginning to experience headaches, anxiety, and insomnia, because ongoing conflict with several employees involving theoretical differences regarding a project was beginning to affect him. He also wanted to seek her assistance about an important personal matter. He told Dr. Ubermacher that a few months earlier he had been contacted by a 19-year-old man claiming to be his son from an earlier relationship. It was true that 19 years ago he had sired a son, whom he and the boy's mother gave up for adoption at birth, and he was well aware that a rendezvous with the young man might eventually occur. He wished to play whatever role he could as a mentor, but he was concerned about how this new development might affect his current wife and children. He was also ambivalent about the extent of his own involvement in the son's life at this point and about the prospect of an old girlfriend, the son's mother, who also had surfaced recently and was living in the same city, reentering his life.

Dr. Ubermacher began feeling understandably overwhelmed with the needs of this family. Although she was competent to treat the problems presented, she saw a clear need for couples therapy in addition to the individual concerns of the members. It rapidly became too complicated for her to attempt to treat all of the family members; after presenting this case at a weekly staff meeting, she was able to see how she had overextended herself. She referred certain family members to other therapists at the agency and in the community and narrowed the scope of her work to include only the 11-year-old. This decision allowed for good confidentiality and clear lines of accountability in all the therapy relationships.

1. Why might accepting the 9-year-old twins, the 11-year-old boy, and the mother and father in treatment concurrently for the array of symptoms be contraindicated from both an ethical and clinical point of view?
2. Would this standard prohibit treating all the members of the family if the setting were rural and very few mental health resources were available?
3. Describe the clinical, ethical, and legal implications and conflicting roles inherent in treating, in individual therapy, a husband and wife who eventually decide to get a divorce?

10.03 GROUP THERAPY

When psychologists provide services to several persons in a group setting, they describe at the outset the roles and responsibilities of all parties and the limits of confidentiality.

If you provide group therapy, be sure to include thorough informed consent at the outset, including, at a minimum, the following information:

- an explanation of the relationship that you will be having with group members, as well as the professional role that you will be playing, and the expected roles of the group members;
- a description of your responsibilities and any responsibilities of group members, as they may apply; and
- a discussion about confidentiality and its limitations—what the legal exceptions to confidentiality are for you (e.g., revelations about suicidality, child abuse, or intent to harm another) and any expectations of participants regarding disclosures to outsiders about what is revealed in the group.

VIGNETTE

It was Dr. Jones's normal policy to have an individual meeting with each new candidate for his therapy group, prior to the first group meeting, to prepare him or her for the experience and assess his or her appropriateness for the group. He would discuss the goals, ground rules, and expectations that applied to members and to himself and would also provide them with a printed handout that described these matters and anticipated many of their questions.

Because Dr. Jones was a member of the American Group Psychotherapy Association and was listed in the National Registry of Certified Group Psychotherapists, he abided by their joint ethical guidelines and, of course, any other standards of this Ethics Code that might apply to group work. His review of these important matters included the following topics:

- the purpose and goals of the group therapy meetings, stated in general terms yet in enough detail so as to educate prospective group members about what to expect;
- how the group functions, what one might hope to achieve by participating in it, and related matters;
- the nuts and bolts of the meetings, such as their length, the duration of the group (unless open ended), and other relevant information;
- the fee and financial arrangements as well as the terms for a reduced fee (if a sliding scale is permitted);

- his policy about maintaining privacy and confidentiality of all disclosures in the group;
- his ethical and legal obligations to take action if harm is imminent (e.g., disclosures about suicidality, intent to harm someone, child abuse, etc.);[1]
- group members' understanding about confidentiality and their commitment to refrain from discussing with outsiders disclosures made in the group, as a means of promoting trust and furthering the potential depth of the group;
- the policy of prohibiting physical interactions between group members and the importance of refraining from acting out angry feelings (group therapists may differ in their policies about physical contact); and
- agreement about avoiding dual roles and refraining from socializing with each other outside the meetings or engaging in a secondary relationship with each other (e.g., business dealings, romantic relationships, etc.) during the course of the group (group therapists may differ in their policies about group members socializing with each other outside of group meetings).

Dr. Jones took the time to thoroughly discuss each of these topics in sufficient detail so as to reduce prospective participants' uncertainty about joining the group. His intention was to form an alliance with the prospective candidate that focused on his or her personal goals, not the group's goals. The main purpose of this screening interview was to determine whether and how the candidate might achieve his or her goals within the group setting. Sometimes, several meetings would be required to accomplish this.

Once in awhile a candidate would wonder if Dr. Jones ever used information that was revealed in the group. He explained that he occasionally teaches a graduate-level group psychotherapy course and draws on experiences in the group to amplify the theoretical material. However, he always altered the facts (topic under discussion) and any identifying features of group members (name, age, gender, professional role, ethnic origin, etc.) so that anonymity would be preserved. He also routinely informed his students that he had altered the information to protect the privacy of group members, so that they would not mistakenly assume that he was revealing confidences or discussing someone whom they thought they could identify.

Naturally, using vignettes in publishing articles or books on the subject of group psychotherapy necessitated a similar deliberate deception and possibly additional safeguards as well. Dr. Jones usually informed group members that he engaged in research, writing journal articles or books that may include descriptions of group experiences that, in fact, constituted an amalgam

---

[1]Please check the legal requirements in your state concerning confidentiality and mandated reporting.

of many experiences in different groups. (If there were ever a particular incident that would lose a great deal by significantly altering the details, he would seek, without coercion, the written consent of the group members to include such a vignette in his writings, and he would do so only after the individuals had ended their participation in the group or the group itself had terminated.)

With such a clear introduction to the general goals, ground rules, and ethical guidelines, prospective group members generally felt secure in at least tentatively beginning to participate in the meetings. Of course, all concerns and apprehensions were not dispelled in the first meeting; these took some time to clarify and resolve. Issues of trust and authority were revisited over the course of many weeks, on many different levels. By providing such clear and thorough informed consent, Dr. Jones was confident that he had done his best to describe what might be anticipated in the group meetings and how the goals of each participant might be approached, at least in a general way.

1. Would Dr. Jones have to conform to the ethical guidelines of the American Group Psychotherapy Association if he were not a member of that organization?
2. What other ethical standards of this Ethics Code might also have a bearing on conducting group therapy?
3. Is it necessary to have printed handouts on informed consent for group members? How else might you document that you provided adequate informed consent without using handouts?
4. How might Dr. Jones handle the disclosure of illegal activity by a group member that had never been discovered, such as cheating on one's income tax, embezzling a large amount of money from a company, or shoplifting expensive items?
5. What are the ethical and clinical implications of promoting or discouraging social interactions by group members outside of scheduled group meetings?
6. How do you conceptualize your professional role as a group therapist? Does your professional role with a former group member ever really end, considering the type of group therapy you provide and your theoretical orientation; that is, would it be ethically acceptable to develop a romantic relationship with a former group member? Friendship? Business relationship?

10.04 PROVIDING THERAPY TO THOSE SERVED BY OTHERS

In deciding whether to offer or provide services to those already receiving mental health services elsewhere, psychologists carefully consider the treatment issues and the potential client's/patient's welfare. Psychologists discuss these issues with the client/patient or another legally authorized person on behalf of the client/patient in order to minimize the risk of confusion and conflict, consult with the other service providers when appropriate, and proceed with caution and sensitivity to the therapeutic issues.

> You may see clients or patients who are currently in treatment with other therapists, but always reflect on the wisdom of offering a second therapy— how best to undertake this—and always give major consideration to the client's or patient's welfare. Discuss these issues with the client or patient (or his or her parent or guardian) in advance, so as to reduce any confusion or conflict, and be sure to collaborate with the other health care professionals when doing so is in the patient's best interest. Proceed with caution and sensitivity to the clinical issues, as therapy can become confusing or even sabotaging unless it is well coordinated.

VIGNETTE

Mrs. Jacqueline Spratt, a portly middle-aged woman diagnosed by Dr. Firstly with borderline personality disorder, decided to secretly seek additional treatment for weight loss with Dr. Secundo, a reputed expert in this area. In her phone conversation with Dr. Secundo, she informed him that she was already seeing Dr. Firstly but was emphatic in her request that he not collaborate with her other therapist or let him know that he also would be treating her. When Dr. Secundo brought up the subject, she specifically said that she would refuse to sign a consent form permitting such contact. Furthermore, she volunteered that in other therapies in the past she had covertly consulted a secondary therapist for one reason or another, and it seemed to work out fine.

Dr. Secundo initially thought that he could work effectively with Mrs. Spratt, and that the Ethics Code now permitted such concurrent consultations with different therapists (as opposed to the previous edition of the code) as long as appropriate coordination or collaboration occurred, if needed. However, the longer he remained on the phone with her, the more doubtful he became that this arrangement could work.

As the truth came out, it appeared that Mrs. Spratt had a strong attachment to Dr. Firstly, and her motivation for losing weight was primarily based on a desire to enhance her physical appearance so that Dr. Firstly might find her more attractive. She stopped just short of saying that she wanted to have a romantic relationship with him, but clearly this was in her mind, and it seemed that she was in the firm grip of an erotic transference with her therapist. Dr. Secundo told her he would consider meeting with her, under the circumstances, but wanted to think it over for a day and call her back. Mrs. Spratt, ever optimistic, consented to this proposal.

Dr. Secundo carefully weighed the merits of beginning therapy for weight loss under these circumstances. He consulted with a colleague who was quite experienced in treating borderline patients. The colleague discussed an array of potential problems involved with commencing treatment under secretive pretenses and the potential for further manipulation as the treatment got under way. He reminded Dr. Secundo of the likelihood of further "splitting" or pitting one therapist against the other, later on, when it suited the patient to reveal that she was seeing Dr. Secundo. Although it might be possible to serve as a therapeutic resource to the woman in addition to helping her lose weight, the risk of ultimately complicating treatment with a borderline patient who had had many therapists in the past, and who currently felt as though she were in love with her treating therapist, seemed too great.

Dr. Secundo telephoned Mrs. Spratt back and informed her that he had decided against accepting her as a patient under her stipulations that collaboration with Dr. Firstly would be ruled out. He explained that the dual therapies might be confusing to her because of the potential different orientations of each therapist. His program of weight loss, he explained, involved not only consistent behavioral interventions but also psychotherapy that could go on for a considerable period of time. He also told her that, in his opinion, to maximize the effectiveness of both treatments, both therapists should have her consent to consult with each other on an as-needed basis. He gently recommended that she might consider discussing her feelings for Dr. Firstly directly and consult with him on the goal of weight loss as well. He further stated that he would be happy to provide treatment to her in the future if she felt she could comply with open collaboration between him and Dr. Firstly.

1. How would you deal with a situation in which your new patient informs you, after three sessions, that she has been seeing another therapist for over a year?
2. Discuss the potential value of Dr. Secundo accepting Mrs. Spratt into treatment for weight loss, under her terms, and how it might possibly be beneficial in the long run. Can you make a valid argument for doing so?
3. How do you think that initiating therapy with a fundamental deception might have an impact later in treatment, with a patient diagnosed with borderline personality disorder? Would you consider accepting this patient under her conditions if her diagnosis were different?

10.05 SEXUAL INTIMACIES WITH CURRENT THERAPY CLIENTS/PATIENTS

Psychologists do not engage in sexual intimacies with current therapy clients/patients.

Never engage in sexual activities of any kind with your current therapy patients or clients, regardless of whether it provides pleasure, and regardless of who initiates it. Of course, this prohibits sexual intercourse, but it would also prohibit the following: touching them or yourself sexually, asking them to touch you or themselves sexually, discussing or focusing on sex unnecessarily, revealing your own sexual activities or fantasies, and anything else that might sexualize the relationship. Remember, because sexual stimulation is often subjectively determined (and you do not know what is arousing to your patient), be especially careful about participating in a full body hug or any verbal or nonverbal behavior that could be confusing or ambiguous and pull for a sexualized interpretation by your client or patient.

VIGNETTE

Camille was a 39-year-old woman married, for the second time, to an alcoholic man who was beginning to become physically abusive. She began therapy with Dr. Mellow for the purpose of exploring how to either improve the relationship with her spouse or how to overcome her despondency and separate from him. As she progressed in therapy over the months, she became more personally secure and less compelled to seek her husband's approval and always try to please him at her own expense. Around this time she also noticed the emergence of strong feelings for Dr. Mellow and found herself thinking about him often with gratitude and affection. She knew that he was recently divorced, and she entertained the thought that he might possibly be interested in having an affair with her some day.

Although Dr. Mellow had steadfastly refused her invitation to meet at a nearby bistro for a glass of wine, he seemed to maintain a special interest in her, and he had always had a very warm and friendly demeanor, in her opinion. After all, she reasoned, he always was attentive to her feelings, was very nurturing, he helped her to make important changes in her life, and he frequently wore shirts of her favorite color.

One day, after a particularly difficult therapy session in which Camille revealed her strong attachment to Dr. Mellow, she ended the session by giving him a slow, sensual hug. Dr. Mellow found her seductiveness compelling, to be sure, and began to feel some stirrings within him that had been absent for too long a time in his life. For several hours following her departure from the office, he was left with confusing and conflicted feelings.

To help process this event, including his own sexual feelings for Camille, Dr. Mellow contacted his old mentor, a trusted senior psychologist with whom he had had many valuable conversations in the past. He took the time to discuss the entire course of therapy, his feelings, boundaries, her attraction for him, his own solitary life, and other matters. These discussions were important in helping Dr. Mellow to achieve insight and find a way of continuing to remain comfortably in the role of therapist without being swept away by his client's intensity or his own needs. He also knew well the research on erotic countertransference, that affairs with patients are generally very harmful to patients over time, and that psychologists who engage in them are frequently sued or become the target of formal ethics complaints after such relationships come to an end.

The meaning of Camille's loving feelings for him was explored over time, in therapy, in a variety of ways, and was revealed to her in a manner that helped her gain insight yet continue working with him as her therapist. This included interpreting and reviewing her immediate set of circumstances, such as the transition in her marriage, her dependency needs, and the inherent supportive behavior on Dr. Mellow's part as her therapist. He was, in the end, able to be an excellent resource to Camille by remaining her therapist, not by having an affair with her.

Later on, Dr. Mellow also found it useful to attend a workshop on sexuality in therapy, as a refresher course, for helping to manage his own feelings of attraction to clients such as Camille in the future. He also came to some realizations about the quality of his own life. He could see that his own social and personal needs had been on the back burner so long that he had begun to use clients for his own gratification, in subtle ways. Shortly after this episode, Dr. Mellow had his first date since his divorce, and he was delighted to discover that there was life outside of the 50-minute therapy hour.

1. How might you deal with a grateful client who has a romantic attraction to you and shows this with a hug or a kiss?
2. What message could be conveyed to a client if the therapist initiates a hug or a touch?
3. Considering age, gender, diagnostic category, cultural values, and other variables, when might it be appropriate to touch a client or patient, and how? Is it ever appropriate with adult clients or patients?
4. If Dr. Mellow had reciprocated Camille's sensual hug, would he have irrevocably changed his role for Camille? What steps might he take to remedy the situation at that point?

10.06 SEXUAL INTIMACIES WITH RELATIVES OR SIGNIFICANT OTHERS OF CURRENT THERAPY CLIENTS/PATIENTS

Psychologists do not engage in sexual intimacies with individuals they know to be close relatives, guardians, or significant others of current clients/patients. Psychologists do not terminate therapy to circumvent this standard.

Never fall in love with, or begin a sexual relationship with, someone whom you know is a close relative (e.g., parent, brother or sister, divorcing or estranged spouse), guardian, or significant other (boyfriend or girlfriend) of a current therapy client or patient. Also, avoid the temptation to end therapy with your client or patient prematurely, just so that you could then "ethically" begin such a romantic relationship with the person in question.

VIGNETTE

Mrs. Ann Banden had brought her 11-year-old son, Reggie, to Dr. Rick Blue for treatment of his anxiety and depression shortly after Reggie was diagnosed with Type 1 diabetes. Reggie had much apprehension about the changes in his daily regimen—medical interventions such as daily blood tests (the "dreaded" finger sticks), radical changes to his diet, not being permitted to attend social events on his own until his dietary regimen was well established, and other major changes. In addition, Mrs. Banden had recently lost her husband of 14 years to an affair with a business colleague over the previous year, and he had moved away to another state. This was indeed a time of major transition for this little family.

Weekly therapy sessions with Dr. Blue helped Reggie gradually to gain some control over his needle phobia and to make progress with his adjustment disorder and provided Mrs. Banden some reassurance, for the first time, that things might actually improve. Dr. Blue was an experienced child therapist, and his manner was affable and nurturing. It was clear that his therapy with Reggie was helping and that he was becoming an important fixture in the Banden family. Also, he had a special empathy for Reggie's mother, as he had recently ended a relationship with his significant other of 4 years and was finding his empty house to be more than he could comfortably bear.

It was Dr. Blue's habit to also meet periodically with the parent or parents of his clients. Mrs. Banden asked permission to bring her sister Mary to a session, as she was an important part of the family, lived close by, had a loving relationship with Reggie and took care of him every afternoon while Mrs. Banden was at work, and needed some guidance in dealing with all the changes in Reggie's life. During the course of this meeting Dr. Blue found himself feeling quite attracted to Mary, yet he was able to maintain his professional focus for the session. Privately, he felt relieved that Mary was not his patient, as the chemistry between them was palpable and, he thought, had the potential of interfering significantly with his work.

During the course of the session, Mrs. Banden's cell phone rang: Reggie had had a minor bicycle accident on the way home from school and needed her help. She promptly left the meeting, leaving it up to Mary to be her proxy for the remaining half hour. Mary spoke of her deep gratitude for all that Dr. Blue had done for her nephew. After raising her questions about her role with Reggie, as he moved through this difficult transition, and as the session drew to a close, Mary said that she had one last question (as though she had been reading Dr. Blue's mind). Admitting that she was usually not quite this bold, she innocently inquired if it would be ethically acceptable to go for a quick cup of coffee together in the restaurant downstairs—her treat. Dr. Blue at first demurred, but then surprised himself by accepting her offer; it was the end of his work week, Mary was not technically a patient of his (he reasoned), the night had nothing else to offer, he was tired, and she was all too wonderfully feminine for him to decline.

Over coffee, the discussion initially centered on Reggie but soon moved to more personal matters. Dr. Blue had been struggling with chronic neck pain from an automobile accident of several years before and periodic depression as well. Mary had been divorced for 5 years and was finding it impossible to meet a good man who was also interested in children. The afternoon cup of coffee merged seamlessly into happy hour. Because it had been 24 hours since his last drink of alcohol, Dr. Blue felt relieved to begin imbibing again, relapsing into comfortable old habits that helped dull his neck pain and soften his depression. The mutual attraction heightened, "Dr. Blue" became "Rick," and he shed his professional role, and his customary good judgment, and soon the couple took to the crowded, noisy dance floor, in each others' arms. One thing led to another, and in the space of a scant 12 hours, the two had traversed the distance from a professional relationship to the most intimate one imaginable.

The weeks that followed were difficult for each family member. Reggie overheard part of a loving telephone conversation between his aunt and his therapist and felt confused about the ensuing relationship. He felt some odd feelings of resentment beginning to stir and a sense of betrayal as well. For the past year he had grown very close to his aunt, who was at his house 5 days a week. They had all faced their losses bravely and had grown quite close, in the absence of father and husband in the household. Now he felt a curious kind of threat emerging, whereby he was losing his aunt's attentions to another man and at the same time potentially losing his therapist's full commitment, as Dr. Blue now appeared more eager to see Mary than him. Mary's sister had ambivalent feelings about the situation. She had trusted Dr. Blue's professional judgment up until the present, yet wondered how he could maintain his objectivity now that he was dating her sister.

Dr. Blue, for his part, was soon aware of his own conflicted feelings and how they influenced Reggie's treatment. Indeed, he began to feel more fatherly toward Reggie than like a therapist, and he found himself advising Reggie how he might alter his behavior at home to better comply with his aunt's and mother's needs. This was a far cry from the initial focus of treatment—Reggie's adjustment disorder with depression stemming from both the postdivorce sequela and his recent diagnosis of diabetes. The focus of treatment clearly had strayed, as Dr. Blue could no longer be impartial, and his competence to help Reggie was undermined. Things came to a head one day when Reggie missed his therapy appointment and went out to drink a large chocolate milkshake instead, resulting in an episode of hyperglycemia.

It was with great difficulty that Dr. Blue was ultimately able to transfer Reggie's care to a different therapist, a female colleague, who could eventually help the boy resolve his complex feelings of loss and resentment. Dr. Blue had always considered himself to be a highly ethical therapist and had never had a complaint brought against him. However, because of a combination of personal and situational factors, he suffered a major lapse of judgment, and learned, too little, too late, about the importance of preserving the frame of therapy and avoiding behavior that might threaten it. He also developed an awareness of his alcohol dependency, due in part to Mary's input, and began to take steps toward his own rehabilitation.

1. What danger signs might Dr. Blue have noticed early on that could have made a difference in both his professional and personal lives?
2. Consider the ethical pitfall of going out for a cup of coffee with a relative of your teenage patient—Aunt? Uncle? In-law? Grandparent? Distant cousin? Godfather or godmother?
3. What might be the clinical, ethical, and legal implications for Dr. Blue if Reggie's self-destructive act had been fatal?
4. What range of rehabilitative experiences would you recommend for Dr. Blue?

10.07 THERAPY WITH FORMER SEXUAL PARTNERS

Psychologists do not accept as therapy clients/patients persons with whom they have engaged in sexual intimacies.

Never accept former lovers as patients no matter how much time has passed since your last contact. There are usually plenty of other therapists you can refer them to who can be objective and competent. Assume that having had a sexual relationship with someone irrevocably alters your ability to provide competent therapy to that person, even though this might not necessarily be the case. At the very least, you may invite significant problems if your former lover decides to bring a complaint against you or sue you, if the therapy does not go well.

VIGNETTE

A pain management clinic in a local hospital referred Mr. Ecks to Dr. Helpim for nonmedical treatment of cluster headaches. After a short telephone intake, Dr. Helpim realized that this was an old boyfriend with whom she had a brief relationship during her graduate school days 20 years before. After some moments of hesitation, she agreed to accept him into treatment for biofeedback and stress management, with the private rationale that because she would not be conducting psychotherapy with him, she was not risking impaired judgment or competence. In that way, she reasoned, she would be keeping within the spirit of this ethical standard. It was true that she had been his lover years before, but she would not be offering him psychotherapy now, only biofeedback and stress management.

The two seemed to work well together for the eight biofeedback sessions, despite the significant memories for each that were triggered when Dr. Helpim would touch his head, neck, shoulders, and hands to tape on the biofeedback leads. Mr. Ecks even jokingly remarked that it seemed "just like old times" when on one occasion she asked him to remove his tie to properly attach the EMG leads to the back of his neck. That comment notwithstanding, the treatment progressed satisfactorily until Mr. Ecks began discussing a major stressor in his life, namely, his second marriage. As a result of exploring this life issue with her patient, Dr. Helpim realized that he manifested many narcissistic traits; she also discovered that he had recently developed a cocaine habit. He was ready and willing to discuss any aspect of his life, thinking that his former girlfriend probably knew him better than anyone and thus would be able to help him. Dr. Helpim, however, found it increasingly difficult to remain objective and could see clearly that he needed (and wanted) individual psychotherapy.

As the biofeedback training drew to a close and the stress management discussions merged into therapy, she found that her patience for Mr. Ecks's self-indulgence, so characteristic of her work with other patients, was beginning to wane. At times, she had quick flashes of frustration and even resentment with his arrogant behavior and blatant disregard for the feelings of others. Her frustration and confused feelings increased when he began to disclose the details of his complex sex life with his wife and several other women, with whom he would regularly use cocaine; sometimes, his motives appeared exhibitionistic, and at other times they seemed to be a call for help. On several occasions, Mr. Ecks chose to nostalgically revisit some of their own shared intimate moments of the past, for which he seemed to have an excellent memory—the unusual places they had made love; her difficulties with orgasm; and her initial reticence to experiment with group sex, which he considered "typical New England uptightness."

Dr. Helpim was flooded with negative feelings after this last session, in which sex seemed to surface as the primary focus and Mr. Ecks seemed bent on teasing her about their past relationship. She realized that no good purpose would be served by continuing to meet with him. At the next session, she pointed out that although the biofeedback training had been effective, psychotherapy was out of the question, because they had a past together and, at least for her, it was intruding on the treatment. She explained that she could not provide competent therapy and had decided she needed to refer him to another colleague, if he desired to have psychotherapy. After reviewing the progress that he had made to date, and preparing for termination, over Mr. Ecks's objection that he was "just starting to look forward to these weekly sessions," Dr. Helpim provided the names of several colleagues to consult for individual psychotherapy. She also recommended that he consider entering a chemical dependency program for his cocaine addiction, as he seemed to be unaware of the risks and unmotivated even to address the issue. She was relieved when the treatment came to a close, another sign for her that termination and referral was indeed a wise choice. She could see, with hindsight, that she never should have accepted Mr. Ecks as a patient in the first place, even for the supposedly limited scope of carrying out biofeedback training and stress management.

1. Would there be any risks to your competence in providing psychological assessment services to a former lover? Does this standard prohibit it?
2. How would you have dealt with a patient such as Mr. Ecks who attempts to manipulate the power relationship within therapy (as a borderline patient might)?
3. How would you determine whether to accept an individual into therapy with whom you never had a sexual relationship but did have a friendship some years before?
4. What are the problems with accepting a former lover into treatment that supposedly is not psychotherapy (i.e., hypnosis for migraine headaches, biofeedback for pain control, consulting for parenting a difficult child, therapy with your former lover's child or spouse, or therapy with your former lover's family member)?

10.08 SEXUAL INTIMACIES WITH FORMER THERAPY CLIENTS/PATIENTS

(a) Psychologists do not engage in sexual intimacies with former clients/patients for at least two years after cessation or termination of therapy.

If you cannot seem to help yourself from falling in love with your former client or patient, you must wait for 2 full years to pass since your last professional contact before engaging in sexually intimate behavior. However, be aware that this standard basically says that *any* posttermination sex is unethical, except in the most unusual of circumstances. It should not be seen as implying that sex is acceptable after 2 years. It might be far wiser to assume that it is always risky and foolish to begin a romantic or sexual relationship with someone you have seen as a client or patient, no matter how much time has elapsed. (Also be aware that some states have laws specifying a longer amount of posttermination time that must elapse before a sexual relationship may begin, and some say that such relationships may never begin.) Bear in mind that there are many cases on record in which the former patient has sued her former therapist, or complained to a licensing board, after the romance has gone bad, and won. Your best guideline (although not stated in this standard) is the following: Once you accept someone as a client or patient, forever forfeit any thoughts of romance with him or her, no matter how much time has elapsed. Look elsewhere for love.

VIGNETTE

Dr. Roamer had been treating Julie, a 29-year-old woman with a history of childhood sexual molestation, for nearly 2 years. Over time, he found himself being increasingly drawn to her, as he had been to several other patients, the longer therapy went on. Her special way of dressing, and her seductive behavior, seemed to be having its inexorable effect. Julie's many years of paternal incest in childhood had resulted in poor boundaries, and as an adult she found herself repeatedly having affairs with men who were in a position of authority or power over her: her parish priest, several university professors, her boss, and a black belt karate instructor. She felt a strong sexual attraction to Dr. Roamer, and she let him know this, unambiguously, by her behavior.

Dr. Roamer knew of the ethical prohibition against sex with current patients, and the 2-year posttermination rule, but he privately thought that the American Psychological Association had no right to restrict a psychologist's actions and freedom of choice to do whatever he or she pleased after terminating therapy with a patient. After all, he reasoned, there would be no formal relationship any more after therapy concluded, and consenting adults should be free to do whatever they like with each other.

Near the end of one session, Dr. Roamer brought up the issue of his strong admiration and attraction for Julie and suggested that he might be able to be more help to her outside the consulting office than inside it. From that moment on, their relationship was irrevocably changed. Needing no further provocation, Julie rose from her seat, glided over to Dr. Roamer, placed her hands on his face, with her body close to his, and gazed excitedly into his eyes. They kissed a long and passionate kiss. Dr. Roamer informed her that he was "not really" permitted to do this because she was currently a patient. He paused. At that point, she quickly suggested that she had been feeling much better, thanks to Dr. Roamer's help, and "wasn't real sure that therapy was necessary any more"; indeed, she felt quite exhilarated and very special that Dr. Roamer, her own psychotherapist, would fall in love with her. She told him that she had always felt a strong spiritual connection with him, from the moment they met. They quickly agreed that therapy should formally terminate and that they should continue their meetings under different circumstances.

Dr. Roamer had a meager comprehension of the concept of boundaries in psychotherapy and convinced himself that he understood the need for stopping therapy completely before their relationship could go any further; hence, the formal termination, complying, in principle, with the requirements of Standard 10.05, Sexual Intimacies With Current Therapy Clients/Patients. He suggested that they meet for dinner the next night and consider the next step. It was on that occasion that they agreed to pursue their new and thrilling relationship.

The romance lasted approximately 10 months, during which time Dr. Roamer grew weary of Julie's mood fluctuations, neediness, alcohol abuse, and increasingly demanding behavior. The affair ended suddenly one day, with a cold telephone call from Dr. Roamer. This resulted in much disappointment and feelings of dejection for Julie and stimulated unpleasant memories and feelings from past rejections. She became deeply depressed and angry, and she ultimately attempted suicide twice over the following 3 months. During the following year, she brought a formal ethics complaint against Dr. Roamer. She charged that he had improperly terminated his therapy with her, failed to wait 2 years posttermination to begin a romantic relationship, and inflicted significant harm on her by sexualizing the relationship even while she was still a patient of his. She claimed that he also had violated a number of other ethical standards while he was her therapist, prior to the affair. She had kept a journal of the treatment sessions and used her writings to attack his manner of conducting therapy.

Dr. Roamer attempted to defend himself on the grounds that Julie was really a former patient, not a current one, and that it was she who had initiated the romantic relationship, not he. After all, she was the one who had kissed him in that final session, and she was the one who said she wished to terminate treatment. Trying to hedge his bets, he attempted to make the point that he felt a professional obligation to convert their therapy relationship into a love relationship because it seemed to be more therapeutic for her in the long run to do so.

Dr. Roamer's defense was immaterial. He had broken the 2-year rule, no matter what his rationale may have been. Of equal importance, he had shown utter disregard for the dynamics of psychotherapy and proper termination by essentially abandoning his therapy patient in the interest of beginning a romantic relationship. He seemed to capitalize on the significant power differential that might have been a factor in Julie's initial attraction for him, but he did nothing to explain, interpret, or defuse the intensity of the interaction for his patient. Neither did he refer Julie to another therapist, or consult one himself, to examine the feelings that were interfering in treatment. Instead, he chose to act on his own sexual attraction to his current patient by first converting her to a former patient and then disregarding the 2-year posttermination rule and agreeing to become her lover. He was ultimately expelled from the American Psychological Association for his blatant disregard of the ethical rule that resulted in significant harm to a patient.

1. How might Dr. Roamer have addressed, in the early stages of therapy, Julie's overly sexual manner of behaving and dressing?
2. What steps might Dr. Roamer have taken to help himself cope with Julie's powerful sexuality, as he became aware of his attraction to her?
3. Would the use of a female cotherapist ever be appropriate, for a period of time, in this situation?
4. What are the ethical, clinical, and legal consequences of admitting to your patient that you feel sexually attracted to him or her?
5. What might be some of the ethical, clinical, and legal consequences if Dr. Roamer had terminated therapy, referred Julie to another therapist, and then contacted her 2 years later, to begin a romantic relationship?

10.08 (b)

Psychologists do not engage in sexual intimacies with former clients/patients even after a two-year interval except in the most unusual circumstances. Psychologists who engage in such activity after the two years following cessation or termination of therapy and of having no sexual contact with the former client/ patient bear the burden of demonstrating that there has been no exploitation, in light of all relevant factors, including (1) the amount of time that has passed since therapy terminated; (2) the nature, duration, and intensity of the therapy; (3) the circumstances of termination; (4) the client's/patient's personal history; (5) the client's/patient's current mental status; (6) the likelihood of adverse impact on the client/patient; and (7) any statements or actions made by the therapist during the course of therapy suggesting or inviting the possibility of a posttermination sexual or romantic relationship with the client/patient. (See also Standard 3.05, Multiple Relationships.)

Sex with a former client or patient is so fraught with complications, no matter how much time has elapsed, that you should probably avoid it altogether, even after 2 years, no matter how strong your feelings may be. If you decide to pursue an intimate relationship after the requisite amount of time has passed, you had better be prepared to prove that you have not exploited your former client or patient by taking into account at least the following seven factors:

1. the length of time since therapy ended (e.g., at least 2 full years);

2. the type of therapy you provided and its duration and intensity (e.g., biofeedback, short-term intervention for anxiety, long-term psychodynamically oriented treatment);

3. how the treatment ended (e.g., natural termination or premature termination in the service of hastening a romantic relationship);

4. the former client or patient's history (e.g., history of childhood sexual abuse or other major boundary violations later in life);

5. the person's current mental health (e.g., current depression, life crisis or major transition, or some other condition resulting in impaired judgment and placing you in a position of undue influence—if they were not your client or patient they never would have considered taking up with you in the first place);

6. the likelihood that beginning an intimate relationship could harm the person in the long run (e.g., recapitulate boundary violations of the past, cause a relapse of symptoms by retroactively inhibiting the results of therapy as you step out of your therapist role, cause some other kind of harm or major relapse if the romantic relationship goes bad); and

7. whether you made any statements or behaved in a way during therapy (over 2 years before) that might have suggested a posttermination romance (thus affecting the course of treatment and potentiating a premature termination; e.g., making indirect comments about a future romance, giving nonverbal cues, such as initiating hugs and touching).

VIGNETTE

Dr. Waerie was being consulted by Laura, a 35-year-old high school teacher and single mother of two who was grieving over her father's loss and experiencing stress-induced headaches and backaches. The treatment was multifaceted and consisted primarily of supportive psychotherapy, with a behavioral focus on stress management and training in progressive muscle relaxation. No Axis II disorder was present, and Laura had a good premorbid history.

As the treatment progressed, Dr. Waerie found himself growing increasingly attracted to Laura. He had been experiencing his own major life transition, having been recently divorced and now adapting to a new living situation away from his children and formerly happy home. As his growing fondness for his patient increased, he began to have such frequent thoughts about her that it started to affect the treatment. He decided that he might benefit by consulting one of his favorite supervisors of 10 years before. He also contacted a psychologist who was well published in the area of erotic countertransference and had several telephone consultations with him over a 2-week period. As a result of these consistent efforts, Dr. Waerie was able to successfully resolve the intensity of his feelings so that he could continue treating Laura successfully. After 6 months of therapy, Laura decided to end treatment, feeling very pleased with the results.

Three years later, while Dr. Waerie was attending a professional conference on learning disabilities, he encountered Laura once again. She was a high-functioning and successful teacher, was in good mental health, and was obviously very grateful to Dr. Waerie for the work he had done with her 3 years before. The two agreed to get together over coffee, and Dr. Waerie found himself disclosing things to Laura about himself that he had never before discussed with a patient or former patient. Up until this point, Laura actually knew very little about Dr. Waerie as a person, although she had been curious at times. The more they talked, the more they discovered that there seemed to be a mature but strong attraction for each other. Their intimacy grew in the weeks that followed, but Dr. Waerie's ethical conscience gnawed at him. He was concerned that he was possibly being exploitative of Laura because she was a former patient.

He again decided to consult someone to help him think through the issues. He chose a colleague who specialized in couples therapy to help him explore the possibility that he might be abusing his power or authority as a former therapist by pursuing a relationship with Laura. He also considered having some couples sessions with the colleague, if Laura were willing, or possibly attending a series of workshops for couples. He was hoping to equalize any residual power differential that might have been left over from the therapy relationship 3 years before. He wished to step out of his role of therapist completely by openly revealing his weaknesses and foibles to Laura and exploring with her his personal wants and needs.

It would be fair to say that Dr. Waerie took every reasonable precaution to avoid exploiting his former patient. Then, and only then, he reasoned, could their developing friendship and affection for each other have the best chance of maturing into a mutually gratifying relationship, if it was to be. Even so, every once in awhile he had the nagging (obsessive?) thought that he might be exploiting Laura, and even placing himself at risk later on, if the relationship should deteriorate and if Laura should overreact, because of the former patient–therapist dependency, by bringing a complaint. Having served on ethics committees before, Dr. Waerie knew that these things did happen, and he was doing his best to avoid such a scenario.

1. If Dr. Waerie had not sought out any professional resources early on, when he felt himself becoming attracted to Laura, what problems might he have encountered?
2. Because Dr. Waerie was going through a divorce, with all the concomitant stresses and reactions, would he have been well advised to seek therapy or monitoring of his professional prac-

tice of some sort, even if he had no attraction to any clients or patients? Discuss the pros and cons from clinical, ethical, and legal points of view.

3. Considering the type of therapy you conduct, and the way you establish relationships with clients and patients, consider what steps you might take, 2 or 3 years after terminating, that would help neutralize any lingering power differential without also negatively influencing the effects of therapy.

4. Was Dr. Waerie being overly obsessive in his concern about Laura's welfare and his own professional risk? What criteria should he use to make this judgment call?

10.09 INTERRUPTION OF THERAPY

When entering into employment or contractual relationships, psychologists make reasonable efforts to provide for orderly and appropriate resolution of responsibility for client/patient care in the event that the employment or contractual relationship ends, with paramount consideration given to the welfare of the client/patient. (See also Standard 3.12, Interruption of Psychological Services.)

Read employment contracts and managed health care contracts carefully so that you understand the agreement about keeping or referring patients when ending your participation in the contract. Remember, the details are important. You have some shared ethical responsibility, in these situations, for the welfare of your former clients and patients and the continuity of their care.[2]

VIGNETTE

Dr. Dawllez was the owner of the ABC Mental Health Group, Inc., a large group practice located in New England. He had not done clinical practice for many years and saw himself primarily as an administrator of the business. He had worked hard to establish contracts for his corporation as a preferred provider with many managed health care organizations and had good working relationships with several nearby hospitals. His business plan included competitively low fees and other incentives for staff, business clients, and individual patients to remain attached to his practice for long periods of time. His focus was clearly on expanding his business connections and increasing the income stream; he appeared to be less interested in patient welfare or mentoring employees.

---

[2]Laws permitting or banning payments to owners of group practices by departing psychologists who take patients with them vary from state to state.

Dr. Dawllez also fostered the notion of "institutional transference" among patients and corporations. He wanted them all to be aware of ABC's supposed dedication and commitment to their needs over a long period of time, regardless of changes in personnel on his staff. He worked at building a good reputation for his company that would draw new patients and hold old ones, even though individual employees might come and go.

An important part of his business plan included actively discouraging his employees from continuing to see patients independently if they left ABC, regardless of whether the patients were participating in a managed-care contract. Some patients had simply chosen an ABC therapist by reputation and had decided to pay for services out of pocket. Because there was no managed-care contract to consider, those patients could readily choose to follow a departing therapist to another location. However, if psychologists decided to leave the group practice, they were required to pay a $600 "transition fee" for each patient who continued to see them privately instead of transferring to another therapist in the group. The policy of requiring a transition fee was not addressed in the original employment contract, however, because this would have violated state law. It was particularly difficult on postdoctoral interns who had worked at ABC for a year or two, were recently licensed, and were hoping to develop their own practice. As an incentive for patients to remain with ABC and see a new therapist, Dr. Dawllez established a company policy of a 25% fee reduction for a period of 3 months. He also required each departing therapist to refrain from establishing a business office within 10 miles of the ABC clinic; this was clearly stated in the employment contract. These business practices constituted a relatively strong incentive for therapists to remain attached to the practice and keep the flow of income predictably constant.

It seemed to matter little to Dr. Dawllez whether a therapist leaving ABC was the best one qualified to continue treating a given patient or whether the patient, having already invested much time, energy, and money in the relationship, preferred to continue seeing that therapist in a different setting. Certainly, for many patients it would have been preferable and least disruptive for the therapy to continue in another setting with their same psychologist rather than being referred to a new in-house therapist. However, therapists who left ABC generally did not choose this alternative; the $600 fee was simply too punitive.

Furthermore, most of Dr. Dawllez's employees did not remember reading the part of the contract about prohibiting a nearby practice when they joined the practice, because it was couched in legal terms and seemed to have remote application, as though it would probably be irrelevant to their situation. This policy obviously did not support patients' freedom of choice in selecting therapists.

It was only a matter of time before several therapists contacted the state licensing board about the questionable business practices of Dr. Dawllez. They were deeply concerned that the best interests of patients were not being considered by such policies and that psychologists were in effect being financially penalized by Dr. Dawllez for attempting to comply with ethical standards in providing for the continuity of care with patients who chose to continue seeing them after leaving his practice. Although there was nothing in the original contract requiring transition fees, these therapists had been informed by e-mail or telephone messages that such was the case, and some of them had, in fact, made payments to ABC for retaining patients when they left. Documentation of the illegal policy was available, via the e-mail transmissions, and there was proof that money had changed hands.

Dr. Dawllez was ultimately charged and convicted of violating a state law that specifically prohibited demanding the payment of fees for the referral of psychotherapy patients. For their part, the therapists who reported Dr. Dawllez were satisfied that they had done everything reasonable to attend to the welfare of their patients while ending their contractual relationship with ABC. They had each joined ABC in good faith, read the contract carefully, and saw nothing in the fine print that portended of the unfortunate scenario that began to unfold when they attempted to leave the group practice.

1. How might you protect yourself when beginning employment with a group practice or managed health care setting, or entering some other contractual arrangement where you find the legalistic language of the contract to be obscure, arcane, or possibly in violation of state or federal law?

2. What questions might you ask of your potential employer at the outset about the disposition of your clients and patients, and their clinical records, in the event that you cease working there? Would you expect this to be documented?

3. Does Dr. Dawllez bear any ethical obligation to see that mentoring is provided to his licensed staff members, either by himself or his designate?

4. Which other ethical standards might apply to Dr. Dawllez's holding patients hostage unless the departing therapist agrees to pay a $600 head fee?

10.10 TERMINATING THERAPY

(a) Psychologists terminate therapy when it becomes reasonably clear that the client/patient no longer needs the service, is not likely to benefit, or is being harmed by continued service.

Enough is enough! Do not provide endless therapy if the patient does not need it, is not being helped in some way, or, even worse, is being harmed by continuing to see you (e.g., financially, by fostering overdependence, or some other way.)

VIGNETTE

Dr. Chronique, a recently licensed psychologist, was providing therapy to Mrs. LeBacque for depression and management of lumbar and thoracic pain of 8 months' duration, the result of a work injury. He had had little formal training in working with chronic-pain patients but was quite competent and experienced in carrying out assessment and psychotherapy. As it happened, he had some fairly rapid success in treating Mrs. LeBacque. After 5 months of biofeedback training and psychotherapy for pain reduction coordinated with medical treatment from a pain specialist, she was feeling much better. Her pain symptoms had decreased by 75%, and she was working nearly full time again. She had responded well to psychotherapy for depression, and her mood was much improved. She was in reasonably good mental health, had no Axis I or Axis II disorder, and was thinking of winding down her therapy.

Although this might have been an obvious time to prepare for termination, Dr. Chronique showed an interest in continuing to work with Mrs. LeBaque, regardless of the fact that there was little she wished to talk about anymore in the sessions and that she had responded extremely well to treatment thus far. His motivation was twofold: First, he was primarily interested in assessment and carrying out long-term psychotherapy, and could always find more to focus on in treatment, and second, at the present time he had few other patients and for financial reasons was reluctant to terminate with any of them. He told Mrs. LeBacque that it would be productive to explore other areas of her life to help maximize her "self-actualization." Specifically, he suggested that she take a vocational inventory test, despite the fact that she was quite pleased with her career path, and that she take the MMPI–2 and several other tests as well. He explained that he would carefully go over all the results with her and that she would not only benefit from further psychological assessment but that she might also be surprised at what she would learn about herself that could affect the quality of her life forever. Dr. Chronique knew that the patient had not expressed an interest in these matters and, to the contrary, that she was concerned about the expense of further treatment in light of her diminished income over the past year. He persevered in his persuasive hard sell nevertheless.

Because Mrs. LeBacque was somewhat passive and dependent, she deferred to her doctor's recommendations; after all, she reasoned, he had been so helpful up until now, and he knew her so well that he would know what is best for her. The additional meeting times were becoming increasingly difficult to schedule, however, and her supervisor at work was beginning to object to the time she took off to see Dr. Chronique. Mrs. LeBacque was hesitant to bring up the subject of ending therapy, especially because he seemed to have such a strong interest in her welfare by conducting additional testing and then scheduling more sessions for providing interpretation. When she finally did mention her desire to end therapy, she was met with assurances by

THERAPY *THERAPY*   321

Dr. Chronique that their work was not quite done—although, he assured her, she was making very good progress, and he promised that they would be finished very soon.

This endless treatment dragged on for 2 more months. Finally, Mrs. LeBacque began to impulsively cancel her appointments, claiming a headache on one occasion and a work emergency on another. Then she went on vacation for 1 week and never called Dr. Chronique on her return. Therapy seemed to have finally stopped, without any formal termination or plan for follow-up.

Dr. Chronique continued to meet with his patient long after her treatment should have ended, causing her to spend several thousand dollars in fees for the last 3 months that may have been unnecessary. The prolonging of treatment seemed be more reflective of Dr. Chronique's professional interests and financial needs (not necessarily in that order) rather than the patient's wishes. Concern for his patient's welfare did not seem to be the prime consideration at this stage of therapy, even though he seemed to communicate a genuine interest in helping her.

1. How would collaborating on establishing treatment goals at the outset of therapy have made a difference in this case?
2. Would you consider Dr. Chronique to be impaired or just inexperienced? How else might he be harmful to patients?
3. What actions would you take, or what would you recommend, if you were in a group practice with Dr. Chronique and several of his patients approached you about his tendency to prolong treatment?

10.10 (b)

Psychologists may terminate therapy when threatened or otherwise endangered by the client/patient or another person with whom the client/patient has a relationship.

You may terminate your treatment with clients or patients who threaten to harm you in some way (e.g., personal injury to you, your family, associates, or harm to your property). The impending threat could come from the person you have been treating or from his or her family members, friends, or associates. In this case, your customary termination procedures obviously will not apply, as therapy has been truncated because of the patient's hostile intent. You have the right to protect yourself from harm.

VIGNETTE

It had been 7 months since Daphne's last hospitalization for suicidality. She was a 29-year-old divorced newspaper reporter in a rural part of Louisiana who had recently relapsed into alcohol abuse and was dropping back into depression. She had begun treatment with Dr. Stocky several months before that, in a flurry of cutting herself with a pocketknife for relief of her most panicky moments. After several sessions, Dr. Stocky had confidently made the diagnosis of borderline personality disorder and, because he was trained in dialectical behavior therapy, was willing to treat Daphne if she would ultimately join the adjunctive group that met weekly. This was his standard protocol for treating individuals diagnosed with this disorder.

Daphne initially resisted her therapist's recommendation to join the weekly group, even though it was presented as a *sine qua non* of therapy. As the weeks went by, she continued to resist and, because of her neediness, Dr. Stocky reluctantly agreed to continue the consultations, if they increased the frequency to two long sessions per week. Not the least of Dr. Stocky's unconscious motivations to depart from his standard protocol was the fact that he had a sister about Daphne's age who also had had a chaotic life and was also in treatment for borderline personality disorder. He wanted to be a help in any way he could, and because he was one of the few therapists in this tiny town who was competent to treat patients like Daphne, he thought she would be worse off if he rejected her as a patient just because she would not participate in the group.

As time went on, Daphne experienced dissociative episodes, both in and out of her therapist's office. The many years of child and sexual abuse by her violent stepfather were taking their inevitable toll and manifesting in every aspect of her life. She was suspended from the newspaper for 3 weeks for cursing at her boss one day when she missed a deadline by 1 hour. A few days later, her boyfriend suddenly moved out of her apartment, taking her TV and other furniture with him, and shortly after that, her alcoholic stepfather left an angry message on her answering machine to "Daffy Daphne," calling her a "slut" and a "loser" and blaming her for forgetting his 60th birthday dinner the week before.

At her Friday afternoon therapy session, while loudly and angrily relating these events to Dr. Stocky, in which, once again, she was being "screwed by self-centered, male bastards of this world," Daphne gradually became more agitated and histrionic. She felt she could not "do this anymore" and "needed a shoulder to cry on." Near the end of the session, she attempted to hug Dr. Stocky, but he gently stopped her, reminding her of his policy about not hugging patients. She pulled away with a shameful glare, sarcastically excusing herself. Then she turned angrily; kicked over a small end table; jammed her finger down her throat and vomited on the carpet; yelled "f___ you"; and stomped out of the office, slamming the door on her way out. An uneasy calm descended on the office.

Dr. Stocky telephoned Daphne at home an hour later but was only able to leave a message on her answering machine. Later that night he received an e-mail note from Daphne; its rambling, ominous tone spoke vaguely of making things difficult for him, as she knew where he lived, and that he'd better "watch out" in the days ahead. On Saturday, he received five more threatening e-mail messages, one hinting that she had called her brother, an ex-con who lived in the next town, and that he would be happy to "have a little talk with the good doctor about rejecting his patients" when they needed affection. He also received an angry, blaming telephone message on his answering machine at work. Concerned, he drove to his office on Sunday afternoon only to find that a rock had been thrown through the window in his office and that the front door to the building had been scratched repeatedly with a sharp object. There was no reason to suspect anyone but Daphne for this damage. When he arrived back home, he thought he recognized her sitting in a parked car across from his house; the car drove off as he approached. Later that night, he saw the same car parked across from his house with someone sitting inside.

Pondering what to do, Dr. Stocky telephoned a trusted colleague that night, and had a long consultation about borderline patients who act out explosively and how to protect oneself against them. He also considered involuntary hospitalization of Daphne, as she obviously seemed to pose a threat to others (himself) and could become suicidal (although she had not threatened this recently). She had made repeated, thinly veiled threats to him, however, so perhaps this would qualify as a Tarasoff situation. Should he break confidentiality, telephone the police and report Daphne's threats, with documentation of the e-mails and voice recording on the answering machine? Should he take out a restraining order against her? Was he still her treating therapist, or was he now a target of her stalking and threats?

Dr. Stocky had never treated such a difficult patient, and he had never been stalked before. He felt that his professional role had rapidly shifted from therapist to victim. Treatment was obviously suspended, and possibly over, as he had become the target of Daphne's transferred rage against other male figures who had broken her trust in the past. He had never feared a patient before, but he was beginning to feel anxious about his and his family's personal safety.

Dr. Stocky was persuaded by his colleague's view that the level of threat, combined with Daphne's emerging pattern of acting out, supported a reasonable belief that she presented a real physical danger to Dr. Stocky and his family. Thus, similar to a situation in which a patient would constitute such a threat to some other member of society, Dr. Stocky would be justified in breaching confidentiality to the extent necessary to have his patient rehospitalized at this time. He, too, believed that any attempt now to reestablish a therapeutic relationship in Daphne's present state would likely be fruitless and might well exacerbate the situation, as he would remain unable to satisfy her demands. While she was hospitalized he would have time to investigate other avenues of treatment that might be effective. Something outside this small community would likely be necessary, because no one locally was qualified to meet her needs. To help further develop a strategy, he also decided to seek the assistance of an attorney to determine whether some form of police intervention might be useful after she was released from the hospital. This recent experience had so unnerved him that he now felt himself without the resources to continue her treatment.

1. How might Dr. Stocky have handled the hug incident differently, in a way that might have been more productive?
2. How would you deal with a client or patient who wished to hug you on one occasion? Regularly after every session?
3. In addition to coping with the real needs of the moment, why is it important for Dr. Stocky to keep an accurate record of events in Daphne's clinical record?
4. What are the relative benefits and risks to Dr. Stocky and to Daphne for each of the following courses of action: agreeing to meet Daphne in his office once again, inviting her into his house for coffee, contacting the police and taking out a restraining order against her, contacting the police or in some other way initiating a mandatory hospitalization, or some other intervention?
5. What steps should Dr. Stocky take to formally terminate his treatment of Daphne?
6. How would Dr. Stocky go about finding a suitable therapist for Daphne, most likely in a different city, as there was none available nearby?

10.10 (c)

Except where precluded by the actions of clients/patients or third-party payors, prior to termination psychologists provide pretermination counseling and suggest alternative service providers as appropriate.

Before ending your work with patients, be sure to discuss their views about therapy and terminating it (i.e., their current psychological needs, alternative resources available to them, possible referrals for different therapeutic experiences if needed) and any other related matters. You need not do this, however, if third-party payors will not provide reimbursement for such a session, or if the patient breaks off treatment, is unwilling, or is otherwise unavailable.

VIGNETTE

Dr. Ender had been providing marital counseling to Mr. and Mrs. Binwith, a couple in their late 40s who had been headed for divorce, for nearly 2 years and was in the process of winding down their sessions. As a part of the process, she carefully reviewed with them their presenting complaints, the major problems in the marriage, the symptoms they each experienced at the outset, progress in therapy, and remaining issues on which to work.

Although the couple had made excellent progress, they still had to be alert to some individual differences and family-of-origin influences that had the potential of causing minor relapses during times of significant stress or transition. Mr. Binwith, when stressed, would characteristically withdraw and stop discussing things with his wife about day-to-day issues. Mrs. Binwith, for her part, had a history of turning to alcohol when under stress, although she had been sober for 18 months and regularly attended AA meetings. She also had an individual therapist whom she saw weekly.

It was important to ascertain if husband or wife could benefit from some other therapeutic work, besides marital counseling, as some individual issues did remain. They all agreed that couples work was not a substitute for individual therapy, yet they had indeed made excellent progress in their individual growth and marital relationship since they had begun treatment, and both Mr. and Mrs. Binwith felt that their marriage was much stronger than it had ever been.

Dr. Ender solicited the Binwiths' input about the marriage counseling, asking for their assessment of the work, and she attempted to determine whether either of them had any interest in other psychological interventions. Mr. Binwith confided that he might find it useful to talk with a therapist about approaching middle age and some ambivalence he had about remaining in his professional field as a computer software engineer. He also had recently been diagnosed with irritable bowel syndrome, and he thought that chronic stress might be a contributing factor to the worsening of his symptoms. Dr. Ender provided the names of several therapists, including a health psychologist who specialized in biofeedback, hypnosis, and similar interventions for physical disorders. She also discussed with him the possibility of participating in an ongoing therapy group, if he wished, to address his tendency, when stressed, to withdraw from people who are important in his life. She suggested he speak with several group therapists to ascertain whether this would be a useful modality.

Mrs. Binwith intended to continue meeting with her individual therapist, as she had for the past 2 years. She was facing the transition of an empty nest at home, as both of her daughters were now away at college. She was considering increasing her part-time job as a substitute teacher in the local school district or possibly exploring a different field altogether. She was pleased with her therapist and would continue working with him. She felt her alcoholism was well under control, and she was strongly committed to continuing her attendance at AA meetings. Dr. Ender consulted with her individual therapist about additional resources and provided Mrs. Binwith the names and phone numbers of a local women's group that she thought might provide a therapeutic experience for her.

Dr. Ender informed Mrs. Binwith that she was willing to provide information to any future therapists whom the couple might consult, on an as-needed basis. She reviewed confidentiality in these situations and the need to sign consent forms if they wished her to contact a new therapist. She requested that even if Mr. Binwith wanted her to collaborate with his individual therapist his wife also sign a release-of-information form, as the discussions would invariably include her and the therapy process as well. They understood this rationale and agreed that it would be no problem.

Finally, they all agreed that additional couples sessions could be scheduled in the future, if needed, and that Dr. Ender would be willing to be available as a resource for them. The last session ended with a feeling of completion and resolution of serious marital dysfunction, enthusiasm for future continued growth, and an appreciation for the strengths that each individual had brought to the process.

1. Why is it important to have a discussion about ending therapy, and what might lie ahead, from a clinical, ethical, and legal point of view?
2. If Dr. Ender knew that Mrs. Binwith was not currently seeing an individual psychotherapist, what might she recommend, in light of her history of chemical dependency?
3. How would you attempt to deal with the usual subjects of termination if the third-party payor refused to provide reimbursement for such a session or the individual was unwilling to pay out of pocket to discuss the termination process?
4. How would you document the usual topics of termination in your clinical record, and what is the importance of doing so?
5. Construct a worst-case scenario for one of your patients who simply stopped coming to sessions and for whom you never had a formal termination session or wrote a letter of termination. What might be the clinical or legal consequences in this case?

APPENDIX A: ETHICS READING LIST

AMERICAN PSYCHOLOGICAL ASSOCIATION
PRACTICE GUIDELINES:

Guidelines for Child Custody Evaluations in Divorce Proceedings (1994)
Guidelines for Providers of Psychological Services to Ethnic, Linguistic, and Culturally Diverse Populations (1993)
Guidelines for Psychological Evaluations in Child Protection Matters (1999)
Guidelines for the Evaluation of Dementia and Age-Related Cognitive Decline (1998)
Guidelines on Multicultural Education, Training, Research, Practice, and Organizational Change for Psychologists (2003)
Record-Keeping Guidelines (1993)
Specialty Guidelines for Forensic Psychologists (1991)

BOOKS

Anderson, J., & Barret, B. (Eds.). (2001). *Ethics in HIV-related psychotherapy: Clinical decision making in complex cases.* Washington, DC: American Psychological Association.

Annas, G. (1989). *The rights of patients: The ACLU guide to patient rights.* Carbondale and Edwardsville: Southern Illinois University Press.

Benjamin, G. A. H., & Gollan, J. K. (2003). *Family evaluation in custody litigation: Reducing risks of ethical infractions and malpractice.* Washington, DC: American Psychological Association.

Bennett, B., Bryant, B., VandenBos, G., & Greenwood, A. (1990). *Professional liability and risk management.* Washington, DC: American Psychological Association.

Bersoff, D. (2003). *Ethical conflicts in psychology* (3rd ed.). Washington, DC: American Psychological Association.

Blackman, J., Cascio, W., Ceci, S., Melton, G., & Miller, M. (1994). *Psychology in litigation and legislation.* Washington, DC: American Psychological Association.

Brabeck, M. (2000). *Practicing feminist ethics in psychology.* Washington, DC: American Psychological Association.

Brodsky, S. (1991). *Testifying in court: Guidelines and maxims for the expert witness.* Washington, DC: American Psychological Association.

Brodsky, S. (2000). *The expert expert witness.* Washington, DC: American Psychological Association.

Ceci, S. J., & Hembrooke, H. (1998). *Expert witnesses in child abuse cases: What can and should be said in court.* Washington, DC: American Psychological Association.

Chatain, G., & Landrum, R. E. (Eds.). (1999). *Protecting human subjects: Departmental subject pools and institutional review boards.* Washington, DC: American Psychological Association.

Committee on Ethical Guidelines for Forensic Psychologists. (1991). American Psychological Association, Specialty Guidelines for Forensic Psychologists. *Law and Human Behavior, 15,* 655–665.

Conley, F. (1998). *Walking out on the boys.* New York: Farrar, Straus & Giroux.

Eyde, L., Robertson, G., Krug, S., & the Test User Training Work Group. (1993). *Responsible test use: Case studies for assessing human behavior.* Washington, DC: American Psychological Association.

Figley, C. R. (Ed.). (1995). *Compassion fatigue: Secondary traumatic stress from treating the traumatized.* New York: Brunner/Mazel.

Fisher, C. (2003). *Decoding the Ethics Code: A practical guide for psychologists.* Thousand Oaks, CA: Sage.

Gabbard, G., & Lester, E. (2003). *Boundaries and boundary violations in psychoanalysis.* Arlington, VA: American Psychiatric Publishing.

Grisso, T. (1988). *Competency to stand trial evaluations: A manual for practice.* Sarasota, FL: Professional Resource Press.

Haas, L. J., & Malouf, J. L. (1995). *Keeping up the good work: A practitioner's guide to mental health ethics.* Sarasota, FL: Professional Resource Press.

Heilbrun, K., Marczyk, G., & deMatteo, D. (2002). *Forensic mental health assessment: A casebook.* Oxford, England: Oxford University Press.

Jacob-Timm, S., & Hartshorne, T. (1991). *Ethics and law for school psychologists* (2nd ed.). New York: Wiley.

Kalichman, S. C. (2000). *Mandated reporting of suspected child abuse: Ethics, law, and policy* (2nd ed.). Washington, DC: American Psychological Association.

Keith-Spiegel, P., Whitley, B. E., Jr., Balogh, D. W., Perkins, D. V., & Wittig, A. F. (2002). *The ethics of teaching: A casebook* (2nd ed.). Mahwah, NJ: Erlbaum.

Kilburg, R., Nathan, P., & Thoreson, R. (1986). *Professionals in distress: Issues, syndromes, and solutions in psychology.* Washington, DC: American Psychological Association.

Kitchener, K. S. (1999). *Foundations of ethical practice, research, and teaching in psychology.* Mahwah, NJ: Erlbaum.

Knapp, S., & VandeCreek, L. (2003). *A guide to the 2002 revision of the American Psychological Association's Ethics Code.* Sarasota, FL: Professional Resource Press.

Koocher, G., & Keith-Spiegel, P. (1998). *Ethics in psychology: Professional standards and cases* (2nd ed.). New York: Oxford University Press.

Koocher, G., Norcross, J., & Hill, S. (1998). *Psychologists' desk reference.* New York: Oxford University Press.

Lakin, M. (1988). *Ethical issues in the psychotherapies.* New York: Oxford University Press.

Lefkowitz, J. (2003). *Ethics and values in industrial–organizational psychology.* Mahwah, NJ: Erlbaum.

Lubet, S. (1999). *Expert testimony: A guide for expert witnesses and the lawyers who examine them*. South Bend, IN: National Institute for Trial Advocacy.

Malone, D. M., & Zwier, P. J. (2001). *Expert rules: 100 (and more) points you need to know about expert witnesses* (2nd ed.). South Bend, IN: National Institute for Trial Advocacy.

McCaffrey, R., Williams, A., Fisher, J., & Laing, L. (1997). *The practice of forensic neuropsychology: Meeting challenges in the courtroom*. Nowell, MA: Kluwer Academic.

Melton, G., Petrila, J., Poythress, N., & Slobogin, C. (1997). *Psychological evaluation for the courts*. New York: Guilford Press.

Pope, K. (1994). *Sexual involvement with therapists: Patient assessment, subsequent therapy, forensics*. Washington, DC: American Psychological Association.

Pope, K. S., Butcher, J. N., & Seleen, J. (2000). *The MMPI, MMPI–2, and MMPI–A in court: A practical guide for expert witnesses and attorneys* (2nd ed.). Washington, DC: American Psychological Association.

Pope, K., & Vasquez, J. T. (1991). *Ethics in psychotherapy and counseling: A practical guide for psychologists*. San Francisco: Jossey-Bass.

Sales, B., & Folkman, S. (2000). *Ethics in research with human participants*. Washington, DC: American Psychological Association.

Sales, B., & Miller, M. E. (Eds.). *Law and mental health professionals series*. Washington, DC: American Psychological Association.

Schoener, G., Milgram, J., Gonsiorek, J., Luepker, E., & Conroe, R. (1990). *Psychotherapists' sexual involvement with clients: Intervention and prevention*. Minneapolis, MN: Walk-In Counseling Center.

Small, R. F., & Barnhill, L. R. (1999). *Practicing in the new mental health marketplace: Ethical, legal, and moral issues*. Washington, DC: American Psychological Association.

Stromberg, C. D. (1988). *The psychologist's legal handbook*. Washington, DC: Council for the National Register of Health Service Providers in Psychology.

VandeCreek, L., & Knapp, S. (2001). *Tarasoff and beyond: Legal and clinical considerations in the treatment of life-endangering patients*. Sarasota, FL: Professional Resource Press.

Whitley, B. E., Jr., & Keith-Spiegel, P. (2002). *Academic dishonesty: An educator's guide*. Mahwah, NJ: Erlbaum.

Winnick, B. J. (1997). *The right to refuse mental health treatment*. Washington, DC: American Psychological Association.

Woody, R. H. (2000). *Child custody: Practice standards, ethical issues, and legal safeguards for mental health professionals*. Sarasota, FL: Professional Resource Press.

Ziskin, J. (1995). *Coping with psychiatric and psychological testimony* (5th ed.). Beverly Hills, CA: Law and Psychology Press.

Zuckerman, E. (2003). *The paper office* (3rd ed.). New York: Guilford Press.

JOURNALS

Ethics and Behavior (Lawrence Erlbaum Associates)
Law and Human Behavior (Plenum Press)
Professional Psychology: Theory, Research, Practice, Training (American Psychological Association)
Psychology, Public Policy, and Law (American Psychological Association)

APPENDIX B: INTERNET RESOURCES

http://www.appic.org/
    (Association of Psychology Postdoctoral and Internship Centers)
http://www.asppb.org/pubs/
    (Association of State and Provincial Psychological Boards)
http://www.nationalregister.com/
    (National Register of Health Service Providers in Psychology)
http://www.psywerx.com/hipaa.htm
    (Health Insurance Portability and Accountability Act [HIPAA]
    Compliancy Information—Synopsis)
http://www.hhs.gov/ocr/hipaa
    (U.S. Department of Health and Human Services, regarding HIPAA)
http://www.nchica.org/HIPAAResources/Samples/Portal.asp
    (North Carolina Healthcare Information and Communications
    Alliance, Inc.; HIPAA documents)
www.kspope.com
    (Contains many excellent articles and downloads by ethicist Kenneth
    Pope, PhD)

REFERENCES

American Educational Research Association, American Psychological Association, & National Council on Measurement in Education. (1999). *The standards for educational and psychological testing.* Washington, DC: Author.

American Psychiatric Association. (2000). *Diagnostic and statistical manual of mental disorders* (4th ed., text rev.). Washington, DC: Author.

American Psychological Association. (1981a). Specialty guidelines for the delivery of services by clinical psychologists. *American Psychologist, 36,* 640–651.

American Psychological Association. (1981b). Specialty guidelines for the delivery of services by counseling psychologists. *American Psychologist, 36,* 652–663.

American Psychological Association. (1991). Specialty guidelines for forensic psychologists. *Law and Human Behavior, 15,* 655–665.

American Psychological Association. (1992). Ethical principles of psychologists and code of conduct. *American Psychologist, 47,* 1597–1611.

American Psychological Association. (1993a). Guidelines for providers of psychological services to ethnic, linguistic, and culturally diverse populations. *American Psychologist, 48,* 45–46.

American Psychological Association. (1993b). Record-keeping guidelines. *American Psychologist, 48,* 984–986.

American Psychological Association. (1996). Strategies for private practitioners coping with subpoenas or compelled testimony for client records and/or test data. *Professional Psychology: Research and Practice, 23,* 245–251.

American Psychological Association. (2001a). *Publication manual of the American Psychological Association* (5th ed.). Washington, DC: Author.

American Psychological Association. (2001b). Rules and procedures. *American Psychologist, 51,* 529–548.

American Psychological Association. (2002). Ethical principles of psychologists and code of conduct. *American Psychologist, 57,* 1060–1073.

American Veterinary Medical Association. (1986). Report of the AVMA Panel on Euthanasia. *Journal of the American Veterinary Medical Association, 188,* 252–268.

Beck, A. (1996). *Beck Depression Inventory.* San Antonio, TX: Psychological Corporation.

Bernstein, E. M., & Putnam, F. W. (1986). Development, reliability, and validity of a dissociation scale. *Journal of Nervous and Mental Disease, 174,* 727–735.

California Business & Professions Code, 2290.5. (1998). In G. Alexander & A. Scheflin (Eds.), *Law and mental disorder* (p. 94). Durham, NC: Carolina Academic Press.

Canter, M. B., Bennett, B. E., Jones, S. E., & Nagy, T. F. (1994). *Ethics for psychologists: A commentary on the APA Ethics Code.* Washington, DC: American Psychological Association.

Derogatis, L. (1993). *Symptom Checklist–90–R*. Minneapolis, MN: National Computer Systems.

Hathaway, S. R., & McKinley, J. C. (1989). *Minnesota Multiphasic Personality Inventory—2*. Minneapolis, MN: Pearson Assessments.

Institute of Laboratory Animal Resources, Commission on Life Sciences (National Research Council). (1996). *Guide for the care and use of laboratory animals*. Washington, DC: Author.

Iversen, I. H., & Lattal, K. A. (Eds.). (1991). *Experimental analysis of behavior*. Amsterdam: Elsevier Science.

Nagy, T. (in press). Competence. In S. S. Bucky, J. Callan, & J. G. Striker (Eds.), *Ethical and legal issues for mental health professionals: Principles and standards*. New York: Haworth Press.

National Commission for the Protection of Human Subjects of Biomedical and Behavioral Research. (1979). *The Belmont report: Ethical principles and guidelines for the protection of human subjects of research* (DHHS Publication No. 8887-809). Washington, DC: U.S. Government Printing Office.

Rothschild, D. A. (2002). My sweet lawsuit: Plagiarism. *Rooftop Sessions*. Retrieved March 1, 2004, from http://www.rooftopsessions.com/Lawsuit.htm

Shor, R. E., & Orne, E. C. (1962). *The Harvard Group Scale of Hypnotic Susceptibility, Form A*. Palo Alto, CA: Consulting Psychologists Press.

Spiegel, H., & Spiegel, D. (1978). *Trance and treatment: Clinical uses of hypnosis*. New York: International Universities Press.

Spiegel, H., & Spiegel, D. (1978). The hypnotic induction profile: Administration and scoring. In H. Spiegel & D. Spiegel (Eds.), *Trance and treatment: Clinical uses of hypnosis* (pp. 45–78). New York: International Universities Press.

Stanford University Sample Consent Form, Human Subjects in Medical Research. (n.d.). Retrieved December 15, 2003, from http://humansubjects.stanford.edu/medical/consent.html

Tellegen, A., & Atkinson, G. (1974). Openness to absorbing and self-altering experiences ("absorption"), a trait related to hypnotic susceptibility. *Journal of Abnormal Psychology, 83*, 268–277.

Title 9 C.F.R., Chap. 1, Subchap. A: Animal Welfare, Pt. 1–3 (1992). U.S. Department of Agriculture.

Weitzenhoffer, A. M., & Hilgard, E. R. (1962). *Stanford Hypnotic Susceptibility Scale, Forms A & B*. Palo Alto, CA: Consulting Psychologists Press.

Wechsler, D. (1997). *Wechsler Adult Intelligence Scale–III*. San Antonio, TX: Psychological Corporation.

INDEX

on conflict between ethics and organizational demands, 22–24
on conflict of interest, 80–83
on conflict involving legal authority, 19–22
on cooperating with Ethics Committee, 29–31
on cooperating with other professionals, 88–89
on delegation of work, 59–61
on delivery of services to organization, 100–101, 102–103
on disclosure, 122–124, 124–125
on education and training programs, 177–179, 179–180, 181–182, 182–184, 185–186, 186–187, 188–189, 189–190, 191–192, 192–194
on emergency service, 52–54
on exploitative relationships, 86–87
on family therapy, 297–299, 299–300
on fees and financial arrangements, 161–162, 162–164, 164–165, 165–166, 167–168, 169–171, 174–175
on group therapy, 301–303
on harassment (general), 70–71
on identification of advertising, 141–142
on improper complaints, 31–33
on informal resolution of ethical violations, 25–26
on informed consent, 90–91, 92–93, 94–96, 97–99
on informed consent for research, 201–202, 208–209
on informed consent for therapy, 292–293, 294–296
on in-person solicitation, 148–149
on interruption of services, 104–105, 318–320
on maintaining competence, 55–56
on misrepresentation in public statements, 132–133, 134–135, 136–137, 137–139, 143, 144–146
on misrepresentation of work, 17–19
models for analyzing, 11–13
on multiple relationships, 74–76, 76–77, 78–80
on payment to journalists, 139–140
on plagiarism, 236–237
on privacy, 119–120, 121–122
on publication credit, 237–238, 239–240, 240–242

on recording, 117–118
on record keeping, 152–154, 154–156, 156–157, 158–159
on release of test data, 270–272
on reporting of ethical violations, 27–29
on research, 196–197, 203–204, 205–206, 207, 210–211, 211–212, 213–214, 214–215, 216–217, 217–218, 219, 220–222, 233–234, 235–236, 244, 245–246
on research use of animals, 222–224, 224–225, 225–226, 227–228, 228–230, 230–231, 231–233
sanctions depicted in, 10
on second therapy, 304–305
on sexual harassment, 68–70
on sexual intimacies and therapy, 306–307, 308–310, 310–312, 313–315, 316–318
on termination of therapy, 321–322, 322–325, 325–327
on test construction, 274–275
on testimonials, 147–148
on test security, 289–290
on third-party request for services, 84–85
on unfair discrimination, 65–67
on unfair discrimination against complainants or respondents, 34–36
Cease-and-desist order, 10
Censure, 9
Child custody assessment, and cultural variables (vignette question), 42
Circumstances, and application of *Ethics Code* language, 6
Citing of original publication, 242–243
Clients
    former sexual partners as, 310–312
    sexual intimacies with, 305–307
    sexual intimacies with former clients, 312–318
    sexual intimacies with relatives or significant others of, 307–310
Codes of Ethics. *See Ethics Code*; Ethics codes
Compensation, for research participants, 199, 202
Competence, 12
    in assessment (vignette), 258
    avoiding deceptive statements about, 133–134

and bases for scientific or professional judgments, 56–58

and delegation of work, 58–61

and failure of health (vignette), 119, 120

maintaining of, 54–56

and personal problems, 61–64

self-question about, 14

staying within boundaries of, 37–39

and areas of expertise closely related to one's own, 45–46

in emergencies, 52–54

and emerging professional areas, 46–48

and forensics, 49–52

and new areas of work, 42–44

and special characteristics of patients, 39–42

in vignette on conflict, 23

in vignette on informal resolution, 25–26

Complainants, unfair discrimination against, 33–36

Complaint process, providing information on, 98, 98n

Complaints, improper, 31–33

Computer

and confidentiality (vignette), 108, 109

and record keeping (vignette), 152, 155–156

Confidentiality, 107–110

and barter associations (vignette question), 171

and consultations, 108–109, 112–113, 126–128

and cooperation with Ethics Committees, 29

and delivery of services to or through organizations, 99, 101

and disclosures, 122–125

discussing limits of, 110–117

and electronic transmission, 114–117

in group therapy, 301, 302

and informal resolution of ethical violations, 24

and information in public domain, 128

and informed consent, 90, 91, 94, 97, 99

and informed consent to research, 198

and informed consent to therapy, 291

and interpreter, 267

and lunch with trainees (vignette), 178

and media presentations (vignette), 145

minimizing intrusions on, 119–122

and multiple relationships, 78

and record disposal, 153

and recording, 117–118

in research (vignette), 204

and record keeping, 154–159

and reporting of ethical violations, 26

and reviewers, 246

and sharing of raw data, 243

and telephone vs. e-mail consultation (vignette), 164

and test materials on Internet (vignette), 283

and third-party request for service, 84, 85

and threatening patient, 324

timely discussion of, 112–113

and transfer to new therapist, 327

in transition after death of therapist, 105

and treatment progress reports (vignette), 166

and use of information for didactic purposes, 128–130

in vignette on conflicts with legal authority, 19–22

in vignette on video-game research, 196

on withholding records for nonpayment, 159–160

Conflict of interest, 80–83

in inducements for research participation (vignette), 210

See also Multiple relationships

Conflicts

between ethics and organizational demands, 22–24

involving legal authority, 19–22

and providing of clinical information (vignette question), 52

personal, 61–64

Consultation, 126–128

in ethical decision making, 13

Context, and application of *Ethics Code* language, 6

Cooperating with Ethics Committees, 29–31

Cooperation with other professionals, 87–89

and confidentiality, 108–109, 112–113, 126–128

Copyrighted materials

in vignette on ethics and organizational demands, 23

in vignette on plagiarism, 236–237

Council on Accreditation of the American Association for the Accreditation of Laboratory Animal Care, 231
Countertransference, erotic, 316–317
Couples therapy, 297–300
    in vignette on recording, 117–118
Court-ordered services, and informed consent, 93–96
Credentials, avoiding misrepresentation of, 135–137
Credit in publication, 237–242
Cultural variables
    in assessment (vignettes), 258, 259–260, 267–268, 276–277, 281
    and boundaries of competence, 39–40
        vignette on, 40–42
"Cutting edge" (groundbreaking) areas of therapy or intervention, 42, 46–48

Data
    adequacy of (self-question about), 14
    duplicate publication of, 242–243
    errors in, 234–236
    importance of methods for coding, 246
    sharing of for verification, 243–246
Death of therapist
    transfer of confidential records at, 158–159
    vignette on, 104–105
Debriefing
    on research, 217–222
        in vignette on child research, 196
        for research assistants carrying out animal euthanasia (vignette question), 232–233
Deceit or deception
    in child research (vignette), 196
    and informed consent for research, 203
    initiating therapy under (vignette question), 305
    in research, 212–217
    self-question about, 15
    See also Public statements
Decision making, ethical, 13–15
Delegation of responsibility, 58–61
    for newsletter (vignette), 238
    and research errors (vignette), 235–236
Delivery of services to or through organizations, 99–103
Denial of reality, self-question about, 15
Department of Veterans Affairs, 11, 107, 122, 152

Diagnosis, accurate reporting of (vignette), 172
Diagnostic and Statistical Manual of Mental Disorders (4th ed., text revision), 138
Differences in real or ascribed social power. *See* Social power, differences in
Dilemmas
    involving legal authority, 19–22
    and vignettes, 4–5
Directives, 9, 10
Disclosures, 122–125
Discrimination. *See* Unfair discrimination
Divorce
    and role conflict, 299
    and video- or audiotaping (vignette question), 118
Documentation of professional and scientific work, 151–152. *See also* Record keeping
Dual relationships. *See* Multiple relationships
Dual therapies, 303–305
Duplicate publication of data, 242–243

Educational aspects, of sanction or directive, 10
Educational programs, non-degree-granting, 142–143
Education requirement, 10
Education and training
    accuracy and adequacy of course content in, 182–184
    assessing of student performance, 189–192
    description of course requirements for, 180–182
    description of programs for, 179–180
    design of programs for, 177–179
    mandatory therapy in, 186–187
        and evaluation of student performance, 187–189
    student disclosure of personal information in, 184–186
e-mail
    and confidentiality, 114–117
    fee for (vignette), 164
Emergencies
    providing service in, 52–54
    and withholding records for nonpayment, 159–160
Emerging areas of practice, and boundaries of competence, 46–48
Errors in published data, 234–236

Harassment, sexual, 67–70
Harm
    avoidance of, 71–73
    from inadequate preparation and train-
        ing (vignette question), 39
    obligation to take action against, 302
    from research (response to), 220–222
    self-question about, 14
    to third party
        as Tarasoff-type situation, 11n.4
        in vignette on reporting of viola-
            tions, 28
    from unjustified scientific judgments, 58
    varieties of, 47, 73n
Harrison, George, plagiarism suit against,
    239n
Health Insurance Portability and Account-
    ability Act. See HIPAA
Higher standard, obligation to adhere to, 5
HIPAA (Health Insurance Portability and
    Accountability Act), 5, 11, 14
    and assessment, 263
    and informed consent, 96
    and informed consent to research, 198,
        200, 202
    and informed consent to therapy (vi-
        gnettes), 91, 95, 98, 293
    and multiple relationships (vignette
        question), 77
    and privacy/confidentiality, 107, 110,
        122
    and record keeping, 152
    and test data release, 269n, 272
    in vignette about complainants, 34–35
    Web sites on, 333
Homogeneity reliability, 275
Homosexuality
    in vignette on conflict over military fit-
        ness, 21, 22
    in vignette on discrimination, 65–67
    in vignette on privacy, 119–120
Humane care and use of animals in research,
    222–233
Human relations. See Conflict of interest;
    Delivery of services to or through
    organizations; Exploitative relation-
    ships; Harassment; Harm; Informed
    consent; Interruption of psychologi-
    cal services; Multiple relationships;
    Sexual harassment; Third-party re-
    quests for services; Unfair discrimi-
    nation

Humor
    and harassment (vignette), 70–71
    in vignettes, 5
Impaired judgment
    self-question about, 14–15
    in vignette on misrepresentation, 19
    vs. willful unethical conduct, 19
Improper complaints, 31–33
Information technology, in vignette on
    boundaries of competence, 46
Informed consent, 89–96
    for assessment, 261–269
        and invalidated instrument, 256
    and barter associations (vignette ques-
        tion), 171
    for biographical material use, 121
    documentation of, 96–99
    for group members (vignette question),
        303
    and peer consultation group, 126
    for recording, 117–118
    and referrals (vignette), 175
    and reimbursement for missed sessions,
        163–164
    in research, 90, 197–202, 207–209
        dispensing with, 207–209
        for recording voices and images,
            203–204
    for therapy, 291–296
        and trainee therapist, 296–297
    vague inducement in (vignette), 212
    in vignette on conflict of interest, 82
Innovative approach, self-question about, 14
In-person solicitation, 148–149
Institutional approval of research, 195–197
Institutional policies, self-question about, 14
Institutional review boards (IRBs), 198
    and nonaffiliated researcher (vignette
        question), 215
Interdisciplinary settings, and confidential-
    ity (vignette question), 128
Internet
    advertising on (vignette question), 138–
        139, 142
    competence nourished from, 55
    and plagiarism, 236–237
    resources on, 333
    test materials on (vignette), 283
Internship sites, in vignette on education and
    training, 178, 179
Interpretation services, 282, 284

Interpreter, informed consent for (assessment), 264, 265–266
Interruption of psychological services, 103–105, 318–320

Journalists, payment to for publicity prohibited, 139
Journals, in maintaining of competence, 55
Journals on ethics, 332
Language
    fashioning of for *Ethics Code*, 6
    vernacular, 7
Law(s)
    and confidentiality, 107, 110–111
    conflicts over, 19
    of copyright, 236
    and disclosure, 124
    and fee practices, 162–164
    concerning guardianship or conservatorship, 265n
    and informed consent to therapy, 293
    on payment to group practices by departing psychologists, 318n
    self-question about, 14
    and sharing of raw data, 244
    and test security, 289
    and threat of harm, 302
    on time between end of therapy and sexual relationship, 313
    on use of animals in research, 222
Legal action, against psychologists, 9
Legal issues, 11–12
Lennon, John, plagiarism suit against, 239n
Litigation
    and competence in forensics, 49–52
    and hypnosis (vignette), 55–56

Malpractice insurance
    and experimental areas of practice (vignette question), 48
    and licensing board investigation (vignette), 120
    limits of, 283–284
    and sanction, 10
Managed health care program
    and billing practices (vignette), 163
    and financial restrictions (vignette), 165–166
    and interruption of therapy, 318–320
Mandated reporting, 110–111, 111n
Mandatory therapy, in education or training programs, 186–187

and evaluation of student performance, 187–189
Manipulation, self-question about, 15
Marital therapy. *See* Couples therapy
Media, payment to for publicity prohibited, 139
Media presentations, avoidance of deception in, 143–146
Military fitness, in vignette on conflicts with legal authority, 19–22
Minors, as research participants, 199
Misuse or misrepresentation of psychologists' work, 17–19
Monetary payment, 10
Money matters. *See* Fees and financial arrangements
Moral considerations. *See at* Ethical
Multiple (dual) relationships, 73–80
    and delegation of work, 58, 59
    in education and training programs, 185–186, 186–189
    in family therapy, 299
    and group therapy (vignette), 302
    and inducement for research participation, 210
    self-question about, 15
    and supervising of assistant (vignette), 193–194
    and testimony as expert witness (vignette question), 52
    in vignette on confidentiality, 127
    in vignette on informal resolution, 25–26
    See also Exploitative relationships; Sexual intimacies

National Register of Health Service Providers in Psychology, 91
    Web site of, 333
Non-degree-granting educational programs, accurate description of required, 142–143
Nonpayment, withholding records for, 159–160
Notes, psychotherapy, 152–153

Objectivity, loss of, self-question about, 14
Organizations, delivery of services to or through, 99–103
Other corrective actions, 10

Parental consent

in vignette on child of divorced parents, 94–96

in vignette on confidentiality, 108

in vignette on documentation of informed consent, 97–99

in vignettes on child research, 93, 196

Patients

former sexual partners as, 310–312

sexual intimacies with, 305–307

sexual intimacies with former patients, 312–318

sexual intimacies with relatives or significant others of patients, 307–310

spouse of patient (and confidentiality), 111

Payors and funding sources, accuracy in reports to, 171–173

Peers, consultation with, 13

Personal information, student disclosure of, 184–186

Personal problems or conflicts, and competence, 61–64

Plagiarism, 236–237

Beatles' members accused of, 239n

duplicate publication as (vignette), 243

from student's thesis (vignette), 86

Practice guidelines

of American Psychological Association, 333

self-question about, 14

Prejudice, self-question about, 15

Press, payment to for publicity prohibited, 139

Press presentations, avoidance of deception in, 143–146

Privacy

and disclosures, 122–125

and informed consent to research, 198

minimizing intrusions on, 119–122

of students and supervisors, 184

and taping (vignette), 118

and third-party requests for services, 84

in vignette on confidentiality, 109

See also Confidentiality

Privileged communication, 122

Probation, 10

Professional issues, 12–13

Professional judgments, bases for, 56–57

Psychological services

delivered to or through organizations, 99–103

interruption of, 103–105, 318–320

See also Therapy

Psychotherapy, conflict of interest in (vignette), 80–81

Psychotherapy notes, 152–153

Publication credit, 237–242

Public statements, avoidance of falsity or deceit in, 131–133

and compensation to journalists, 139–140

about credentials, 135–137

and descriptions of workshops or non-degree-granting educational programs, 142–143

and identification of advertising, 141–142

and media presentations, 143–146

in statements made by others, 137–139

and testimonials, 146–148

about training and experience, 133–135

Radio, payment to for publicity prohibited, 139

Radio presentations, avoidance of deception in, 143–146

Reading list on ethics, 329–333

Recording, 117–118

in research (informed consent in), 203–204

Record keeping, 151–154

confidentiality in, 154–159

and disposal, 153, 154–156

and withholding records for nonpayment, 159–160

"Record-Keeping Guidelines" (APA), 153, 155

Referrals

to colleagues with special competence, 40

and disclosure, 123

and fees, 173–175

demanding payment of fees for, 319–320

following up on, 88

in vignette on delegation of work, 59–60

Regulations

conflicts over, 19

self-question about, 14

Rehabilitative aspects, of sanction or directive, 10

Release-of-information form, 122, 123

Reporting

ABOUT THE AUTHOR

Thomas F. Nagy received his PhD from the University of Illinois at Champaign–Urbana in 1972. He is currently in independent practice in Palo Alto, California, is an assistant clinical professor in the Department of Psychiatry and Behavioral Sciences at the Stanford University School of Medicine, and is on the staff of Stanford's Center for Integrative Medicine. For the past 25 years, Dr. Nagy's professional activities have focused in part on ethical issues for psychologists. He has served as chair of the Illinois Psychological Association Ethics Committee (1982–1986), was a member of the American Psychological Association (APA) Ethics Committee (1985–1987), served on and chaired the APA Ethics Committee Task Force that revised the "Ethical Principles of Psychologists and Code of Conduct" (1986–1992), was a member of the California Psychological Association Ethics Committee (1988–1993), and currently serves on the Ethics Committee of Stanford University Hospital. He was also an oral examiner for the California Licensing Board for 10 years and has participated in forensic work as an expert witness and consultant to attorneys for many years.

Dr. Nagy provides psychological services and ethical consultation to psychologists, attorneys, educators, and consumers. He is a fellow of APA Division 29 (Psychotherapy) and Division 42 (Psychologists in Independent Practice) and is also a fellow in the Society for Clinical and Experimental Hypnosis. He is the recipient of the Illinois Psychological Association's Special Award for Outstanding Contribution to the Profession of Psychology (1986) and the Santa Clara County, California, Award for Significant Contributions to the Field of Psychology by a Psychologist (1999). He has been interviewed on radio, TV, and print media on the subject of ethics in the practice of psychology in a variety of settings. Dr. Nagy has written on ethical issues related to professional competence, managed health care, and psychology over the Internet and is a coauthor of *Ethics for Psychologists: A Commentary on the APA Ethics Code* (Canter, Bennett, Jones, & Nagy, 1994).